Aging Well

The Complete Guide to Physical and Emotional Health

JEANNE WEI, M.D., PH.D.
SUE LEVKOFF, SC.D.

John Wiley & Sons, Inc.

New York • Chichester • Weinheim • Brisbane • Singapore • Toronto

In memory of Alice and George, and to Michael and David

J. Y. W.

*I dedicate this book to my 83-year-old mother and my 87-year-old father,
who have taught me a lot about how to grow old and live life to the fullest.*

S. E. L.

This book is printed on acid-free paper. ∞

Published by John Wiley & Sons, Inc. Published simultaneously in Canada

Design and production by Navta Associates, Inc.

Joan Mimi's poem "Can You Imagine," on page 307, reprinted with permission, Northwest Care-giver newsletter, Fall/Winter 1998, Legacy Community Health Education, Portland, OR.

The information contained in this book is not intended to serve as a replacement for professional medical advice. Any use of the information in this book is at the reader's discretion. The author and the publisher specifically disclaim any and all liability arising directly or indirectly from the use or application of any information contained in this book. A health care professional should be consulted regarding the reader's specific situation.

Library of Congress Cataloging-in-Publication Data:

Wei, Jeanne Y.
    Aging well : the complete guide to physical and emotional health / Jeanne Wei, Sue Levkoff.
      p.   cm.
    Includes bibliographical references and index.
    ISBN 0-471-32678-X (alk. paper)
      1. Aged—Health and hygiene.   2. Middle aged persons—Health and hygiene.
    3. Self-care, Health.   4. Aging.   I. Levkoff, Sue.   II. Title.

RA777.6.W43 2000
613'.0438—dc21
                                              99-050257

Printed in the United States of America

10 9 8 7 6 5 4 3 2 1

CONTENTS

FOREWORD

As I speculate on why I was asked to write the foreword for *Aging Well,* I might assume that it is because I am a subject for study. In this role, I can't help but sound an optimistic note about the process of aging. I recently was privileged to become an octogenarian. Some years ago—long before I thought I might attain such exalted status—while writing a chapter on human development, I came upon an observation by the British writer Frank Swinnerton:

For me, it is a great privilege to be an octogenarian. The high fevers of life are over, and unless his facilities are badly rusted (which is not the experience of my octogenarian friends) the man of eighty-odd begins every day free from the anxieties, angers, and frustrations which beset his juniors. He is no longer love-sick; he has not to jostle with the crowds on train or street car; he has time to "stand and stare." Further satisfactions follow. He is still richly alive; and having experienced nearly a hundred years of rich and turbulent history, sees the present in perspective, as more than a detail in the tremendous stream of time.

Today, I probably would have a bit of a disagreement about standing and star-ing. For example, by university statutes I became emeritus, but I didn't retire. More and more, my colleagues remain energized in most of their customary activities as they become emeritus.

But I must move away from anecdotes lest I be accused of entering my anec-dotage. What we need to address are the complex issues of aging in our soci-ety—a central concern not alone of our professions, but also of our body politic, as candidates for public office illustrate as they vie for the support of older Americans.

It is fortuitous that concerns over our aging are so prominent, for we are growing older faster than we are growing younger (and the baby boomers haven't yet arrived). A few demographic trends should be recalled: life expectancy has increased from 48 years at the turn of the century to 75.8 years in 1995. We must continue to strive to reduce the 5-year lag for men as well as the relative lag among minorities of diverse ethnic backgrounds. These demo-graphic changes weren't entirely anticipated. I can recall reading articles by respected demographers in the 1970s suggesting that the great gains in life expectancy were over because of the striking reductions in mortality—especially from the infectious diseases—in the early decades of the century. They were predicting that there would be little increase in the period beyond age 65. The data, of course, have proven them wrong. The period beyond 85 years constitutes the single most rapidly growing group in our population. We haven't yet quite made an accommodation to these changes.

We are ultimately interested in improving health and the quality of life, and this book differs from others in that it gives older and younger persons alike the tools they can use to take control of their own health and maintain independence for as long as possible. Certainly health habits related to smoking; alcohol and drug use; exercise; nutrition; and immunizations for influenza and pneumonia have much to do with function as we grow older. *Aging Well* is a wonderful guide to better health through knowledge of the latest research in all of these areas.

Being free of illness does not necessarily ensure quality of life, though. Mobility, independence, cognitive function, psychological state, social relations or networks, assume great importance. Significantly, the elderly often do not associate absence of illness with health. In fact, good health has been defined in nonmedical terms. For example, a person might say, "I feel great, I am mobile, I can remember more people and places even though I have high blood pressure. I love my bridge club and my walking partners."

Recent research studies show that it is possible to improve and maintain physiological performance, sense of well-being, and quality of life, and we are understanding more about how to enhance function. The goal of aging well is now very much within our reach. This is an exciting time indeed.

Julius B. Richmond, M.D.
Professor of Health Policy, Emeritus
Harvard Medical School

Former U.S. Surgeon General and
former Assistant Secretary of Health,
U.S. Department of Health and
Human Services

PREFACE

If you or someone you love is a senior citizen, you're in good company. Every day in the United States, about 3,000 people turn 65 years old, and 2,000 people who are older than age 65 die, resulting in 1,000 new members of the over-65 population. This population of seniors is expected to keep growing, so that by the year 2030, close to 25% of the people in the United States will be age 65 or older.

The rest of the globe is also "graying" rapidly. By 2020, most people in Japan will be over the age of 65, and China will have 250 million people over age 60.

While we are all growing older, our health care system is in a state of flux. You may find simple checkups with your primary care doctor to be complicated by the maze of insurance or Medicare coverage, sometimes confusing diagnostic tests, and seemingly disjointed referrals to specialists who may not appear to communicate well with each other regarding your health care. Too often, we come away from a visit to our physician with a prescription for a specific ailment, but not a clear idea of other steps that we can take to improve our all-around health and well-being.

Furthermore, not all doctors have special training in the disorders that are particular to the older person. In fact, some researchers have estimated that we currently need to triple the number of primary care physicians with special training in geriatric medicine serving the existing population of elders. However, the dearth of specialists is expected to continue, in part because there are not enough faculty members in medical schools who can teach courses in geriatrics. Thus, it's more important than ever for each of us to learn as much as we can about what normal aging is, what kinds of physical and psychological changes we can expect as we grow older, and what we can do to stay healthy for as long as possible. Having such knowledge will empower us to be our own best advocates in the health care world in the years to come.

A number of excellent guides to aging have been written since the mid-1990s. Thomas Perls and Margery Silver wrote *Living to 100: Lessons in Living to Your Maximum Potential.* This book defies the long-held myth that sickness and dementia are inevitable parts of aging. The authors pass on lessons that they have learned from healthy centenarians about how to stay healthy to the maximum life span for which we have the genetic potential.

Christine Cassel edited a volume entitled *The Practical Guide to Aging: What Everyone Needs to Know.* It covers an array of topics, from managing medical problems to making living arrangements.

John Rowe and Robert Kahn wrote *Successful Aging,* which featured the MacArthur Foundation study demonstrating the importance of lifestyle choices in maintaining health and vitality for seniors.

As Leon Trotsky once said, "Old age is the most unexpected of all the things that happen to a man." We've written this book to help you and perhaps your older parents to prepare for the unexpected. For each major system of the body, we've described ways that you can maintain and improve your health, as well as various illnesses that you may one day encounter. In the chapters that follow, you'll find a complete guide to the latest treatment options for the problems that you may confront.

In addition to presenting these health issues, we feel that it is equally important to address some of the other challenges and experiences that may lie ahead, including retirement, decisions about where to live, the process of caregiving, risks to your safety and your rights under the law, end-of-life decisions that you may need to make, and the potential loss of loved ones.

Finally, we discuss the latest research on therapies that some day may be used to help us stay more youthful and healthy for a longer period of time.

Many individuals have helped us along the way. Much of this book is based on the research of our colleagues at Harvard and elsewhere. Helen Rees turned our dream into reality. Tom Miller and John Simko, our editors at John Wiley & Sons, guided us toward the goal with enthusiasm and provided us with valuable advice for improving the organization of the book. We are deeply grateful to one of the most talented writers, Sharon C. Hogan, for her insight, energy, patience, and encouragement. Kathleen McKenna and Elizabeth Willingham also added a great deal of energy and clarity in the development and writing of this book. Dr. Yeon Kyung Chee provided exceptional assistance in researching material. Jessica Meltzer and David Knauss kindly gave us expert and patient assistance with final manuscript preparation. Last, we are indebted to our patients and their families for giving us the inspiration to write this book. We are most appreciative of all of their contributions.

PART ONE
AGING WELL

*Human aging is the sum total of all experiences and adaptations that
a person undergoes from conception to death, including the complex
processes of development, maturation, and attainment of wisdom.*

J. Wei

When she was 55 years old, Elsie Frank went back to work to help educate her fourth child.

At 60, she moved to Boston to be closer to her children, one of whom was going through a divorce and needed a hand in looking after her three little girls.

At 70, she retired from a job that she loved in order to help her oldest son, Massachusetts Congressional Representative Barney Frank, campaign in a very tight political race. Although she'd never done any public speaking before, she overcame her initial nervousness and time and again rose to speak out on the podium.

Today, at 86, Elsie Frank works as a volunteer to provide housing for homeless elders and serves as an advocate in many other organizations for the elderly. In addition to being a valuable source of wisdom and support for her family and friends, her views on Social Security and Medicare are sought by community leaders and politicians alike.

As she has grown older, the needs of Elsie's family and community have grown, too, but she hasn't retreated from taking an active role in the lives of the people around her. Instead, she has continued to step forward to help out, and in so doing, she has remained vital and connected in a remarkably positive way. She loves life.

We don't all have to become good public speakers in order to enjoy success in our later years, but we can learn a lot from Elsie's example of aging well by living well. In this chapter, we talk about some different ways to look at what aging is, and about how we can keep our lives healthy, dynamic, and productive.

How We Age

What comes to mind when you think of aging? Do you think of a downhill slope, an uphill climb, or simply another bend in the road? Research has shown that aging is a very complex, multifaceted process. Let's look at how this stage of life is viewed by *gerontologists,* specialists who study aging and have expertise in treating the problems of older people.

Chronological Age

Chronological age relates to the number of years that we have lived since we were born. Several factors have a role in our longevity, including our sex and our genes. The average life expectancy for women in the United States who were 65 years old in 1980 is 83.7 years; for men who were 65 in 1980, it is 79.8 years.

Although there is no single explanation for this sex difference, there are clear indications that men tend to die sooner than women from certain diseases and conditions (such as coronary artery disease). Smoking, the most preventable cause of death in the world, is more prevalent among men than women. Unfortunately, however, lung-cancer deaths in women have been rising, due to increased smoking by women. Gender differences in lifestyle and health maintenance might partly contribute to the fact that women enjoy longer lives. However, living longer may not necessarily be a cause for celebration because twice as many women as men live at or below the poverty line, the median income of older women is only 57% of that for older men, and 41% of women over the age of 65, in contrast to 16% of older men, live alone.

In addition to sex differences, some other genetic factors also appear to influence the aging process. One of our colleagues, Thomas Perls, has done some fascinating research with the "oldest old"—those over age 95 years—and has found that many of these individuals are mentally and physically healthier than their somewhat younger peers in their 80s and early 90s. It's possible that these people have some genetic advantages that help them to overcome or cope with diseases.

How long and how well we live are not determined by any one single factor, however. Although our sex and our genetic makeup may partly contribute to average life expectancy, factors such as environment, lifestyle, and how we care for our health are actually even more important.

Biological Age

Another way of looking at aging is to consider our *biological age,* which has more to do with our physical condition. For example, there appears to be a relationship between aging and "programmed cell death" (*apoptosis*) which seems to be an essential part of the life of multicellular organisms such as humans. However, the variations due to a person's susceptibility to disease and his or her genetic makeup make it difficult for researchers to find a single explanation for physical decline with the passage of time. The aging process affects each individual differently, and it even occurs at different rates among various body systems within a single individual. Moreover, the decline in function in one organ does not necessarily mean that others in the same body will decline, too.

Finally, gerontologists sometimes refer to *behavioral age,* which relates to how old we act and how old we think of ourselves as being. Behavioral age involves a person's ability to function independently. You've probably met two people who have the same medical diagnosis—such as arthritis or heart disease—and yet they radically differ in how well they function. One may be quite disabled and completely dependent on others to get through the day, while the other, in spite of some limitations, may be completely self-sufficient and may be able to perform *activities of daily living* (e.g., bathing, eating, dressing) with little or no difficulty.

Behavioral Age

A person's ability to function, rather than his or her disease, affects the person's quality of life. Although we may encounter illnesses along the way, growing old is not the same thing as "functional decline." This book will help you to optimize and strengthen your *functional reserves,* so that when one area of your body is affected by illness or disease, your functional levels in other areas do not suffer.

Now let's look at some of the normal age-related changes and syndromes that tend to occur most commonly in older individuals.

Normal Changes in Later Life

In our later years, our organs sometimes may not work to the capacity that they did when we were younger; hence, certain conditions may affect us with greater severity. Bacterial pneumonia, for instance, can become quite serious because of our reduced lung function. Over time, our hearts may become less efficient, as scar tissue may take the place of healthy muscle tissue. We may experience hardening of the arteries, or atherosclerosis, too. The chapters that follow offer specific suggestions for countering these changes with exercises, a good diet, and regular medical care.

Organ Function

According to the Baltimore Longitudinal Study on Aging, which tests more than 2,200 men and women every other year for physical and mental functioning, short-term memory in certain individuals tends to decline somewhat over time after age 70. Some individuals over the age of 70 may also experience a slightly reduced ability to solve problems. As you'll discover in Chapter 6, though, our brains have plenty of cells to spare, and there are many things that we can do to strengthen our brain power. It's important to note that some forms of forgetfulness are also *not* related to increasing age; in fact, they are highly treatable and even curable.

Memory Loss

We may lose bone mass as we get older, so fractures may be more likely if we fall. Also, changes that occur in the spinal nerves may make it slightly more difficult for some of us to maintain balance. We may also experience a loss of muscle tissue as we age, especially if we have not exercised. Chapter 9 describes steps you can take to maintain or improve your musculoskeletal fitness, including the benefits of supplemental calcium and vitamin D, as well as different types of exercises that can be helpful, no matter how late in life you begin to do them.

Musculoskeletal Changes

Urinary and Bowel Function

Our kidneys, which help to keep water and electrolytes in balance in our bodies, can become slightly less efficient over time. Our bowels can also develop problems, partly because of long-term consumption of refined foods, inadequate amounts of fiber, and laxative use. Roughly half of all Americans over the age of 80 develop a condition called *diverticulosis* (herniations through the muscular part of the colon). You can take steps to avoid kidney and bowel problems by embracing a healthier lifestyle. Chapters 11 and 13 discuss these problems in more detail and provide some useful recommendations for managing them.

Sensory Changes

Vision. As we discuss more extensively in Chapter 7, the lenses of our eyes become more opaque and stiff as we get older. At about age 40 or so, a condition called *presbyopia* may develop when the lens is less able to focus at various distances the way it used to do. Close vision may become problematic, and bifocals may be needed.

Cataracts, glaucoma, and other eye problems are also more likely to appear with the passage of time. However, decreased vision is not necessarily a normal part of aging, and many of these conditions are highly treatable.

Hearing. Long-term exposure to noise in the environment can cause mild to moderate damage to the inner ear and may cause a condition called *presbycusis,* or sensorineural hearing loss, especially in the higher frequency range. Chapter 7 discusses the latest therapeutic options for this condition and for other hearing problems that some of us may encounter later in life.

In spite of these potential age-associated changes, with a positive attitude and an ounce of prevention, we can and should function well and continue to live meaningful lives.

Not long ago, Elsie Frank remarked, "Although we may never be able to prevent aging, we at least are learning how to keep it from reducing the quality of our lives. Nothing can prevent us from readjusting our sights as we grow older. All of life is a readjustment to age. . . .

"What people have to remember is that just because we are older it doesn't mean that we have lost our sense of humor, our sense of pleasure, or our dignity. It's important that we do not give up control and [that we] continue to put our best foot forward. I've always felt I could affect my aging process, and I've been working hard at it."

In the next several chapters, we discuss how you, too, can take charge of your own aging process and step forward to a healthier and more fulfilling future.

CHAPTER 2
HOW TO AGE SUCCESSFULLY

*To know how to grow old is the masterwork of wisdom, and one
of the most difficult chapters in the great art of living.*

Henri Amiel (1821–1881)

The key to aging successfully involves reaching for a level of physical, social, and psychological well-being that is pleasing to both ourselves and others. We may also strive to age productively by remaining as active as possible in all three spheres. A physically sedentary, mentally inactive, and socially isolated lifestyle, in contrast, may lead to an unhealthy cycle: It can contribute to disabilities that can make it even more difficult to remain engaged in the world around us.

*The sum of the whole is this: walk and be happy; walk and be healthy. The
best way to lengthen our days is to walk steadily and with purpose. The
wandering man knows of certain ancients, far gone in years, who have
staved off infirmities and dissolution by earnest walking—hale fellows,
close up on ninety, but brisk as boys.*

Charles Dickens (1812–1870)

Physical Exercise

If we want to remain independent, and if we want to continue to have the physical wherewithal to carry our own groceries, vacuum our homes, and walk to the corner store, we need to get some form of exercise. If we don't, we will lose strength, stamina, and eventually our physical independence.

Even if we've never been physically fit, starting an exercise program in our later years can still definitely confer a number of benefits for our bodies and minds. Muscle strength training, even in frail elders who already have car-

Why It's Important

diopulmonary or musculoskeletal disease, can result in greater mobility, improved balance and gait, improved cardiovascular function, and improved cognitive function. It also can decrease mental stress and improve emotional well-being.

One of our colleagues, Maria A. Fiatarone, has also linked weight-lifting exercises to increases in strength and effective prevention of bone loss (*osteoporosis*) in women after menopause. Another study in 1999 showed that the strength of a man's hand grip—a good measure of overall strength—between the ages of 45 and 68 was a good predictor of disability 25 years later. Hence, it makes sense for us to invest in our future health now.

There are many types of exercise programs available, but don't let the array of fancy choices overwhelm you. The most important thing to do is to *start*. You don't have to join an expensive health club or take up the latest fitness fad to strengthen your body. Walking, an excellent form of exercise, is just as beneficial.

We tell our patients that physical activity should be habitual and light or moderate in intensity, and it should last a minimum of about 20 to 30 minutes a day, for at least three to four days per week.

We live on the third floor, and I climb the stairs—there's 34 steps—and I try to go out every other day. I don't want to push it too hard, but on a day when I'm not going out I do the stairs. My doctor told me that walking down *is not such a good form of exercise: it really isn't good for strength building, it can increase one's risk of falling, and it can even cause muscle injury. So I usually take the elevator going down and walk back up again.*

When I go down to get the mail, I take the elevator down and then walk back upstairs again. So that's my own way of getting my exercise. If I can walk it, I walk it.

Roger, age 82

Getting Started

Before embarking on a new exercise regimen, be sure to talk with your doctor about your plans. He or she will want to examine you for any heart or muscle problems, as well as any diseases that you may have or medicines that you're taking that could have an effect on, or be affected by, your exercise routine. If you have chest discomfort, uncontrolled diabetes, shortness of breath, certain heart problems, a bone fracture, or fever, you may need to forgo your workouts for the time being.

After you've gotten the okay from your doctor, consider working with a trainer at a health club, YMCA, or senior center to help you customize an exercise program to your particular needs. Remember to progress *gradually*.

Exercise Options

There are many different ways to go about the pursuit of fitness, from climbing an extra set of stairs on your own to joining an aerobics class at a local gym. Everyday activities such as raking leaves and gardening are also forms of exercise.

Elsie Frank, the energetic elder whom we introduced you to in Chapter 1, notes that "it costs a lot of money to go to the gym. I had a neighbor who had joined the YMCA and wanted me to go with her, and I said, 'No, Sophie, because I get my exercise by walking . . . you know, you go to the gym and get home and drive to the market and drive home with your bundle. . . . Well, that's how I get my exercise—I just get it differently.' "

If you do engage in a regular exercise program, fitness experts recommend that you keep three important parts of this activity in mind: warm-up, the exercise itself, and cool down. The first and last parts should each last about 5 to 10 minutes and should include stretching and slow movements such as walking, swimming, or rowing. The cool-down period also should involve some relaxing, deep breaths.

The exercises themselves may include endurance, strength, or flexibility training, or all of these forms of physical activity.

Endurance training, or *aerobic exercise,* is a type of exercise that is designed to strengthen your *cardiorespiratory efficiency;* in other words, it will help to keep your heart and lungs in good shape by helping your body make good use of oxygen. Such exercises include walking, cycling, skating, dancing, and water exercise. These are called "low-impact" aerobics because they do not involve the more intense workout of the muscles and joints that occurs during "high-impact" aerobics, such as jumping rope and jogging.

By using lots of muscles to do repeated exercises, you can raise your heart rate. As you gradually build up your strength, you can increase the length of this part of your exercise session. Endurance training is good for everyone, but it's especially beneficial for people with non-insulin-dependent diabetes mellitus, high blood pressure, osteoporosis, and heart disease.

Strength training, also known as *weight training* or *resistance training,* can help you to enhance your muscles' strength. These exercises involve moving your joints through a full range of motion against increasing amounts of resistance. Hand weights, dumbbells, and even beanbags can be used to perform these smooth, controlled exercises. Exercise weight machines at fitness centers can be used, too.

We recommend that you have a fitness expert help you to get started with resistance training because if done incorrectly, these exercises can be harmful. You should learn a variety of routines and vary them from day to day so that you don't use the same muscles two days in a row.

Flexibility training involves slow, focused movements to stretch the muscles, tendons, and ligaments that affect the motion of your joints. Once you learn to do flexibility exercises (such as flexing your shoulders and knees), you can do them just about anywhere.

No matter what form of exercise you choose, while you're working out, be sure to dress comfortably, wear comfortable shoes, and drink plenty of fluids. Also, get medical assistance right away if you develop shortness of breath or sudden pain.

Some Precautions

Are You Still Avoiding Exercise? If you don't exercise, what's keeping you from this worthwhile activity? The accompanying sidebar lists some common reasons that people give for not exercising—and some suggestions for overcoming these barriers to good health.

Overcoming Barriers to Exercise

Exercise is hard work.

Pick an activity that you enjoy and that is easy for you.

I don't have the time.

You can gain a lot from just three 20-minute sessions per week. Could you give up three TV shows each week?

I'm usually too tired for exercise.

Tell yourself, "This activity will give me more energy," and it probably will!

I hate to fail, so I won't start.

Physical activity is not a test. You won't fail if you choose an activity that you like and you start off slowly.

I don't have anyone to work out with.

Maybe you haven't asked. A neighbor or coworker may be a willing partner. Alternatively, you can choose an activity that you enjoy doing by yourself.

There's no convenient place.

Pick an activity that you can do at a place that is convenient. Walk around your neighborhood or do exercises with a TV show or a videotape at home.

I'm afraid of being injured.

Walking is very safe and is excellent exercise. Choose a safe, well-lit area.

The weather is too bad.

There are many activities that you can do in your own home, in any weather.

Exercise is boring.

Listening to music during your activity will keep your mind occupied. Walking, biking, or running can take you past lots of interesting sights.

I'm too overweight.

You can benefit regardless of your weight. Pick an activity that you are comfortable with, such as walking.

I'm too old.

You're not too old. It's never too late to start. People of any age can benefit from physical exercise.

Source: Adapted from Project PACE, *Physician-Based Assessment and Counseling for Exercise.* San Diego, CA: San Diego State University and San Diego Center for Health Interventions; 1999. Used with permission of the publisher.

I have a four-wheeled cart. I walk to the supermarket, load up the cart, and walk home. My favorite exercise is this: I don't push that cart into the apartment. I take two cans at a time, pick them up, and bring them into the kitchen . . . this is a little exercise gem.

Viviane, age 74

Nutrition

One of the best ways to age well is to eat well. Elsie Frank says, "Since concentrating on good nutrition, I know that I've turned my life around. I have the buoyancy, energy, kick, and all-around good feeling now that I did not have when I was younger."

Do you feel energized by your healthy diet or do you suspect that there may be room for improvement? Take a minute to go through the accompanying checklist to help you identify areas that may need some work.

Determining Your Nutritional Health

	Yes
I have an illness or condition that made me change the kind and/or amount of food I eat.	2
I eat fewer than 2 meals per day.	3
I eat few fruits and vegetables, or milk products.	2
I have three or more drinks of beer, liquor, or wine almost every day.	2
I have tooth or mouth problems that make it hard for me to eat.	2
I don't always have enough money to buy the food I need.	4
I eat alone most of the time.	1
I take three or more prescribed or over-the-counter drugs a day.	1
Without wanting to, I have lost or gained 10 pounds in the past six months.	2
I am not always physically able to shop, cook, or feed myself.	2
Total	

Instructions: Read the preceding statements. Circle the number in the *yes* column for those that apply. Add up the circled numbers to get your total nutrition score. If it is

0–2	Good! Recheck your nutritional score in 6 months.
3–5	You are at moderate risk. See what you can do to improve your eating habits and lifestyle. You can get help from your local office on aging, senior nutrition program, senior citizens center, or health department. Recheck your nutritional score in 3 months.

6 or more   You are at high nutritional risk. Talk with your doctor, dietitian, or other qualified health or social-service professional about this checklist.

Source: Adapted from *The Nutrition Screening Initiative* (educational material and office aids for screening elderly patients for nutritional deficiencies). Washington, DC: Nutrition Screening Initiative. Reprinted with permission of the Nutrition Screening Initiative, copyright 1993.

Improving Your Diet

How did you do? If you appear to be at nutritional risk, you can immediately make changes to your eating habits. We recommend the following changes.

Avoid excesses or imbalances of foods. Your body needs approximately 1600 to 2400 calories, or about 25% fewer calories than it did when you were 25, but just as many nutrients. In fact, research has shown that the best diets for older people include 20 different food types per week!

Just as when you were younger, you need to find a balance such that you eat enough protein, vitamins, and minerals—but not so much food that you gain too much weight. Obesity itself can create a number of health problems, such as high blood pressure, diabetes, and arthritis.

The energy that we require to keep our essential body functions going (the basal metabolic rate) usually drops by about 20% between the ages of 20 and 90. Because of these changes in our bodies' energy requirements, the American Dietetic Association has created a food pyramid (Figure 2.1).

Figure 2.1
The Food Pyramid

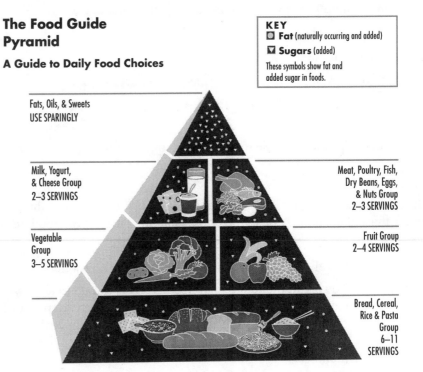

The Food Guide Pyramid

A Guide to Daily Food Choices

KEY
▢ **Fat** (naturally occurring and added)
◪ **Sugars** (added)
These symbols show fat and added sugar in foods.

Fats, Oils, & Sweets
USE SPARINGLY

Milk, Yogurt, & Cheese Group
2–3 SERVINGS

Meat, Poultry, Fish, Dry Beans, Eggs, & Nuts Group
2–3 SERVINGS

Vegetable Group
3–5 SERVINGS

Fruit Group
2–4 SERVINGS

Bread, Cereal, Rice & Pasta Group
6–11 SERVINGS

As this pyramid shows, you should consume a variety of foods, with far more servings of grains than sweets and fats. Eat lots of fruits and vegetables. Consume sugar and salt in moderation only. Reduce your alcohol intake (grape juice is an excellent substitute).

Adjust your caloric intake to maintain a healthy weight. Your consumption of fat should be less than 30% of your total calories—and 8% or less of your calories should come from saturated fats such as cream, meat, cheese, and butter.

Consume enough calcium to decrease your risk of bone loss. In addition to calcium from foods such as yogurt, skim milk, broccoli, and cheeses (e.g., parmesan, cheddar, American), we recommend that postmenopausal women and older men take supplements of 800 to 1500 mg of calcium every day.

Make sure that you *get enough folate, or folic acid,* an important vitamin found in oranges, strawberries, spinach, avocados, and some breads, cereals, and pastas. Eating enough of this B vitamin can protect you from anemia.

Take Vitamin D to prevent bone fractures. In addition to getting some vitamin D from the sun and consuming this vitamin through certain fortified products such as milk, we recommend that you take 600 to 800 international units of this vitamin every day.

Take Vitamin A for healthy skin and to prevent poor eyesight from worsening. Vitamin A is found in eggs, whole-milk products, and green and yellow vegetables such as spinach, kale, broccoli, squash, and carrots. If you eat a good variety of vegetables, you will probably get enough of this vitamin.

Add extra fiber to your diet to combat a sluggish digestive system. Fruits and vegetables, whole-grain breads and cereals, and beans are all good sources of fiber.

Remember to *drink fluids* because you may not always feel thirsty when you actually need to drink. Water, juice, and noncaffeinated teas are great choices.

Read food labels. Elsie Frank says, "I refuse to be self-conscious about questioning new food products, about being so particular about the foods I ingest. It is my body that will suffer if I am not careful, it is my quality of life that is at stake. Derogatory remarks supposedly made in jest while I am reading labels from items I take off the supermarket shelves do not intimidate me!"

Figure 2.2 shows you how to read a food label. Serving sizes on these labels are similar among similar products, so half a cup of one brand of rice, for example, can be compared to half a cup of another brand of rice.

Shop for foods that are low in saturated fat, cholesterol, and sodium. Pay particular attention to the number of calories per serving and the amount of calories from fat. Remember that your daily intake of fat should be no more than 30% of your total calories. (This translates to roughly 65 grams if you are on a 2000-calorie diet and approximately 40 grams if you are on a 1200-calorie diet).

In addition to what you eat, how you eat is also important. Studies have shown that those who eat breakfast and don't snack very often live longer than those who don't! Also, try not to eat a big supper and then fall asleep shortly

Figure 2.2

The Food Label at a Glance

This food label carries an up-to-date, easy-to-use nutrition information guide. It is required on almost all packaged foods. The guide serves as a key to help in planning a healthy diet.*

Serving sizes are now more consistent across product lines, are stated in both household and metric measures, and reflect the amounts people actually eat.

The **list of nutrients** covers those most important to the health of today's consumers, most of whom need to worry about getting *too much* of certain nutrients (fat, for example), rather than too few vitamins or minerals, as in the past.

The labels of larger packages may tell the number of calories per gram of fat, carbohydrates, and protein.

Nutrition Facts
Serving Size 1 cup (228g)
Servings Per Container 2

Amount Per Serving

Calories 260   Calories from Fat 120

	% Daily Value*
Total Fat 13g	**20**%
Saturated Fat 5g	**25**%
Cholesterol 30mg	**10**%
Sodium 660mg	**28**%
Total Carbohydrate 31g	**10**%
Dietary Fiber 0g	**0**%
Sugars 5g	
Protein 5g	

Vitamin A 4%	•	Vitamin C 2%
Calcium 15%	•	Iron 4%

* Percent Daily Values are based on a 2,000 calorie diet. Your daily values may be higher or lower depending on your calorie needs:

		Calories:	2,000	2,500
Total Fat	Less than		65g	80g
Sat Fat	Less than		20g	25g
Cholesterol	Less than		300mg	300mg
Sodium	Less than		2,400mg	2,400mg
Total Carbohydrate			300g	375g
Dietary Fiber			25g	30g

Calories per gram:
Fat 9 • Carbohydrate 4 • Protein 4

*This label is only a sample. Exact specifications are in the final rules. Source: Food and Drug Administration, 1994

Calories from fat are shown on the label to help consumers meet dietary guidelines that recommend people get no more than 30 percent of the calories in their overall diet from fat.

% Daily Value shows how a food fits into the overall daily diet.

Some daily values are maximums, as with fat (65 grams *or less*); others are minimums, as with carbohydrates (300 grams *or more*). The daily values for a 2,000- and 2,500-calorie diet must be listed on the label of larger packages.

Health Claims: Food labels are allowed to carry information about the link between certain nutrients and specific diseases. For such a "health claim" to be made on a package, the FDA must first determine that the diet-disease link is supported by scientific evidence.

Health claim message referred to on the front panel is shown here.

"While many factors affect heart disease, diets low in saturated fat and cholesterol may reduce the risk of this disease."

Frozen Mixed **VEGETABLES** *in sauce*

• Low Fat
• Cholesterol Free
• Good Source of Fiber
See back panel for nutritional information

"While many factors affect heart disease, diets low in saturated fat and cholesterol may reduce the risk of this disease."

Ingredients: Broccoli, carrots, green beans, water chestnuts, soybean oil, milk solids, modified cornstarch, salt, spices.

NET WT. 8.9 oz. (252 g)

Claims: While descriptive terms like "low," "good source," and "free" have long been used on food labels, their meaning—and their usefulness in helping consumers plan a healthy diet—have been murky. Now FDA has set specific definitions for these terms, assuring shoppers that they can believe what they read on the package.

Ingredients are listed in descending order by weight, and the list is required on almost all foods, even standardized ones like mayonnaise and bread.

thereafter. Eat smaller amounts than you used to if you find that your weight is rising steadily.

Smoking

The use of tobacco is the most important single preventable cause of death in most countries around the world. By giving up this habit, you can reduce your risk (and your loved ones' risk) of stroke; coronary heart disease; chronic obstructive pulmonary disease; asthma; lung, bladder, pancreatic, cervical, and oral cancers; ulcers; and peripheral artery disease. Furthermore, if you take estrogen replacement therapy, you can decrease your risk of hip fracture by quitting smoking.

Quitting Works!

Researchers Philip Cole and Brad Rodu attribute the drop in some cancer deaths from 1990 to 1995 to the reduction in smoking among American men. This change in behavior has resulted in a 3.9% reduction in lung cancer and a 2% decline in other smoking-related cancers.

While lung-cancer deaths continue to rise in women, the rate of rise has slackened slightly since the mid-1990s. We hope that the cancer deaths in women will show a similar trend to that of men in the future, as smoking among women declines.

How to Stop

You will not lower your risk of heart disease simply by switching to cigarettes that have reduced amounts of tar and nicotine. Giving up smoking altogether is the best thing you can do for your health. If you have been unable to stop smoking, consider a smoking-cessation program. If you smoke because of stress, such a program can show you different ways to manage life's pressures.

A recently marketed drug called buspirone (Zyban or Wellbutrin) has been found effective in helping people lose the desire to continue smoking. Ask your doctor about this drug. Some minor side effects, such as skin rashes, may occasionally occur.

Nicotine gum and nicotine patches may also be helpful. However, they have associated side effects and *contraindications* (that is, they should not be used at all if you have certain health conditions). Use these products only if you are under the care of a physician or other health care provider.

Alcohol

Drinking alcohol may be associated with falls and accidental injury, heart-rhythm disorders, stroke, urinary incontinence, confusion, delirium, and a host of other conditions. We thus advise our patients to limit their alcohol intake to less than the equivalent of one small glass of wine per day. In Chapter 6, we talk more about ways to reduce your alcohol consumption.

Safe Sex

You may think that your days of worrying about the consequences of sex are over now that you're older, but safe sex means more than pregnancy prevention. According to the federal Centers for Disease Control and Prevention, 11% of all acquired immune deficiency syndrome (AIDS) cases diagnosed in 1995 involved Americans over age 50. Just under half of these cases were the result of homosexual encounters. One fifth of these cases involved heterosexual contacts. Also, the number of older women infected with the human immunodeficiency virus (HIV) is steadily rising.

How can you protect yourself from HIV infection and other sexually transmitted diseases (STDs)? You can either abstain from sex or avoid sex with partners who may be infected. If you are sexually active, the most important precaution is to always use latex condoms for sexual contacts, especially if practicing anal sex.

Some physicians may have a difficult time initiating conversations with their older patients about sex, but that should not deter you. It's up to you to educate yourself about these issues and also to ask your doctor openly about any questions that you may have. You'll find some useful guidance in Chapter 5.

Medications

A Look Inside Your Medicine Cabinet

Every few months, go through all of the medicines in your home, and look at the expiration dates on the bottles. Discard any old drugs, and ask your pharmacist if you're unsure whether any are still okay. Outdated medicines can be harmful!

Where do you store your medicines? We now know that keeping them in a bathroom cabinet is not a good idea because the moisture and heat created there can affect them. It's better to store them in a cool, dry place, such as a hall closet or a kitchen cabinet (as long as it's not located near the stove).

How many prescription and nonprescription drugs (such as vitamins, cold medicine, laxatives, antacids, and sleeping pills) are you taking? When was the last time you reviewed all of these medicines with your doctor? It's possible that you may be taking more than you need.

The next time you have a checkup, write down, or better yet, bring with you to the doctor's office all of the drugs that you take on a regular basis. Then ask your doctor,

- Which side effects should I be aware of?
- Is there a chance that any of these drugs might interact with each other?
- Are there any foods that I should eat or not eat while I'm taking these medications?
- Am I taking these drugs at the right time of day?
- Will any of these medicines make me especially sensitive to sunlight?
- Do I really need to be taking all of the drugs that I've been taking?

You should also make sure that you know how to read the labels on your prescriptions, and ask your doctor about anything on the label that you're unsure about (Figure 2.3).

When you're taking your medicine, always check the label to make sure that you're taking the correct one. If you find it difficult to read the print on the medicine label, talk with your pharmacist about whether he or she can provide a large-print label, perhaps on a bigger bottle. If taking several different medications at different times of day, you might want to get a medication box to place

Figure 2.3 *How to Read a Prescription Drug Label*

Greenville Pharmacy
Phone: 541-4598

This is the name and telephone number of the drug store. Always feel free to call your pharmacist if you have *any* questions about your prescription.

No. 1236544
Date: 5/2/2000

You can refer to this prescription number and the date when the prescription was filled if you need to discuss this medication with your pharmacist.

For: Cindy Riffe

#100 Phenytoin 50 mg capsules

This prescription is for 100 capsules of a drug called phenytoin, and each capsule contains 50 milligrams.

Drugs have both general, nonproprietary names (generic names) as well as their brand, or trade, names. In this label, "phenytoin" is the generic name. This drug is also sold under the trade name "Dilantin." It's a good idea to ask your doctor for both names. The generic form generally costs less than the trade form. Pharmacies can charge different amounts for drugs, so you may also be able to save money by shopping around. Also, if you will be taking the medicine for a long time, ask your doctor whether he or she can prescribe a large quantity of the drug so that you can save some money (and reduce your trips to the drug store for refills).

Take one capsule three times a day for seizure control.

You may wish to ask your doctor or pharmacist about how many hours apart you should take this drug. Is it safe to take it with breakfast, lunch, and dinner, or should the doses be taken literally every 8 hours?

Dr. Nancy Gilson

This is the doctor who wrote the prescription.

Expiration: 5/2/2001

Pay careful attention to expiration dates on all of your medicines. They may no longer be effective and in some cases may be harmful if taken past their expiration date.

all the pills in their appropriate slot (morning, afternoon, and evening), so that you can keep track of which medicines you have taken. Each of us has probably had the following experience: You are holding your medication container and you have no idea as to whether you just took it. It's usually better not to take an additional dose without first consulting your physician because medicine stays in your system. It's better not to double up—instead wait and then take it at your next prescribed time. A medication box would help you avoid such a predicament.

Also, never take medicine in the dark! Finally, never trade or share medications with friends, relatives, or neighbors. It is not good for you or them and can add to the confusion of everyone.

Drugs That Can Keep You Well

Now that you've checked with your doctor about whether you're taking too many drugs, are you sure that you're taking enough of the right ones? For example, as you will see in Chapter 6, doctors often reduce the amount of depression medication after a person is doing well, but maintenance therapy frequently requires ongoing therapeutic doses. In addition to the medicines that can cure our ills, there are some good ones that can prevent certain conditions, such as heart attack and osteoporosis.

Aspirin. Taking an aspirin a day sometimes can keep the cardiologist away. Specifically, some studies have shown that men and women who take a regular, low dose of aspirin (80 to 160 mg per day) have a lower risk of heart attack and possibly stroke than those who don't. We talk more about such measures in Chapter 4.

Estrogen. As you'll read in Chapter 9, estrogen can help to prevent bone loss and fractures in postmenopausal women. It may also protect women from urinary-tract problems and from some kinds of heart disease, it may alleviate mood changes, and it may reduce the risk of Alzheimer's disease.

Immunizations

Did you know that many of the diseases that vaccines can prevent are more dangerous to adults than to children? Unfortunately, though, many adults think that they have outgrown the need for immunizations—even though about 90% of deaths due to influenza and pneumococcal infections occur among people who are 65 and older.

Tetanus and Diphtheria

Tetanus, a disease caused by bacteria that enter the body through a cut, and *diphtheria,* a contagious bacterial disease that affects the throat and windpipe, can be dangerous. More than 60% of tetanus infections (also called "lockjaw") occur in people who are 60 years old or older.

Generally, the vaccines for these two types of infection are administered together. We recommend that our patients receive tetanus and diphtheria (Td) booster shots every 10 years. You may also need to get a booster shot if you have a severe puncture wound.

Influenza, or the flu, is a very contagious disease that is caused by a virus. Younger people may experience fever, sore throat, aches and pains, and a runny nose when they get the flu. In older people, however, this virus can have more serious consequences, such as dehydration, pneumonia, delirium, congestive heart failure, diarrhea, and weight loss.

Flu

Most people should get flu shots every year. However, if you are allergic to eggs you should *not* receive the flu vaccine because the vaccine is cultured in an egg medium (see Chapter 12).

Older people are more likely than younger people to develop *pneumococcal disease,* a bacterial infection that can affect the lungs (pneumonia), the blood (bacteremia), or the brain (meningitis). These infections can be quite severe in the elderly. It's wise to be vaccinated against pneumococcal disease beginning at age 65 and to consider repeating the vaccination every six years. Other than some minor soreness at the injection site, most people have no side effects from the vaccine.

Pneumococcal Disease

Speak with your doctor about whether you should receive the hepatitis B vaccine. This vaccine generally is recommended for people who are traveling to areas where this virus is endemic (widespread), patients who are on dialysis, and patients who are exposed to blood or other body fluids from infected persons.

Other Immunizations

You should also make sure that you're up to date on your vaccinations against measles, mumps, and rubella.

If you're traveling abroad, ask your doctor about whether you need other vaccinations or prophylactic medications (for example, against malaria).

Adults should have yearly comprehensive physical exams and screenings to check for dental, vision, and hearing problems; other conditions such as high blood pressure, malnutrition, and thyroid disease; and breast, cervical, prostate, or colorectal cancer, as well as mental health problems.

Physical Exams

In addition to your physical examinations with a doctor, don't forget to see a dentist at least once per year. One study indicated that nearly half of older people have undetected dental disease. Flossing is very important for your health. Regular dental visits can help you to address tooth decay, gum disease, and dry mouth, all of which are common problems in the older mouth (see Chapter 16).

Dentistry

You can take measures to make your living space as safe as possible. In Chapter 18, we suggest several ways to eliminate the risk of falls and burns in your home. Investing a little time in assessing the safety of your home can do more than protect your physical health—it can help you to maintain your independence.

Accident Prevention

Here are some practical things that you can do to prevent accidents:

• Wear low-heeled shoes that have good traction.

- Don't walk in socks or stocking feet because you'll be more prone to slipping.
- Be conscious of toys on the floor when children come to visit, and watch out for your and other people's pets.
- Make sure not to leave garden tools and hoses outside after you've been using them.
- When you have a lot to carry, divide large loads into smaller ones.
- When you've been lying down, sit up gradually; likewise, when you've been sitting, rise to a standing position gradually.
- See your eye doctor regularly to make sure that you have the correct prescription.
- Remove scatter rugs.
- Remove electrical cords from the path where you might walk.

Car accidents are another major problem. Seatbelts are a must. Only one third of people over age 65 wear seatbelts! Bicycle and motorcycle helmets are also essential.

Staying Involved

We need the constant ebb and flow of wavelets of sensation, thought, perception, action and emotion, lapping on the shore of our consciousness.

Whatever we are, . . . we preserve it best in the experience of many things.

Christopher Barney (1917–)

Now that we've looked at some of the steps that we can take to age well physically, let's address the other part of living and aging well—a healthy mind and soul. Winston Churchill once said, "We make a living by what we get, but we make a life by what we give." Any time is a wonderful time in your life to give. It is truly more blessed to give than to receive.

Albert Schweitzer observed, "I don't know what your destiny will be, but one thing I know: the only ones among you who will be really happy are those who will have sought and found how to serve. . . .The purpose of human life is to serve, and to show compassion and the will to help others."

At age 79, Elsie Frank helped found the Committee to End Elderly Homelessness. She and six other women started this organization with $100. They have transformed two empty houses (and are in the process of transforming a third) into apartments for low-income elders.

Today Ms. Frank says, "Talk about aging well! It is such a feeling of satisfaction to have been able to do that, to walk into that building, to see all those people. They each have their own apartment—nothing makes you feel as good."

Almost one in five Americans age 65 and over engage in unpaid volunteer work for organizations such as churches, schools, or other civic groups. Sharing one's resources, skills, and experience can help both the giver and the receiver to grow.

Sixteen percent of men and 8% of American women also participate in the labor force after age 65. We explore this option further in Chapter 17.

I have four children, and if I'm at a family gathering, I want to be able to participate in the conversation instead of complaining about my pains and ailments. It's important to show that you know what they're talking about. And all that also can help to promote "connectedness."

Mary, age 79

Aristotle once wrote, "Education is the best provision for old age." There are opportunities for continuing education all around us: the public library, a writing class, free lectures, the Internet. Consider asking a friend or family member to join a club or take a class with you. We guarantee that even in some small measure, it will help to enrich both of your lives. Mental exercises are as important as physical exercises.

The true way to render age vigorous is to prolong the youth of the mind.

Mortimer Collins (1827–1876)

Staying Connected

In some ways, strong connections with friends and family, participation in social activities, and availability of social support can be as important as or more important than physical exercise and other activities. One of our colleagues, Lisa Berkman, has shown that those who don't stay closely connected to others experience greater declines in physical and mental functioning. Conversely, social factors can modify the effects of various health problems that we may experience.

The average age when women become widows is 56 years, and many women live for an average of 18 years after their husbands have died. In 1997, almost half of American women over age 65 were widows.

In contrast, divorced and widowed men may remarry quickly. Men who do not remarry have a higher death rate than those who do.

In Chapter 17, we talk more about ways to remain close to others by participating in social clubs, joining "visiting groups," and maintaining telephone contact with friends and family members. In so doing, you'll be better able to manage stress, and you'll strengthen your ability to cope with health problems.

The tree of deepest root is found
Least willing to quit the ground;
'Twas therefore said by ancient sages
That love of life increased with years,
So much that in our later stages,
When pains grow sharp and sickness rages,
The greatest love of life appears.

Hester Lynch Piozzi (1741–1821)

Changing Behaviors for a Healthy Life

What changes do you think are necessary to make your life healthier and happier? Do you want to spend more time with friends, volunteer at the local hospital, enroll in a class, or eat a healthier diet?

In a study of middle-aged Americans, another colleague, Paul Cleary, found that it can be quite difficult to try to make major lifestyle changes to prevent various health problems. Only one in five persons who tries to change behavior actually succeeds the first time. For instance, the average smoker tries to quit four to seven times prior to quitting permanently. Trying to lose weight or to quit smoking may be the most difficult changes of all.

James O. Prochaska has developed a theory called "stages of change," which includes five steps to changing behavior:

1. *Precontemplation* involves being conscious of the ill effects of one's behavior (for example, being aware that smoking causes lung cancer).
2. In the *contemplation* step, a person considers changing. This stage can last a long time. One study of 200 smokers showed that most remained in this stage for two years.
3. *Preparation* involves planning to take definite steps to change within a given time. It can be helpful to set a certain date to make a change. If you've tried to change a particular behavior before and you haven't succeeded, this may be a good time to figure out what went wrong.
4. *Action* occurs when you take steps to change the behavior.
5. *Maintenance* involves the prevention of relapse. It begins six months after taking action and can last a lifetime. You can learn to recognize and avoid those triggers of undesirable behaviors that can cause you to relapse.

One of us (SL) suggests that the "stages of change theory" doesn't go far enough to help people with lifetime behavioral change. We believe that behavioral change occurs best when attempted in a supportive social environment that enables rather than inhibits individuals in adopting and continuing positive behavioral change. So, think about the roadblocks that tend to interfere with your ability to achieve your goals. Do you want to exercise three times every week? What types of impediments may prevent you from doing so? What can you do about these obstacles? What will you need to do to get back on track if something stands in the way of helping you to meet your goals?

You can begin to make some improvements. Take on one concern at a time, and find a friend, counselor, or physician to help you strategize and stay motivated. Take what was once a roadblock and turn it into an enabler! Don't give up. Don't let go. Keep trying, even if you don't succeed fully the first time. As long as you keep trying, you will continue to make progress, and eventually you will succeed. Don't be disheartened if you fail a few times. Just keep trying. You will eventually succeed.

In the next chapter, we discuss some ways to find the best health care and tap into the resources that are available to help you succeed.

There is no short-cut to longevity. To win it is the work of a lifetime.

Sir James Crichton-Browne (1840–1938)

*There is a wisdom in this beyond the rules of physic. A man's
observation, what he finds good of and what he finds hurt of,
is the best physic to preserve health.*

Francis Bacon (1561–1626)

Just as when you were younger, at this stage of your life your doctors should
support you in your efforts to prevent illness, as well as to treat any health problems you may have. You and your doctor are a team. The job of this team is to
help you to stay well, maximize your independence, and maintain a high quality of life.

Is this your experience? Do you have a comfortable relationship with your
primary care physician? Do you feel that he or she is doing as much to keep
you healthy as to cure what ails you, or do you feel that your visits to your doctor are rushed and impersonal? Does the task of negotiating your way through
today's complicated and expensive health care system seem so overwhelming
that you put off or avoid checkups altogether?

Part of the problem is that most doctors don't specialize in treating seniors.
Therefore, to get the most from your trips to the doctor's office, you need to
learn to communicate with your doctors so that they can relate to your experience of illness beyond diagnostic categories of disease.

Health Care Options

As you know, the U.S. health care system is in flux, and some of the options
presented in this book may not be available at this time to all readers. This guide
is therefore meant to illustrate the range of choices you might be given.

Medicare

Medicare is an insurance program created in 1965 to assist older Americans and
some disabled individuals in paying for health care. If you are receiving Social
Security benefits, you are probably eligible for Medicare, too.

How It Works. Major transformation is occurring in the organization and delivery of health care today, but as of this writing, Medicare benefits are broken into two parts: Part A (Medicare Hospital Insurance) and Part B (Medicare Supplemental Medical Insurance). Part A covers some hospital, skilled-nursing facility, home health, and hospice care. It also pays for blood products. Part B covers a portion of doctors' bills and pays for some prescription drugs.

If you are a beneficiary of Medicare, you can usually opt for either a fee-for-service plan or a managed care plan. The following sections describe how these two choices may differ.

Traditional Fee-for-Service Medicare. In a fee-for-service plan, you see a physician who treats you and bills you directly for care. One plus of this system is that you usually can choose any licensed doctor or hospital that is certified by Medicare.

Indemnity plans are the most common fee-for-service plans. Generally, you pay a deductible, as well as any costs that are not covered or that surpass those that are approved by Medicare. The different types of indemnity plans include

- *Hospital indemnities.* Hospital indemnity plans pay a fixed amount for each day that you spend in the hospital, up to a preset number of days or a preset payment amount. Some plans also offer coverage for surgery or skilled nursing home care.
- *Medical/surgical expense plans.* Generally these plans pay a certain amount for various medical conditions and surgical procedures.
- *"Specific disease" plans.* Similarly, these plans pay a certain amount only when you need treatment for one disease (such as cancer) or a certain group of diseases (such as heart diseases).
- *Disability plans.* These plans pay a set amount for each month that you are out of work due to illness.
- *Long-term care insurance (LTC) plans.* Such plans pay a set amount for each day that you require nursing home, home health, hospice, adult day care, and other services (see Chapter 18).

Managed Care Plans and Medicare. Medicare also contracts with private health insurers such as health maintenance organizations (HMOs) to provide care to seniors. In so-called "managed care" plans, you enroll in an HMO, preferred provider organization (PPO), or point-of-service (POS) plan.

For a fixed price, this plan covers preventive care (for example, annual physical examinations and immunizations). Patients generally pay monthly premiums as well as minimal copayments each time they see the doctor or have a prescription filled. These plans may be less expensive than fee-for-service plans.

The potential down side to managed care is that in some cases you have less say in choosing your doctor than you would under a traditional fee-for-service plan. If you want to visit a physician who is outside your managed care network of doctors, you may have to pay for part or all of the visit yourself.

These organizations also may try to keep costs down by limiting what they consider to be unnecessary services. They may, for instance, agree to pay for fewer days for recovery in a hospital than other plans might. Sometimes they also may limit home-care services.

The positive part of their efforts to contain costs, however, is that Medicare managed care plans tend to emphasize preventive care, so they may cover all or part of the cost of a health club. This is how these types of plans differ:

- *HMOs* usually have their own doctors and sometimes hospitals. You may be able to visit one facility to see all of your doctors and specialists. Sometimes, several groups of doctors' offices and other health facilities are linked together in an HMO network.
- *PPOs* generally are more expensive than HMOs. These managed care plans provide care through networks of physicians—these doctors are not centralized in one facility as they may be with HMOs.
- *POS* plans are a type of PPO. With a POS plan, you can go outside the plan's network of providers, and the plan will still pay a certain portion of the charges. However, you will have to pay more for this flexibility.
- *Individual practice associations (IPAs)* generally don't have their own medical staff. Rather, they have contracts with several physicians who have their own medical practices. You choose one primary care doctor from their list of contracted physicians, and that doctor can refer you to any specialists that you may need to see.

To find out more about the managed care plans where you live, call your state insurance counseling office or Medicare. If there are a few different managed care plans to choose from in your area, you can compare their benefits, as well as the premiums and copayments that you will be required to pay if you join.

Like doctors, HMOs are certified. You can check with the National Committee for Quality Assurance (their phone number is 202-955-3500) to find out whether the HMO that you're interested in is accredited.

Public Health. In some communities, neighborhood community health centers serve individuals regardless of their level of income. Sometimes, they also offer free or low-cost immunizations for all. You can easily find out more by calling your city or state commission of health or Department of Medical Assistance.

When looking into managed care health plans, here are some questions that you may want to consider:

Which Health Plan Is Good for You?

- Do I have any preexisting health conditions that might stand in the way of total coverage?
- Is my doctor in the plan? How many other doctors does this plan include?
- How expensive is the plan? How much do the monthly premiums cost? What are my other monthly costs?

- What are the benefits of the plan?
- Are visits to the emergency room covered?
- Are drugs covered? How expensive are drug copayments?
- How much would my medications cost me under this or another plan?
- How expensive are office-visit copayments?
- How can I switch back to fee-for-service Medicare if I'm not satisfied with this plan? Will I have to wait for a certain length of time to disenroll from the plan?
- Will I need to get a referral every time I need to see a specialist?
- What type of coverage will I have if I travel a lot or live out of the state for part of the year?

Medicaid

Another federal health-insurance program, *Medicaid,* provides coverage for people who are over age 65 with low incomes, as well as for individuals of all ages who are blind or otherwise disabled. Sometimes, patients who have had Medicare coverage may switch to Medicaid when they have exhausted their own financial resources to pay for medical bills or nursing home care.

Health Plans for Active and Retired Military Personnel

For members of the military and those who have retired from military service, the government also provides health care through veterans' hospitals and through the Civilian Health and Medical Insurance Program of the Uniformed Services (CHAMPUS). Also, the Veterans Health Administration provides care to veterans through 22 Veterans Integrated Service Networks (VISNs). These patients also are covered by Medicare.

Private Health Insurance

In addition to the health plans just described, there are other private health insurance plans to consider. For instance, many people purchase "Medigap" health insurance that supplements the expenses (such as copayments and deductibles, dental exams, and home health care) that are not covered by Medicare. Medigap plans are usually for patients who have chosen fee-for-service, rather than managed care plans.

Because Medicaid coverage is generally more extensive than Medicare, if you qualify for Medicaid, you probably won't need to buy supplemental Medigap insurance. Also, if you do purchase one of these supplemental policies, we recommend that you buy just one, because usually having more than policy does not give you any additional coverage.

Medigap plans are regulated by federal and state laws, and many states control the number of different Medigap plans that are available. This makes it easier for patients to comparison shop among the different plans. Contact your state insurance commission to help you review the different private supplemental insurance options that are available in your area.

While you're exploring your choices, keep the following considerations in mind:

- Does this plan have "preexisting condition" exclusions? In other words, will the policy cover health problems that you already have—not just ones that you may develop in the future?
- Do you really need this coverage, or do you already have another comprehensive policy? Again, two policies generally aren't necessary. On the other hand, if you want to switch from one Medigap policy to another, don't cancel the first one until you're certain that the second is in place.
- Beware of agents who tell you that their policies are sponsored by the government. State laws regulate insurance policies, but states do not sell them.
- Make sure that the insurance company is licensed in your state. Call your state insurance department before you sign anything.
- Pay only by check, money order, or a bank draft made out to the insurance company (not to the agent). Make sure that you have the agent's and the company's names, addresses, and telephone numbers.

Once you've chosen a health plan and a physician, you may find it helpful to write down the following information to help you keep track of the paperwork that tends to follow (and sometimes precede!) most visits to the doctor:

- Your Medicare claim number
- The name, claims address, and policy number of your supplemental health insurance plan, if you have one

The American Association of Retired Persons (AARP) also recommends that you keep the following type of payment record:

Controlling the Paper Trail

Know Who Will Pay the Bills

Payments for Visits to the Doctor and for Prescriptions

Doctor/prescription	Date	For	Cost
Dr. Smith	5/12/99	Office visit, EKG	$100

You can monitor your medical expenses carefully by recording the following for each visit to the doctor or each prescription filled.

Doctor Visit Record

Charge	I paid ($/date)	Claim filed w/Medicare	$ approved by Medicare	$ paid by Medicare	Claim filed w/other insurer	$ paid by other insurer
$100	none	5/12/99	$100	$80	6/13/99	$20

Source: Adapted from AARP, *AARP Health Care Campaign,* 1992. Reprinted with permission.

Help Your Doctor's Office to Help You with Claims

Before you visit your doctor, call to confirm that your health insurance will pay for the doctor's office visit. Usually, there is a financial counselor in the office who can advise you and assist you.

Here are some other things to keep in mind about Medicare coverage:

1. Providers (your doctors) usually must file the initial claim to Medicare.
2. Call your doctor's office to confirm that they filed your claim. If you haven't received a Medicare "explanation of benefits" statement within two months, call Medicare (1-800-638-6833) and find out why.
3. If your claim is denied, find out why (from Medicare). You may need to ask your doctor to change or justify the claim or to file an appeal.
4. Be sure to tell both your provider and Medicare if you have an employer-based health care plan that pays first before Medicare.
5. If you have Medigap insurance, give the policy number or numbers to your doctor's office so that they can put that information on the Medicare claim form. Medicare may automatically forward your claim to your Medigap insurer for processing.
6. You may need to forward your claim to your insurance company by yourself.
7. Outpatient hospital charges are sometimes higher than those approved by Medicare. Talk with your hospital financial counselor if necessary.

Source: Adapted from AARP, *AARP Health Care Campaign,* 1992. Reprinted with permission.

Know How to Appeal for Coverage

What if, after you've chosen a managed care plan, you find that the plan will not pay for services that should be covered through Medicare, or it won't provide the services that you need? If your HMO denies you coverage for medical services that you and your doctor believe to be medically necessary, ask your HMO to put this denial in writing, then contact the membership office of the plan itself. Your local Social Security Administration office, state insurance counseling office, and area agency on aging can help you, too. Finally, you can appeal the decision through an independent arbiter appointed by the U.S. government. In October 1999, Congress passed legislation that would increase federal protection of medical consumers and give them the right to sue HMOs for deaths and injuries resulting from denied treatment or poor care.

Traditional and Alternative or Complementary Medicine

Traditional doctors include doctors of medicine (M.D.s) who can diagnose illnesses, prescribe medications, and in certain instances perform surgery. The American Medical Association also recognizes doctors of osteopathic medicine (D.O.s) as fully qualified primary care doctors. Osteopathic physicians are trained and licensed to practice complete medical care just as M.D.s are. The difference between these two types of doctors lies in the philosophy that underlies their training: Osteopathy emphasizes good body mechanics and the ability of the healthy body to heal itself from disease. D.O.s also prescribe medication and perform surgery.

Primary care physicians—both M.D.s and D.O.s—can refer you to many different types of specialists, such as a *geriatrician,* who specializes in caring for seniors, or a *geriatric psychiatrist,* who can help with emotional and psychological problems.

More and more, Americans are turning to *alternative,* or *complementary, healers* for everything from back problems to cancer. The accompanying sidebar lists some of the different types of nontraditional forms of therapy that are available. Many of these therapeutic options are not covered by certain health-insurance plans. Always check with your plan ahead of time to see what they will cover.

Acupuncture uses tiny needles to stimulate energy in the body.

Homeopathy involves the use of plants and minerals to encourage the body to heal itself.

Naturopathy generally stresses the use of natural elements, such as water, sunshine, and fresh air, and sometimes physical manipulation (such as chiropractic therapy—described later in this list) and electrical stimulation to heal the body. Practitioners of naturopathy usually don't encourage the use of medicines and surgery.

Massage therapy can improve your circulation, ease your aches and pains, and make you more relaxed by loosening up contracted muscles. Research has also shown that massage—a dose of human touch—can have wonderful therapeutic benefits for people who may feel depressed and alone.

Ayurvedic medicine is a traditional Indian form of treatment that employs exercise, herbs, massage, and dietary changes to create a sense of balance in the body.

Chiropractic therapy uses manipulation of the spine and the muscles and joints surrounding it to take away headaches and back pain. Sometimes serious injuries such as stroke or spinal cord paralysis may result from this manipulation, especially in persons with neck or back conditions. You should discuss this therapy with your doctor first.

Nontraditional (Alternative or Complementary) Medicine

If you're "in the market" for a new doctor, talk with your friends and loved ones and other health care workers about their recommendations.

Your local hospital or medical society also may have a physician referral service. If you live near a major medical center or teaching hospital, you can contact individual departments for doctors who are taking new patients.

Sites relating to health on the Internet may be good resources, but the information may not always be the most reliable. One Internet site that does provide accurate, useful guidance is www.abim.org. This site by the American Board of

Finding a Doctor

Where to Find a Physician

Internal Medicine lists which doctors in your area are "board certified," which means that they have passed certain exams that prove their expertise in internal medicine or specialties such as geriatrics. Your public library also may have this information in book form in the reference section in the *Directory of Physicians in the United States* and the *Official American Board of Medical Specialties Directory of Board-Certified Medical Specialists*.

Questions to Ask When You're Choosing a Doctor

Selecting a new physician is an important decision requiring careful consideration. You may find it helpful to make a list of traits or factors that are most important to you, and then consider your options against this list before you make your final selection.

When you've found a few physicians who appear to be good choices, call their offices and ask about their background, location, office hours, and billing policies. If the doctor is taking new patients, ask for an informational appointment (you may have to pay for this).

Consider the following questions:

WHAT IS THE PHYSICIAN'S BACKGROUND AND SPECIALTY? When and where did the doctor go to medical school? How long has he or she been practicing medicine? Is he or she board-certified in a specialty such as internal medicine or geriatrics?

CAN YOU COMMUNICATE WITH THIS PHYSICIAN? Do you feel that he or she listens to you and shows you respect? Do you feel comfortable talking about very personal and sensitive subjects with this person? For example, do you feel that you can discuss your sexual activities openly with him or her? Could you tell him or her about your feelings about entering a nursing home, your end-of-life wishes, or dying? Would you feel more comfortable if your doctor was of the same sex, ethnicity, or religious background as you are?

DOES HE OR SHE SEE MANY OLDER PATIENTS? What are his or her views on including the patient's family members in decisions about care? Will he or she continue to serve as your doctor if you enter a long-term health care facility (see Chapter 18)? Most importantly, what are his or her views on aging? Does he or she feel that memory loss, incontinence, or depression are to be expected as we get older? As you'll discover as you read this book, these conditions are *not* part of the normal aging process—and in many cases they can be treated. If this physician does not seem to take your concerns seriously, find another one.

WILL THIS DOCTOR SPEND ENOUGH TIME WITH YOU? It's fair to ask how long his or her average visits with patients are.

DOES THE PHYSICIAN HAVE HIS OR HER OWN PRACTICE, OR DOES HE OR SHE BELONG TO A GROUP? Is this doctor taking new patients? How difficult is it to get an appointment? Does he or she see patients every day? Who will cover for your doctor after hours or when he or she is away?

WHICH HOSPITAL IS THIS DOCTOR AFFILIATED WITH? Is this hospital conveniently located? Does it have a good reputation? Can it provide the services you may need?

WHAT ARE HIS OR HER FEES AND BILLING PRACTICES LIKE? What do the doctor's fees include? Will his or her office bill your insurance provider directly, or will you need to pay at the time of the visit?

Once you've chosen a physician, go ahead and set up an appointment for a physical.

GET DIRECTIONS. One way to maximize your time with your physician is to prepare ahead of time for getting to the doctor's office. If you've never been there before, ask the doctor's secretary to send you good instructions or go through such directions with you by phone. Also feel free to ask about parking, the distance from the doctor's office to the subway or bus stop, and whether there is an elevator in the building if the office is not on the first floor.

BEAT THE TRAFFIC. When scheduling your doctors' appointments, consider your energy level and the most convenient time of day for you to travel to the doctor's office—and request an appointment for that time of day.

GATHER YOUR MEDICAL RECORDS. If you have several other health providers, ask ahead of time which medical records the doctor would like to see, and request—as soon as possible—that this information be sent to your new doctor right away. Then call to see whether it's been sent. In addition to the names and addresses of your other doctors, make sure you have all relevant insurance information and your Social Security card with you. If your new physician would like you to fill out a medical history form, ask whether his or her office can send it to you in advance so that you'll have plenty of time to fill it out.

BRING A NOTEBOOK. Bring along notes about any symptoms that you may be having (including when and how often they occur and what remedies seem to help), a list of questions for the doctor, as well as a list of the drugs (both prescription and nonprescription) that you may be taking. You should also gather up all of the medications that you've been taking and bring them along to show the doctor. Finally, bring along the name, address, and phone number of the pharmacy that you prefer to use.

BRING A COMPANION. Bring along a friend or loved one. It will be nice to have the company and to help you remember what the doctor said. If English is not your first language, bring someone who can serve as a careful translator, or request one.

KNOW YOUR HEALTH HISTORY AND THE HEALTH HISTORY OF YOUR FAMILY. Did you stop smoking 20 years ago? It's helpful to have a list of which immunizations, medical conditions, and operations you've had, and whether you have allergies to any medications. Your doctor may also ask about the general health histories of your immediate family members.

TELL HIM OR HER ABOUT ANY RECENT CHANGES IN YOUR LIFE, GOOD OR BAD. Did your son get married? Did you just gain a grandchild? Did your husband or wife die recently? Have you been having trouble sleeping? How is your

Getting the Most out of Your Doctor Visits

Before the Visit

During Your Appointment

appetite? Do you notice any dizziness or headaches after taking certain medications? Your doctor will want to know all of this information.

This doesn't mean that you need to give your doctor your whole life story! Be honest about your concerns, however, and be sure to mention any details that may help the doctor to help you. Ask as many questions as you need to ask until you feel that you understand his or her advice.

TAKE NOTES. Note-taking will make it easier to remember what happened during the visit. Some people feel that note-taking is too distracting, and they find that taping the visit helps them to keep the details straight. Of course, you'll need to ask your doctor's permission before you do this.

ASK QUESTIONS, THEN ASK AGAIN. Don't hesitate to ask your doctor to draw a picture of what he or she is talking about, give you a written list of important things to remember, provide you with a pamphlet full of information, or recommend a book about your condition. If your hearing isn't as good as it used to be, tell the doctor if you can't hear what he or she is saying.

ASK ABOUT ANY SPECIAL TESTS THAT YOUR DOCTOR RECOMMENDS. If your physician recommends that you undergo a diagnostic test or tests, make sure that you understand what the test is for before you leave his or her office. Key questions to ask are

- What type of information will this test provide?
- Where will the test be performed?
- How should I prepare for it?
- When will the test results be available?
- Is the test expensive? How much will insurance cover, and how much will I pay?

IF YOUR DOCTOR PRESCRIBES DRUGS FOR YOU, make sure that you have the answers to the following questions:

- What is the medicine for?
- How much and how often should I take it? How long will I need to take it?
- Can or should I take it with or without food?
- How should this medicine be stored?
- What should I do if I miss a dose?
- Are there are any potentially harmful interactions with drugs that I'm already taking?
- Are there any side effects or risks to be aware of?
- How often should I see the doctor to check on how this medicine is working after I've started taking it?
- Are there any pamphlets available so that I can read about this drug if I have any questions?
- Is this medicine expensive? Are there any generic drugs or less expensive drugs that I can take instead?

Call the doctor's office if you have any questions.

If you're taking medication and you're having a bad reaction to it, or if it doesn't appear to be working, let your doctor know. Never stop taking a medication without speaking with your physician about it first.

Following is a useful chart to help you remember essential information about the drugs that you are taking.

My Medicines

Drug	For	Appearance	Began	Prescribed by	Dosage	Notes
Isosorbide dinitrate (Isordil, Sorbitrate)	Heart	green circle	7/2/00	Dr. Smith	30 mg	Take with food

If your primary care physician recommends that you see a specialist—a cardiologist for a particular heart problem, for example—your primary care doctor will make a referral to a specialist so that the cost of your visit to the specialist is covered by your health care plan. You or your friend or family member may need to make sure that your specialist receives your medical records from your primary care doctor, and vice versa. Especially if the specialist is not in the same group as your regular doctor, it's very important to make sure that these physicians communicate regarding your situation so that they can work as a team to give you optimal quality care. Just as with your primary care doctor, you should feel free to ask a specialist about his or her diagnosis and treatment recommendations.

If your primary care physician or specialist recommends surgery, you may want to seek a second opinion (or you may need to if your insurance company requires it). It's not at all unusual to do so, and you needn't be concerned that your doctor will be offended if this is what you decide to do. In fact, he or she may be able to provide you with the name of another doctor or specialist who can assess your situation also.

If both doctors recommend surgery, these are the important questions that you'll need to ask:

- What is this operation for?
- Is it an *outpatient procedure* (which means you'll be able to go home not long afterwards to recover, without having to spend the night in the hospital) or is it an *inpatient operation*? If it is the latter, how long would you expect me to stay in the hospital?
- Where will this operation take place?
- Will you, my doctor or specialist, perform this operation? If not, who will?

- What are the success rates for this surgery? Are there any common complications that I should be aware of?
- How can I prepare for it?
- What will my recovery period be like?

| **In the Hospital** | If your illness or operation requires that you stay in the hospital overnight or longer, find out as much as possible ahead of time about the particular hospital at which you'll be staying. For instance, is it a teaching hospital, where you might be seen by medical students, interns, residents, and fellows, as well as your own doctor? How often can you expect to see your own physician? What is the nurse-to-patient ratio? |

| **After Hospital-ization** | Depending on the type of health coverage you have, you may qualify for a number of different types of care after you leave the hospital. |

| **Home Health Care** | If you need short-term care after hospitalization, and you have some help at home already (from a family member or friend, for example), a home health care aide, nurse, or in some cases a physician can make house calls to oversee your care in your own home. You may be able to rent equipment (such as a hospital bed or commode), and services such as meals and housekeeping may be provided by the home health agency. |

| **Rehabilitation Hospital or Acute Hospital Rehabilitation Unit** | There are fewer free-standing rehabilitation hospitals now than there were in the past because they are so expensive to run. However, these facilities play an important role in providing care for patients with complex health problems (such as a stroke) that may require them to receive more intensive care than might be available in other care options. |

| **Subacute Care Units** | Subacute care is a growing field that includes skilled care provided after hospitalization. This option is best for patients who do not need to be in the hospital or a long-term care facility, but who are not yet ready to return home after experiencing an acute illness such as congestive heart failure, a musculoskeletal injury, or stroke. Subacute care sometimes, but not always, involves rehabilitative or nursing home care. Besides subacute care, you may hear the following terms used to refer to this type of health care: skilled care, intensive therapeutic care, transitional care, extended care, and restorative care. |

Your health care team will recommend a subacute-care facility for you before you leave the hospital. These are the questions you and your family may wish to ask at this time:

- How is the facility organized in terms of patients who are there for short- and long-term care? We have found that facilities that have a special unit for short-term care can be more motivating for some patients.
- Which hospital is the facility affiliated with?

- Who is the medical director of this facility? Who are the doctors? Will you be able to see your own doctor?
- Are there rehabilitation therapists on staff? If so, how often is therapy offered?
- Will my insurance plan cover the costs of this facility?

When you or a loved one is ill or just not feeling well, you want to do the right thing and get the best possible care. How do you determine whether that care is at your doctor's office or the emergency room? Although that may sound like a simple question, when you are in a real-life situation, it's not always easy to figure out what you should do. Our best answer is that if you or a loved one has a sudden, acute change, even something subtle such as slightly slurred speech, you should not hesitate to call your doctor immediately and, if so instructed, go straight to the emergency room. On the other hand, if you or they are suffering from persistent symptoms, such as a nagging cough or dizziness, it is best to contact your doctor's office and seek their advice on what to do. If you have trouble getting through to your doctor or health care provider, then you'll need to use your best judgment, but if the situation changes suddenly or becomes worse, please go to the nearest hospital. You should not worry that you will be inconveniencing anyone.

What Is an Emergency?

Stella called her mother's doctor's office on a Friday morning to say that her 79-year-old mother, Mildred, had just vomited profusely, then passed out and woke up with a bloody nose and incoherent speech. She didn't know what she should do and didn't want to call an ambulance before speaking with the doctor. She was told by the doctor's office to call an ambulance immediately and proceed with her mother to the nearest emergency room.

Stella then called the office back about 20 minutes later and said that her mother was much better and that she'd decided not to call the ambulance. They had been to the emergency room before, she explained, and had been stuck waiting most of a day before Mildred was seen. Neither of them wished to repeat that experience. She then asked whether her mother could be seen the next week in the clinic.

Stella was told that a sudden event such as the one her mother had just had was not something that could wait for an appointment in the doctor's office. When she and Mildred still expressed a reluctance to go and a concern that the situation wasn't really an "emergency," an ambulance was called by the office to take Mildred to the nearest hospital.

Mildred was admitted to the hospital, where she remained for several days while being treated for a stroke.

In the case of Stella and her mother, Mildred, it was necessary that she go straight to the emergency room to get the immediate care that was required. The story of Tom and his father, James, is an example of a non-urgent visit to the emergency room.

James is an 82-year-old man who suffers from very mild dementia and lives at home with his son Tom and Tom's wife, Susan. James had been in bed for most of the week with a bad cold and didn't move around much except to go to the bathroom and for meals. He didn't have a fever but did have a cough and runny nose. On Wednesday afternoon, he got up out of bed to go to the bathroom and became dizzy and had to sit down. He told Tom about the incident, and Tom became concerned.

Tom called the doctor's office, explained what had happened, and was told that a nurse would call him back shortly. When the nurse called back a few minutes later, there was no answer at the house. Tom had decided to take his father to the emergency room.

Several hours later, the doctor received a page from the emergency room, stating that James was being sent home and that he'd suffered a dizzy spell after he'd risen from his bed too quickly. They'd run all sorts of tests and found no new changes with him other than the common cold.

It was correct for Tom to be concerned about his father's health and for him to be willing to seek prompt treatment. It would, however, have been equally appropriate in a situation such as this for him to have spoken with the nurse and then had his father seen in the office that afternoon or the next morning.

Staying in Charge of Your Health Care

We must never say that health conditions are good, but must rather ask ourselves constantly whether they are as good as they could be.

Henry E. Sigerist (1891–1957)

As we explore in Chapter 20, there are several legal documents available so that you can ensure that your loved ones and doctors will be clear about your preferences even if one day you cannot communicate with them as you can now. Living wills and durable powers of attorney for health care are two forms of "advance directives" that we describe in more detail later on in this book.

If you don't already have such documents in place, think about what your preferences are, and begin to talk now with your family and physicians about your choices.

PART TWO

USER'S GUIDE TO THE AGING MIND AND BODY

CHAPTER 4
YOUR HEART

When man is serene and healthy
The pulse of the heart flows and connects,
Just as pearls are joined together or like a string of red jade—
Then one can speak of a healthy heart.

Huang Ti (2697–2597 B.C.)

You may have heard the story about the woman who went to the doctor because of some pain in her right knee. The doctor said, "Well, what do you expect? You're 90 years old!" She replied, "But my left knee doesn't hurt, and it's 90 years old, too."

How many times have you heard such negative messages about your aging body—even from doctors and nurses? When you have aches and pains, do you take these words to heart and write off your discomfort as part of getting old? Or do you, like the woman in this story, believe that your body can and should be well—and assert your right to feel better?

It's sometimes hard to stay positive when we're constantly bombarded with less-than-hopeful attitudes about aging and with frightening information about health problems that affect the older population. We're sure you've heard the statistics about heart disease, for instance: Nearly half of people over age 75 may have some form of it. In fact, heart disease is the number-one killer of older adults in the United States—that's at least one third of a million people every year.

Although it is true that the likelihood that we will develop, suffer from, and possibly die of a heart disorder *does* increase as we age, there are many ways that we can slow or even partly reverse the age-related changes that can lead to heart disease. Also, even if we do develop a heart problem, it's important to remember that heart disease—unlike many other chronic conditions such as emphysema or arthritis—may be very treatable and potentially even partly reversible. We can either allow heart disease to be extremely crippling or even lethal, or, with proper advice and treatment, we can live well in spite of it. Is a heart problem keeping you or a loved one at home, in bed, or confined to a chair? Is it standing in the way of an active, exciting lifestyle? It doesn't have to, and it shouldn't.

In this chapter, we talk a little bit about the way your heart works, what happens to it as you get older, and the symptoms, diagnosis, and treatment options for various heart problems. We also talk about things that you can do to make and keep your heart well.

How Your Heart Works

Your heart's job is to pump blood through your body. It's the driving force behind the circulatory system. Your heart continuously pumps, relaxes, then pumps again; this accounts for the *ba-boom* of your heartbeat.

Two major pumps (the ventricles) and two minor pumps (the atria) make up your heart muscle. The right side of your heart receives blood that is depleted of oxygen from all parts of your body and sends it to your lungs, where it picks up oxygen. Then the blood (now saturated with oxygen) returns from the lungs to the left side of your heart, where the left major pump (ventricle) moves it through the aorta and out to the rest of your body.

The blood from your heart travels throughout your body in vessels that are called *arteries.* Arteries branch into smaller vessels called *arterioles,* and finally into even smaller vessels, called *capillaries.* Within each organ, it is through these tiny capillaries that much of the oxygen and nutrients is exchanged for carbon dioxide and metabolic waste products, respectively, in your tissue.

As the blood continues to travel along, beyond the capillaries, the vessels grow larger again. They are now called *veins.* Veins enable the blood to continue to move through your body's major organs and then back to your heart, where the process begins all over again. All the while, the blood vessels and your heart are restoring the nutrients that your body needs and removing the waste that it doesn't.

Age-Related Changes

The Heart Muscle

Your heart pumps blood, or contracts, only one third of the time. The rest of the time, it is relaxing. As you grow older, your heart still contracts as well as it did when you were younger, but it may take longer for your heart to relax between contractions.

When the heart's relaxation capabilities are slowed, the rate at which the heart chamber fills with blood also decreases. At age 70, your heart will probably fill at about half the rate it did when you were 30. If your heart cannot fill with blood as efficiently as it needs to in order to keep pumping, you may be at risk for developing congestive heart failure.

When your heart beats faster (for example, during physical activity, illness, or fever), your heart's relaxation time is shortened even further. Young people can readily tolerate an increase in heart rate, but in older people, this rate increase could lead to fatigue and shortness of breath. In those who cannot raise the heart rate sufficiently to maintain an adequate blood pressure, even normal activities such as standing up or sitting up from a lying-down position, eating a meal, or using the toilet could result in dizziness or occasionally even fainting.

Another change that happens as we age is that the arteries may not be as distensible as they used to be, so the older heart usually meets greater resistance as it pumps. This will require the heart to work harder. Over time, your heart may lose some of its ability to fully adapt to all these changes.

The Arteries

Like much of the rest of our bodies, our arteries tend to stiffen with age. Artery walls do not expand as well as they used to because of decreased elastic tissue and increases in muscle and scar tissue; increased stiffness due to a fibrous protein called *collagen;* and calcium deposits. Midway through the artery wall, the smooth-muscle cells grow bigger and more plentiful, so that the wall becomes thicker and somewhat more rigid. The older heart, in turn, needs to supply more force to propel the blood forward through these thickened, stiffened, and less elastic arteries.

Blood Pressure

The force that is created when blood is pumped from your heart into your arteries is partly reflected in your blood pressure. As we grow older, we face a greater risk of developing elevated blood pressure, *hypertension.* This condition affects more than half of the over-70 population. Hypertension means that your heart is pumping blood against more resistance and is therefore working more than it needs to; this extra effort may lead to increased risk of coronary heart disease, congestive heart failure, stroke, and kidney failure.

Risk Factors for Heart Disease

Even if you have a history of good health and no cardiovascular risk factors (see the sidebar below), aging itself represents a risk factor for heart disease. A sedentary lifestyle and a diet that is high in fat may also exacerbate some of the changes that occur with aging and further contribute to your chance of developing heart problems.

Risk Factors for Heart Disease

- High blood pressure (hypertension), blood pressure above 140/90 millimeters of mercury (mmHg); or *systolic hypertension,* which means that the systolic pressure (the top number) is above 140, while the bottom number may be normal (below 90).

- Diabetes (especially for women), which adversely affects the small arteries and arterioles and may also be associated with elevated cholesterol

- High levels of serum cholesterol (total cholesterol above 240 mg/dl) and low-density lipoprotein (LDL) cholesterol (above 160 mg/dl), or LDL/cholesterol ratios above 0.6

- Decreased high-density protein (HDL) cholesterol levels (below 35 mg/dl in men and below 45 mg/dl in women)

- Age (older than 65 years)
- Smoking
- Obesity

Heart Specialists

Some heart diseases may act differently in the old compared to the young, and sometimes these health problems need to be treated differently. To take good care of your heart, you should have regular physical exams with your primary care physician and, if necessary, see one or two specialists to help you manage cardiac problems whenever they arise.

Heart and lung specialists are very well trained to advise you and your physician. *Cardiologists* are heart specialists who have spent at least six or seven years of additional training after medical school just to learn as much as they can about heart problems. This extra period of study includes a three-year residency in internal medicine, followed by a three- to four-year fellowship in cardiovascular diseases.

Similarly, *pulmonary specialists,* doctors who specialize in chest and lung problems, do a three-year internal-medicine residency and a two- to three-year pulmonary fellowship to gain clinical experience after medical school.

Cardiac surgeons spend four years after medical school studying general surgery and four more years after that learning about heart operations.

In addition to these specialists, at some point, you may need someone to help you coordinate your health care, especially if you have complicated medical problems. A *geriatrician* may be an excellent counselor. He or she may work as a primary care physician, be on staff in a hospital, and/or serve as an outpatient consultant. Like the other specialists we have just mentioned, a geriatrician spends additional time (usually at least five or six years after medical school) to gain extra clinical training and experience in his or her specialty—learning about the aging process and how to care for older persons.

How can you make sure that your doctor is qualified? Doctors need to take national board examinations in order to be certified in a given specialty. Specialists in cardiology and geriatrics must take additional board exams in their area of expertise; this testing process is overseen by the American Board of Internal Medicine. Surgeons must also take board exams that are overseen by the American College of Surgeons. To find out whether your doctor is "board certified," you can call the doctor or clinic that your doctor is affiliated with, or call 1 (800) 776-2378 or check an Internet website: www.certifieddoctor.org or www.abim.org.

Types of Heart Disease

Coronary Artery Disease

Coronary artery disease (CAD) is an appreciable narrowing of the arteries that supply the heart; this narrowing hinders or blocks blood flow. It happens when the inside lining of the arteries is thickened with fat and cholesterol deposits.

Each year, at least half of all people age 75 years and older who go to a doctor's office see a physician for heart disease.

SYMPTOMS. Many women with CAD first experience some chest discomfort or pressure (this is also called *angina pectoris,* whereas the initial acknowledged symptom for men may be more often that of a prolonged, unrelenting chest pressure associated with a heart attack (or myocardial infarction, see pp. 50–51). Women tend to lag behind men by an average of 10 to 15 years in developing CAD symptoms and by about 15 to 20 years in experiencing a first myocardial infarction.

DIAGNOSIS. To diagnose CAD, your doctor may use electrocardiography (ECG, or EKG), echocardiography, an exercise stress test, and possibly angiography to assess the extent and the effects of CAD on your heart and vessels. These diagnostic tests and others are described in more detail in the sidebar beginning on page 44.

TREATMENT. If your doctor determines that you have CAD, he or she will probably prescribe anti-anginal medicines and will probably also encourage you to make certain changes in your lifestyle. Dietary changes to reduce fat consumption to 30% of total caloric intake, weight control, regular exercise, and smoking cessation are generally recommended for treating CAD. Your physician may also prescribe medication to lower your cholesterol level, if needed.

For some postmenopausal women, estrogen replacement therapy may be recommended. Estrogen has been shown to be helpful for maintaining the integrity of the inner lining of the blood vessels (the endothelium) in some cases. Once the endothelium is diseased, clots can form easily in the vessel walls, and this can put you at risk for a future heart attack or stroke.

Procedures or operations that are sometimes used to treat people with CAD include:

- *Angioplasty* to open up the arteries
- *Coronary atherectomy* to remove fatty deposits inside the arteries
- *Intracoronary stent placement* to hold open an artery that was once closed, so that blood can continue to flow through it
- *Transmyocardial revascularization* to open up blocked areas with laser beams
- *Coronary artery bypass graft (CABG)* to circumvent a blockage in a coronary artery

Angina Pectoris

An 82-year-old woman once was completely homebound. She led a very restricted life because she could only go from her bed to a chair. She was having some discomfort due to angina, so her doctor recommended an angiography test to look at her heart vessels, and she ended up undergoing an angioplasty procedure to open up the clogged arteries.

Afterward, she became a new person: She got out of the house, started volunteering at her local senior center, went shopping for her neighbors, and completely redecorated her house. She was so delighted with her new self that she sent "before" and "after" photos of herself to her doctors. CAD is potentially a very treatable problem!

J.W.

Electrocardiography

Electrical impulses are responsible for each beat that your heart makes. Electrocardiography (ECG or EKG) is a common test used to assess the function of the heart by measuring its electrical activity.

An ECG is a *noninvasive test;* that is, it's done with equipment outside of your body. It is painless and does not cause electrical shock. For a resting ECG, a doctor or nurse will ask you to lie still and breathe normally. He or she may wipe certain areas of your chest with an alcohol pad to remove oils on the skin and then attach electrodes that can detect your heart's electrical impulses.

An *exercise ECG (stress test)* is used to assess your heart function during physical activity. Bicycle and treadmill testing are two forms of exercise ECGs. Your doctor will first do a resting ECG and then will have you exercise on the bicycle or treadmill while electrodes are attached to your chest. This type of testing is not painful, but it can be tiring. You should be sure to get plenty of rest the night before you take an exercise ECG test, and avoid smoking, drinking alcohol or caffeinated drinks, and eating a meal right before the test. Dress comfortably. Sometimes, if you are not able to exercise due to other conditions such as arthritis or weakness, a chemical stress test may be recommended. If so, you will get an injection of a drug that has the same effect as exercise.

Echocardiography

An echocardiogram is another painless, noninvasive test that involves the use of sound waves to produce images of the heart. A transducer (a device that can sense the motion of the heart) is placed on several areas of the chest. This device generates brief pulses of high-frequency sound that go through the chest to the heart and back. These echoes are used to produce a two-dimensional image of the heart. An echocardiogram can be done at your bedside or in an echocardiography laboratory.

Transesophageal echocardiography (TEE) provides an even clearer view of the heart than a regular echocardiogram. A scope is inserted into the esophagus, behind the heart. This type of test requires mild sedation and local anesthesia, so you should not eat or drink anything for 8 to 10 hours before or 2 hours after a TEE scan. A TEE may produce mild throat discomfort, which usually does not last longer than a few days. This discomfort can be relieved by antiseptic spray or throat lozenges.

Doppler Test

A Doppler test is a sound wave test that can be used to give information about the flow of blood within either a heart chamber or a blood vessel. It is often used to complement the echocardiographic evaluation.

Cardiac Catheterization

A catheter can be inserted into the heart in order to assess any damage to or abnormalities in the heart and its surrounding vessels. This procedure is usually performed in a laboratory set up just for that purpose. If you undergo this test, you shouldn't eat or drink for at least four hours beforehand. In the cardiac catheterization room, you will lie on an x-ray examination table for approximately two hours for the procedure.

Cardiac catheterization is usually not painful, but it may be tiring. Risks from this procedure include clot formation, arrhythmias, infection, and an allergic reaction to the contrast medium, which contains iodine. You should discuss these risks with your physician before the procedure.

Computed Tomography

Scans done by computed tomography (CT) show the differences between bone and soft tissue. Several images are obtained by x-rays, and a computer reassembles the image data into a three-dimensional picture. This type of testing is painless.

Angiography

Angiography involves the intravascular (into a vein or artery) injection of a contrast medium (dye) before an x-ray film is taken to look at the blood vessels. This test is usually painless and brief. Some patients experience a transient sensation of flushing and warmth while the contrast medium is injected. Patients who have sensitivity to such dyes may need to take some medication before they take this test; if you are concerned about having such sensitivity, talk with your doctor.

Cardiac angiography (also called angiocardiography) involves injection of the contrast medium into the heart (the left ventricular chamber) during cardiac catheterization. X-ray films are then used to study the movement of the contrast agent from the heart into the aorta.

Coronary angiography (also called coronary arteriography) is a test to look for blockages in the coronary arteries surrounding the heart.

Cineangiography also involves the injection of a contrast medium into a blood vessel. Radiographic imaging techniques are then used to produce moving images of the flow of blood through the vessel.

Positron Emission Tomography

Positron emission tomography (PET) is a scanning test that involves injection of radioactive chemicals into your veins before images are taken. You will need to fast for four hours before the scan, and you will need to be motionless during part of the test. This type of diagnostic test takes between two and three hours.

Magnetic Resonance Imaging

A magnetic resonance imaging, or MRI, test uses a strong magnetic field and radio waves to produce multidimensional images of the structures of the heart. You must take off all metal items (for example, jewelry and eyeglasses) before an MRI scan. If you have a pacemaker, you cannot have this type of test because the magnetic field of the MRI could damage the pacemaker. During the scan, you will lie on a table inside the MRI machine for approximately one hour. If you tend to feel claustrophobic, your doctor may give you a sedative to help you relax.

Chest X-ray Studies

X-ray tests are routinely done for people with heart problems. Two standard views are usually taken, with one from back to front, and one from the side.

Radionuclide Imaging Scans

Radionuclide scans are x-ray pictures that can provide more information than normal x-ray films. During these painless tests, a small amount of radioactive isotopes are injected intravenously into the blood vessels. These isotopes are carried by the blood into the heart, and the radioactivity inside the heart can be detected by an external camera that then creates a high-resolution image.

Thallium scans are x-ray picture tests that involve a very small amount of radioactivity, and they are often used for heart scans to identify regions of insufficient blood supply (underperfusion) in the heart. Thallium imaging can be done alone or before or after an exercise ECG.

Radionuclide ventriculography is another type of test that creates images of the heart ventricular structures and shows how well the heart is contracting.

Vein Studies

Some of the studies of venous circulation include:

- *Phlebography,* in which a radio-opaque dye is injected into your veins, and then an x-ray film is taken to view them
- *Doppler flowmetry,* a test that measures the blood flow through your veins
- *Plethysmography,* a test that reveals how your veins are affected by the blood flowing through them

---

Angina pectoris, or chest pressure or discomfort that is caused by insufficient blood supply to the heart muscle, is present in about 10% of older persons. It is often the first sign of CAD and may in some instances herald the development of a subsequent heart attack.

SYMPTOMS. Angina appears similarly in the young and the old. Whereas younger people usually complain of chest pressure first, shortness of breath may be a more common first symptom among older people. If you are an older person, you also may experience sweating, palpitations, and, rarely, fainting. Other symptoms may include sudden coughing during times of emotional stress, increased fatigue, and (rarely) confusion.

Sometimes, if pain or discomfort does occur, it may feel as if it's coming not from your chest, but from your abdomen or back. Because these symptoms can be hard to pinpoint, many older people (especially women) tend to delay getting much-needed medical attention.

DIAGNOSIS. To diagnose angina, the tests are similar to those for CAD. Your doctor will ask you about your medical history and will talk with you about your symptoms. He or she may request several tests, including an ECG, blood tests, a standard exercise treadmill test with an ECG, a chest x-ray, and echocardiography or radioisotope imaging. A coronary angiography evaluation may also be recommended. These tests were described in more detail on pages 44–46.

TREATMENT. Angina is a warning signal that a part of the heart is not receiving enough oxygen or nutrients, and if untreated, a heart attack could occur in the future. Your physician will probably advise you to take immediate steps to prevent one. Excellent ways to do so include quitting smoking, losing excess weight, reducing stress in your life, and embarking on a sensible diet and exercise program.

There are also a number of medications that can help to treat your angina:

- *Beta blockers* are sometimes prescribed if you have both angina and high blood pressure or angina and rapid heartbeat because they reduce your heart's demand for oxygen and tend to slow down your heart rate. Common beta blockers include propanolol, atenolol, metoprolol, and timolol. A more recently approved beta blocker is carvedilol.
- *Vasodilators* work by dilating your blood vessels. A commonly used vasodilator is nitroglycerin, a nitrate that comes in patch, paste, and pill forms. You may be prescribed a nitroglycerin tablet to put under your tongue before you begin certain physical activities (such as showering or shaving) if they tend to bring on angina for you.
- *Calcium antagonists,* or *calcium channel blockers* such as nifedipine, diltiazem, verapamil, and amlodipine, may also be useful. These agents work by reducing the amount of constriction in your arteries.
- *Antiplatelet drugs* such as aspirin, ticlopidine, or similar agents decrease the likelihood that you will develop blood clots, so they can lower your risk of a stroke or heart attack.
- *Anticoagulants,* which are also sometimes called antithrombotics, such as heparin (including low-molecular-weight heparins) or warfarin, also reduce your risk of developing blood clots.

Table 4.1 describes some of the common applications and side effects of drugs used to treat heart diseases. Medications that are used to treat angina may sometimes lead to fainting, light-headedness, fatigue, and dizziness, so always discuss possible side effects with your doctor before taking a drug for the first time.

Not just people with angina, but also most people over age 50 who don't have contraindications, should take low-dose aspirin to prevent the formation of blood clots that can lead to strokes and heart attacks. Aspirin can also reduce your risk of developing dementia and colon, breast, or prostate cancer.

An Aspirin a Day, or Every Other Day

Ask your doctor how much and how often you should take this type of antiplatelet medication. We recommend starting at a daily dose of 81 mg.

Table 4.1 Commonly Prescribed Drugs for Heart Problems

Type	Generic name/trade (brand) name	Prescribed for	Side effects
ACE inhibitors	captopril (Capoten); enalapril (Vasotec); lisinopril (Prinivil, Zestril); quinapril (Accupril)	Aortic insufficiency; hypertension; congestive heart failure; MI; mitral regurgitation	Hypotension, cough, skin rash, dizziness, high potassium
Alpha blockers	doxazosin (Cardura); terazosin (Hytrin); prazosin (Minipress)	Hypertension	Postural hypotension, dizziness, fainting, headache
Angiotensin receptor antagonists	losartan (Cozaar); valsartan (Diovan)	MI; CHF; hypertension	Hypotension, dizziness
Anticoagulants	warfarin (Coumadin); heparin; enoxaparin (Lovenox)	Arrhythmias; MI; stroke; blood clots	Bleeding
Antiplatelet agents	acetylsalicylic acid (aspirin); abciximab (ReoPro) and eptifibatide (Integrilin) (new drugs that are also called glycoprotein IIb–IIIa inhibitors)	Arrhythmias; angina; MI; stroke	Bleeding, stomach upset
Beta blockers	metoprolol (Lopressor); timolol (Blocadren); atenolol (Tenormin); propanolol (Inderal); carvedilol (Coreg)	Angina; hypertension; MI; CHF; arrhythmias	Depression, confusion, wheezing, diarrhea, impotence, fatigue, insomnia
Calcium channel blockers	amlodipine (Norvasc); diltiazem (Cardizem); nifedipine (Procardia); verapamil (Calan, Isoptin); bepridil (Vascor); nicardipine (Cardene)	Aortic insufficiency; angina; hypertension; MI; CAD; arrhythmias	Dizziness, low blood pressure, fluid retention, itching, constipation

Commonly Prescribed Drugs for Heart Problems (continued)

Type	Generic name/trade (brand) name	Prescribed for	Side effects
Central sympathetic blockers	clonidine (Catapres); guanabenz (Wytensin); guanfacine (Tenex)	Hypertension	Sedation, dry mouth, blurry vision, headache, low blood pressure, dizziness
Digitalis	digoxin; digitoxin	Heart failure, atrial fibrillation	Confusion, nausea, anorexia, headache, visual disturbances
Diuretics	hydrochlorothiazide (HydroDIURIL); chlorthalidone (Hygro-ton); furosemide (Lasix); bumetanide (Bumex); ethacrynic acid (Edecrin); metola-zone (Zaroxolyn); spironolactone (Aldac-tone); triamterene (Dyrenium); amiloride (Midamor)	Hypertension; CHF; fluid retention	Urinary incontinence, low sodium, low potassium
Vasodilators	nitrites; nitroglycerin (Nitrolingual, Nitro-gard); isosorbide dinitrate (Isordil, Sorbitrate); hydralazine (Apresoline); minoxidil (Loniten)	Angina; congestive heart failure; MI	Hydralazine: headache, nausea, dizziness Minoxidil: fluid reten-tion, hair growth
Anti-arrhythmics	amiodarone (Cordarone); adenosine (Adipex); esmolol (Brevibloc); flecainide (Tambocor); quinidine (Quinidex); procainamide (Procanbid)	Atrial fibrillation; atrial flutter; ventricular tachycardia	Irregular rhythms, low blood pressure, rash, tremors, nausea, liver dysfunction, thyroid disorders

Myocardial Ischemia

Myocardial ischemia occurs when there is an insufficient supply of blood to the heart due to blockage or constriction of the coronary arteries. This condition can arise because excess fatty deposits called *atherosclerotic plaques* line and narrow the inside of the arteries, or because the coronary arteries do not dilate sufficiently in response to an increased demand for blood flow. These arteries with reduced flow can be further compromised when a plaque ruptures and a blood clot forms at the site, thereby occluding or nearly occluding the artery.

SYMPTOMS. Fewer women than men experience exertion-induced chest pressure as the first symptom of myocardial ischemia. Most women have less typical symptoms, such as jaw pain, heartburn, abdominal discomfort, and nausea and fatigue. They also experience shortness of breath and chest pressure (angina) at rest more often than men do.

In frail older women, the first major indications of myocardial ischemia are often extreme weakness, confusion, anxiety, and agitation.

DIAGNOSIS. In addition to a thorough history and physical examination, your doctor may have you get an ECG. Exercise treadmill testing with echocardiography is sometimes recommended for both men and women to screen for myocardial ischemia. Your doctor may also have you get a high-resolution radioisotope test called a thallium scan to view your heart. Coronary angiography may sometimes also be done. These tests were described in more detail on pages 44–46.

TREATMENT. To reduce your risk of developing a heart attack or irregular heart rhythms because of myocardial ischemia, your doctor will probably encourage you to do the following:

- Reduce your blood pressure through lifestyle changes and possibly medication (see Table 4.1).
- Lose weight
- Stop smoking
- Modify your diet to reduce your fat and salt intake and to eat more fruits, vegetables, and high-fiber foods
- Take antithrombotic drugs such as aspirin or warfarin to prevent blood clots from forming
- Lower your cholesterol with lifestyle changes or medication, or both

Myocardial Infarction

Acute myocardial infarction is the medical term for a heart attack. Heart attacks generally occur when a narrowed or partially blocked atherosclerotic artery develops a blood clot, often at the site of a ruptured plaque, that cuts off the flow of blood and damages the heart muscle. The severity of the attack depends on the extent of the damage to your heart.

In younger people, men are three times more likely than women to suffer heart attacks. Above the age of 70 years, however, the numbers even out to nearly one to one. Myocardial infarction (MI) occurs in women more commonly after menopause. In older women over age 65, MI may be associated with more complications, and they often occur while the person is at rest. Women who smoke have three times the risk of an MI, as compared to non-smoking women.

SYMPTOMS. Approximately one fourth of all people who experience acute MI do not have symptoms that are readily identifiable as being classic symptoms of a heart attack. Therefore, if you don't feel "quite right," or if your loved one just doesn't feel good or is uncomfortable and thinks perhaps he or she has indigestion, consider the possibility that this discomfort could be related to the heart—and seek medical advice promptly.

Symptoms of MIs that may occur in older people include:

- Severe, unrelieved chest pressure (this is not necessarily the first, major symptom of a heart attack in an older person)
- Pain in the back, neck, jaws, abdomen, left arm, or shoulder
- Sweating
- Confusion, agitation
- Fainting
- Stroke
- Dizziness
- Weakness
- Persistent vomiting
- Shortness of breath, cough

Patients with diabetes often do not have chest pressure with heart attacks. They may feel weak or "unwell."

If you have symptoms suggestive of a possible heart attack, DON'T WORRY ABOUT INCONVENIENCING SOMEONE. Please seek help immediately.

Sometimes, as we get older, we allow ourselves to have decreased expectations of our health, so that we accept pain or discomfort more readily because we think that it's inevitable. Otherwise highly functioning persons, including some physicians, have sometimes downplayed their chest discomfort. They may think it's only indigestion, and they lay down to rest. Unfortunately, sometimes it's more serious. A poor outcome in these cases perhaps could have been avoided or ameliorated if the person had picked up the telephone to let someone else know that he or she wasn't feeling right. Don't hesitate to call your daughter, son, friend, neighbor, or other caring person. Medical care is available to help you. You just need to let someone know that you need it.

DIAGNOSIS. In addition to blood tests, your physician will probably do an ECG to diagnose an MI. Other tests that may be done include radionuclide scan, PET, MRI, echocardiography, and TEE (see pp. 44–46).

TREATMENT. After a heart attack, your doctor may prescribe medications such as

- Beta blockers
- Nitrates

- Calcium channel blockers
- ACE (angiotensin-converting enzyme) inhibitors
- Angiotensin receptor antagonists
- Anti-inflammatory drugs (such as aspirin or related compounds) (Recent studies have shown that aspirin given to adults after a myocardial infarction reduced deaths by a third to a half.)
- Anticoagulation therapy (heparin, including low-molecular-weight heparins or warfarin)
- Thrombolytic drugs (including anti-platelet agents)

More information about these drugs can be found in Table 4.1.

A Promising Drug Therapy for Heart Attacks

"Clot-busting," or thrombolytic, drugs such as streptokinase or tissue plasminogen activator (TPA) in some cases may be sufficient for breaking up the clot formed by platelets and clotting proteins that are blocking blood flow to an area of the heart. In other situations, they may not do an adequate job.

What is needed in those situations are more effective agents to prevent further formation of a clot. A relatively new type of drug, called a "glycoprotein IIb–IIIa inhibitor," can be more successful, especially when it's combined with the standard clot dissolvers (see Table 4.1). Two glycoprotein IIb–IIIa inhibitors are "abciximab" (the trade name is ReoPro) and "eptifibatide" (Integrilin). These so-called "super clot busters" work directly on the blood platelets, preventing them from becoming activated, thereby preventing the development of more blood clots.

In some instances, this drug therapy can be as successful at clearing clogged arteries as balloon angioplasty (described in the subsequent "Procedures" section of this chapter). Preliminary findings suggest that these glycoprotein inhibitors may also be helpful in preventing complications following heart surgery. Future research will probably study the effect of oral glycoprotein IIb–IIIa inhibitors.

Available procedures that may be done after a heart attack include percutaneous transluminal coronary angioplasty (PTCA, also called "balloon angioplasty"), atherectomy, and stent placement, as well as laser myocardial revascularization. Surgery would entail CABG. (See the discussion of coronary artery disease for more information regarding these procedures; see also the subsequent "Procedures" section of this chapter.)

After a heart attack, your doctor will also encourage you to slowly and gradually increase your level of activity. When exercising, remember to warm up slowly, work out carefully, and cool down gradually. Light activity such as walking or stretching after exercise may help to prevent muscle injury.

Some people become depressed after a heart attack because they may have led an active, successful life until they were suddenly stricken. They may wake up in the hospital with intravenous (IV) lines and instrumentation everywhere, and be afraid that their life, as they knew it, is over. We might compare this depression to that which some women might experience after the birth of a child. Although you will not undergo postpartum hormonal fluctuations after having a heart attack, the lack of sleep and the psychological adjustment to this major life event can cause a similar sense of gloom.

If you find that you're feeling low, sad, and down in the dumps after a heart attack, tell your doctor. Let your friends and family members know that you need their support. Just as with postpartum depression, it may seem as though your life is falling apart, but things will definitely get better, and you will be able to regain control and return to the active life that you had before.

Cholesterol is a steroid substance found in animal cells and body fluids. Two types of cholesterol are important to keep in mind: high-density lipoprotein (HDL) and low-density lipoprotein (LDL). HDL can actually be protective against heart disease. LDL cholesterol, in contrast, is a risk factor for coronary heart disease. Cholesterol is less of a risk factor in old age than it is in middle age.

What about Cholesterol?

Should you have your cholesterol checked frequently?
If you have a prior history of CAD, abnormal results on an ECG, an enlarged heart (which can be seen on a chest x-ray film), angina associated with exertion, or a clinical diagnosis of angina pectoris or heart attack, you should have your cholesterol checked every year.

On the other hand, if your ECG results are normal, a chest x-ray film shows that you have a normal heart size, you have no cardiac symptoms, and you are older than 80, cholesterol checks may not be necessary.

What should you do if your cholesterol level is high?
If your doctor tests your blood cholesterol and finds an LDL level higher than 130 mg/dL, your doctor may recommend that you switch to a diet that is low in saturated fat. Therefore, you should eat less red meat, fried foods, saturated fats and oils, and whole milk, cheese, or other dairy products. If dietary changes do not bring your LDL level down, drugs such as cholestyramine and colestipol may be recommended.

Fortunately, the HDL cholesterol, or "good cholesterol," can be as beneficial for older people as it can be for younger people. If your HDL level is low (below 35 mg/dL), you may be able to bring it up to a good level with regular exercise.

Irregular heartbeats (also called arrhythmias or dysrhythmias) can lead to problems called "conduction disorders," which are aptly named because the healthy heart is like an orchestra in which all of the players are keeping perfect time. If

Irregular Heartbeats (Dysrhythmias)

one section of the orchestra skips a beat, though, all of the players may be thrown off, and a good conductor will have to get everyone back into the right rhythm.

Your heart can get out of rhythm even if it's healthy, or you may have irregular heartbeats because you have some form of heart disease. You may not be aware of any symptoms of this disorder, or you may have chest discomfort (angina), dizziness, fainting, heart palpitations, and/or shortness of breath.

There are different kinds of arrhythmias; most are more common in older than in younger people. The types of irregular heartbeats are designated by which part of the heart they originate from and whether the abnormal rhythm is fast or slow. During times of rest, an adult's heart usually beats 60 to 80 times every minute. The term *bradys* is Greek for "slow," and *tachys* is Greek for "swift." Hence, *sinus bradycardias* are slow heart rhythms (generally less than 60 beats per minute) that originate in a part of the atrium called the sinus node. Likewise, *atrial tachycardias* are rapid heartbeats (more than 100 beats per minute) that originate in the atrium (the upper chamber of the heart).

The sidebar below lists the types of irregular heartbeats that can originate in the atria, the atrioventricular junction (where the atria meets the lower chamber of the heart, or the ventricles), and the heart ventricles.

What Kind of Irregular Heart Rhythm Might You Have?

Some irregular heart rhythms originate in the *atria,* the upper chambers of the heart that receive blood from your veins and transfer it into the ventricles. These irregular rhythms, which are also called *atrial dysrhythmias,* can lead to the following disorders: atrial flutter, atrial fibrillation, paroxysmal atrial tachycardia, and sick sinus syndrome

The irregular heart rhythms that originate between the atria and the ventricles (the part of your heart that propels the blood forward to your arteries) are called *atrioventricular junction arrhythmias.* These irregularities can lead to conditions called atrioventricular blocks.

Irregular heart rhythms that originate in the ventricles are called *ventricular dysrhythmias.* They can lead to the following disorders: premature ventricular contractions, ventricular tachycardia, and ventricular fibrillation.

Atrial Dysrhythmias

Now let's consider the different kinds of irregular heart rhythms that may arise from the upper chambers of the heart.

Atrial Flutter. *Atrial flutter* involves rapid heart contractions (200–320 beats per minute). This dysrhythmia is considered to be an intermediate heart rhythm because it will either progress to atrial fibrillation (which we describe next), or convert back to a normal heart rhythm. In older people, this condition is often caused by CAD (see pp. 42–43) or by chronic obstructive pulmonary disease (COPD; see Chapter 12).

SYMPTOMS. Atrial flutter may cause no symptoms, or it may cause weakness, fatigue, light-headedness, palpitations, chest pressure, nausea, or shortness of breath.

DIAGNOSIS. Your doctor will be able to detect the irregular rhythm of your atrial flutter on physical examination, and he or she can determine that this irregular beat is atrial flutter (rather than another form of dysrhythmia) by having you undergo an ECG.

TREATMENT. If you have this type of irregular heart rhythm, your doctor will probably want to treat it, even if it does not cause any symptoms at this point. This is because atrial flutter increases your risk of stroke and of congestive heart failure, even when it's not associated with symptoms initially.

Your doctor may prescribe for you drugs such as quinidine or procainamide plus either digoxin, a beta blocker, or a calcium blocker (see Table 4.1), or he or she may give you a type of electrical shock called cardioversion to regulate your heartbeat.

Atrial Fibrillation. *Atrial fibrillation* is a discoordinated, irregular, sometimes rapid heart rhythm that arises from various sites within the atria. We can think of atrial fibrillation as being similar to a chaotic orchestra in which no one is paying attention to the conductor (in this case, the area of the heart called the sinus node), and the woodwind, string, and percussion sections are all playing at their own paces.

Atrial fibrillation becomes more prevalent as we advance in age and is quite common in people older than 75. It may be caused by a hormonal imbalance (such as hypothyroidism or hyperthyroidism) or by imbalances of salts (called electrolytes) in your blood. Atrial fibrillation can also be a result of another heart problem such as a heart attack (myocardial infarction), high blood pressure (hypertension), or congestive heart failure; or of a lung disorder such as emphysema, pneumonia, pulmonary embolus, or severe asthma.

In some cases, atrial fibrillation is the result of a serious problem such as a stroke or a blood clot in the lung (pulmonary embolus), so it's very important to have this condition treated right away and to have it monitored carefully.

SYMPTOMS. You may have no symptoms of atrial fibrillation at all, and your doctor may discover it when taking your pulse or doing an electrocardiogram (ECG). Alternatively, you may go to see your doctor because you have been feeling weak, dizzy, fatigued, or short of breath. Another symptom that you may or may not have is palpitations, or a rapid thumping sensation in your chest.

DIAGNOSIS. If your doctor suspects that you have atrial fibrillation, he or she probably will ask you questions, including your medical history, and will give you a physical examination. He or she may also do some blood tests, take a chest x-ray, and have you obtain an ECG.

TREATMENT. If your atrial fibrillation is caused by another problem, that *primary* problem may be taken care of first. For example, if your doctor finds that you have a thyroid imbalance, you may be given medication to bring your thyroid hormone level into the normal range. Atrial fibrillation is a very treatable condition! Your physician will get your heart rate and blood pressure under control, and he or she will try to restore your heartbeat to its normal rhythm with medicine and sometimes with an electrical pulse (cardioversion, see p. 60). Sometimes a pacemaker placement with electroablation (interruption of abnormal rhythm pattern) may be recommended.

In general, two types of commonly used drugs are prescribed for this type of irregular heart rhythm: medicines to regulate the heartbeat, and blood-thinning medicines to prevent stroke. Medicines to regulate your rhythm disorder include procainamide, digoxin, flecainide, amiodarone, calcium channel blockers, and beta blockers. Drugs to prevent stroke include warfarin (Coumadin) and possibly low-dose aspirin (for those who are at high risk of falls or bleeding and cannot take warfarin). You'll find more information about these drugs in Table 4.1.

Your doctor may need to do blood tests frequently when you first start medicines such as warfarin so that your dose can be adjusted. After you've been taking blood-thinning medication for atrial fibrillation for a while, your doctor may still test your blood, but less frequently, perhaps every four weeks or so. You will probably also need to obtain an ECG every three or four months. You may need to take the medication for quite some time, but once your heart rhythm is back under control, you can golf, swim, and play tennis again just as you always have.

Paroxysmal Atrial Tachycardia. *Paroxysmal atrial tachycardia,* sometimes also called *paroxysmal supraventricular tachycardia,* is a sudden, rapid heart rate (usually 140–190 beats per minute).

Symptoms. If you have this kind of irregular heart rhythm, you may or may not be able to feel a fluttering in your chest. You may or may not have chest discomfort and feel weak or fatigued, and sometimes you also may experience shortness of breath. For attacks that come on suddenly, you should probably lie down.

Diagnosis. The diagnosis of paroxysmal atrial tachycardia (PAT) is made by physical examination and by ECG.

Treatment. Usually this type of arrhythmia is treated with medications such as adenosine, beta blockers, calcium channel blockers, or amiodarone. Sometimes PAT may be treated with electroablation (interruption of an abnormal pattern of electrical signal transmission).

Sick Sinus Syndrome. If your doctor tells you that you have *sick sinus syndrome,* he or she doesn't mean that you have a sinus infection! Rather, you have an irregular, slow heart rhythm that occurs more commonly with advancing age.

There are a few variations on the sick sinus tune. You may have a slow heart rate alternating with a fast one (this is called "bradytachy"), or you may simply have an extremely slow rate ("severe sinus bradycardia"). Sometimes, there also can be a slow sinus rate with a further delay in the transmission of the electrical impulse through the part of the heart called the atrioventricular node (this delay is called "atrioventricular block").

This syndrome may sometimes be associated with other types of heart problems, including CAD—although having sick sinus syndrome doesn't necessarily mean that you have another type of heart disease.

SYMPTOMS. If you have sick sinus syndrome, you may or may not feel weak or fatigued and have heart palpitations, dizziness, fainting, and chest discomfort.

DIAGNOSIS. Your physician can diagnose sick sinus syndrome by physical examination with an ECG and possibly further electrophysiological studies, as needed.

TREATMENT. If you have symptoms of this disease, your physician may need to adjust the dosage of medicines that you are already taking (or discontinue them altogether), give you other medicines, or possibly recommend a pacemaker to regulate your heart rhythm (see the sidebar below).

What Does a Pacemaker Do?

A *pacemaker* is a device that helps to recruit the cells in the heart to synchronize their timing of electrical firing, or "depolarization," to make it easier for the heart muscle to contract in an orderly fashion. A pacemaker accomplishes this by sending out little pulses of electrical currents at a preset rate (usually between 60 to 80 times per minute).

There are single-chamber and dual-chamber pacemakers. More people today are receiving the dual-chamber pacemaker, which places an electrical wire, or lead, in both the right atrium and the right ventricle; this usually ensures a more coordinated contraction than a single-lead pacemaker can provide.

If you need a pacemaker, you will be given anesthesia so that you won't feel anything during this procedure, which may last for a few hours. The surgeon then will put the leads of the pacemaker through a vein into your heart. These tiny leads will be connected to your pacemaker box, which will be implanted in a little pocket under the skin on your anterior chest, not far from your shoulder.

After this procedure, you may feel a little local skin discomfort that will be readily treatable with pain medicine. Usually, antibiotics are also given for a short period of time after a pacemaker is implanted, to reduce the (tiny) risk of infection.

Once your pacemaker is in place, you will need to see your doctor regularly, about every three or four months. In the meantime, as with any medical condition, if you don't feel quite right, you should call your doctor. Sometimes, you may also have to see your physician to have the pacemaker lead checked or possibly adjusted.

Most people do beautifully after they get the pacemaker, and for the most part, you can resume your normal everyday activities, with two exceptions: You should not go near microwave ovens or through airport metal detectors because a magnet inside these machines could interfere with the function of your implanted metal pacemaker.

You may wonder how a pacemaker differs from another device called an *implantable heart defibrillator.* There is actually a big difference between these two heart regulators. A pacemaker sends an extremely small electrical impulse to the cells in the heart. Once a few of these cells are depolarized, they work just as normal cells should.

In contrast, an implantable defibrillator, which is a less common device, "listens" to your heart rhythm all the time, and if the rhythm gets chaotic because of a serious arrhythmia such as ventricular tachycardia or fibrillation, the defibrillator will send out a small to moderate jolt to take command of the whole heart and synchronize all the cells. Like a pacemaker, an implantable defibrillator is a very effective device.

Atrioventricular Junction Dysrhythmias

Atrioventricular Blocks: First-Degree and Second-Degree Blocks. To work properly, the heart depends on a regular flow of electrical impulses from the atria to the ventricles. If a problem (such as scarring) occurs in the area between these two parts (that is, in the *atrioventricular junction*), these electrical impulses may be slowed down or blocked for prolonged periods of time.

First-degree atrioventricular block, the least severe of the atrioventricular (AV) blocks, occurs commonly in older people. These usually mild prolongations in the flow of electrical impulse from the sinus node to the AV node may be caused by natural age-related changes; by drugs such as beta blockers, calcium channel blockers, and digoxin; by electrolyte or hormone imbalances (such as hypothyroidism); or by illness. It may also occur in association with CAD.

If you have a first-degree AV block, you probably will not have symptoms and you may not need treatment. However, if you are taking medications such as beta blockers, calcium channel blockers, or digoxin, your doctor may need to adjust the dosage.

Second-degree atrioventricular block means that there is a more serious delay of the conduction of electrical impulses through the AV node. This type of block may be caused by drugs such as beta blockers, calcium channel blockers, or digitalis; by insufficient blood supply to the heart due to blockage or constriction of the coronary arteries (this is also called "acute ischemia"); or by damage to the heart tissue due to a heart attack (myocardial infarction). Viral infections, electrolyte abnormalities (salt imbalances in the blood), and hormone imbalances (such as hypothyroidism) may also occasionally lead to second-degree AV block.

SYMPTOMS. You may or may not have symptoms of this disorder (such as weakness, fatigue, chest discomfort, shortness of breath, or fainting).

DIAGNOSIS. In addition to a physical examination and an ECG, your doctor may wish to request additional electrophysiological diagnostic studies if you are having symptoms. Irregular heart rhythms can also be diagnosed over the telephone using a special heart-rate monitor.

TREATMENT. Your physician or heart specialist may need to adjust or discontinue the medications that you're taking (such as digitalis, beta blockers, or calcium channel blockers). Also, in certain situations when you have symptoms such as fainting, you *may* need to get a pacemaker to regulate your heartbeat more closely.

Third-Degree Atrioventricular Block. In this form of AV block, which is much less common than the other two forms, the electrical impulses are not getting from the sinus node through the AV junction adequately; consequently, there is no coordination between the atria above this junction and the ventricles below it. In fact, the two parts of the heart (atria and ventricles) are depolarizing and contracting independently of each other.

This condition, which is also called "complete heart block," can be caused by medication, acute ischemia, other illnesses (such as viral infection), an extreme salt (electrolyte) imbalance in the blood, or rarely, a transient increase in vagal tone such that the sinus rate is slower than the AV rate.

SYMPTOMS. You may or may not have symptoms such as dizziness and fainting, chest pressure, weakness, or fatigue.

DIAGNOSIS. As with the other forms of AV block, your doctor will be able to diagnose this disorder with a physical examination and an ECG.

TREATMENT. Your physician may prescribe for you a drug such as atropine or a related compound such as scopolamine, and he or she may also recommend a pacemaker for you, especially if you are having symptoms.

Ventricular Dysrhythmias

Ventricular dysrhythmias are irregular heartbeats that originate in the heart's ventricles. They include premature ventricular contractions, ventricular tachycardia, and ventricular fibrillation.

Premature Ventricular Contractions. *Premature ventricular contractions* are heartbeats due to cells in the ventricle that depolarize, or play a note in the band before they are supposed to. These types of irregular heartbeats are very common among older people. They generally do not need to be treated unless they cause symptoms. Premature ventricular contractions may be caused by natural age-related changes, heart disease, ischemia, salt imbalance, hormonal disorders, or illness.

SYMPTOMS. If you do experience symptoms of this type of irregular heart rhythm, you may feel a thumping or flip-flop in your chest occasionally, or if the irregular beats are more frequent, you may feel weakness, fatigue, chest discomfort, or faintness.

DIAGNOSIS. As with other arrhythmias, your doctor can diagnose premature ventricular contractions by physical examination and ECG.

TREATMENT. If treatment is required, your doctor may prescribe an antiarrhythmic medication such as a beta blocker or calcium blocker, amiodarone, or procainamide. Sometimes reducing your caffeine and alcohol intake and getting more sleep will do the trick or at least will help to improve the situation.

Ventricular Tachycardia. *Ventricular tachycardia* is a rapid heartbeat (between 100 and 150 beats per minute) that requires immediate attention, especially if you have CAD. With proper antiarrhythmic medication and possibly an implantable heart defibrillator, though, you can live quite well with this type of disorder. Ventricular tachycardia may be caused by insufficient blood supply to the heart (ischemia), chronic disease of the heart muscle (cardiomyopathy), or CAD.

SYMPTOMS. If you have ventricular tachycardia, you may feel faint or weak, and you may even lose consciousness. Some individuals with this condition feel a pounding or thumping in their chest, but others do not. If you have had these arrhythmias in the past, you may be able to sense when they are coming on; if so, you may have been instructed to cough or to pound your chest regularly to help to temporarily maintain blood flow (and to try to convert the dysrhythmia to a normal rhythm). This action will also call attention to your distress, because you will probably need emergency medical care.

DIAGNOSIS. Your doctor will be able to diagnose your ventricular tachycardia by physical examination, ECG, and possibly further electrophysiological tests.

TREATMENT. For this type of problem, intravenous antiarrhythmic drugs (see Table 4.1) and/or *electrical cardioversion,* a form of electric pulse with a device called a *defibrillator,* may be necessary. Fortunately, around the world, defibrillators are becoming increasingly available, not just in hospitals and ambulances, but also elsewhere in our communities and even on airplanes. There is also a movement afoot to teach more people how to use these devices.

After your heart rhythm has been brought under control, your doctor may prescribe antiarrhythmic medication to keep it that way. He or she may also need to treat the underlying heart condition (such as cardiomyopathy or CAD) that may have led to this type of arrhythmia. An implantable defibrillator may also be recommended for you.

Ventricular Fibrillation. The most serious arrhythmia, *ventricular fibrillation,* is a very rapid and erratic heart rhythm that requires immediate medical attention with defibrillation. Now, with the availability of implantable heart defibrillators, people with chronic ventricular tachycardia/ventricular fibrillation can be successfully resuscitated and can do quite well for many years. Ventricular fibrillation may be the presenting sign of CAD, heart attack, or other serious underlying heart problems.

SYMPTOMS. Loss of consciousness is the major symptom, and it happens rapidly. Sometimes a patient may feel unwell before the episode, but usually there is not much warning.

DIAGNOSIS. The diagnosis is made by physical examination and ECG. Researchers are trying to identify risk factors for these types of arrhythmias, but the timing of such events may be difficult to predict, even in people who have had them before.

TREATMENT. Fortunately, we now have implantable defibrillators that really work and save lives. As we mentioned in a previous sidebar, this device senses when your heart rhythm goes haywire, and it sends a small jolt to your heart. This jolt can be likened to a coach who blows a whistle so that everyone will stop what they are doing and pay attention. This pause gives cells in the heart a chance to reset and for the heart to get its own rhythm going again, under the direction of a pacemaker, either natural (in the sinus node) or implanted, in the form of a device.

Implantable defibrillators work together with antiarrhythmic medications (see Table 4.1) to help to keep your heart rhythm regular. After you have been treated for ventricular fibrillation, you will need to have regular follow-up appointments with your doctor and heart specialist, but you can—and should—resume most of your daily activities. Your doctor will probably tell you, "don't be afraid to go out and do things," because staying active is actually much better for your health. You may or may not be able to continue driving a car. Ask your physician.

Congestive Heart Failure

Congestive heart failure (CHF), which is also called simply "heart failure," occurs when the heart is not able to pump blood sufficiently to meet the needs of the body. This condition is the most common cause of hospitalization and rehospitalization among adults over age 65.

A number of cardiac problems can lead to heart failure. They include a heart attack, CAD, heart valve disease such as aortic or mitral valve stenosis or regurgitation, and high blood pressure. Stress, obesity, irregular heart rhythms (arrhythmias), infections, anemia, and lung disease may contribute to CHF, too. Although CAD is common in older people with CHF, half of those who die in CHF do not have significant coronary disease. Therefore, CHF should *not* be equated with CAD.

CHF is six times more common among persons 65 to 74 years of age than among those 45 to 54 years old. Not surprisingly, more than 75% of cases of overt heart failure in older people are associated with high blood pressure or CAD. Thus, heart failure is prevalent among older persons not only because of advanced age but because these other diseases are also more prevalent in the elderly.

Until relatively recently, we thought that CHF in older persons developed as a result of the heart's inability to contract. Now we know that impaired heart-muscle relaxation (diastolic dysfunction), not impaired heart-muscle contraction (systolic dysfunction), is the major cause of heart failure in the older person, especially in women over the age of 75 years.

SYMPTOMS. Typical symptoms of CHF, which are similar in younger and older people, include shortness of breath, coughing, the feeling of suffocation, ankle swelling, frequent urination at night, and sweating. Older persons are more likely to also experience other symptoms, such as somnolence, confusion, disorientation, weakness, and fatigue. Any existing dementia may worsen.

Symptoms often develop during exertion. If you don't get much exercise, the signs and symptoms of CHF may sometimes not be apparent until the disease is at a later stage, and it manifests itself at rest.

DIAGNOSIS. In addition to a physical examination, your doctor may use a chest x-ray, ECG, Doppler echocardiography, or radionuclide scanning techniques (see pp. 44–46) to diagnose CHF.

TREATMENT. If you have suffered an exacerbation from sudden heart failure, you may need to stay in the hospital for a few days for observation and treatment.

In the event that your CHF is caused mainly by an impairment in the heart's ability to contract (that is, you're suffering from "systolic dysfunction"), your doctor will probably prescribe for you rest, oxygen if needed, and drugs such as digitalis, diuretics, vasodilators such as nitrates, and ACE inhibitors such as captopril and enalapril. Prolonged bedrest may be harmful, so you'll probably be advised to sit with your legs elevated when you're not walking around. If your doctor determines that your heart's contractility is preserved but its ability to relax is impaired (you're suffering from "diastolic dysfunction"), he or she may wish to prescribe low doses of medications such as beta blockers, calcium channel blockers, ACE inhibitors, nitrates, or very low-dose diuretics.

Usually systolic dysfunction is accompanied by at least some degree of diastolic dysfunction, especially in older persons and in those with CAD or hypertension. Both systolic and diastolic function will improve with treatment.

An 81-year-old man had been diagnosed 25 years ago to have cardiomyopathy with extensive and severe CAD. At that time, he saw many well-respected cardiologists, and they told him that his disease was widespread and inoperable, and that he would just have to deal with the poor prognosis of his condition. At that point, he had difficulty just getting out of bed, and he was limited to a bed-to-chair existence.

Well, this man was intelligent and motivated, and he wasn't willing to accept that prognosis. He started reading everything he could find about his disease, and he began a slow and gradual exercise program on his own and worked on his diet. Today he still has his severe coronary heart disease, and he still has intermittent atrial fibrillation, but he now has more physical strength and endurance than many of his peers who don't have heart disease. He chops wood, can outwalk his healthy wife, and has been able to maintain his large yard and work on his home all by himself for the past 3 years.

This doesn't mean that you shouldn't listen to your doctor, but you should never get discouraged by any diagnosis, and you should never give up hope and the desire to do better.

J.W.

Cardiomyopathy is a chronic disease of the heart muscle. The three types of cardiomyopathy are dilated, or congestive cardiomyopathy; hypertrophic cardiomyopathy; and restrictive cardiomyopathy.

Cardiomyopathy

Dilated, or Congestive Cardiomyopathy
If your heart can't contract, or squeeze as well as it needs to, the ventricular
chamber of your heart will become enlarged. Doctors sometimes misdiagnose
this condition, which is called *dilated cardiomyopathy,* because it resembles
heart failure that may sometimes be brought on by CAD.

Although this disorder is thought to be rare in older persons, several large
studies have shown that approximately 10% of people with this condition are
older than 65 years.

SYMPTOMS. If you have dilated, or congestive cardiomyopathy, you may tire
easily, and you may develop a tendency to retain fluid, so that your ankles may
swell somewhat. You may also have difficulty catching your breath when you
exert yourself.

DIAGNOSIS. Dilated cardiomyopathy is usually confirmed by echocardiography.

TREATMENT. The treatment of this disorder usually involves drugs such as
ACE inhibitors, vasodilators, diuretics, and antiarrhythmic agents (see Table
4.1). Digitalis may also be effective, especially if you have atrial fibrillation.

Dilated cardiomyopathy may increase a person's tendency to develop blood
clots in the heart, so your doctor may also prescribe anticoagulant drugs to keep
your blood thinned (see Table 4.1).

Hypertrophic Cardiomyopathy
The next form of long-term condition involving the heart muscle is *hypertrophic cardiomyopathy*. In this type of disease, the ventricular chamber does
not enlarge, but the ventricular wall thickens. Hypertrophic cardiomyopathy
may be related to conditions such as high blood pressure (hypertension) or narrowing of the aorta (aortic stenosis). It may also be *idiopathic,* which means
that its cause is not clear.

Older women with hypertension tend to develop this form of cardiomyopathy
more often than men do, even if they have the same blood pressure level or the
same degree of aortic stenosis as men. The reasons for this difference are under
study.

Like dilated cardiomyopathy, hypertrophic cardiomyopathy is often misdiag-
nosed in older people. The wrong diagnosis of CAD or pulmonary disease, with
resulting inappropriate treatment, can lead to undesirable complications.

SYMPTOMS. The main symptom of hypertrophic cardiomyopathy is shortness
of breath. Other symptoms include dizziness, chest pain, palpitations, fainting,
and fatigue.

DIAGNOSIS. In addition to a physical examination, your doctor may use an
electrocardiogram (ECG) and echocardiography to diagnose this condition.

TREATMENT. With treatment, the prognosis for older people with hypertrophic cardiomyopathy tends to be better than that of younger people. If you have this condition, you may be given drugs such as calcium channel blockers or beta blockers. You may also receive prophylactic antibiotics, which are given before certain procedures to protect against potential infection of the heart valves (this is a serious heart illness called infective endocarditis, see p. 68). Surgery (myotomy and myectomy, see p. 74) may also sometimes be helpful.

If you have this form of cardiomyopathy, you probably will not take drugs such as digitalis or large doses of diuretics or vasodilators. That's because these agents may exacerbate your condition by reducing the left ventricular chamber size even further, and this reduction in size could prevent the muscle from pumping the blood out effectively.

Restrictive Heart Disease

Restrictive heart disease could be due to a muscle problem (cardiomyopathy) or to a problem with the sac surrounding the heart (pericarditis). *Cardiomyopathy* involves an increased stiffening of the heart muscle. This disorder may result from amyloid heart disease, which is characterized by small ventricular chambers, enlarged atrial chambers, thickened muscle walls, and increased amounts of a fibrous protein called *amyloid* in the heart (this happens more often in older people). Chest radiation therapy (for example, for cancer) occasionally can cause restrictive cardiomyopathy, months or years after it is given.

Sometimes, restrictive heart disease also occurs when the sac that surrounds the heart muscle, called the *pericardium,* develops scar tissue, perhaps because of chronic infection (such as tuberculosis) or other conditions (such as metastatic cancer). Alternatively, the pericardial space may be filled up with fluid that then prevents the heart from functioning normally, such as may rarely occur in cases of severe kidney failure.

SYMPTOMS. There may not be symptoms until the disease is quite extensive. Fatigue, weakness, and shortness of breath may be the associated symptoms. Until late in its course, this disorder rarely causes impaired heart function.

DIAGNOSIS. The diagnosis of this disorder may be made by physical examination, ECG, and echocardiography.

TREATMENT. Although there is no magic bullet for restrictive cardiomyopathy, your physician may give you medicines to optimize your heart's function. These medicines may include low doses of diuretics or vasodilators. He or she may also encourage you to reduce your salt intake slightly in order to lessen your risk of developing CHF. Sometimes, in rare cases of restrictive heart disease due to chronic infection (such as tuberculosis), metastatic cancer, or kidney failure, a *pericardial window* (a small opening in the sac surrounding the heart muscle) may be made, to help relieve the symptoms.

Valvular Heart Disease

When the four valves of your heart are working as they should, blood flows through your heart and lungs smoothly in a single direction. Valvular heart diseases disrupt this process by blocking the blood, restricting its flow through narrowed (*stenosed*) valves, or allowing it to go backward (*regurgitate*).

Common valvular heart diseases in older persons include aortic stenosis, chronic aortic regurgitation, acute aortic regurgitation, mitral stenosis, mitral valve prolapse, mitral regurgitation, mitral annular calcification, and infective endocarditis. Tricuspid valve regurgitation may also occur, especially in the presence of mitral- or aortic-valve disease.

Aortic Stenosis

Narrowing of the aortic valve, or aortic stenosis, is a potentially very treatable problem.

SYMPTOMS. Sometimes this condition may coexist with CAD. Symptoms of aortic stenosis include chest pressure (angina pectoris), dizziness or fainting with exertion, shortness of breath, atrial fibrillation, and CHF.

DIAGNOSIS. The diagnosis of aortic stenosis may be made by physical examination and echocardiography.

TREATMENT. Surgical aortic-valve replacement is often required for treating aortic stenosis in older people, especially if you experience worsened symptoms such as fainting, angina, shortness of breath, or atrial fibrillation and CHF, and the ECG shows that your heart is thickened.

If you receive a mechanical heart valve, you may be given long-term blood-thinning therapy with a drug called warfarin. If you receive a biological valve (usually made from pericardium or heart-valve tissue of cow or pig), you might not need to take long-term warfarin.

Having a prosthetic valve can increase your risk of developing endocarditis, or valve infection, so after such an operation, you will usually need to take antibiotics before dental or surgical procedures.

Another surgical option to discuss with your doctor is called *percutaneous aortic valvuloplasty*. This procedure involves placement of a catheter across the aortic valve. A tiny balloon on the catheter is then placed across the narrowed valve and inflated gently, to crack open the calcified valve. Although this operation can temporarily alleviate the symptoms of aortic stenosis, it usually only provides a short-term benefit, and the symptoms and narrowing of the valve may recur within 6 to 12 months.

Years ago, a family member of a physician knew that an aortic-valve replacement would help her but was afraid that if she told people how old she really was, the surgeon wouldn't do the procedure. She understated her age and said that she was 79. She underwent her valve operation, and afterward confessed that she was really 92. By telling this story, I don't mean that you should lie about your age. Rather, you should not let age be a deterring factor against your potential medical options.

J.W.

Aortic Regurgitation (or Aortic Insufficiency)

Sometimes, blood that is supposed to flow from the ventricle into the aorta is pushed back into the left ventricle because of a leaky aortic valve. This condition, which is called *aortic regurgitation,* may be commonly caused by rheumatic heart disease, valve infection (infective endocarditis), or high blood pressure. Other possible causes include a structural abnormality from birth and genetic disorders involving connective tissue.

SYMPTOMS. If you have aortic regurgitation, you may experience weakness, fatigue, decreased exercise tolerance, and shortness of breath.

DIAGNOSIS. This problem can usually be diagnosed through a doctor's examination, echocardiography, and Doppler studies.

TREATMENT. Medical treatment options for aortic insufficiency include vasodilators, diuretics, ACE inhibitors, and digitalis. Your doctor may also want to monitor your condition every 12 months or so. If you are an older person with no symptoms of chronic (long-term) aortic regurgitation, aortic-valve replacement may not be necessary, but if you develop progressive CHF, either chronic or acute, as a result of this defect, you may need to undergo eventual valve replacement. Also, if your aortic regurgitation is abrupt in onset (i.e., it comes on suddenly and severely), prompt valve replacement may be necessary.

Mitral Stenosis

The *mitral valve,* which is so called because it resembles the mitre hat of a cardinal or pope, is also known as a *bicuspid valve,* being composed of two triangular-shaped flaps through which blood passes from the left atrium to the left ventricle. Narrowing of the mitral valve (also called *mitral valvular stenosis*) in older people usually results from rheumatic heart disease, which typically occurs in one's youth, often before the age of 20 years, although it may not create clinical problems until several decades later. This condition is more common in women than in men.

SYMPTOMS. If you have mitral stenosis, you may have heart palpitations, a cough, and shortness of breath.

DIAGNOSIS. The diagnosis of mitral stenosis in older persons involves physical examination and echocardiography and Doppler studies.

TREATMENT. If you have this condition, your doctor may prescribe diuretics and possibly mild salt restriction initially, as well as beta blockers to keep your heart rate down. If you are experiencing atrial fibrillation, a common consequence of mitral stenosis, your physician may also recommend digitalis and anticoagulants to keep blood clots from forming in the enlarged left atrium.

If you have atrial fibrillation, your doctor may also try to regulate your heart rhythm with chemical or electrical efforts (cardioversion, see p. 60). Later on, valve replacement or balloon valvuloplasty may be considered to fix the narrowed valve, if needed. Valvuloplasty is similar to angioplasty; both use balloons to dilate a narrowed passage, but the size and duration of balloon inflation differ.

Mitral Valve Prolapse

Mitral valve prolapse, a common and usually benign abnormality, tends to occur more often in women than in men. In this disorder, part of the mitral valve leaflet bulges into the left atrium when the heart contracts during systole. This defect could occur because of valvular leaflet redundancy. It could also be due to prior injury to the part of the heart muscle that controls the opening and closing of the valve (called papillary muscle). In some cases, the mitral valve prolapse could lead to *progressive mitral regurgitation* (in other words, more and more blood will flow in the wrong direction, backward into the left atrium).

SYMPTOMS. Symptoms of mitral valve prolapse may be minimal or may be substantial and may or may not include chest discomfort, irregular heart rhythms (arrhythmias), and CHF (cough and shortness of breath).

DIAGNOSIS. To diagnose this type of disorder, your doctor will probably give you a physical examination and possibly tests that include chest x-ray, echocardiography, and ECG (the results of your ECG may or may not be normal if you have this condition).

TREATMENT. If you have irregular heartbeats with mitral valve prolapse, your doctor will give you antiarrhythmic drugs to regulate your heart rhythm. You may also be given prophylactic antibiotics before dental procedures to protect against potential infection of the valve (endocarditis) if you also have mitral regurgitation. Finally, your physician may prescribe antiplatelet therapy to prevent the development of blood clots and thereby reduce your risk for stroke or heart attack.

Mitral Regurgitation

If you have *mitral regurgitation,* which is also called *mitral incompetence,* you have a leaky mitral valve that allows blood to flow backward from the left ventricle to the left atrium. This inadequate valve closure could be due to several problems, including rheumatic heart disease and CAD.

SYMPTOMS. You may have no symptoms of mitral regurgitation, or you may have palpitations, chest discomfort, weakness, fatigue, or shortness of breath.

DIAGNOSIS. Mitral regurgitation can be diagnosed easily with clinical examination and Doppler echocardiographic evaluation.

TREATMENT. If you have mitral regurgitation, you may be given drugs called ACE inhibitors, vasodilators, and diuretics to decrease the aortic resistance against which the heart must work. You may also be given prophylactic antibiotics before dental visits to prevent infection of the valve (endocarditis).

If your mitral regurgitation becomes severe, you eventually may need to have valve replacement surgery.

Mitral Annular Calcification

As we age, calcium deposits can accumulate around the ring of the valve opening between the two chambers of the heart. This condition, called *mitral annular calcification,* is common in older people (especially in older women) and is usually benign.

SYMPTOMS. Most people do not experience symptoms with this condition.

DIAGNOSIS. The diagnosis of mitral annular calcification may be made by chest x-ray and/or echocardiography.

TREATMENT. Usually, medical and surgical treatment are not necessary for this condition.

Infective Endocarditis

Infective endocarditis, an inflammation due to bacterial infection of the heart, is more common among older people than younger people. Your risk of developing this type of infection is highest if you have another disease that's affecting either your aortic or your mitral heart valve. This infection can be serious.

SYMPTOMS. If you have infective endocarditis, you may have no symptoms, or you may have a flulike illness (fever and fatigue), or you may feel very weak.

DIAGNOSIS. To diagnose infective endocarditis, your doctor will request blood cultures for microorganisms, as well as an ECG, chest x-ray, and Doppler echocardiography. Once this condition has been diagnosed, these tests may also be done for follow-up monitoring.

TREATMENT. If you have infective endocarditis, you may require intravenous antibiotics for several weeks, as well as possibly other medications if you have symptoms of CHF. Sometimes, in very severe cases, valve replacement may be considered, after completion of a course of antibiotics.

Congenital Heart Disease

Congenital (from birth) heart problems that are seen in older persons include atrial septal defect, ventricular septal defect, coarctation of the aorta, and patent ductus arteriosus.

Atrial Septal Defect

An *atrial septal defect (ASD),* or a hole in the heart wall between the left and right atria, is the most common form of congenital heart disease in older people.

SYMPTOMS. If you have an ASD, you may have no symptoms or you may have irregular heartbeats (atrial flutter or atrial fibrillation, see pp. 54–56) or symptoms of CHF, such as cough, sweating, shortness of breath, confusion, weakness, or fatigue.

DIAGNOSIS. An ECG, echocardiogram, and radiologic studies such as chest x-ray or radionuclide scan may be helpful in diagnosing an ASD.

TREATMENT. If you have symptoms of an ASD, your physician may prescribe medications such as those given for CHF and/or irregular heart rhythms (see the preceding sections). You may also be prescribed prophylactic antibiotics for dental procedures. If needed, you may also undergo surgery to patch the tiny hole in your heart.

Ventricular Septal Defect

A congenital *ventricular septal defect (VSD)* is a hole (usually very tiny) in the wall that separates the left ventricle from the right ventricle. In an older person, this defect is less common than an ASD. If present since birth, it is usually extremely small, and it usually does not require surgery. If your VSD was acquired after a heart attack, then management will be different, and surgery may be needed.

SYMPTOMS. The symptoms of a VSD are similar to those of an ASD.

DIAGNOSIS. To diagnose a VSD, your doctor will probably have you obtain an ECG, echocardiogram, and radiologic tests such as chest x-ray.

TREATMENT. Surgery to close the hole may be required if your symptoms become severe. Your doctor may also give you prophylactic antibiotics to protect against infection of the heart valves (infective endocarditis, see p. 68).

Coarctation of the Aorta

Some people are born with an abnormally narrow segment in a portion of the *aorta* (the large trunk that carries blood from the heart to the arteries). There are few undiagnosed new cases of this condition—called coarctation of the aorta—in people older than 50 years.

SYMPTOMS. If you have coarctation of the aorta, you may have high blood pressure. Some people with this disorder also have aortic stenosis (see p. 65).

DIAGNOSIS. To diagnose this problem, your doctor may check your blood pressure and have you get an ECG and an echocardiogram. Sometimes, further radiologic studies are also done.

TREATMENT. Surgery to repair the narrowing is usually recommended. More than half of those who undergo surgery will experience improvement. If you have this operation, the results of your exercise stress tests (see pp. 43–44) will probably be monitored regularly, and you will probably be checked periodically.

Patent Ductus Arteriosus

A *patent ductus arteriosus (PDA)* is usually heard as a continuous murmur across the upper anterior chest. If you have a small PDA and no symptoms, your doctor will monitor you (by ECG and Doppler studies, see pp. 43–44) and he or she may give you prophylactic antibiotics to prevent infective endocarditis (see p. 68). If you have symptoms such as shortness of breath, an irregular heart rhythm, palpitations, and weakness, surgery may be recommended.

High Blood Pressure (Hypertension)

Blood pressure readings, which are calibrated in millimeters of mercury (mmHg), consist of two numbers (for example, 140/90 mmHg). The top number is called the *systolic level,* and the bottom number is called the *diastolic level.*

Hypertension (systolic pressure above 140 mmHg with normal diastolic pressure, or systolic pressure above 140 and diastolic pressure greater than 90 mmHg) is the greatest risk factor for heart disease in older adults. It's also a major risk factor for stroke and kidney failure. Hypertension rises in prevalence with age and may occur in over half of persons over the age of 70 years.

SYMPTOMS. You may have no symptoms at all and discover at an annual checkup that you have high blood pressure. Sometimes, headaches may be a symptom of high blood pressure. However, in spite of the word "tension" in "hypertension," you may have high blood pressure even if you are very relaxed —only a blood-pressure monitor will be able to tell for sure.

DIAGNOSIS. The test for blood pressure, which is quick and painless, should be done at least once a year if you don't have high blood pressure and more frequently if you do. A doctor or nurse will put a blood-pressure cuff around your arm above your elbow. He or she then will pump air into the cuff and read the measurement as the air flows out.

Your blood pressure varies from day to day and tends to rise when you have been exercising or experiencing stress. So, if your blood pressure reading is high, your physician will probably want to check it again three or four times over a six- to eight-week period before making a final diagnosis. He or she will probably also measure your blood pressure while you are in different positions (lying down, standing, and sitting). For younger adults, the average blood pressure is 120/80.

If the systolic pressure (the top number) is high, but the diastolic pressure (the bottom number) is normal, you may have a condition called "isolated systolic hypertension." You definitely need to be treated for this condition to reduce your risk of stroke or heart attack.

TREATMENT. Most cases of high blood pressure cannot be cured altogether, but they can be controlled. Sometimes, certain medical problems will cause *secondary hypertension,* which may go away completely when the original medical problem is treated.

Treatment of hypertension is the best way to prevent heart disease. If you have a mild case, you may be able to lower your blood pressure through lifestyle changes without taking any drugs at all. Your doctor may suggest that you try the following lifestyle changes:

- Lower your body weight.
- Switch to a no-added-salt diet (but don't eliminate salt from your diet altogether), and ensure that your diet includes plenty of calcium, magnesium, and potassium.
- Get more exercise.
- Don't drink alcohol.
- Consider relaxation techniques such as meditation, yoga, or breathing exercises.

Drugs for treating high blood pressure include:

- Diuretics—generally effective, with few side effects when taken at low doses; especially good for women during and after menopause because they may block the excretion of calcium from the kidneys
- Alpha blockers—a good choice for people who also have diabetes or for men with urinary frequency due to an enlarged prostate
- Beta blockers

- Calcium channel blockers
- ACE inhibitors
- Central sympathetic blockers
- Aspirin
- Angiotensin receptor antagonists

More information about these drugs can be found in Table 4.1.

Your doctor will want to monitor your blood pressure often after you have started taking medication. In some cases, home blood-pressure monitoring is also available.

- What should you do if you forget to take your daily dose of medicine for your heart? Don't double the dose. Instead, call your doctor for advice.
- Don't wait until you are out of medicine before asking for a refill. Always try to request a refill at least three working days before you will run out of the medicine.

Low blood pressure (e.g., a reading of 110/70 or less) can cause symptoms in older people. Hypotension is not a disease in itself, but rather a sign that disease, medications, or simply aging itself are affecting your body's ability to regulate your blood pressure. Ironically, high blood pressure often leads to low blood pressure in the elderly, because medications for hypertension can lead to excessive drops in pressure. The use of drugs such as antidepressants, nitrates, antianxiety medications, and diuretics can also cause hypotension.

Low Blood Pressure (Hypotension)

In *orthostatic hypotension,* which occurs in 20% to 30% of older persons, your blood pressure drops when you change from a lying down or sitting position to standing up. Health problems that can result in prolonged periods of inactivity or bedrest also can lead to this type of hypotension.

In *postprandial hypotension,* your blood pressure drops substantially between 15 minutes and 90 minutes after you have eaten. It's probably more common than orthostatic hypotension. To relieve this problem, try eating frequent, small meals consisting of low-carbohydrate, high-protein foods; not drinking alcohol; and drinking plenty of water and juice.

SYMPTOMS. Sudden drops in blood pressure may cause fainting, dizziness, weakness, angina, falling, and even—in severe cases—stroke.

DIAGNOSIS. Just as with high blood pressure, your doctor will need to measure your blood pressure several times to determine whether you have hypotension. He or she will want to take your blood pressure at least one half hour after you have eaten or taken medication. Your blood pressure will be measured after you have been lying down for at least 15 minutes, then right after you have stood up, and again, while you are standing, a few minutes later.

TREATMENT. If you haven't experienced any symptoms of hypotension, but your doctor discovers during a physical examination that you have low blood pressure, he or she will probably suggest that you stop or reduce medications that may be causing this problem. If hypotension is causing you to feel dizzy or faint after meals, you should take your cardiovascular medicines between, rather than with, meals. If you don't have severe CHF, increasing your salt consumption may also be helpful. Drinking tomato juice is an especially good way to do this, because it is high in sodium content.

You may also be taught some exercises to help increase your blood pressure. Slowly rising from a sitting to a standing position will decrease your risk of fainting or falling. Other remedies for low blood pressure include wearing elastic stockings and raising the head of your bed slightly.

In addition to these nonmedical solutions, if you have *orthostatic hypotension,* your doctor may prescribe drugs such as a mineralocorticosteroid called fludrocortisone acetate. In rare instances, nonsteroidal anti-inflammatory drugs (NSAIDs) such as ibuprofen may be slightly helpful.

For *postprandial hypotension,* your physician may recommend drugs such as caffeine and related compounds. It may be best, however, to change to frequent, small meals, and to plan to put your legs up and rest for about one and one half hours after eating.

Venous Disorders

Varicose Veins

Varicose veins are a common problem, especially among people in their 50s and 60s. You may have inherited your tendency to develop varicose veins, or you may have experienced some form of trauma or inflammation that has brought on this problem.

SYMPTOMS. In addition to their unattractive appearance, varicose veins can cause itching, aching, and swelling. They can also put you at risk for developing blood clots.

DIAGNOSIS. Your doctor will examine your legs and may confirm the diagnosis of varicose veins with various tests, including phlebography, Doppler flowmetry, and plethysmography (see p. 46).

TREATMENT. Your physician may prescribe compression stockings, worn below the knee, to apply pressure to your ankles. You should also avoid wearing tight clothes around your torso and standing still for long periods of time. Take walks, and keep your legs elevated when you are sitting down.

Your doctor may recommend the use of *sclerotherapy* to close the veins. This measure, which involves the injection of a drug into the veins, will not solve the problem altogether, but it may improve the look of and feeling in your legs. After this procedure, you may need to wear bandages for about six weeks.

For more severe varicose veins, a surgeon can *ligate* (tie off) the main saphenous vein and remove the smaller varicose veins in your legs. This procedure, which occasionally may have complications (such as bleeding, infection, and nerve damage), usually involves an overnight hospital stay.

Deep Venous Thrombosus

Another type of venous disorder that involves blood clots, called *deep venous thrombosus (DVT)*, could give rise to blood clots (called *pulmonary emboli*) in the lungs. In many cases, this unsuspected potential killer can be prevented by walking around, wiggling your toes, and flexing your calf muscles during train, plane, or car rides—even if your journey only lasts one and a half hours.

SYMPTOMS. If you have a DVT, you may have no symptoms, or you may have pain in the leg or shortness of breath, and you may feel faint.

DIAGNOSIS. If you experience any of these symptoms, your doctor may check to see whether the blood flow in your veins is decreased or blocked. One way is through angiography (see p. 45) to measure the resistance of the blood flow. The other way is to use ultrasound to view your blood vessels.

TREATMENT. If you have had a DVT, your doctor will probably prescribe blood thinners such as heparin or warfarin to prevent clots from forming in the future. If you're at increased risk for DVTs, you should also be vigilant about wiggling your toes! If you've had a stroke, arthritis, or other condition that makes it difficult or impossible to move your legs and feet, move your arms instead. Doing so will still help to increase the flow of your body's natural circulating blood thinners to your legs.

We also recommend that you drink lots of fluids, especially if the weather is warm or you are in a hot indoor environment. As we age, our kidneys don't hang on to sodium as well as they did when we were younger, so drinking adequate amounts of fluids and taking in enough salt to replace the lost sodium is important to prevent dehydration and a condition called *hyponatremia* (low sodium in the blood). Dehydration may make you more susceptible to clot formation, and hyponatremia may also increase your risk of falls. Tomato juice can be the ideal drink to help to prevent both of these conditions, because one 8-ounce serving can provide 30% of your daily requirement of sodium.

Procedures

In addition to medications, many other options are available to treat your heart disease. They range from minimally invasive coronary artery bypass procedures (to open up blocked arteries) to laser ablation and novel gene therapies (to stimulate the growth of healthy new blood vessels in the heart).

Coronary Artery Bypass Graft

If you have symptomatic heart disease, you may benefit from bypass surgery, or coronary artery bypass graft (CABG). This operation involves either removing a vein from the leg and attaching its two ends to the blocked coronary artery or redirecting an artery from the inside of the anterior chest wall to the heart, to allow the blood flow to bypass the blockage in that artery.

If you are a candidate for CABG surgery, you may wish to weigh the benefits and risks involved carefully. CABG may provide you with a longer life, decrease your chest discomfort (angina) and your need for medications, and probably enable you to be more active. However, complications of CABG include bleeding, infection, stroke, myocardial infarction (heart attack), blood clots, organ failure, and in rare cases, death.

People older than 70 years, especially women, have a higher postoperative complication rate from CABG than younger people. They may require a longer period of assisted ventilation, or a pacemaker, or they may develop bleeding, stroke, and sepsis. However, 90% of older people without other major health problems may enjoy at least a five-year survival without chest discomfort after CABG.

As always, you should discuss your options with your doctor.

Myotomy and Myectomy

In rare cases, a procedure that involves *cutting* (*myotomy*) or *excision* (*myectomy*) of a portion of the heart muscle is done for conditions such as hypertrophic cardiomyopathy. This procedure also has been applied recently to patients with dilated cardiomyopathy. The idea is that with less muscle mass, the heart muscle may be able to contract better. This procedure has been done with varying success.

Percutaneous Transluminal Coronary Angioplasty

Each year, more people age 65 or older are successfully undergoing percutaneous transluminal coronary angioplasty (PTCA, also called "balloon angioplasty") procedures for CAD. PTCA is a less invasive intervention than open-heart surgery. An x-ray film helps the physician to direct a catheter through an artery in the patient's leg up to the blocked coronary artery. The doctor then inflates a small balloon on the tip of the catheter, which opens up the artery. The success rates of this technique for older people are comparable to those for younger people. Although the risk of complications may be higher for them than it is for younger people, it is usually not different from that seen with bypass surgery.

Intracoronary Stent Placement

Sometimes, after PTCA has been done to open up a coronary artery, a small wire mesh tube, or *stent,* is inserted into the artery to keep the formerly constricted area open.

Coronary Atherectomy

Coronary atherectomy is a procedure that removes fatty deposits that are clogging the coronary arteries. A catheter with a tiny rotating device takes out these plaques from the inside of the artery wall. This procedure is often followed by balloon angioplasty and possibly stent placement for optimal results.

Transmyocardial Laser Revascularization

A new and effective procedure for the treatment of CAD involves the use of laser beams to open up blocked areas of the heart. This technique, which is called *laser ablation,* or *transmyocardial laser revascularization,* may be a good alternative for people whose blocked arteries are not accessible by PTCA.

Laser ablation involves the creation of a number of small channels from the left ventricular chamber through the heart wall. These channels allow oxygenated blood to flow through the ischemic heart muscle. It has been reported to result in the relief of ischemia and in the growth of new blood vessels.

Heart Transplantation

Heart transplants generally are not done for people over the age of 70 years. For people under age 70, though, this procedure, which has been used for 30 years with great success, is a very feasible and viable surgical option for end-stage cardiomyopathy. It involves substantial planning on the part of you (the patient), your family, and your doctor.

Unfortunately, the demand for donor hearts exceeds the supply by a large margin. Researchers are currently actively exploring other related therapies, such as tissue transplantation and nonbiological heart replacement. Many of these new options offer great hope for the future treatment of heart disease.

Angiogenesis is the process by which new blood vessels are created from existing ones. Research is still ongoing to explore the possibilities of a new technique called *myocardial angiogenesis,* but preliminary results suggest that it may be a useful intervention for treating myocardial ischemia. This gene-therapy procedure involves the administration of *growth factors* (proteins or genes that encode these proteins) to the area of blockage. The area then can be stimulated to form new collateral blood vessels in the heart to enhance blood supply and thereby improve heart functioning.

Myocardial Angiogenesis

We're fortunate to live in an era in which new medical and surgical treatments for heart disorders are developing rapidly. Even more important, we have the ability, on our own, to substantially slow or even partly reverse many of the age-related changes in our hearts by the choices that we make with regard to our lifestyle. A good attitude, regular medical checkups, an exercise program, and proper nutrition can all go a long way toward keeping our hearts healthy.

So What Can We Do about Heart Disease?

If we believe that growing old can be a healthy process, our heart rate and blood pressure will listen to that message. Our memory, mathematical ability, and self-confidence will stay strong. If we have a good self-image, we'll even be able to walk better. Having a positive outlook and believing that we can and should be well are probably more powerful than any of the drugs, surgery, and mechanical devices available to us.

Attitude Is Key

Regular visits to your doctor are also very important. We frequently hear of patients who cancel medical appointments because "they're too sick to get out of bed." Others see no need to go to a doctor if they're feeling "perfectly fine."

Yet, as we've mentioned throughout this chapter, many heart disorders (such as irregular heart rhythms) may only be detected through a careful medical examination. Also, if you already have been diagnosed with heart disease, it's very important to see your physician regularly to make sure that you are taking the correct dosages of medication and to keep an eye on your condition. Close monitoring by a qualified primary care doctor or a specialist who is trained in managing heart problems is an essential part of staying well.

Regular Checkups

A sedentary lifestyle is one of the most prevalent cardiac risk factors for older adults. In contrast, those who exercise tend to have higher levels of physical and mental performance, lower percentages of body fat, and a lower resting blood pressure and heart rate than nonconditioned older people. Those who are fit also have lower rates of myocardial infarction and heart failure.

Muscle strength training can contribute to greater mobility, improved bal-

Exercise

ance and gait, and better emotional well-being. Even activities such as walking and gardening can have beneficial effects. Physical activity should be habitual and light or moderate in intensity, and it should last a minimum of 20 to 30 minutes, at least three days per week.

Smoking Cessation

Cigarette smoking is a major risk factor for heart disease. Fortunately, the risk of heart disease associated with smoking is lowered dramatically within two years after a person stops smoking. Also, the benefits of quitting are maintained with older age.

If you choose to stop smoking, look for a program that can both help you quit and help you with weight reduction through diet and exercise.

Good Nutrition

It's best to eat a diet that includes a good variety of foods, with relatively little fat (less than 30% of total calories) and cholesterol. Eat lots of fruits, vegetables, and grains, and only modest amounts of sugar, salt, and alcohol (less than the equivalent of one small glass of wine per day).

Learn about the nutritional content of foods (see Figure 2.1), and consider asking your doctor for a referral to a registered dietitian.

What about Fat?

Regardless of whether you are a man or a woman, if you have too much fat around your abdomen, you are at a disadvantage when it comes to risks for heart disease. If, on the other hand, your fat is concentrated around your hips and buttocks, you may have less of a risk of developing heart disease.

Not all fat is bad for you, though. Older people with very low cholesterol levels can also develop serious disease, perhaps in part because the very low cholesterol level may be indicating the presence of another disease (or diseases). Talk with your doctor about your cholesterol level and about whether your weight is in a healthy range.

Estrogen

Hormone replacement therapy with estrogen may help older women prevent coronary artery disease, osteoporosis, and hip fracture. Before deciding about estrogen therapy, however, you should be aware of the reasons not to take estrogen. If you have breast cancer or a family history of breast cancer or endometrial cancer, you should not take this hormone. Even without a family history of these cancers, there is a low risk of developing endometrial cancer, a potential risk of developing breast cancer, and a small risk of developing vaginal bleeding. For more information about estrogen therapy, see Chapter 5.

National and Regional Support Groups for Heart Disease

American Heart Association, 7272 Greenville Avenue, Dallas, TX 75231; Tel. (800) AHA-USA1.

National Heart, Lung, and Blood Institute Information Center, P.O. Box 30105, Bethesda, MD 20824-0105; Tel. (301) 251-1222

National Institute on Aging Information Center, P.O. Box 8057, Gaithersburg, MD 20898-8057; Tel. (800) 222-2225 or (800) 222-4225 (TTY)

CHAPTER 5

YOUR REPRODUCTIVE SYSTEM

Youth, large, lusty, loving—youth full of

grace, force, fascination,

Do you know that Old Age may come after

you with equal grace, force, fascination?

Walt Whitman (1819–1892)

Why would some people find the following personal ad from a Virginia newspaper amusing—or perhaps somewhat shocking?

Old Lady Wanted

DWM, 70, 6 ft 2 inches, 175 lbs., wants to meet a discreet, sexy, broad-minded, fun-loving lady 50–80.

Stereotypes about the elderly abound, but that of the "dirty old man" and the prudish matron (who certainly wouldn't be interested in a sexual relationship with each other) can make you fear that the inevitable physical changes in your reproductive system will not only rob you of an important source of pleasure in your life but even change your personality.

Some might say that facing the changes in sexuality that accompany aging seems like a challenge you just can't win. If you try to safeguard your physical attractiveness—and maybe even hide the signs of aging with hair color and exercise—your attempt might seem to be a foolish effort to revive your youthful vigor (particularly if you buy a sports car!). If you give any indication of having a sex life, you might even be considered inappropriate and strange.

If you don't try to fight the gray hair, wrinkles, and flab, however, will your love life suffer? Also, what about the changes in your body that you can't delay or cover up? We know that women's interest in sex may change (some experience a decrease, and some an increase) due to the hormonal changes ushered in with menopause. Also, some men may find a reduction in their ability to perform sexually due to biological changes, such as changes in the local circulation and, occasionally, prostate enlargement.

Actually, the effects of aging on the reproductive system may vary widely from person to person and over time. Many of the negative consequences can be improved, some with medication and others with nonmedical treatment.

You also have other allies in your effort to stay sexually happy and healthy:

- An open mind and positive attitude can help you overcome negative social attitudes about sexuality in older people.
- Educating yourself about changes in your reproductive system can help you move past the myths about a decline in sexual interest and performance.
- Assertively seeking treatment for any troublesome conditions that arise can keep your whole body in better shape.

Yes, it is possible, and certainly worth it, to take these steps to preserve—and even develop—that private part of your life that has always played a large and important role in your romantic and loving relationships with others.

How Your Reproductive System Changes as You Age

Women

Hormonal Changes of Menopause

During the reproductive years, the pituitary gland in the brain generates hormones that usually result in a new egg being released from its follicle in the ovary each month. The follicle also increases production of the sex hormones estrogen and progesterone, which in turn stimulate the creation of a uterine lining that nourishes the fertilized egg after conception.

Once you reach your mid-30s, the number of eggs released and the hormones produced tend to decline, and usually by your late 40s, these changes may cause irregular menstrual cycles and unpredictable heavy bleeding. These skipped periods are the result of decreased levels of progesterone, the hormone that breaks down the uterine lining when fertilization doesn't occur. We call this transition *perimenopause,* and you may be too distracted by career and family at this time in your life to even notice these gradual changes.

These changes don't occur in exactly the same way at exactly the same time in all women. Some women experience symptoms severe enough that they need medical treatment for this "change of life." Other women notice almost no changes other than those in their menstrual cycles.

By the time you reach your early to mid-50s (the average age at which women have their last period is between 50 and 52), your periods will stop completely, though estrogen production will continue to some extent. Your genes appear to determine the age at which you will reach menopause—not your race, socioeconomic status, age at which you first began your period, or number of prior ovulations. Smoking does cause an earlier menopause, however, as do chemotherapy and exposure to pelvic radiation.

The accompanying sidebar summarizes the physical changes and problems that some women may experience as a result of normal hormonal changes due to aging. Next, we discuss ways to manage these symptoms of menopause so that they don't disrupt your life.

Physical Changes of Menopause

Reproductive System
Vaginal dryness, which can lead to irritation and pain; shrinkage of the reproductive organs (smaller ovaries, marked reduction in size of the uterus, shortening and narrowing of the vagina, shrinkage of the vulva, reduction in size of the clitoris)

Urinary System
Thinning of organ tissues, leading to increased incidence of bladder infections and stress incontinence (see also Chapter 11)

Musculoskeletal System
Osteoporosis—weakening of bones due to loss of estrogen (see also Chapter 9)

Skin Changes
Thinning of the skin and possibly delayed wound healing

Cardiovascular System
Increased risk of heart disease due to loss of the protective effects of estrogen and the changes of levels of fats (lipids) in the blood of postmenopausal women (see also Chapter 4)

Managing the Side Effects of Menopause

Hormone Replacement Therapy and Its Alternatives. Hormone replacement therapy (HRT) uses the female hormones estrogen and progesterone to control many of the unpleasant effects of menopause. Some studies show that HRT can also stop bone loss and thus combat osteoporosis. It may also reduce the risk of death by cardiovascular disease.

Since its first use in the 1940s, HRT has been somewhat controversial because the scientific reports about its effectiveness and safety have been mixed and incomplete. More conclusive evidence is needed before we can recommend HRT for all menopausal women, but we can say now that it improves the short- and long-term quality of life for *some* women. Women in the United States today can expect to live on average about 30 years—nearly 40% of their lives—after menopause, so the development of safe and effective therapy for menopausal symptoms has tremendous public health considerations.

We present the benefits of HRT in Table 5.1. Because HRT is not for everyone, we also provide alternative ways to cope, both with medication and without. You should discuss the details of HRT with your physician.

Table 5.1   **The Benefits of Hormone Replacement Therapy (HRT)**

Symptom	Effect of HRT	Alternatives
Mood changes: irritability, anxiety, depression, insomnia and/or vasomotor symptoms ("hot flashes"), caused by falling estrogen levels; affect about three fourths of women; last 1 to 2 years after menopause for most women but can last as long as 10 years; can disrupt both daily activities and sleep	Systemic estrogen therapy is very effective; symptoms may return if therapy is stopped abruptly; a drug called medroxyprogesterone is also effective	A medicine called clonidine; supplemental soy protein (discussed in the text); dressing and sleeping in breathable layers that can be easily removed; drinking cold water at the start of a flash
Vaginal and urinary tract changes: vaginal dryness and itching that can make sexual intercourse painful; urinary urgency and incontinence	Systemic estrogen therapy is very effective; in addition to oral estrogen tablets, estrogen may also be applied topically (as either a cream or a suppository)	Water-soluble lubricants (such as K-Y Jelly); regular physical exercise; bladder training (see Chapter 11)
Osteoporosis: bones becoming thin, fragile, and highly prone to fracture; affects 5–6 million women in the United States; caused by loss of estrogen (see Chapter 9)	Estrogen therapy is very effective	Drugs called bisphosphonates and raloxifene (an estrogen-like medicine without some of the side effects of estrogen); dietary supplementation with vitamin D and calcium; weight-bearing exercise
Cardiovascular disease: the leading cause of death for women (see Chapter 4)	Inconclusive, but some studies show that women who use HRT have a 50% lower risk of developing heart disease than those who don't	Control of cholesterol levels through diet, exercise, and sometimes medication; control of high blood pressure through diet and medication

The major potential risks of HRT—and some have not been definitively proven—include the following:

- *Breast cancer.* It is believed that long-term exposure to estrogen may increase the risk of breast cancer, but whether HRT increases the risk is still being studied. Use of estrogen for less than five years appears to confer no additional risk and may reduce mortality. If you have a family history of breast cancer, you should not take HRT.

- *Uterine (endometrial) cancer.* If it is used without the addition of the hormone called progestin (which contains progesterone), estrogen therapy increases the risk of developing uterine cancer.
- *Blood clots.* HRT can be dangerous in women who previously have experienced blood clots or stroke.
- *Gallbladder disease.* Estrogen increases the risk of developing gallstones.

Some women avoid HRT altogether because they fear the risks involved or because they don't want the related hassle of monthly periodlike bleeding. Whether you will have this bleeding, which is generally briefer and lighter than menstrual bleeding, depends in part on how long you had stopped having periods completely before you began HRT.

Other effects of HRT may include deep venous thromboses (DVT), leg cramps, and, in asthmatic patients, increased bronchospasm. Many women who start taking HRT may stop taking the medication after one or two years in part because their doctor didn't explain fully the importance of its long-term health benefits. For most women, we believe that these benefits outweigh the risks.

Your family health history (for example, if your mother had breast cancer) and your personal health and life experiences (such as when you had your first child and the results of your most recent Pap smear and mammogram) play a role in deciding whether HRT may be right for you. When discussing HRT with your doctor, you should let him or her know whether you have ever been diagnosed with cancer and whether there is a history of cancer in your family.

Exercise and Diet. While we can't recommend HRT for all menopausal women, we can safely say that exercise and diet are allies that all women can use to combat the effects of menopause—and, of course, aging in general. Regular physical exercise can help you protect both your bones and your heart. Studies have shown that weight-bearing exercise as simple as walking and running can even help you recover bone tissue lost through the years. It can also raise the levels of good (high-density lipoprotein, or HDL) cholesterol in your blood. There's more, too: Exercise will help you sleep better, will help you control your weight, and will help improve your mood through the release of endorphins, the feel-good hormones.

Researchers have also been paying more attention to the effect of diet on menopausal symptoms since it was noted that Japanese women, who consume a large amount of soy protein, have few undesirable symptoms of menopause. In one study, supplemental soy protein was shown to relieve hot flashes by 45% after women had been taking it for three months. The effect appears to be due to the presence of natural compounds called *phytoestrogens* in the soybean plant. While we can't conclusively make a soy prescription until there's more definitive research, we recommend the inclusion of soy protein in the diets of menopausal women. A little extra tofu certainly can't hurt you!

We also recommend that all menopausal women strive to eat a healthy diet of fruit, vegetables, and whole-grain cereal products, that they eat foods low in fat and cholesterol to decrease the risk of cardiovascular disease, and that they take calcium supplements (1,000–1,500 mg per day) to ward off bone loss and osteoporosis.

Menopause and Mental Health

You might remember the controversial episode of the 1970s television sitcom *All in the Family,* in which Edith Bunker's emotional symptoms of menopause served as a source of exasperation to her husband Archie, who demanded that she be done with "the change" instantaneously. While the show broke ground by focusing on a formerly taboo topic, it also portrayed some of the stereotypes and myths surrounding the emotional effects of menopause.

Menopausal women may, but do *not* necessarily, become more moody or depressed than other women. If you experience insomnia, irritability, depression, or anxiety during the menopausal years, keep in mind that other events common at midlife, such as the loss of a parent or having the youngest child leave the nest—not necessarily just hormonal changes—may be causing you to feel upset also. In either case, we would encourage you to talk with your doctor about these concerns. Your doctor will take your complaints seriously and will not dismiss them as hysterical or emotional outbursts from a neurotic person.

Men Men do not usually experience a "male menopause," per se, or a distinct change in reproductive capability, as women do. As with women, however, the symptoms of changes in the reproductive system of the male vary widely from man to man.

Some studies indicate that men experience a decrease in levels of *testosterone*, the male sex hormone that produces the masculine traits of body hair, large muscles, a deep voice, and aggression. Other studies, however, show that low levels of testosterone are not necessarily linked to aging; some older men have low levels and some don't, just as some younger men have high levels and some don't. Interestingly, testosterone levels are declining slightly worldwide each year, probably because of environmental factors.

Once men enter their 60s and 70s, their ability to father children is reduced due to decreased production of viable sperm. This reduction is due in part to a thickening of connective tissue in and occasional collapse of the tubes within the testes through which sperm is delivered to a duct called the *vas deferens.*

It used to seem as though only a few movie stars such as Clark Gable and Cary Grant were fathering children in their golden years. Now we see lots of men fathering children in their 60s, 70s, and beyond. One reason for this increase is the rise in the effectiveness of reproductive technology, which can allow men and women previously classified as "infertile" to conceive with the help of laboratory techniques that can, among other procedures, concentrate the numbers of sperm.

Older men may produce less pre-ejaculatory fluid and experience less forceful ejaculation at orgasm. They may also find that their libido decreases and that the need to release sexual tension through orgasm occurs less frequently. The change in reproductive function that probably worries you most, however, is the loss of penile erectility, or impotence.

Origins and Symptoms of Impotence

About 25–50% of 65-year-old men and 50–70% of 80-year-old men are *impotent*; that is, they are unable to achieve and maintain an erection when desired. Many people believe that impotence is a natural part of the aging process resulting from changes in the male reproductive system. Actually, for older men as well as younger men, impotence is usually caused by disease in other organ systems of the body, or from medicine or surgery used to treat those conditions. Both smoking and depression are known to increase the risk for impotence. The accompanying sidebar lists the most common causes of impotence. Next, we'll discuss some effective ways to treat impotence, which have been developed recently.

- Diseases: atherosclerosis ("hardening of the arteries"), diabetes mellitus, underdeveloped testes (*hypogonadism*), high blood pressure (*hypertension*), vascular disease, Peyronie's disease (structural disorder of the penis), high cholesterol (*hypercholesterolemia*), kidney disease, liver disease (cirrhosis)

- Trauma (from lumbar disk disease and surgical procedures such as rectal surgery and removal of the prostate [*prostatectomy*])

- Psychosocial causes: depression, alcohol use, lack of sexual knowledge or poor techniques, deterioration of relationship with sexual partner, smoking

- Drugs: anticonvulsants, antibiotics, antiarrhythmics, antihypertensives, antianxiety agents and hypnotics, antidepressants, antipsychotics, diuretics, cold and allergy medications, narcotic analgesics, gastrointestinal agents (e.g., anticholinergics and antispasmodics), central nervous system stimulants, and miscellaneous medicines (Acetazolamide, Baclofen, Clofibrate, Danazol, Disulfiram, estrogens, interferon, Naproxen, progesterone)

Common Causes of Impotence

Treatment of Impotence

Before your doctor can treat impotence, he or she will need to diagnose the cause of the problem by taking the following steps:

- Taking a detailed health history
- Performing a complete physical examination
- Taking blood tests to measure levels of testosterone, thyroid-stimulating hormone, and possibly other hormones
- Performing an ultrasound scan to look at the blood vessels in the penis
- Performing a study to find out whether your penis becomes erect while you

are sleeping (you can do this test at home by placing a ring of postage stamps around your penis; if the perforations are broken in the morning, an erection has occurred). These results would indicate that your impotence is likely not caused by a physical problem.

About 10% of cases of impotence are caused not by a physical condition, but by an emotional or psychological one. If your doctor determines that your problem is not physical, he or she may advise you to seek psychological counseling or behavioral therapy, preferably with your sexual partner. In addition to improving sexual function, both types of counseling can help you with depression and anxiety.

The most well-known medical therapy for impotence is sildenafil (Viagra), which was approved by the U.S. Food and Drug Administration (FDA) in March 1998 and has received a tremendous amount of media attention. There are two important caveats about the drug to keep in mind when considering its use:

1. Viagra does not have an effect on impotence caused by emotional and psychological reasons.
2. At the time of this writing, a number of deaths have been associated with the use of Viagra. The majority of these deaths occurred in patients with CAD who were taking drugs called nitrates. If you are taking nitrates in any form, consult your doctor before taking Viagra.

In addition to these concerns, you also should be aware of the commonly reported adverse effects of Viagra: headache, flushing of skin, and indigestion. In spite of the downsides to this drug, in many places, the need for Viagra has outstripped the supply. The majority of our patients who have taken Viagra have been pleased with the results, and they seem to be asking for the maximum amount of this drug that their insurance will pay for.

Before assuming that Viagra is the only treatment for impotence, though, you should consider other therapies for impotence caused by physical problems:

- *Self-injection therapy* (*intracavernous pharmacotherapy*), in which you inject drugs called vasoactive compounds directly into your penis. This therapy, which usually causes an erection in 5 to 10 minutes, is generally effective if you have mild to moderate, but not severe, vascular disease.
- *Vacuum tumescence devices,* which use suction to pull blood into the penis and cause an erection.
- *Binding devices* made of metal, leather, or rubber, which are designed to slow the outflow of blood at the base of the penis. These devices usually help patients with mild impotence, but some people cannot tolerate the discomfort that they may cause.
- *Penile revascularization surgery,* which is still experimental and is performed only on patients with identifiable blood-vessel blockages.
- *Testosterone injection or transdermal* ("through the skin") *patches,* which may increase libido, in addition to improving erectile dysfunction in certain

cases. These preparations are currently under study in older men, but preliminary results suggest that they may be beneficial for men with impotence.

- *Penile prostheses,* which can produce an erection but may not provide sensation if you have neurologic damage. These are for patients who do not meet with success in trying other medical therapies.
- *Gels,* which may contain vasodilating compounds such as papaverine or prostaglandin E1, can increase local blood flow to the penis and thereby treat impotence. The success rate has been variable, depending on the cause and degree of erectile dysfunction.

> *Age does not protect you from Love.*
> *But Love, to some extent,*
> *protects you from Age.*
>
> Jeanne Moreau (1929–)

Sexual Behavior and Response

In a society obsessed with both youth and sex, it's not surprising that many of us assume that the two go hand in hand, and that our sex life will deteriorate as we age. This is not necessarily the case. For many people, sexual interest and activity continue throughout the later years; one survey of men and women age 65 and older found that 74% engaged in sexual activity at least once a week. There is no automatic event in the process of aging that definitively shuts down sexual function.

It's true that certain normal changes in your body can affect your sex life, but being informed and discussing them with your partner and physician can usually solve the problems caused by those changes. More important, the two ingredients that contribute to a healthy, happy sex life at any age are necessary in the older years: good health and a happy relationship with a healthy partner.

Normal Changes in Sexual Response

In both men and women, whether they are heterosexual or homosexual, the response to stimulation is usually slowed with aging. Men will experience a gradual slowing of erections and will require more direct stimulation, and it will usually take longer to have another erection after orgasm. The force of the orgasm and the amount of ejaculate generally decrease. Women also require a longer time to reach sexual excitement, and the loss of estrogen after menopause contributes to vaginal dryness, which can lead to pain during intercourse. A water-soluble lubricant can help with this problem.

Communication between sexual partners is especially important as these physical changes begin to affect response and behavior. A man may assume that his partner's lack of lubrication means she's not interested or stimulated, when in fact the freedom from birth control and pregnancy worries that comes after menopause may make her more relaxed and interested in sex. The fact that they no longer have children living at home may give couples more time and energy for sex, so being open with each other can help overcome the physical changes so that you can take the sexual relationship into a new stage of response and expression of feeling.

Good Health and Your Sex Life

Poor health affects your sex life at any age, so if your sex life is not satisfying, it may be because of the effects of disease, surgery, or medication you are taking, not just the fact that you are growing older. Table 5.2 highlights medical conditions that commonly affect sexuality in older people and some suggestions for limiting these negative effects.

Relationships and Sexuality

Recently an 82-year-old woman began a new sexual relationship two years after her husband passed away. She was worried about her inability to reach orgasm. Her sex life with her husband of 48 years had been very satisfying to her.

She was worried that she might have a physical problem, but her physical examination indicated that she was in good health. Her doctor suggested that she seek psychological counseling because sometimes long-term grief over the loss of a spouse can impair one's ability to find an intimate and relaxed connection with another person.

A satisfying sex life requires a complicated but compatible mix of biological, psychological, and social factors at any age. Couples who have experienced some sexual problems or a less active sex life while younger will probably do the same as they grow older. As we said earlier, talking directly with your partner about the normal physical changes that accompany aging is the healthiest path to take, but this may be hard to do if intimacy has not been a comfortable part of the relationship. Such issues may be best addressed by psychological counseling for both of you.

One way to put a positive spin on the normal changes of aging is to *enjoy* the increased amount of time it takes for you each to become fully aroused, and to work together to explore new techniques that could bring increased sexual satisfaction.

For many older women, the issue isn't an unsatisfying relationship but the lack of a relationship at all. Because women usually live longer than men, about 60% of older women don't have a spouse (vs. 20% of men), and many women who are married have husbands with health problems that may preclude an active sex life.

Older lesbian women and gay men may also report a decrease in sexual activity because they lack a healthy partner. If both partners are healthy, and the relationship is no longer satisfying, counseling may be an option.

In addition to striving for openness about sexual issues with your partner, it's also very important for you to feel comfortable talking about these issues and questions with your physician. Once a physician asked a 61-year-old patient whether she was sexually active, and she said, "Not really, I just lie there." Although some people might find this reply humorous, the information that she provided was really very helpful, and her comment was a good starting point for discussion.

Table 5.2   Illnesses and Surgical Procedures that May Affect Sexuality

Medical condition	Effect on sexuality	Treatment
Diseases		
Arthritis	May interfere with physical performance	Trying different positions; avoiding sex during periods of the day when pain and stiffness are worst
Emphysema and chronic bronchitis	Shortness of breath affects performance	Rest; supplemental oxygen
Prostatitis (inflammation of the prostate gland)	Pain, leading to diminished desire	Antibiotics, warm sitz baths, prostatic massage, Kegel exercises (described in Chapter 11)
Diabetes mellitus	Impotence	Strict control of diabetes
Coronary artery disease (CAD)	Eight- to 14-week recuperation period needed after heart attack; impotence; fear of causing another heart attack by having sexual intercourse	Reassurance from physician that sex is safe (heart attack during sex occurs 20 times in a million); exercise program to improve heart function
High blood pressure (hypertension)	Impotence	Antihypertensive drugs that don't impair sexual response
Parkinson's disease	Lack of desire; impotence	A drug called levodopa can improve sex drive and response in some men
Surgical Procedures		
Hysterectomy	Six- to 8-week recuperation period; depression causing loss of desire	Psychological counseling and support groups
Mastectomy	Depression causing loss of desire	Psychological counseling and support groups
Prostatectomy	Six-week recuperation period; impotence (sometimes due to nerve damage, sometimes psychological)	Psychological counseling and support groups
Colostomy and ileostomy	Emotional reaction causing loss of desire	Psychological counseling and support groups

Source: Adapted from R. N. Butler, M. I. Lewis. Sexuality in old age. In *Brocklehurst's Textbook of Geriatric Medicine and Gerontology* (5th ed.). London: Churchill Livingstone, 1998.

Risks for Sexually Active Adults

You should be aware of the risks associated with sexual activity even as you age; many can affect you just as much as they did when you were younger.

Pregnancy and Birth Control

When one of our colleagues had her first child at 34, she went into the labor and delivery room and saw her name up on a board. It said, "senile primigravida." She knew from her medical training that a *primigravida* was a woman who was giving birth for the first time—but *senile*?! Her doctor explained that at that time, a patient over the age of 32 could be given that label. These days, they no longer call you "senile."

Women are increasingly bearing children into their 40s, but these births are not without risk to mother and baby. Older pregnant women are at increased risk of developing gestational diabetes and high blood pressure (hypertension), simply because the likelihood of both diseases increases with age. Cesarean sections are also more common when older women give birth; anatomical changes in the pelvis that accompany aging may be partly responsible.

The psychological implications for mother and child are usually positive, however. While some older parents worry about being close to retirement when their children go to college, children seldom think or worry about the age difference between them and their parents—all parents seem old to kids! If you're having children later in life, remember that your children will be able to benefit from your maturity and wisdom, and that you're lucky to have kids around to keep you young.

Unfortunately, if you want to avoid the risk of becoming pregnant during your perimenopausal years, your options for birth control are somewhat limited. Birth control pills that contain a combination of the hormones estrogen and progestin are contraindicated in women 35 or older who smoke heavily; have diabetes or high blood pressure; or are at increased risk of blood clots. Women over the age of 39 should try not to take them at all to avoid the risk of developing a blood clot, especially if they have any of the aforementioned risk factors, migraine headaches, or systemic lupus erythematosus. Use of progestin-only contraceptives or intrauterine devices may be safe alternatives. Surgical sterilization through tubal ligation or vasectomy is among the most common birth control methods used by perimenopausal-aged couples.

It's also important to remember that if you are not in a mutually monogamous sexual relationship, you should always use a condom, even if you or your partner is postmenopausal or has been surgically sterilized. Otherwise, you put yourself at risk of potential infections with a sexually transmitted disease—no matter what your age.

AIDS and Other Sexually Transmitted Diseases

As an older adult, you may think you are not at risk for becoming infected with the human immunodeficiency virus (HIV), which causes the acquired immune deficiency syndrome (AIDS). The truth is that according to the Centers for Disease Control, the 50 and older age group is the fastest-growing segment of

HIV-infected patients, with a 71% increase between 1992 and 1994. Throughout the AIDS epidemic, older adults have composed about 10% of the total AIDS patient population.

In the early years of the epidemic, older adults were probably more likely to become infected by receiving unscreened blood transfusions. More recently, they are contracting the virus the same way younger people do—through unprotected sexual contact and injecting drugs with contaminated needles and syringes. Unfortunately, only recently have health care workers recognized that the need to educate older Americans about the risks of HIV infection is just as great as it is for younger people.

Another troubling factor is that AIDS sometimes goes undiagnosed in older patients because its symptoms can be confused with those of other diseases common in older people. For example, weight loss and fatigue might be attributed to depression, or mental confusion might be considered a symptom of Alzheimer's disease. *Pneumocystis carinii* pneumonia could be mistaken for lung disease. Misdiagnosis can delay treatment, endangering the patient further.

Some studies have indicated that older AIDS patients may tolerate drug therapy poorly and that their prognosis may be worse than that of younger patients. However, old age may not necessarily be associated with more rapid progression of AIDS. Older patients who do not have medical problems unrelated to AIDS (these are called "comorbid conditions") and who take antiretroviral therapy can have a more hopeful prognosis. Thus, *if you are diagnosed as being HIV-positive, do not assume that because of your age you are past the point of being treated successfully with drugs that can stave off the onset of full-blown AIDS. Discuss with your doctor the possibility of antiretroviral therapy because you will probably do well on it.*

As at any age, to limit the risk of contracting HIV infection, be sure to use a condom during sexual intercourse unless you are in a mutually faithful relationship with an uninfected partner. Your life depends on it!

If you have multiple sexual partners, practicing safe sex can also limit your chances of contracting other sexually transmitted diseases (STDs), such as syphilis, some forms of hepatitis, and gonorrhea. Older AIDS patients often have a history of these other STDs. One 62-year-old patient who was recently treated for an STD was surprised that he continually contracted gonorrhea from his young girlfriend; he mistakenly thought that he was having "safe sex" because he was taking antibiotics for another condition.

Sexuality and Nursing Homes

Even though many older people living in nursing homes experience some kind of physical or mental disability, it's likely that their need for intimate physical contact with a loved one remains intact. Nevertheless, in many long-term care facilities, even married patients live in separate rooms, and there is insufficient respect for the patients' privacy. Even in nursing homes where accommodations are made for men and women to be alone together, there may not be staff members who are understanding and supportive of expressions of sexuality.

It's also important to bear in mind that people who are living in nursing homes are experiencing a dimension of life that in many ways may not be different from the life that they may have experienced before they entered this type of facility. There are people who get married in nursing homes and people who get divorced there. Recently a 96-year-old man divorced his wife (age 84) after 60 years of marriage while they were living in a nursing home together. They both felt that their quality of life was better after the divorce.

If your mother or father is in a nursing home and you are his or her guardian, it may be especially difficult for you to address these complex issues, especially if your parent or his or her partner is cognitively impaired. There are many factors to consider: your own feelings about your parent's sexuality; your parent's needs, regardless of his or her age, marital status, or mental condition; and the feelings, needs, and rights of his or her partner.

We would advise you to support your dad or mom as best you can and try to think about his or her wishes and needs, even if they may not be what you would want. On the other hand, you are your parent's guardian and best advocate, and what you say absolutely counts, so seek the advice of the nursing-home staff, your parent's physician, and counselors who can provide you with guidance.

Sometimes, medical intervention can be helpful in such instances. For example, a 92-year-old man, recently widowed, was making suggestive verbal and explicit physical gestures toward his young female caregivers (nurses and nurses' aides). His doctor discussed this behavior with him at length, and he said that he missed his wife, who had died two years earlier. After several counseling sessions were attempted, without much success, his doctor prescribed a very low dose of the hormone estrogen for him. Within two weeks, his inappropriate behavior decreased.

James was an 83-year-old man who had been treated in the hospital for congestive heart failure, arthritis, and other problems, including a stroke. When he returned to his nursing home, I went to visit him.

From a distance, I saw him walk (with the help of a walker) with incredible determination and focus toward a woman at the other end of the hallway, who seemed to be waiting for him. I was impressed to see him moving this well so soon after he had gotten out of the hospital. I was delighted to see how much initiative and resolve he had.

At that point, I didn't realize that James and Dorothy, another patient at the nursing home, were boyfriend and girlfriend. A few weeks later, I heard that Dorothy's daughter had discovered James and her mother in an intimate embrace. The daughter was very upset and wanted to take her mother out of the nursing home. Yet in this case, Dorothy and James were consenting partners, and her daughter eventually was able to accept that idea.

I think of what a powerful motivating factor this relationship was for James. Nobody else could have gotten him to walk up the hallway like that!

J.W.

We learn through our painful experiences with family and friends—and sometimes ourselves—that cancer is a significant problem in older people. An in-depth discussion of cancer of the reproductive organs is beyond the scope of this book, but we briefly outline the most common types, the risk factors for each, and the most common treatments.

Cancer of the Repro-ductive Organs

Prostate cancer is second only to lung cancer as a cause of cancer death in men. Age is the strongest risk factor, with 82% of cases occurring in men over age 65. A family history of the disease and the patient's race are also risk factors; African-American men have a 50% higher incidence than European-, Hispanic-, or Asian-American men. Smoking and a diet high in animal fat are also associated with increased risk. We recommend eating fruits, green and yellow vegetables, legumes, and tomatoes to decrease the chances of getting this type of cancer.

Prostate Cancer

In the early stages of prostate cancer, men usually have no symptoms. Even if you do find that you have a slower or weaker urine stream, a need to urinate more frequently, or pain in the groin area, you may not have prostate cancer, but rather a more common condition called benign prostatic hypertrophy (BPH), which occurs as the prostate enlarges. Because early detection improves the chances of curing the cancer, it's important to see your doctor if you do have symptoms, though, and to be screened by having a digital rectal examination and possibly having the levels of prostate-specific antigen (PSA) in your blood measured. There is some controversy about the value of the PSA test (levels of PSA tend to go up progressively with age, and elevated levels do not necessarily mean that a person has prostate cancer). You should discuss it with your doctor. The results of neither test are definitive, so diagnosis is usually confirmed by transrectal ultrasound-directed needle biopsy.

There are several treatment options for prostate cancer:

- *Observation and follow-up.* This option may be best for men 85 years or older who have cancer that is confined to the prostate and whose life expectancy at the time of diagnosis is less than 10 years.
- *Radical prostatectomy, or removal of the prostate.* This option is often chosen by men in their 50s, 60s, and 70s who have cancer confined to the prostate and are otherwise healthy. Unfortunately, the potential complications of this surgery can sometimes include urinary incontinence and impotence.
- *Radiation therapy.* This is another option for men with cancer confined to the prostate. Impotence may be likely after this treatment.
- *Hormone therapy.* This treatment suppresses testosterone production by removal of the testes or with drugs; this treatment may also result in impotence and decreased libido.

If you are faced with making the choice of therapy, be sure to get a second opinion. Don't rush your decision-making process. Talk with people who have previously experienced prostate cancer, and read as much about the disease as you can. For more information about prostate cancer, call the National Cancer Institute (NCI) at 1-(800)-4CANCER.

Testicular Cancer

Cancer of the testes is rare, usually affects young men between 15 and 35 years of age, and is more common in those with an undescended testicle, an under-developed testicle (for example, due to a viral infection such as mumps), or a family history of testicular cancer. European-American men are at slightly increased risk, compared to African-, Hispanic-, or Asian-American men.

The chances of surviving testicular cancer can be high (approximately 95%) if the cancer is diagnosed early. Self-examinations are very important for finding it early. If you feel a small, hard, pea-shaped mass or swelling, or a change in the way it looks or feels, or if there is a heavy feeling or any pain in the testicle, it does not necessarily mean that you have testicular cancer, but it would be good for you to see your doctor to have it evaluated, for your own reassurance.

Uterine Cancer

Uterine (or endometrial) cancer is the most common gynecological cancer, and about three fourths of affected patients are postmenopausal. Fortunately, the death rate due to uterine cancer is decreasing, and because this cancer is usually diagnosed at an early stage, the rate of cure is high (85% survival rate at 5 years). Obesity, lack of childbearing, late menopause, high blood pressure (hypertension), and diabetes are all risk factors for the disease.

Taking birth control pills or HRT that combine estrogen and progesterone tend to decrease the risk. It is important to note that taking estrogen without progesterone ("unopposed estrogen") *increases* the risk of developing uterine cancer.

Most patients with uterine cancer will have abnormal uterine bleeding; they may also have pain in the pelvis, back, or legs; and possibly bladder or rectal symptoms. Weight loss and general weakness also may occur.

An endometrial biopsy is required for diagnosis, and treatment depends on the stage of the cancer. Patients in the early stages will have a hysterectomy with removal of both fallopian tubes and ovaries; patients with more advanced cancer will undergo radiation after this surgery.

Ovarian Cancer

Ovarian cancer is less common than uterine cancer but is more likely to cause death because it rarely causes symptoms in the early stages. The median age at diagnosis is 61.

The risk of ovarian cancer is associated with the number of ovulation cycles a woman experiences; drugs or conditions that suppress ovulation decrease the risk of the cancer. Thus, having more than one child, taking birth control pills, breastfeeding, and disorders that inhibit ovulation are preventive, and women who do not have children and who have a late menopause are at increased risk. A family history is also a risk factor, as are a high-fat diet and a history of mumps infection before the age at which menstrual periods begin.

When symptoms appear, they are usually nonspecific gastrointestinal disorders such as indigestion, nausea, a feeling of fullness after eating very little, and a change in bowel habits. Diagnosis may be helped by the use of ultrasound tests.

Treatment includes removal of the uterus (hysterectomy); removal of the ovaries, uterine tubes, and ligaments of the uterus (adnexectomy); and removal of part of the abdomen called the omentum (omentectomy)—followed by chemotherapy.

Cervical Cancer

Even though cervical cancer is highly preventable through screening (Pap smears) and treatment of premalignant lesions, cervical cancer still accounts for about 20% of all gynecological cancers. The average age of the patient at onset of the disease is 45 to 55. Risk factors include age, race (African-American, Hispanic, and Native American women have an increased risk), smoking, long-term contraceptive use, and engaging in sexual activity at an early age.

Tissue and cell changes that lead to cervical cancer are caused by *human papilloma virus (HPV)* infection, a sexually transmitted disease that causes genital warts. HPV is very common, but many cases do not produce noticeable symptoms—thus, screening with Pap smears is very important. Fortunately, HPV infection progresses to cancer in less than 1% of women.

Treatment of invasive cervical cancer includes both surgery (hysterectomy) and radiation.

Hysterectomy

The removal of the uterus, or hysterectomy, is one of the most common major surgical operations in the United States, although in recent years, these procedures have been done less frequently. Most of these operations are performed for women in their early 40s. About 25% of American women over age 60 have had a hysterectomy. Although most hysterectomies were done through an abdominal incision (75%), an increasing number are now being done vaginally; this procedure is called "laparoscopically assisted vaginal hysterectomy."

If you are told that you need a hysterectomy, you should first seek a second opinion. One condition that always requires a hysterectomy is uterine cancer (about 10% of hysterectomies). *Fibroids*—benign tumors—may cause excessive bleeding and account for one third of hysterectomies. Endometriosis that causes severe pain is another common reason for hysterectomy. Prolapsed uterus may also warrant a vaginal hysterectomy.

There are different reasons and procedures for performing a hysterectomy. The most important thing to do is to learn as much as you can about this procedure and to seek a second opinion.

For more information, call the Gynecologic Cancer Foundation, 1-800-444-4441.

From the brain only, arise our pleasures, joys, laughter and jests, as well as our sorrows, pains, griefs and tears. . . . It is the same thing which makes us mad or delirious, inspires us with dread or fear, whether by night or by day, brings sleeplessness, inopportune mistakes, aimless anxieties, absent-mindedness, and acts that are contrary to habit. These things that we suffer all come from the brain, when it is not healthy.

Hippocrates (460–377 B.C.)

Just as with our physical health, there are many myths surrounding time's effect on our brain's health. Here are two of them:

1. *Forgetting where you put your keys is just part of getting old.* Usually, it's not. In fact, this sort of lapse in memory may indicate nothing or that something transient and reversible is affecting you—possibly something as simple as the fact that perhaps you're tired, distracted, or taking two drugs that do not interact well.
2. *Older people need less sleep.* Wrong again! "Senior discounts" should apply to restaurant prices and theater tickets—not to the number of hours that you need to sleep every night. Although waking up more frequently during the night and having difficulty getting back to sleep *are* more common in later life, you still need as much sleep as you did when you were younger. So don't resign yourself to being tired much of the time—there are proven strategies to help you get the restful sleep that you need.

This chapter is intended to dispel the foregoing and other common misconceptions about aging by clarifying what's normal and what's not.

We start by describing how the brain might change as we grow older. Then we look at some proactive things that we can do to keep our minds sharp. Finally, we explore the various challenges to mental acuity—such as memory loss, confusion, poor mood, and emotional struggles—that we may encounter. More often than not, there are excellent treatment options available to help us manage these difficulties when they arise.

The human brain is a world consisting of a number of explored continents and great stretches of unknown territory.

Santiago Ramon y Cajal (1852–1934)

How Does Your Brain Age?

Our brains may actually shrink by as much as 5–10% as we get older. This doesn't mean that we're destined to become less intelligent, though. In fact, certain mental abilities (such as an expanding vocabulary) can *increase* in 1 out of every 10 people in their 80s and 90s.

Even if our brains do get a bit smaller with time, we still have plenty of gray matter to work with. With remarkable insight, poet Emily Dickinson described the brain as being "wider than the sky"—and she was right: Like the stars in space, our brains hold an almost unimaginable number of cells and connections. This wonderfully complex living microprocessor contains about 100 billion nerve cells (*neurons*), as well as billions of *glial cells,* which support these neurons by supplying them with nutrients and many other molecules to help them function well. Thus, even though some of our brain cells may die as we age, an abundant supply of others is available to take their place.

Our nerve cells communicate with each other via electrical impulses that travel across junctions called *synapses.* These impulse messages, which are transmitted by chemicals called *neurotransmitters,* might move less efficiently from one neuron to another as we get older, and these slight delays can affect our ability to solve problems and remember information quickly. A bit later in this chapter, we also talk about how decreased amounts of certain neurotransmitters can lead to particular feelings of sadness or confusion—and we discuss therapeutic ways to make up for these chemical deficiencies. Right now, though, we look at the essential ingredients for feeding a healthy brain.

What Can You Do to Keep Your Mind Fit?

Maintaining a balanced diet, staying physically and mentally active, getting enough rest, and attending to our health problems may not absolutely guarantee that we will keep our minds and memories intact forever, but working at keeping our whole bodies fit can have many benefits for our brains. These measures can maintain and support the chemical messengers and blood supply that are essential to mental functioning and can help to keep us alert and energized. Here are some specific steps that you can take to make the most of your brain power: Eat well, get exercise, sleep well, and get treatment for medical problems.

Eat Well

There may not be a miracle diet for mental fitness, but research has shown that we'll do best if we follow the ancient sages, who advised people to "do nothing in excess." You already know that consuming too much sugar, salt, and caffeine is bad for you. In addition to eating and drinking these substances in moderation (and minimizing your intake of alcohol), we recommend the following steps:

Eat plenty of fruits and vegetables. Vitamins, especially those found in fresh foods, are important for healthy functioning of the brain. Although multivitamin pills can be beneficial, we really can't say for sure how much of the vitamins in these pills and capsules is absorbed from the gastrointestinal tract. Vitamins in food are much better, because they're *bioavailable*—that is, most of the vitamins are accessible and useful to your body.

Make sure you're getting enough of the right vitamins. Although eating vitamin-containing foods is the best way to obtain these nutrients, it's sometimes hard to get enough of certain vitamins from our diet. This may be especially true of important nutrients such as *vitamin E,* which has been shown to slow the rate of memory decline in patients who are in the early stages of memory loss such as Alzheimer's disease. Vitamin E is also an *antioxidant,* which means that it helps protect the brain cells and blood vessels that carry oxygen-rich blood to our brains.

Eating broccoli, spinach, peanuts, and vegetable oil will provide you with some vitamin E. A number of our patients—even if they are taking a multivitamin—also take an additional 400 international units of vitamin E two times each day (for a total of 800 international units).

Vitamin C is another important antioxidant that's good for our small blood vessels (capillaries). Vitamin C is *water soluble,* which means that it isn't stored in our bodies for very long. Therefore, in addition to consuming fresh fruits and vegetables that contain this vitamin, you may want to take an additional 60 mg per day. Most multivitamins contain this much vitamin C per pill.

Folic acid, or *folate,* may help to prevent "hardening of the arteries" (*atherosclerosis*). This agent is also essential for the synthesis of choline, from which an important neurotransmitter called *acetylcholine* is formed. A shortage of this chemical messenger can make us confused, so foods that contain choline-building folic acid (such as cereals and fortified bread products, broccoli, spinach, and orange juice) are good "foods for thought." Most people can also get enough folate (400 micrograms per day) from multivitamins.

Finally, whole *B vitamins* (thiamine, riboflavin, niacin, vitamin B_6 [pyridoxine], and vitamin B_{12} [cobalamin]) are also essential for good functioning of the central nervous system. Thiamine, in particular, which is found in whole grains, rice, beans, and potatoes, among other foods, helps to synthesize acetylcholine and keeps nerve fibers and neurons healthy. Too little of this vitamin may lead to a depressed mood. Like vitamin C, the B vitamins are water soluble, so it's important to get enough of them every day. We advise our patients to consume whole grains, vegetables, and a multivitamin daily.

Don't forget the minerals. Most multivitamins—and many foods, such as fish and fresh vegetables—contain minerals such as magnesium, copper, phosphorus, and iron. Magnesium is especially good for maintaining the nerve impulses in our brains. A lack of this mineral has been linked to confusion and restlessness. Copper helps to maintain *myelin,* a protective cover that surrounds some nerve fibers. Phosphorus is essential for metabolism, and iron is required for metabolism and for building *hemoglobin,* an important component of red blood cells.

You may want to review your usual diet to make sure that you're getting enough of these crucial nutrients. If you're concerned about mineral deficiencies, talk with your doctor about whether you should be taking a supplement.

DRINK MILK. Besides being an excellent source of protein, milk and other foods that contain calcium, such as calcium-fortified orange juice, spinach, and salmon, are good for you. Not only will these foods keep your bones strong, but they may also help to maintain the nerve cells that transmit chemical messages in the brain. Again, if you're unsure about whether you're getting enough calcium from your diet, talk with your physician.

EAT ARTERY-FRIENDLY FOODS. You're probably aware of how important a low-fat diet can be for maintaining a healthy heart. Remember, though, that arteries also supply the brain with well-oxygenated blood, so a diet that is good for your heart is also good for your brain. To keep both of these organs healthy, avoid fatty foods such as cheese, which may clog up your arteries.

EAT ONLY MODERATE AMOUNTS OF SALT AND SUGAR. Don't eliminate salt and sugar entirely from your diet—some is essential—but don't overdo it, either. Talk with your doctor about how much of these substances is right for you, especially if you have conditions (such as high blood pressure, kidney problems, and diabetes) that can be affected by your salt and sugar intake.

APPRAISE THE VALUE OF HERBAL ADDITIVES. The labels on natural health products that are sold in health-food stores, pharmacies, and supermarkets may promise you everything from sharpening your thinking to protecting you from the common cold. Some people swear that certain of these products—such as choline supplements, shark cartilage, ginkgo, and ginseng—improve their mental and physical functioning.

These preparations may or may not be beneficial for some individuals; more good-quality scientific studies need to be done before we can be more clear about how much, for whom, and for what conditions they are really effective. Until then, it's important to keep in mind that most herbal or alternative drugs are not federally regulated or standardized. Consumers cannot be sure about the exact ingredients, concentration, quality, or bioavailabilty of such compounds. For instance, five brands of echinacea could all contain different amounts of this substance, and your body might not absorb each preparation in the same way. So you can't necessarily assume that what's on the bottle label is exactly what your body will get.

Many preparations also contain a variety of added ingredients that are labeled inactive (*inert*). The problem is that it may be difficult to know what these inert substances are, and not all of them may actually be inactive, especially in persons who may have allergies to certain foods or other substances.

It has been reported from time to time that ingestion of these preparations has resulted in serious side effects. For instance, some people would take over-the-counter tablets of the essential amino acid called tryptophan to help them get to sleep. Several years ago, one lot of this drug contained a toxic, related compound that ended up causing severe disability and long-lasting joint and muscle pain in some of the people who took it.

Herbal remedies may also interact negatively with other medications that you may be taking. Once a patient who suffered from depression was taking a blood thinner called *warfarin* to protect her from developing blood clots. Her daughter noticed that the patient was becoming more depressed, and so she gave her mother an herbal medication that she thought might boost her mother's energy and mood.

The herbal preparation reacted with the blood-thinning medication to such an extent that it actually completely reversed the blood-thinning effect, and our patient developed a blood clot in her arm that required emergency surgery to save her hand. Now when she wants to try new medications, this patient tells us first, so that we can monitor more closely for potential drug interactions.

USE MODEST AMOUNTS OF CHEMICAL FLAVOR ENHANCERS. MSG is a type of salt that may be used as a food additive to enhance the flavor of some foods. It is thought to work by stimulating receptors on the tongue and nerve cells (*neurons*) in the brain. Some people actually get headaches or allergic reactions after ingesting MSG. More research needs to be done regarding MSG's full effects on the brain, but for now, it would be reasonable for you to use this flavor enhancer in modest amounts. Also, try adding natural spices (such as oregano, cinnamon, paprika, or pepper) to make your food more appealing.

Get Exercise   In addition to a good diet, physical activity is a wonderful way to help keep your mind working to its best potential. Physical activity also keeps our hearts healthy and improves our circulation so that blood can fully circulate in our brains. When we exercise, chemicals called *endorphins* are released from the brain. Endorphins heighten our sense of well-being and leave us with a good sense of accomplishment. Furthermore, tests that have been done on people before and after they exercise show that physical activity improves mental functioning and sharpens our senses and motor reflexes, too.

Getting more exercise does not mean that you have to train for running a marathon or swimming across the English Channel! You don't have to invest in an expensive health club or embark on an elaborate physical regimen. Simply taking a walk several times a week is fine. See your physician before you start any new exercise program. Remember to start out very slowly and gradually increase your level of activity as you build up your tolerance over time. Don't push yourself when you don't feel right.

In *Macbeth,* the great bard Shakespeare described sleep as the "Balm of hurt minds. . . . Chief nourisher in life's feast." Indeed, nothing is more essential for the optimal functioning of our minds and our memories than sleep. **Sleep Well**

Why do many people believe that we need less sleep as we grow older? This misconception arises from the fact that older people tend to nap more during the day and sleep fewer consecutive hours at night. This change may be due in part to the alterations in the daily rhythm of a number of our hormones and body functions (such as core body temperature), which some of us may experience. Our colleague Charles Czeisler has reported that these alterations can affect our sleep-wake cycle during a 24-hour period.

As we get older, it may take longer for us to fall asleep when we lie down, and it may be more difficult for us to stay asleep for a length of time. We may wake up more frequently during the night and then find it more difficult to fall back asleep again or to get additional good-quality sleep.

To add to this unrestful cycle, some of us may occasionally experience brief (5- to 10-second) interruptions in breathing during sleep. This condition, called *sleep apnea,* may benefit from further evaluation and treatment. Often, it is very treatable and will improve function of many other systems once it's treated. Fatigue due to insufficient sleep may also lead to an increase in snoring for some people, and it may contribute to *restless leg syndrome,* or discomfort in the lower extremities, which may further interfere with sleep.

None of these age-related changes mean that we need less sleep as we get older, though. In fact, we need about as much restful sleep as we always have. If we don't get it, we tend to not be quite ourselves. If you are getting less than the "40 winks" that you require, here are some strategies that you might want to try:

GET MORE PHYSICAL EXERCISE. We just described the benefits of physical activity for mood and mental functioning. Exercise has also been found to be more effective than sleeping medicines for many seniors, so try to exercise, by walking, for example, even when you feel a little tired.

Gregg Jacobs, of the Sleep Disorders Center of Boston's Beth Israel Deaconess Medical Center, recommends that you exercise late in the day before dinner (but not less than three hours before you go to bed), because physical activity raises your body temperature, and then, a few hours later, your body temperature drops to a level that is conducive to sleep.

CUT BACK ON CAFFEINE. If you're having trouble sleeping, drink fewer caffeinated beverages after 12 noon, and don't drink any caffeinated beverages after 4 P.M. because this stimulant can stay in your system for many hours, interfering with sleep.

MAKE YOUR BEDROOM A GOOD PLACE TO SLEEP. Be sure to sleep in a dark, quiet place. Eyeshades and earplugs may be helpful if your room is too bright or if your surroundings are too noisy. A cool, well-ventilated bedroom will also help to keep your body temperature down to a level that may help you to stay asleep.

AVOID THOSE AFTERNOON NAPS. Some people feel more refreshed after a short nap in the afternoon. Others find that forgoing naps during the day helps them to sleep better at night. If you're a napper but are having trouble sleeping after the sun goes down, you may want to try skipping your afternoon nap for a few days.

DRINK WARM MILK OR NONCAFFEINATED TEA IN THE EVENING. In addition to calcium and protein, milk contains an essential amino acid called *tryptophan,* which is a natural sleep inducer. Others swear by chamomile or mint tea. You may want to try different (nonalcoholic) drinks in the evening to see which has the most soothing effect for you, but don't drink too much fluid just before bedtime, because it may interrupt your sleep by increasing your need to urinate.

DECOMPRESS SO THAT YOU CAN REST. Rest and sleep go hand in hand, so try to find relaxation techniques that are effective for you. Some people find that meditation, reading a book, or listening to certain kinds of music may be soothing. Others may find that taking a leisurely stroll, imagining a beautiful scene, or taking a warm bubble bath about an hour and a half before bedtime can be calming and may promote sleep. Prayer, breathing exercises, or massage may also be helpful. Whatever works for you, get into a routine that you like, and indulge in it regularly!

DON'T DRINK A NIGHTCAP. Try to minimize your use of alcohol, and don't drink alcohol after 6 P.M. because several hours after drinking, when the level of alcohol in your blood goes down, you may find yourself more awake, and you may have trouble falling back to sleep.

DON'T READ OR WATCH TELEVISION WHILE IN BED. Researchers have found that if you use your bedroom just for rest, and if you go to bed only when you are tired, you will sleep better. If you're still awake after 15 or 20 minutes, get out of bed and read or listen to music under dim lighting until you feel sleepy again.

DON'T TRY TO CATCH UP ON SLEEP. On weekends, vacations, or other times when you have the opportunity to sleep later than usual, go to bed at your usual time and don't sleep more than an hour later than you usually do. You can't really replace the sleep that you may have lost on previous nights, and you may find that oversleeping may actually make you more tired.

IF YOU TAKE SLEEPING PILLS, DON'T TAKE THEM EVERY NIGHT. Despite their name, sleeping pills may actually cause insomnia if you use them continuously for long periods of time. Therefore, if you do take medicines to help you sleep, try not to take them every night, and skip one or two nights per week on a regular basis.

Many sleeping pills are sold over the counter, but if you use these medicines, you should still talk with your doctor about which type is most appropriate for you. We generally recommend sleeping pills that are *short acting,* so that they don't linger in your system and give you a hangover the morning after you've taken them. Also, agents such as diphenhydramine (Benadryl) or triazolam

(Halcion) might not be good for some people because these drugs have been found to increase confusion, especially in those over age 50.

IF YOU TAKE MELATONIN, BUY A REPUTABLE BRAND. Although its benefits are still unclear, many people swear by *melatonin,* a natural hormone that our brains secrete in direct response to changes in the level of light in our environment. A shortage of these chemicals in our brains may be responsible for the depressed feelings that may occur during the winter when there is little sunlight. This hormone is also related to a neurotransmitter called *serotonin,* which is essential for maintaining our mood balance. Melatonin supplements are available as over-the-counter drugs, and people sometimes take these supplements to help them sleep, or to ward off the disruptions in the sleep cycle that can occur during travel across several time zones.

Some studies have shown that melatonin at low doses (less than 1 mg) may be beneficial (and may have relatively few side effects), but research is still ongoing. Like the other herbal and alternative medications described earlier, it's important to consider the issues of preparation, purity, and bioavailability when purchasing this type of unregulated drug. High doses of melatonin (above 3 mg) occasionally have been associated with negative side effects such as confusion, headache, or nightmares.

ABOVE ALL, MAKE GOOD, SOUND SLEEP A PRIORITY. Scientific studies have shown that Shakespeare was right: There is no substitute for sleep. This "balm" and "nourisher" is good for our brains, and it helps us to function better all around.

Get Treatment for Medical Problems

Several medical conditions are known to cause or contribute to cognitive decline. Therefore, one of the best things that you can do to keep your mind healthy is to make sure that the rest of your body is healthy, too. Several disorders can adversely affect your mind.

SEVERE ANEMIA. A low blood count, or *anemia,* is one of the most common and readily treatable causes of acute confusion or delirium in older persons. Your physician can tell with a simple blood test whether you are anemic; if you are, this condition may be very reversible with medical treatment or dietary supplements, or both.

THYROID PROBLEMS. *Hypothyroidism,* an underactive thyroid gland, can make you feel low and lethargic. *Hyperthyroidism,* an overactive thyroid gland, can also make you feel tired and depressed, and it can alter your thinking. Again, a blood test can tell your doctor whether your thyroid hormones are at the proper level. Sometimes, it only takes replacement or reduction of this hormone to restore a wonderful sense of energy.

HIGH BLOOD PRESSURE. High blood pressure (*hypertension*) may be harmful to the brain in several ways. It may impair the circulation of blood in the brain, even if the arteries to this important organ are not clogged with fatty deposits. If there is plaque in an artery that leads to the brain, a sudden blockage could result in at least a temporary loss of oxygen and nutrients (ischemia), and these deficiencies could damage and destroy brain cells. Hypertension is also associated with a greater prevalence of breathing disturbances during sleep (e.g., sleep apnea).

HIGH CHOLESTEROL. You probably know that high cholesterol can put you at risk for a heart attack (see Chapter 4). It can also affect the arteries that lead to the brain by clogging them with plaque and increasing the likelihood of blood clots and strokes. Blood thinners such as aspirin can reduce the stickiness of blood platelets and may help to prevent these serious outcomes. See Chapter 4 for further guidelines regarding acceptable cholesterol levels and suggestions for lowering high cholesterol levels.

IRREGULAR HEART RHYTHMS. Like high cholesterol, irregular heart rhythms (arrhythmias) can also reduce and interrupt the supply of blood and oxygen to the brain. See Chapter 4 for a complete discussion of the types of arrhythmias and the therapeutic options available to treat them.

What about When the Brain Is Not Well?

Perhaps you've always maintained a nutritious diet, you've stayed physically fit, you've seen your physician regularly, and through the years you've carefully taken whatever medicines have been prescribed to keep yourself healthy. Is there still a chance that you'll have difficulty remembering information as you get older? Yes, but just as with other health problems that you have had in your lifetime, effective treatments are often available to address these challenges. Next, we discuss the problems that we may encounter and the treatment options that can help.

Memory Problems

Although some people do experience short-term memory loss as they age (this is called age-associated memory impairment or benign senescent forgetfulness, and it does *not* necessarily lead to Alzheimer's disease), you and your family should not assume that problems such as forgetfulness go hand in hand with getting old. Rather, you may have any of a number of potentially very manageable conditions, including medication side effects, mild cognitive impairment, depression, delirium, stroke, and possibly Parkinson's disease.

Can Your Memory Loss Be Helped by Estrogen?

An 88-year-old former high-school teacher was experiencing increased memory lapses, urinary tract infections, and urinary incontinence. We prescribed a low daily dose (0.3 mg) of the hormone estrogen, and her symptoms improved significantly. Her husband, a 91-year-old former attorney, noticed how much his wife's memory had improved, and he asked his doctor for an estrogen prescription also. He started taking it and noticed that his own thinking seemed to become clearer.

Indeed, research has shown that when estrogen is removed from an animal or a human (by removal of the ovaries, for example), there may be more memory losses; when estrogen is replaced, there may be at least a partial restoration of memory function, and neurons in the brain then may also make new connections with other neurons. Although estrogen replacement therapy does not appear to improve memory in people with chronic dementia, it may help them feel better and consequently function better.

Is it unnatural to take supplemental estrogen? Estrogen and related compounds are naturally occurring proteins in both animals and plants. Some women prefer to eat vegetables and soy-protein-rich tofu, which contain estrogen-like compounds, rather than to take pills.

Estrogen is not the only alternative, however. Other good options are exercise, sleep, meditation, nutritious foods, calcium, vitamins, blood-pressure-lowering agents, bisphosphonates, selective estrogen receptor modulators (SERMs), and lipid-lowering drugs, as needed.

According to the American Psychiatric Association, *delirium* is a cognitive disorder that is marked by wandering attention, disorganized thinking (such as rambling, irrelevant, or incoherent speech), and sometimes memory loss and disorientation. People with delirium may seem less alert and may have difficulty with sleeping. Unlike Alzheimer's disease sufferers, patients with delirium may have lucid periods alternating with impaired mental functioning off and on throughout a day; their deficit does not steadily worsen, but waxes and wanes. This disorder, which is often caused by infection or drug toxicity, generally develops suddenly, may last longer than was previously thought (up to six months), and is usually reversible. In most cases, delirium can be treated, but only after the underlying cause or, more likely, multiple causes of the syndrome are treated.

Dementia is another syndrome that involves cognitive decline. This slowly developing syndrome involves diminishing memory, as well as trouble with language, motor activities, orientation, judgment, planning, or organization. Many cases of dementia are highly treatable, and any symptoms of this disorder demand a careful workup to identify these potentially reversible causes. *Alzheimer's disease,* the most common form of dementia, is a chronic condition that tends to get steadily and progressively more severe. Symptoms include memory loss, the inability to perform routine tasks, disorientation, a decline in communication skills, and impaired judgment. It's possible to have Alzheimer's disease and delirium or Alzheimer's disease and depression.

Delirium versus Dementia: What Are the Differences between These Disorders?

Confusion (Delirium)

> In bodily disease a wandering mind
> is often found; devoid of reason then,
> The patient raves and roams delirious.
>
> Lucretius (96–55 B.C.)

Memory changes may occur at different rates for different people, but increasing confusion is *not* a normal part of aging. Rather, it is a symptom of an underlying disorder, just as a fever is not a normal part of aging but may be a symptom of infection, which needs to be treated.

Acute confusion may be caused by a number of factors, including vision and hearing loss, heart disease, a change in environment, infection, anemia, malnutrition, metabolic disorders such as kidney and liver disease, head trauma, pain, or stroke. It may also be caused by the interactions of several drugs taken at once. Older persons (people over 85 years) with chronic medical problems and multiple medications, and individuals with sensory, memory, or functional deficits, are at greatest risk of developing this problem.

Acute confusion, sometimes called *delirium,* develops suddenly over hours to days and fluctuates in severity over a 24-hour period. A person with this disorder may have brief periods of lucidity alternating with an inability to pay attention. He or she may have visual hallucinations and disorganized thinking, and he or she may engage in rambling or incoherent conversation. A person with delirium may be quiet and withdrawn or upset and agitated.

A doctor can assess for delirium by taking a careful history and giving a physical examination. The examination will include a *mental status examination* to identify preexisting impaired cognitive function and a more specific test for the presence of delirium, as well as some laboratory tests. Information from an informant such as a spouse or close friend familiar with the person's prior cognitive function is necessary in order to determine whether the symptoms are new or are exacerbations of preexisting ones.

In order to treat delirium, physicians search for the factors that caused it. This search may present challenges because the symptoms of confusion may persist for several weeks in certain patients, even in the absence of new contributing factors. If the cause (such as inappropriate medicine use) is determined and corrected, this type of confusion usually can be reversed.

Memory Loss (Dementia)

The term *dementia* is sometimes used as a general, non-specific term that is applied to a number of different disorders, including memory loss, depression, and delirium. Some form of dementia is thought to affect approximately 10% of adults over age 65. We define dementia as a progressive condition that involves an increasing inability to remember or think or reason clearly. Other symptoms may include:

- Difficulty remembering appointments and recent experiences and conversations
- A tendency to misplace things increasingly often
- Difficulty accomplishing tasks that have several steps, such as cooking
- Disorientation
- Trouble expressing ideas or opinions, difficulty finding the right word for an object or concept
- Unusual behavior (for example, acting more irritable or more passive than usual)

In time, this problem can begin to severely affect a person's ability to manage everyday life.

Reversible Dementias. It is important to carefully diagnose the cause of a person's dementia because some causes are treatable, or at least partly reversible. Just as with delirium, reversible dementias may be caused by medications, alcohol, hypothyroidism, dehydration, problems of metabolism, or infection. Often, stopping the medication, taking an antibiotic for an infection, or correcting a condition such as hypothyroidism with hormone replacement therapy can be effective in treating the resulting dementia.

Progressive Dementias. Many dementias may not be reversible, but if correctly diagnosed, some symptoms can be treated, and the person's quality of life can be greatly improved. The progressive dementias, some of which we explore in more detail below, include Alzheimer's disease (the most common form of dementia); Lewy body dementia; vascular (multi-infarct) dementia; Parkinson's disease; alcohol-related dementias; Pick's disease (a rare degenerative brain disorder that is similar to Alzheimer's disease in its progressive course); and Huntington's dementia, a hereditary degenerative brain disorder. Huntington's dementia (formerly called Huntingon's chorea), which may first cause symptoms in people over age 50, may begin with personality changes, depression, and clumsiness and may progress to movement problems and slurred speech.

Alzheimer's Disease

Alzheimer's disease is a progressive degenerative disease that alters the brain and may dramatically affect a person's behavior. In the United States, it is the fourth leading cause of death in older adults. In 1906, a German physician and neuropathologist named Alois Alzheimer (1864–1915) identified certain anomalies in the brain of a woman in her 50s who suffered from dementia. Our colleagues Dennis Selkoe and Brad Hyman have reported that the brains of patients with Alzheimer's disease usually have increased numbers of distinct *plaques*—or deposits of protein on the outside of cells—and *neurofibrillary tangles*—bundles of threads that take the place of nerve cells (neurons).

Risk Factors. Alzheimer's disease affects an estimated 6–8% of all people age 65 and older and an estimated 25–45% of people over age 85; 60–80% of people with dementia have Alzheimer's disease. Although scientists are still investigating the causes of this disease, which appears to affect men and women in equal percentages, they do know something about its predisposing factors. The two main risk factors are

- *Age.* The risk of getting Alzheimer's disease increases exponentially with age and doubles with every decade after age 65 years. It is usually diagnosed in people older than 65, although rarely it is diagnosed in people in their late 30s or in their 40s or 50s.

- *Family history.* Most people with Alzheimer's disease do *not* come from families that have been affected by this disease. In some cases, however, especially in patients with *early-onset disease* (Alzheimer's that strikes when a patient is in his or her late 30s or 40s), Alzheimer's may be inherited. Researchers are investigating the genetic component to this disease.

Symptoms. Memory loss, diminished language skills, gradual loss of judgment, disorientation, and personality changes are some of the symptoms of Alzheimer's disease. Others are listed in the accompanying sidebar. This disease progresses at different rates in different individuals. From the time symptoms begin until the patient eventually dies, there is a range of 3 to 20 years, with an average of 8 years.

Seven Warning Signs of Alzheimer's Disease

1. Asking the same question repeatedly
2. Telling the same story, word for word, over and over again
3. Forgetting how to do complex things that one used to do without conscious effort, such as cooking or playing games
4. Losing the ability to pay bills or balance the checkbook
5. Getting lost in familiar places or misplacing household objects
6. Neglecting to bathe or wearing the same clothes repeatedly, but insisting that one has bathed or that unwashed clothes are clean
7. Depending on another person to answer questions or make decisions that one would have made without help in the past

Generally, the first signs of Alzheimer's disease involve difficulty in managing one's everyday life. It may become increasingly troublesome to cook dinner, balance a checkbook, or drive to the store without getting lost. As the disease progresses, a person may grow more forgetful and may have trouble finding the right words to express himself or herself. The ability to plan and organize becomes more elusive.

Roughly half of people with this disease may also, at some point, become suspicious of others. They may feel that they are being persecuted or imprisoned, they may suspect that things are being taken from them, and they may believe that their spouse is being unfaithful. This paranoia can come and go. In later stages of the disease, wandering, aggression, and sometimes hallucinations may occur.

Diagnosis. There is currently no single definitive test of a living patient to diagnose Alzheimer's disease. However, in order to assess the severity of the disease and to confirm that a person most likely has Alzheimer's disease and not some other form of dementia, the doctor may give a patient several different kinds of tests, including:

- A health history and physical examination
- Blood and urine tests
- Neurological and mental status tests
- Chest x-ray films and an electrocardiogram (ECG)
- Computed tomographic (CT) and electroencephalographic (EEG) scans
- Psychiatric or neuropsychological tests

Alzheimer's disease is a gradually progressive condition, so a doctor may ask the spouse or caregiver to keep track of the person's behavior and symptoms over time. Once a diagnosis of Alzheimer's disease is made, it is also important to be on the lookout for other health problems, such as depression or hearing loss, that may exacerbate the person's memory loss.

What's the Relationship between Aluminum and Alzheimer's Disease?

You may have read or heard that exposure to aluminum may lead to Alzheimer's disease. In fact, about a decade ago, considerable media attention was given to the idea that deodorants containing aluminum chlorhydrate or aluminum-containing cookware might not be safe for this reason.

Although this issue remains somewhat controversial, as of this writing, there is no scientific proof that aluminum and Alzheimer's disease are causally related. Although there sometimes are deposits of aluminum in cells or parts of cells that have been injured, it's still unclear whether these deposits mark the site of cell injury due to other causes or they actually caused the damage.

Treatment. There are currently two drugs—tacrine (Cognex) and donepezil (Aricept)—that have been approved by the FDA for the treatment of Alzheimer's disease. These drugs, which work by sustaining levels of the neurotransmitter called *acetylcholine* in the brain, can help with memory impairment and behavioral problems in people with mild to moderate dementia symptoms, but they will not cure the disease.

Other medications are available to lessen the person's agitation (e.g., aggression, combativeness), depression, and anxiety and to promote sleep and rest. Drugs may also be prescribed for symptoms of paranoia and hallucinations. These are similar to the drugs that may be prescribed for people with thought disorders or schizophrenia. Patients with Alzheimer's disease may sometimes respond to them. Also, it has been reported that high doses of vitamin E (1,000 international units taken twice per day) may also help to slow down the course of Alzheimer's disease.

In addition to medical treatment with drugs, the person with Alzheimer's disease can greatly benefit from "habilitation therapy," which was developed by our colleague Paul Raia. The aim of habilitation therapy is not to cure or restore persons with dementing illness to what they once were (in other words, *rehabil-itation*), but to maximize their functional independence and morale by mini-mizing difficult behaviors and eliminating excessive disability that might exacerbate symptoms of Alzheimer's. For caregivers, the primary task is learn-ing to value and focus on what is still there, and not to dwell on what the person has lost. When cognitive functions involving memory, reason, language, per-ception, and motor control are declining, what remains? The capacity to feel and express emotion persists far into the disease process. Activities including reminiscence, art, music, and pet therapy have been very beneficial in bringing about positive emotions and improving function and well-being. Caregivers also can promote good feelings by helping the person with communication skills and behavioral management, and by providing a safe environment over the course of the day (for specific guidelines, see the sidebar below).

Because of the progressive nature of this disease, the person with Alzheimer's and his or her family need to do what they can to sustain his or her quality of life and to ease the possible negative impact of the illness on the patient's family. The patient should see his or her primary care physician regularly. Some family members and caregivers have found it easier not to tell the patient about the appointment until they are almost at the doctor's office because, especially late in the disease, some patients may become agitated at the idea of going to see a doctor "for no reason." Also, it may be helpful to schedule the appointment at a time of day when the patient's energy level and attitude are at their best.

How You Can Help Your Loved One with Alzheimer's Disease

- Try to be patient; try to be tolerant.
- Try always to be respectful. People with Alzheimer's disease are likely to be more aware of and sensitive to their problem than you may think. Don't be condescending. Never treat him or her like a child.
- Help your loved one to review his or her health care directives (such as living wills) while he or she still has the mental capacity to do so (see Chapter 20).
- Identify a trusted friend or family member who can help to manage the per-son's financial bills and transactions.
- Encourage the person to maintain or increase his or her level of physical and social activity.
- Provide a structured environment with visual aids for orientation, such as clocks and calendars.
- If you need more help, arrange for a home health aide several times a week.
- For patients with late-stage Alzheimer's disease, wandering can be a concern. Name tags and medical-alert bracelets can be helpful, as can complicated locks and cues such as stop signs on doors to discourage wandering.
- Determine when the person should curtail and cease to drive, and anticipate his or her transportation needs once driving has stopped.

- Determine whether the person could be in a better living situation (see Chapter 18), and investigate options for long-term care. Most people with progressive memory loss eventually will require care in a long-term residential facility.

- Seek treatment for related problems, such as depression, lethargy, hallucinations, incontinence, agitation, insomnia, and wandering.

- Promptly address issues related to the person's job (if he or she is still working) and responsibilities at home or in the community.

- Explore community-support groups for caregivers, as well as possibilities for respite care.

- Explore Internet sites for information on and resources for Alzheimer's disease and other dementias.

Vascular Dementia

Vascular dementia (or multi-infarct dementia) is another common cause of memory loss. High blood pressure is often a contributing factor in these cases. Small blood vessels in the brain may become blocked, causing tiny, undetectable strokes. Vascular dementia may be present in up to about 20–40% of all dementias; when it is present together with Alzheimer's disease (it frequently is), it may be called "mixed dementia." This disorder may be treatable with blood pressure medications and aspirin.

Symptoms. If you find that your loved one is behaving abnormally or having a difficult time putting things in the right places (for example, putting orange juice instead of syrup on the pancakes), he or she may have had a stroke in an area of the brain that alters executive function. You should take him or her to the doctor.

Diagnosis. Doctors base a diagnosis of vascular dementia on a number of tests, including CT, MRI, and MRA (magnetic resonance angiography).

Treatment. Medical treatment for vascular dementia and stroke prevention includes blood-thinning medications: antihypertensives, anticoagulants, and aspirin. Some surgical options also have been tried with various degrees of success.

Parkinson's Disease

In people with Parkinson's disease, cells in a small part of the brain called the *substantia nigra* are not able to make sufficient amounts of a neurotransmitter called dopamine. This lack of neurological signaling affects the way a person moves his or her limbs, and in late stages, it can also lead to memory loss. Parkinson's disease can also be accompanied by dementia and depression. The incidence of Parkinson's disease becomes increasingly prevalent with age. The average age at which it begins is 55, and it affects 2.5% of people at age 80. There may be several different causes of Parkinson's disease, including long-term use of drugs such as haloperidol (Haldol) and certain types of progressive cellular damage to the nervous system (such as damage that occurs with a condition called *progressive supranuclear palsy*).

Symptoms. Slurred speech; shaking (tremors) at rest; stiffness in the face, joints, and limbs (so that it may be difficult to write neatly); muscle aches; difficulty with balance; slowed movement (*bradykinesia*); difficulty with walking; difficulty with swallowing; and weight loss are all symptoms of Parkinson's disease. Generally, the shaking at rest begins in one arm on one side of the body early in the course of the disease, then it gradually spreads to both sides of the body. These resting tremors usually affect the arms rather than the legs, and they tend to decrease or disappear when the person moves intentionally.

Diagnosis. To diagnose Parkinson's disease, a physician must do a careful physical examination because, unlike many other illnesses, the diagnosis is based primarily on the symptoms that we just described and on medical signs such as an absence of facial expression, infrequent blinking, slow reflexes, and altered gait, rather than on laboratory or radiological tests.

Treatment. Treatments for Parkinson's disease include drug therapy, surgical therapy, emotional support, and diet and exercise.

DRUG THERAPY. Many different types of medicines are available for people with Parkinson's disease. Your doctor can determine which one or ones are best for you, according to the severity of your disease and what types of symptoms you may be experiencing.

In Parkinson's disease, the *substantia nigra,* the part of the brain that creates the neurotransmitter called dopamine, experiences substantial cell loss. A drug called L-dopa (levodopa, Sinemet or Madopar) can replace dopamine with miraculous effects. Several weeks of treatment with this drug may be required before the patient experiences the full therapeutic benefits of a reduction in muscle stiffness and immobility.

An antiviral drug called amantadine is sometimes prescribed for patients with mild Parkinson's disease. There is a low incidence of side effects from this drug.

Drugs called *anticholinergics* may be used to stop the tremors of Parkinson's disease. These agents, which include trihexyphenidyl (Artane) and benztropine (Cogentin), may cause side effects such as memory impairment and confusion, and they are not commonly prescribed for older people.

Researchers have also produced chemical agents such as selegiline (Eldepryl, Deprenyl), which can slow down the degeneration of the brain cells that produce dopamine. This drug, which may be given with levodopa, causes few side effects. Other promising new therapies include pramipexole (Mirapex), ropinirole (Requip), and tolcapone (Tasmar).

In addition to these drugs to treat the symptoms of Parkinson's disease, your physician may also prescribe medications to address the depressed mood that may accompany this disorder.

CELL TRANSPLANTATION. Recently, human and pig nerve cell transplants into the affected region of the brain have met with impressive success in some patients. In the future, gene therapy and cell engineering may be developed to treat the underlying disease process in Parkinson's disease as well as in other neurological conditions such as stroke and seizure disorders.

SURGICAL THERAPY. It may be possible to partly control the symptoms (tremors) of Parkinson's disease by surgically removing cells from a part of the brain (called the *globus pallidus*) that controls voluntary movement of muscles. This method has been effective in some patients.

ELECTRICAL STIMULATION. The FDA recently approved a type of device called a *neural stimulator implant,* which acts like a heart pacemaker to create small electrical jolts to different parts of the brain. Our colleague Dan Tarsy has reported that these devices may be very helpful in controlling tremors.

EMOTIONAL SUPPORT. In addition to drug and surgical treatment options, support groups or simply contact with another family that has some experience with this disease can help to build emotional and psychological coping skills. Counseling with a psychologist or social worker may also be beneficial.

DIET AND EXERCISE. Although there is no specific anti-Parkinson's diet, it is clear that eating foods that contain a lot of fiber and drinking large amounts of fluids will help to ease the constipation that often accompanies and exacerbates this disease. Stretching and strengthening exercises such as walking and swimming can also help to relieve discomfort and stiffness in the back, hip, and shoulders.

Memory Loss Caused by Alcohol

Alcohol depresses the central nervous system and interferes with our ability to think clearly. Drinking excessive amounts of this chemical can also lead to stupor, coma, and serious withdrawal symptoms such as tremors, hallucinations, and seizures. Excessive alcohol can take away a person's ability to live independently and in some cases can reduce his or her lifetime by as much as 15 years.

"Too much alcohol" means something different when you're 75 than it did when you were 20 because older people begin to show the effects of alcohol at lower levels, they don't have the same metabolism that can work to detoxify the effects of alcohol, and they also have less reserve to compensate for alcohol's effects.

How many alcoholic drinks is too many? The National Institute on Alcohol Abuse and Alcoholism recommends that for older people, one drink per day may be too much in some cases, especially in older women. One drink is one can of beer or ale (12 oz.), one shot of hard liquor (1.5 oz.), one glass of wine (5 oz.), or one small glass of sherry, liqueur, or aperitif (4 oz.). We recommend that you decrease your alcohol consumption to even less than one drink per day because of its cumulative negative effects.

And no one should drink alcohol if they have struggled with drug or alcohol problems in the past, if they have diabetes or heart failure, or if they are taking medications that can intensify the effects of alcohol.

Eleven Good Reasons to Drink Less Alcohol

1. It causes high blood pressure, which increases your risk of stroke.

2. It increases your risk of developing irregular heartbeats (*arrhythmias*), including atrial fibrillation, and makes your blood platelets stick together; these conditions may increase your risks of stroke and heart disease.

3. It kills brain cells.

4. It makes you unsteady on your feet and increases the likelihood that you may fall.

5. It increases your risk of developing pneumonia because alcohol paralyzes the hair cells in your airways, thereby impairing their ability to clear normal secretions or saliva (which contain bacteria). When this happens, bacteria have a chance to set up house.

6. It tends to interrupt the signaling of one neuron to another in your brain, and it contributes to memory problems.

7. It may also adversely affect your body's infection-fighting white blood cells.

8. It may cause urinary incontinence.

9. It may disrupt sleep. If you drink a nightcap, you may wake up several hours later and have difficulty getting back to sleep. This occurs because when the alcohol level in your blood begins to drop, its initial suppressive effect on the *reticular activating system* (an area of the brain stem that controls your wakefulness and alertness) disappears, and this may cause you to have a rebound effect and become wide awake around 2 A.M.

10. It kills cells in your liver, which can lead to scarring or cirrhosis.

11. It can lead to impotence. ("The mind is willing but the body is weak." –W. Shakespeare)

What about the studies showing that alcohol has protective properties? Be careful because a number of these studies actually were at least partly funded and supported by liquor companies. Even if some studies may suggest that red wine is good for the heart, exercise and a healthy diet are even better, and they do not have the negative effects of alcohol that are summarized above.

Thus, given all of the potentially harmful things that alcohol may do to you, we recommend that you minimize your alcohol intake. There are better alternatives. For example, exercise is still better for both your heart and your brain than alcohol will ever be, and grape juice is just as good for you as red wine is.

Risk Factors. Older men are more likely than older women to have problems with alcohol. White women (with high income levels) are more likely to use alcohol and prescription drugs than are African- or Hispanic-American women. In all cases, alcohol is more of a problem for those who have lost their husbands or wives through separation, divorce, or death than for those who have not. Other risk factors for older people include abuse of alcohol, nicotine, or prescription drugs earlier in one's life; depression; and a family history of alcoholism.

Symptoms. Initial symptoms of an alcohol problem include depression, irritability, upset stomach, weight loss, malnutrition, memory loss, insomnia, and self-neglect. As the condition worsens, additional symptoms may include incontinence; stomach problems; heart, liver, or kidney disease; pancreatitis; cancer; and a compromised immune system (leading to infections such as pneumonia).

Diagnosis. In younger people with alcohol problems, employers and sometimes the courts may identify a problem with alcohol and may refer a person for treatment. In older people who may not work or end up in trouble with the law because of their drinking, however, alcohol abuse and alcoholism are often underrecognized. This is especially a problem with elders, particularly older women, who live alone or are homebound. Older women tend to drink less in public than in private, and alcohol may be more toxic for women than for men because their lower body weights and slower alcohol metabolism result in higher blood-alcohol concentrations, even if they drink less alcohol than their male counterparts.

Even doctors often misdiagnose alcoholism as depression, anxiety, or diabetes. As a result, the first realization that a person has a drinking problem may not occur until he or she ends up in the hospital because of a broken hip or a car accident. Also, during brief doctor's visits, patients, their families, and their physicians may place a greater emphasis on more tangible health problems, such as heart disease or diabetes, than on potential substance abuse.

Sometimes, family members of older adults are also embarrassed about the person's drinking and do not do what is necessary to have the person treated. Some people view alcoholism as a private family matter. Others view social drinking as an acceptable behavior that can bring little harm to an older person. These views are not correct. Older people who drink too much are more likely to be depressed and are at increased risk for serious health problems such as high blood pressure, stroke, heart attacks, cirrhosis of the liver, and gastrointestinal bleeding.

Treatment. Although giving up drinking altogether is a worthy goal, just cutting back is a great start. Mature adults can have as much (or more) success in reducing or eliminating alcohol from their lives as younger people. Initial treatment for people with alcohol problems may include interventions and counseling. *Interventions* involve meetings among a counselor, the person who is struggling with an alcohol problem, his or her family member or friend, and sometimes a doctor.

A counselor may also be able to help the person identify the factors such as grief or loneliness that have led to seeking the comfort of alcohol. He or she may be able to suggest activities that do not involve drinking, such as old hobbies or volunteer opportunities, and may suggest strategies for avoiding situations that lead to drinking, such as too much time alone.

Relatively informal counseling with a doctor to more structured therapy also may be helpful. The goal of this approach, known as *brief intervention,* is to motivate the problem drinker to change his or her behavior, *not to blame.* Education about negative consequences of alcohol and coping strategies for stress resulting from late-life changes is essential to enhance the effectiveness of treatment. The indication of success can be flexible, allowing drinking in moderation, while total abstinence is desired. Brief intervention usually consists of three visits over a 12-week period. In the first session, future goals are set to reduce drinking, to assess health habits and reasons for drinking, and to develop strategies for cutting down. In the following sessions, current drinking patterns and other interventions such as pharmacotherapy are reviewed.

Sometimes, it's necessary for the patient to stay at a hospital for a while to safely withdraw from alcohol or other drugs. In some cases, drugs such as naltrexone (ReVia) are given to prevent relapses.

Dementia Pugilistica

Because of changes in our balance and gait as we get older, our risk of falling is greater than that of younger people. Recurrent falls or head injuries can cause a type of brain damage called *traumatic brain injury,* which may in later years manifest as memory loss and cognitive impairment called *dementia pugilistica.* This condition sometimes occurs in individuals (such as construction workers or athletes) who may have had a history of prior head trauma.

As we age, we have less subcutaneous tissue to cushion our falls, as well as less brain tissue as a reserve when we experience head injuries. Thus, if you've fallen and bumped your head, it's important to let your doctor know.

When Driving Becomes an Issue

Unfortunately, doctors don't have a good test that will indicate clearly at which point it is no longer safe for patients with cognitive problems to drive. People who have mild dementia should be strongly encouraged to curtail or stop driving altogether. Others with moderate or advanced mental impairment definitely do not belong behind the wheel. A sense of loss of freedom and control that are associated with driving can be devastating for anyone. Appreciation of how much driving means to that person is key. Planning together with the family for their transportation needs is often helpful and critically important to enable the patient to feel supported and cared for, and to feel less of a loss of control.

Depression

Everyone feels blue or "depressed" from time to time. Sometimes, though, these sad feelings may continue for days, weeks, or months, and they can affect your relationships and interest in activities that used to provide fulfillment. This type of sad feeling, or depression, is *not* normal. In fact, for the most part, it's an illness that is as treatable as, for example, a sinus infection.

Depression can affect you suddenly, literally out of the blue, or it can be triggered by problems that many older people will encounter at one point or another: Loneliness, isolation, loss of health, and grief over the loss of loved ones are major triggers. An estimated 1 million persons 65 years old or older are depressed. In addition to its effect on your family, work, and social life, depression can become quite disabling. It lowers life expectancy and is associated with a greater risk of heart disease.

Although untreated depression can lead to serious health problems, it's important to remember that most people can be treated for depression and will recover from it. Seeking help for this medical illness is thus an important and positive step.

Mood Changes

- Family history of depression
- Substance abuse (particularly alcohol)
- Loss of a spouse
- Chronic pain
- Financial difficulties
- Medical illness
- Lack of social support

Risk Factors for a Mood Disorder, such as Depression

Symptoms. Often, people who are depressed do not realize that they are, so those around them need to pay attention to the signs of depression and help their friend or family member to seek help from a doctor or a mental-health professional.

Psychologists and psychiatrists diagnose depression if a person is experiencing a depressed mood that lasts for two or more weeks, or problems with five or more of the following:

Is It Depression?

- Insomnia or sleeping more than usual
- Sad dreams
- Diminished interest or loss of pleasure in hobbies, social activities, work, or sex
- Feelings of guilt, hopelessness, or worthlessness

- Fatigue or loss of energy
- Trouble concentrating, remembering, or making decisions
- Increase or decrease in appetite or weight
- Sluggishness, listlessness, apathy
- Agitation
- Thoughts of suicide, attempted suicide, or recurrent thoughts of death

Source: Adapted with permission from the *Diagnostic and Statistical Manual of Mental Disorders,* fourth edition. Copyright 1994 American Psychiatric Association.

Diagnosis. Depression may be related to another medical problem (such as heart disease, stroke, or thyroid dysfunction) or to medications, so doctors generally do a thorough physical examination and review of medicines that a person is taking in order to determine whether an illness or drug is causing depressive symptoms.

Treatment. Treatments include the management of other medical problems, counseling, antidepressants, and electroconvulsive therapy.

TREATMENT OF OTHER MEDICAL PROBLEMS. Sometimes, depression is caused by another medical problem (such as a thyroid condition) or by the use of too much alcohol or prescription or illicit drugs. When the related condition is treated, the depression may go away also. If the depression persists after the other associated problem has been addressed, though, the depression itself must be treated.

COUNSELING. Psychotherapy may be helpful when a person has issues that a counselor, geriatric psychiatrist, or psychotherapist (especially one who is trained in helping older people) may be able to help him or her address. Therapies such as cognitive behavioral therapy can also teach a patient new coping skills and behavior modification strategies. *Reminiscence and life review therapy* can help a person put past experiences in perspective in order to go forward in a healthy and positive way. Other types of therapy include *behavioral therapy* to work on changing behaviors that can lead to (or exacerbate) depression; *cognitive therapy* to work on positive thinking; and marriage counseling.

ANTIDEPRESSANTS. Medication is sometimes prescribed by a medical doctor or a geriatric psychiatrist in order to help a person whose depression cannot be helped by counseling alone. The earlier antidepressant drugs (called tricyclics) can have side effects that include drowsiness, constipation, blurred vision, dizziness, and dry mouth. Always tell your doctor if you experience any side effects from medication. He or she may adjust the dosage or give you another medicine instead. The newer antidepressant medicines (referred to as SSRIs) have fewer side effects and usually are well tolerated by older persons.

Unlike aspirin for a headache, antidepressant medications may take a long time to work. It's not unusual for people who are taking these drugs to have to wait up to three months before they see improvement. Even when you begin to feel better, you should never discontinue your medication without consulting your physician first. Many doctors recommend that you remain on a maintenance dose of antidepressants in order to prevent you from slipping into depression again.

ELECTROCONVULSIVE THERAPY. Electroconvulsive therapy (ECT), although rarely used for older people, seems to be fairly well tolerated and effective. Generally, it is used only for those patients who are not responding to medical treatment or are suicidal. ECT is administered in a hospital to patients who have not been helped by other forms of therapy.

Mr. R. experienced his first episode of major depression when he was 45 years old, and during the three decades that followed, he went through several successful trials of drugs, psychotherapy, and electroconvulsive treatment.

Seven years ago when he was 78 years old, he once again experienced a major depressive episode, which did not respond to many trials of medications, combined with psychotherapy. This depression was so severe that he could barely function in any of his normal activities of daily living.

His wife of more than 45 years could not cope and asked the children to try to convince him to undergo shock treatment, which had helped him so much in the past. For six months, he refused, saying that he didn't want to be seen as a "crazy person," and he adamantly refused to be hospitalized for any treatment because he didn't want anyone to know about this "embarrassing condition." The stigma he attached to this illness was so enormous that it prevented him from receiving treatment for at least six months, during which time he grew progressively worse, and his 73-year-old wife became so functionally compromised that the family began to have serious concerns about her continued ability to cope.

When the doctor offered him outpatient shock treatment, he finally consented, though unwillingly. The success of the treatment was remarkable. Not only did his former exuberant personality return, but luckily, in his family's opinion, he was completely unaware of how very depressed he had been.

After ECT therapy, a relapse can often be prevented by the use of antidepressant medications and by regular visits with a doctor.

Bipolar Illness

Some patients who experience depression also have *manic* episodes, in which they feel wakeful, abnormally talkative, and "up." This disorder causes individuals to need less sleep. They may talk nonstop, have grandiose ideas, and take risks that they ordinarily would not take. In between the depressed and manic states, the person may feel completely normal.

Bipolar illness is usually an inherited condition but may also be caused by head injury or other medical problems. A physician will give a complete physical examination and will make a careful diagnosis before developing a treatment plan.

Brain Tumors

Recent studies suggest that malignant primary tumors (cancer) of the brain increase in incidence with increasing age, at approximately 1.2% per year, with the highest rate of increase in those over age 70 years. The most common primary malignant tumor is *glioblastoma multiforme,* which is also the cause of most deaths attributable to brain tumors. *Meningiomas* comprise the majority of the benign brain tumors. One study from Rochester, Minnesota, reported that the incidence of pituitary adenomas increased significantly between 1950 and 1990, but there was no change in incidence trends for other types of brain tumors such as gliomas, malignant astrocytomas, or meningiomas.

The number of cancers diagnosed incidentally by neuroimaging studies has risen since the late 1970s, and new technological improvements may in part account for the increased incidence that has been observed. We will need to collect more data in the coming years for this possibility to be tested.

Symptoms. The general signs and symptoms of brain cancer include headache, nausea, and vomiting, or altered levels of consciousness. Unfortunately, none of these signs or symptoms are specific. Very few patients who have headaches have brain tumors. Headaches that are more often associated with brain tumors tend to be intermittent and moderately severe, and they may be more frequently experienced in the early morning. Maneuvers such as coughing or straining that may increase intracranial pressure may also exacerbate the headache. Vomiting associated with a brain tumor may indicate increased intracranial pressure, or it may be related to the location of the tumor.

Seizures may be the initial manifestation in up to 30% of persons with a brain tumor. However, as is the case with headaches, most persons with seizures do not have brain tumors. The relationship of seizure to the existence of a brain tumor tends to increase with age. Patients with slow-growing tumors are also more likely to have seizures, compared to those with rapidly growing tumors.

The location of the tumor can influence the signs and symptoms that the person with brain tumor will manifest. Those with tumors in the frontal lobes may show changes in attention span, communication, and behavior. More posterior tumors can cause weakness or seizure activity. Tumors in the temporal lobe can cause seizures, weakness, or memory impairment, and there may be associated hallucinations. Those with occipital lobe tumors tend to experience visual changes and sometimes have difficulty in recognizing familiar objects. Parietal lobe tumors can be associated with difficulty in recognizing or writing numerals or letters and sometimes also a lack of awareness of the side of the body that is opposite the side where the brain tumor is located.

Diagnosis. Diagnosis is made by neuroimaging studies, including magnetic resonance imaging (MRI) and computed tomography (CT). Sometimes, contrast enhancement can be helpful. Positron emission tomography (PET) may be important in certain cases, especially those in which radiation treatment (called brachytherapy) or radiosurgery have been given.

Treatment. In addition to biopsy of the tumor, surgery for tumor resection (removal) may sometimes be beneficial, especially for relief of symptoms due to the large size of the tumor. In cases of benign tumors (e.g., meningiomas), surgical cure with complete tumor removal may be possible. However, for brain cancers, surgical resection is usually not for cure, but for symptom relief. Radiotherapy and chemotherapy may be used to help prolong survival. It would be important to discuss these possible treatments completely with your doctors.

When we talk about drug abuse among older adults, we generally are referring to dependency on prescription drugs, rather than on the use of illegal drugs. People over age 65 use more prescription drugs than any other age group. In fact, as many as a third of people in this age group take eight or more prescription drugs every day. **Drug Dependency**

If used under a doctor's direction, *psychoactive drugs* can be beneficial in treating mood disorders, depression, and sleeping problems. However, such drugs may be prescribed inappropriately. Also, people sometimes fail to comply with the doctor's directions about how a medication should be taken. Finally, as with alcohol, prescription drugs have a stronger effect on older people than on younger people; women are especially vulnerable to the effects of these agents.

Errors on the part of both the doctor and the patient can lead to further health problems for the patient. These problems include drowsiness, confusion, depression, and loss of memory. Also, misuse of tranquilizers and of sedating antidepressants can lead to falls and car accidents.

Commonly Used Drugs That May Be Addicting. All of the medications listed in this section interact poorly with alcohol, which is a depressant that can heighten the effects of sedating drugs and can increase a person's dependence on them.

PRESCRIPTION DRUGS. *Tranquilizers* (antianxiety drugs; benzodiazepines) such as diazepam (Valium), flurazepam (Dalmane), and lorazepam (Ativan) may cause side effects such as faulty memory, inattention, and even delirium, which may be mistaken for other disorders such as Alzheimer's disease.

Sedatives (hypnotics) are often prescribed to help a person sleep. However, as we mentioned earlier, changes in the quality of a person's sleep naturally occur with the aging process. People tend to wake more frequently during the night and to sleep fewer hours at a stretch than they did when they were younger. Sedatives may not be effective after they are used for 30 consecutive nights, and people can quickly develop a tolerance to and dependence on such drugs. Therefore, ask your doctor about suggestions for improving your sleep without nightly sedatives (see pp. 99–101).

Antidepressants such as amitriptyline or the new SSRIs are prescribed for depression and other mood disorders.

Narcotic analgesics, such as codeine and morphine, are often prescribed for pain that is not alleviated by over-the-counter drugs such as ibuprofen or acetaminophen.

OVER-THE-COUNTER DRUGS. Although people generally believe that over-the-counter drugs cannot be very harmful because they can be purchased without a prescription, in fact, this is not true, particularly for older persons. Particularly troublesome drugs are antihistamines and cough medications.

Antihistamines, which are usually taken for allergies, can have adverse side effects such as confusion, depression, or dizziness caused by low blood pressure that occurs when a person goes from a lying to a sitting or standing position. When mixed with alcohol, these negative effects can be intensified.

Cough medications sometimes have a high alcohol content or contain pseudoephedrine, so they can have harmful interactions with other drugs or additional alcohol.

Diagnosis. Patients, their families, and even their doctors may attribute symptoms of drug toxicity to other conditions associated with aging: depression, dementia, and declining health. Therefore, we recommend that you tell your physician about all drugs that you may be taking, regardless of whether they are prescription drugs or over-the-counter medications.

Treatment. Withdrawal from some drugs may cause you to experience seizures or delirium. In these situations, you may need to go through the withdrawal process in a hospital.

Questions to Ask Your Doctor or Pharmacist

- What is this prescribed drug for?
- Is a generic drug available that may be less expensive than the trade (brand) name medicine?
- How much of the drug should I take? How often should I take it? How long will I need to take it?
- Are there any side effects that I should know about?
- These are the other medications that I am currently taking. Is it safe to take this new drug with those drugs?
- Should I take this medicine at a certain time of day? Is it important to take it with food, or should I wait several hours after I have eaten?
- Is it safe to drive while I'm taking this drug?
- Can I drink modest amounts of alcohol when I am taking this drug?

Headaches   There are many kinds of headaches, but three kinds are experienced most commonly by older people. These include vascular headache, tension headache, and headaches caused by eye muscle strain.

Vascular Headaches

A headache that is associated with fatigue, visual changes, and limpness of the jaw may be a vascular headache caused by a condition called *temporal arteritis* (inflammation of the arteries). A doctor will be able to confirm this diagnosis by means of a blood test and possibly other tests, including a tiny biopsy of the temporal artery, if needed.

If you have had migraines earlier in your life, you may continue to have them as you age, but if you have not experienced them before, you have a low risk of developing them now. Before the onset of this type of vascular headache, you may experience an aura of flashing lights. Then you may experience a painful headache, usually on one side of the head.

Lying down to rest in a dark room and avoiding bright lights may be helpful. Drugs called beta blockers or calcium channel blockers may be prescribed to prevent the blood vessels from causing this form of headache. A medicine called ergotamine may also be prescribed to prevent the migraine from worsening once it begins.

Tension Headaches

A common type of headache that feels like pressure or a tight band wrapped around the head is called a tension headache. This discomfort may be due to stress, fatigue, or arthritis pain. Analgesics and muscle relaxants may be helpful.

Headaches Due to Eye Muscle Strain and Pain

As we age, our eyes sometimes gaze slightly outward because of a gradual loss of muscle tone. If this occurs and we read or do other close work in the evening when we are tired, our eye muscles can become even more strained. If you wake up with a headache that is especially uncomfortable in your brow and forehead area, or if you have a throbbing, aching sensation behind your eyes, your headache may be related to this form of muscle fatigue.

Your doctor may suggest that you read earlier in the day, and he or she may recommend exercises to strengthen the affected muscles near your eyes.

Epilepsy (Seizures)

Seizures are sudden, brief (one-to-two-minute) periods of unconsciousness from which one awakens, sleepy and confused. *Epilepsy* is a condition in which repeated seizures occur. Epileptic seizures become more common after age 60 years. The major cause of seizures in older persons is prior cerebrovascular disease (stroke). Other risk factors associated with late-onset epilepsy include dementia, brain tumor, infection, trauma, and drug side effects (including excess alcohol). Very rarely, antibiotics and antidepressant and antipsychotic medications have also been reported to be a risk factor for seizures, especially in patients who have had a previous stroke.

The risk of seizures is also increased after traumatic brain injury, especially in those persons over age 65 who suffer brain contusions with subdural hematoma, skull fracture, and loss of consciousness or amnesia for more than one day. Almost 50% of the time, however, the cause of epilepsy in older people may be unclear.

Diagnosis. To diagnose seizures, your physician may have you undergo a test called an EEG to assess brain wave activity and an MRI scan or CT scan to determine whether a tumor, hemorrhage, or abscess is causing the seizures.

Treatment. Treatment currently includes medications and surgery.

MEDICATIONS. If you are diagnosed with epileptic seizures, your doctor may prescribe antiepileptic medications (such as phenytoin [Dilantin] or carbamazapine [Tegretol]) to prevent further seizures. However, the standard antiepileptic medications are not without problems because of their potential side effects, multiple drug interactions, and complex drug metabolism. Also, as a result of age-associated changes in bone turnover and osteoporosis, older persons are at increased risk of fracture during trauma. This predisposition may be worsened by antiepileptic medications because they may further accelerate the loss in bone mass, while also increasing the risk of falls through the drug side effects of decreased balance and gait stability. It is therefore important to see your doctor regularly for careful monitoring and dosage adjustments of the antiseizure medication, as needed.

Although new drugs for the treatment of epilepsy are being developed, more clinical trials are needed for the newer medicines before they can be safely recommended in older persons.

SURGERY. In one third of patients who are not helped by medical treatment for epilepsy, a surgical procedure known as a *partial temporal lobotomy* may be helpful. This entails disruption of the communication from the part of the brain with the seizure focus. This procedure has been found to be as effective for older patients as for younger ones.

Electrical stimulation via an implanted device in the affected part of the brain may also be helpful in some cases.

CELL TRANSPLANTATION. Brain cell grafts using nerve cells are currently being studied for the treatment of seizures. Preliminary results are quite promising.

Stroke   A *stroke* is a sudden partial loss of brain function caused by a blockage (such as a blood clot or a constricted blood vessel) or hemorrhage (due to a broken blood vessel or a ruptured artery— an *aneurysm*) in the brain. These types of strokes cause symptoms that usually last longer than a day. Those that cause symptoms for less than a day and do not cause permanent brain damage are called *transient ischemic attacks,* or TIAs. TIAs, or "ministrokes," may precede an actual stroke, so they should be considered a warning sign, and you should seek treatment.

Deaths from strokes are declining in part because we're doing a better job of managing risk factors such as high blood pressure (hypertension), smoking, and high blood cholesterol levels. Other risk factors include obesity, a history of heart disease, and diabetes.

Symptoms. Symptoms of a stroke may include a sudden severe headache; sudden tingling, numbness, or weakness on one side of your body (these symptoms will occur on the side of the body opposite the side of the brain that was injured); blurred vision; clumsiness and difficulty with balance; difficulty speaking and swallowing; and confusion and memory loss.

Diagnosis. A stroke is a medical emergency that requires immediate attention. Doctors may perform blood tests; CT scans of the brain; and MRI scans (which are sensitive in detecting blockages), angiography, and echocardiography to confirm the diagnosis and determine which area of the brain is affected.

Treatment. Many people who have had a stroke have some spontaneous recovery. However, following a stroke, you may need to spend some time in the hospital to manage complications (such as bowel or bladder problems) and to address potential risk factors for additional strokes (such as hypertension or carotid artery disease). If these are tight blockages in the carotid arteries, carotid endarterectomy may help to prevent a second stroke.

Thrombolysis is currently being performed at major medical centers around the country with good success rates. Carotid artery angioplasty and stent placement are similar to the procedures that have been used in the heart (see Chapter 4), and they are also being performed with good results.

Rehabilitative therapy can also help you to restore lost abilities. Physical therapy may help you to regain muscle strength, balance, and coordination. A speech-language pathologist can help you with speech and swallowing problems, and an occupational therapist can provide exercises to help you work on eye-hand coordination and rebuild skills such as dressing, writing, and bathing. Recovery may take weeks, months, or years.

An estimated 30–50% of people who have had a major stroke will experience depression, but generally, depression after a stroke responds well to antidepressant medications. Stroke support groups can also be helpful for both the patient and his or her family.

New therapies that are currently being tested include cell transplantation using nerve cells; studies of such techniques are showing very favorable results, according to our colleagues Louis Caplan and Julian Wu.

As we age, we need to be extra vigilant not just about our physical fitness, but about our mental fitness, as well. If we're feeling unusually confused or "down," we should seek medical advice just as we do for other medical conditions—without guilt or embarrassment. Chances are, a solution to our problem exists.

Resources

- Alcoholics Anonymous (AA) national office, 475 Riverside Drive, 11th floor, New York, NY 10115; (212) 870-3400 (Refer to your local phone book for the chapter nearest you.)

- The National Institute on Alcohol Abuse and Alcoholism (NIAAA), 6000 Executive Boulevard, Bethesda, MD 20892-7003; (301) 443-3860
- The National Council on Alcoholism and Drug Dependence, Inc., 12 West 21st Street, 8th floor, New York, NY 10010; (800) NCA-CALL (800-622-2255)
- Alzheimers.com (website)
- Alzheimer's Disease Education and Referral Center of the National Institute on Aging, ADEAR Center, P.O. Box 8250, Silver Spring, MD 20907-8250; (800) 438-4380
- National Alzheimer's Association, 919 N. Michigan Avenue, Suite 1000, Chicago, IL 60611; (800) 272-3900; www.alz.org (website)
- National Family Caregivers Association, (800) 804-6604
- Local chapters of the Alzheimer's Association
- Local agencies for aging
- National Stroke Association, 8480 East Orchard Road, Suite 1000, Englewood, CO 80111; (800) 787-6537
- www.biostat.wustl.edu/alzheimer (website), sponsored by the Washington University Alzheimer's Disease Research Center

Specialists Who Work with Geriatricians to Treat Cognitive Problems

Neurologist	Especially helpful for patients with Parkinson's disease, stroke, and seizures; a medical doctor with special training in treating the nervous system
Psychiatrist	Diagnoses and treats mental disorders through psychotherapy and medication; a health care provider who is a medical doctor with special training in psychiatry
Clinical psychologist	Provides psychotherapy for both patients and caregivers; a health care provider with a doctoral degree in psychology and training in counseling
Neuropsychologist	Can help determine the severity of a person's mental impairment and the particular kinds of impairment to enable interventions to be appropriately targeted to enhance function
Social worker	Provides counseling and suggestions regarding community resources
Occupational therapist	Assesses a person's ability to perform everyday activities and provides strategies for maximizing one's capabilities

CHAPTER 7
YOUR SENSES

*The infinite delicacy of the educated senses is almost more
incredible than the compass of the imagination. When they unite
in creation, no shadow is too fleeting, no line too exquisite for
their common engagement and mutual reinforcement.*

(Sir) Clifford Albutt (1836–1925)

Like every other part of our bodies, our senses—our hearing, sight, and sense of taste and smell, as well as our perception of pain—undergo some changes as we get older. In this chapter, we discuss some of the alterations that may occur, and we briefly touch on some of the treatments available for problems that may occur.

Hearing

Older adults find it more difficult to process and isolate sounds than do younger people. It may be difficult to identify a voice or understand a spoken message when there is background noise, for example.

Hearing loss affects 30–80% of American adults over age 65. This decline may be due more to lifestyle than to chronological age. Some researchers believe that the noise and stress of life in industrialized countries tend to promote hearing loss. One study showed that the Mabaans, an isolated community in the Sudan, showed very little hearing loss at ages 60 to 65, as compared with their American contemporaries.

Hearing loss is usually gradual, and you may not notice it until it becomes difficult to hear soft sounds (such as a dripping faucet), or sounds appear to be mumbled, muffled, or slurred. Sometimes, hearing problems also lead to the sensation of a constant hissing or ringing sound. If you are experiencing any of these difficulties, you should see your physician, who may refer you to a hearing specialist (an *audiologist*) for further testing and treatment.

Today there are several types of programs and devices available to help people who have experienced hearing loss, including external hearing aids, implantable hearing devices, assistive listening devices, and lip-reading programs.

HEARING AIDS. Hearing aids, which work by amplifying sounds, may be worn inside the ear, behind the ear, or on the middle of the chest. Three types of hearing aids are available: the older types that can be adjusted with a screwdriver, programmable hearing aids that come with digital amplifiers, and the newer digital hearing aids. Your audiologist can work with you to determine which type is most appropriate for you. You may be able to try your new hearing aids for a trial period before you are required to purchase them.

IMPLANTABLE HEARING DEVICES SUCH AS COCHLEAR IMPLANTS. These new devices, which may be appropriate for people with severe hearing loss who are not helped by traditional hearing aids, make use of a tiny computer that translates spoken words into electrical impulses that stimulate the functioning nerve endings inside the ear.

ASSISTIVE LISTENING DEVICES. Television and telephone amplification systems are two types of devices for people who have difficulty hearing. Other systems make use of flashing lights to alert a person who is hard of hearing that the doorbell is ringing or the smoke detector has gone off. Dogs may also be trained to alert their hearing-impaired owners in response to certain sounds (such as an alarm clock). Another helpful tool is a telecommunication device for the deaf (TDD) system, which can be set up so that you can receive typed rather than verbal telephone messages.

LIP-READING PROGRAMS. In addition to hearing aids and assistive listening devices, an audiologist can help you to understand what people are saying to you by helping you to focus on the speaker. Lip reading (also called speech reading) involves heightening one's awareness of the nonverbal clues such as the speaker's facial expressions and gestures in order to get the sense of what is being said.

OTHER WAYS TO MAKE THE MOST OF YOUR HEARING. These strategies include

- Reading about a play or a movie that you're going to see in advance
- Asking others to speak directly to you (facing you) so that you can hear them better
- Learning how to make the most of the acoustics of every room. At meetings, for instance, it may be easier to hear what's going on if you're sitting next to the loudspeaker, rather than in the front row of the audience.

Sight   Is the world a blur without your glasses? If so, you're not alone. Nine out of 10 older Americans need corrective lenses.

The most common age-related change in the eyes is *presbyopia,* a diminished ability of the lens to focus at different distances. This condition occurs in many of us, and it doesn't seem to matter whether our occupation placed great demands on our eyes or not: a proofreader is no more likely to develop it than an athletic trainer. If you find that you have to hold a book or newspaper farther away in order to focus clearly, you may need a pair of reading glasses, bifocal glasses, or contact lenses; these corrective lenses will likely compensate for this condition.

Roughly 40% of older adults develop *arcus senilis* (a yellowish-white, opaque ring around the periphery of the iris) due to fatty deposits in the membranes. This condition does not interfere with vision, and it may bear no relation to other age-related changes or blood cholesterol levels.

Another common visual change that may develop as we age is a *cataract,* a clouding up of the normally clear lens within the eye. If you develop cataracts and the blurred or spotty vision and increased sensitivity to glare that may accompany them, your ophthalmologist may recommend glasses or a change in your prescription for glasses. If, in spite of glasses, poor vision due to cataracts begins to interfere with your everyday activities, surgery may be recommended. This type of operation, which involves replacing the natural, clouded lens of the eye with an artificial one, is generally very successful in restoring vision. Usually this operation can be done on an outpatient basis. **Cataracts**

In spite of some inevitable age-related changes to your eyes, there are a number of things that you can do to take good care of them:

WEAR SUNGLASSES AND A SUNHAT OR VISOR. Ultraviolet "B" radiation has been associated with an increased risk of developing cataracts, so protecting your eyes from bright sunlight is sensible.

PROTECT YOUR EYES FROM INJURY. Nonfluorescent light bulbs are better than fluorescent ones. Be careful when using pesticides, cleaning solutions, and equipment that may injure your eyes.

DON'T SMOKE. Smokers appear to have a higher risk of developing cataracts than do nonsmokers. They also may be at greater risk of developing macular degeneration (see p. 128).

TAKE CARE OF OTHER HEALTH PROBLEMS THAT YOU MAY HAVE. Conditions such as diabetes have been implicated in cataract formation and retinopathy (see p. 128), so keeping your blood sugar under control may also have a protective effect.

SEE YOUR EYE DOCTOR REGULARLY. Many of the eye problems that we describe next can be treated most effectively in their early stages, so seeing your eye doctor at least once a year is very important.

Even if you do your best to take good care of your eyes, you may develop an eye problem in your later years. In this chapter, we talk about treatment options that are available if this happens. In addition to presbyopia, arcus senilis, and cataracts, other potential vision problems of older people may include glaucoma, macular degeneration, cornea disease, diabetic retinopathy, ischemic optic neuropathy, excessive tearing, and dry eyes.

Glaucoma   The term *glaucoma* refers to a common group of diseases that are marked by gradually increased pressure inside the eye. Our colleague Cynthia Grosskreutz explains that this increased pressure can lead to damage to the *optic nerve* (which relays visual information to the brain) and potentially loss of vision. You may have no symptoms of glaucoma until you experience some vision loss, so it's very important to have regular eye examinations. If your eye doctor does find that you have this condition, he or she may prescribe medications, such as beta blocker eye drops, to lower the pressure inside your eye. Laser surgery is sometimes also used to treat glaucoma.

Macular Degeneration   The *macula* is the part of your eye that is made up of cones; these cones make acute vision possible because they convert light energy into electrical signals that the brain can interpret. If you develop macular degeneration, your vision may become distorted; you may see dark spots, and clear color vision may gradually be lost.

Laser therapy is most helpful in the early stages of macular degeneration. This is another reason why regular eye examinations are so important. Oral antioxidant supplements may also help to retard the progression of this disease.

Cornea Disease   Aging may affect the *cornea,* the transparent part of the eyeball that covers the pupil and iris, before it affects any other part of the eye. The surface of the cornea may become thickened, flattened, and less smooth than it used to be. Also, degeneration of the cells that line the inner surface of the cornea may cause this part of the eye to swell and thereby cause cloudy vision. Sometimes, eye drops that contain saline can be used to reduce this swelling and resulting haziness; in more severe cases, corneal transplants may be done to restore vision.

Diabetic Retinopathy   *Retinopathy* is a degenerative disease of the *retina,* the sensory membrane that lines the eye. At least half of all people with diabetes will develop diabetic retinopathy after they have had diabetes for 7 years. In people who have had diabetes for 20 years, there is a 90% incidence of this eye disorder. Thus, if you have been diagnosed with diabetes, regular eye examinations are a must! Retinopathy may lead to blurriness in the field of vision due to scar tissue formation on the retina.

Laser treatment may slow the progression of this disease by as much as 50–60%.

Ischemic Optic Neuropathy   Diabetes can also lead to a condition called *ischemic optic neuropathy,* in which vision may become slightly impaired or it may become so poor that one may have only faint light perception. The ability to see color may also be reduced. Regular visits to your eye doctor are very important.

Excessive Tearing   Increased sensitivity to light, wind, or temperature may cause excessive tearing. Sometimes it also can be due to an infection and/or blockage of the tear duct. These conditions can be readily treated by your eye doctor. Wearing sunglasses also can help to decrease the tearing due to light sensitivity.

If your eyes become dry and irritated in places where there is low humidity, you may want to try using artificial tears up to four times each day. When buying this product, look for brands that do not contain preservatives because the preservatives may be irritating to your eyes.

Dry Eyes

If an eye disorder has diminished your ability to read a map or to see your watch clearly, you may benefit from some of the new devices that are available to magnify letters, numerals, and images so that you can see them better. The Vision Foundation publishes the Vision Resources List, which gives information on special products and services. Its address is 818 Mt. Auburn St., Watertown, MA 02172. Your *optometrist* (a specialist—not usually a medical doctor—who can examine your eyes and prescribe corrective lenses or exercises) or *ophthalmologist* (a physician who specializes in diagnosing and managing problems of the eye) may be able to recommend suitable aids. (In contrast, an *optician* sells glasses, contact lenses, and other optical items). The following list is a mere sampling of the helpful devices that are available:

Low-Vision Devices

1. Magnifying lenses (In addition to magnifying spectacles, magnifying glasses that you can hold as you read or that are built into a stand so that you can have your hands free to read may change your reading experience dramatically. Some stand magnifiers also come with a built-in light.)

2. Closed-circuit televisions, which can magnify images up to 45 times their size (These can cost a couple thousand dollars but are very helpful for some individuals.)

3. Large-print books, magazines, and newspapers

4. "Talking" watches, computers, and so on

5. Electronic magnifying monitors, which can transform a home computer into a large clock, calculator, or address book

---

If you are unable to see well because of an eye disorder, or if a health problem prevents you from holding a book or turning its pages, you *don't* have to give up the great pleasure that comes from reading novels, biographies, mysteries, how-to books, romances, and more.

Books Are for Everyone

The Library of Congress "talking-book" program records more than 70 popular magazines, as well as more than 250,000 books, on compact discs and cassette tapes. If you enroll in this free program, you may borrow and return these discs and tapes via postage-free mail or through a local library that participates in this program. You can also join book-reading clubs where people read aloud to each other.

For more information (and to apply to this program), contact The National

Library Service for the Blind and Physically Handicapped, The Library of Congress, Washington, DC 20542, or explore the program's Internet site: www.loc.gov/nls.

Taste and Smell

Although we generally do not lose the ability to taste as we get older, we sometimes have a more difficult time gauging taste intensity. In other words, we may be clear about what salty foods taste like, but we may find ourselves adding more salt to our meals in order to make them taste salty enough.

Another sense that is critical for our enjoyment of food is smell. This sense tends to diminish somewhat in our later years. Smoking and certain illnesses or medications may exacerbate this natural decline in sensitivity to odors. Cessation of smoking will not only restore your sense of smell but will also enhance your taste.

If you find that you are adding more salt or sugar to your food than you used to, or if a lessened sense of smell is interfering with your enjoyment of meals, talk with your doctor about referral to a nutritionist, who can provide you with some useful suggestions such as making foods taste more appealing with herbs and spices (rather than with salt, which may be especially harmful if you have high blood pressure).

Pain and Pain Management

The brain is the "citadel of sense-perception."

Pliny the Elder (23–79)

Although pain is not a normal part of the aging process, *chronic* (long-term) pain affects approximately 30-40% of older persons, and the incidence of pain rises with advancing age. Older persons may also present special challenges when it comes to the management of pain. These challenges arise partly because older persons may not seek treatment for their discomfort as promptly as younger people do, because they tend to minimize the discomfort and tend to believe that it is an expected part of aging. In addition, the greater challenge is partly because older patients have an increased incidence of other health problems, sometimes involving several medical problems at the same time.

When doctors refer to *acute pain,* they are speaking of pain that comes on abruptly, is generally not long lasting, and can be treated readily by addressing the underlying health problem that caused it. A common example of acute pain is the discomfort experienced following a traumatic injury. As the wound heals, the pain diminishes. In contrast, *chronic pain* (usually lasting 3 months or longer) may result from conditions that are not easily remedied. Multiple causes may be involved; these may include back problems, arthritis, muscle or nerve problems, vascular disease, and diabetes.

Regardless of whether your pain is acute or chronic, when you talk with your physician about your pain, it may be helpful to describe its intensity on a scale of 1 to 10, and to be as specific as you possibly can be about how the pain feels:

Is it an aching or a throbbing sensation? Where and when is it most apparent? The following information can also help your physician to identify the source of your pain:

- Are there any factors (such as particular stressors) or activities that appear to bring about your discomfort?
- What methods of pain relief have you found helpful?
- Does the pain occur most acutely at a particular time of day?
- Are there any other associated symptoms?
- Where is the pain located? Does it spread to other parts of your body? Other than this particular area of concern, do you have pain elsewhere in your body?
- Have you experienced similar discomfort in the past?
- How long does the discomfort usually last?
- What is your medical history? Have you had any recent illnesses or hospitalizations?
- How does the discomfort affect your mood?
- Do you drink alcohol?
- Do you take analgesic medications? What other medications are you taking?
- Have you been experiencing difficulty sleeping, either with or without pain?
- Have you lost weight recently?
- Have you experienced a change in appetite?
- Are there any gastrointestinal symptoms associated with your pain?
- Do you have allergies?

Depending on the nature and cause of your discomfort, as well as on your other health problems, your physician may prescribe a pain-relieving medication (*analgesic*) for you. Whether or not he or she prescribes a particular pain reliever (such as aspirin, acetaminophen [Tylenol], codeine, or nonsteroidal anti-inflammatory drugs [NSAIDs]) for you will depend on whether you have certain conditions such as heart disease or a history of gastrointestinal problems that may contraindicate the use of some pain relievers. As we discussed in Chapter 2, sharing medicines with others—even common pain relievers—can be risky because not all of these medications are appropriate for everyone.

Stronger pain relievers, such as codeine especially, must be taken with great care, because they sometimes cause more intense side effects (such as confusion and constipation) in older people than in younger people. Always talk with your doctor about the side effects of prescription pain relievers, and make sure you know whether it is safe to drive while taking such drugs.

Physical therapy, water therapy, and sometimes simply concentrating on correct posture may also go a long way toward relieving certain forms of pain. Again, speak with your doctor about whether there are any nonmedical forms of pain relief that may be appropriate for you.

Your physician may recommend that you visit a pain clinic if you are experiencing chronic discomfort. Our colleague Carol Warfield tells us that most older patients who are referred to pain clinics are suffering from lower back pain (see also Chapter 9, on the musculoskeletal system). Such clinics may offer, in addition to nonsteroidal drugs and physical therapy, transcutaneous electrical nerve stimulation (TENS), nerve blocks, and epidural steroid injections.

Good sleep is essential for proper functioning and it also tends to reduce the severity of pain. When one is already experiencing chronic pain, the effect of a poor night's sleep can exacerbate the pain tremendously. A few helpful hints for improving sleep are discussed in Chapter 6.

If, in spite of these measures, your discomfort persists, you may wish to discuss other possibilities with your doctor. Occasionally, surgery may be recommended for pain relief, and if so, it's often very effective. In any case, please don't suffer in silence. It is extremely important that you inform your doctor of your need for more effective pain relief. This is because he or she may be hesitant to prescribe high doses of strong (e.g., narcotic) medicines that may be habit forming and may have other side effects. However, he or she would not want to undertreat your pain either. Therefore, you should call your doctor's attention to the fact that the dose of pain medicine that you are taking is not sufficient. Remember that you are your best advocate. You may also wish to request a referral to a pain specialist.

Sometimes, counseling may be helpful. You may also find that visits with your priest, rabbi, or chaplain may enable you to find the strength to cope. If you are severely ill and experiencing pain, your health care team can provide you with palliative care and comfort, as well as support for both you and your family (see Chapter 20).

The best of all things for earthly men is not . . . to see the beams of the bright sun.

Theognis (c. 545 B.C.)

Nothing affects the visible age of a person's outward appearance quite as much as the amount of time that he or she has spent in the sun. The captain of a swordfish boat, in all likelihood, will take on the visage of an old salt long before an office worker will. Likewise, those who spend their leisure time sun worshipping or strolling across a golf course at high noon may suffer the consequences of *photo* (light) *aging* more quickly than those who prefer to spend their free hours inside a bowling alley or at a library.

Fortunately, though, no matter how you occupied your time in your younger years, it's never too late to start protecting your skin from the harmful rays of the sun. Doing so may keep you more youthful looking and may prevent you from developing some potentially dangerous health problems.

In this chapter, we talk about long-term sun exposure, as well as time's other effects on your skin, hair, and nails.

Your Skin

Most of us take our skin entirely for granted, except when it burns and peels from sun exposure, or breaks out in pimples, or perspires unpleasantly. When we think of it at other times, it is with a vague sense of wonder at so neat and efficient a covering for our insides: waterproof, dustproof, and miraculously— until we grow very old—almost always the right size.

Adapted with permission from *MassPRO Medicare Annual Report*, 1998

How Your Skin Changes as You Age

Approximately 90% of the age-associated changes in the skin are due to photoaging, according to our colleague Barbara Gilchrest. With the passage of time, skin that has been exposed to the sun can become more coarse and wrinkled; this is especially true of fair-skinned individuals. In addition to this photo-aging process, skin may naturally grow thin, dry, rough, and wrinkled as we grow older, partly because we sweat less than we used to, and we have fewer oil glands. Crow's-feet may develop around our eyes because the subcutaneous tissue that supports the skin also tends to become diminished, due in part to loss of collagen.

In our later years, our skin may serve less well as the effective barrier from infection that it once was. Cuts and sores may take longer to heal because our cells may replenish themselves slightly less rapidly when they become damaged or destroyed.

What You Can Do to Take Care of Your Skin

STAY OUT OF THE SUN. The ultraviolet (UV) rays of the sun can damage proteins and fibers called *elastin* in our skin. Over time, this damage can make skin sag, stretch, and bruise more easily. We advise our patients to stay out of the sun altogether between 10 A.M. and 3 P.M. If you must be outside during these hours, wear a hat, sunglasses, and long-sleeved clothing. Also, whenever you venture out into the sunshine, always wear protective sunscreen that has a sun protection factor (SPF) of 15 or higher.

STOP SMOKING. Smoking not only harms our lungs but also can affect our appearance. Perhaps because smoking inhibits blood flow to the skin, people who smoke usually develop more wrinkles than people who don't.

MOISTURIZE. Dryness can lead to many of the skin conditions that may accompany old age. Thus, make sure that the soaps, cosmetics, perfumes, and antiperspirants that you use are not drying your skin further, and use a moisturizing lotion often, especially after showering or bathing.

Problems That You May Encounter

DRY SKIN. In medical jargon, dry skin, which is very common among seniors, is called *xerosis*. This problem can be exacerbated by low humidity, by overheated indoor air, and by bathing too often. Use a humidifier if the air in your home is especially dry. Bathe (no more than once every two days) with warm, rather than hot water. Opt for mild soaps or nonsoap cleansers. Bath oils may seem like a good idea, but they can make the bathtub very slippery and put you at risk for falls. Applying a moisturizer after you bathe may be better and safer.

Talk with your doctor if your skin remains extremely dry despite these measures. He or she may recommend lotions that contain alpha-hydroxy acids to replace lost moisture. Sometimes, vitamins (especially B complex and E) may also be helpful.

ITCHING. Dry skin can lead to another problem of old age: itching. Although itching can be annoying and may even interfere with your sleep, in most cases, it isn't caused by a serious underlying illness. Again, lotions, used regularly, can go a long way toward remedying both dry skin and the itching that it causes. Some laundry detergents may cause more skin irritation and itching. You may want to try a hypoallergenic detergent with fewer additives.

If itching persists despite your use of lotions, see your doctor. Sometimes, itching is related to diseases such as diabetes or kidney disease, and sometimes, medicines that you may be taking can cause or exacerbate itching.

Intertrigo. This type of skin inflammation occurs because of the friction caused by skin rubbing against skin. This condition can make the skin under the arms, in the creases of the neck, in the groin, between the toes, and beneath the breasts become sweaty and itchy. Intertrigo can be made worse by hot weather, incontinence, and obesity.

Air is the best cure for this problem. Wearing light, loose, absorbent clothing and exposing the irritated skin to dry air (by using a hair dryer or fan) for 10 to 15 minutes several times each day can help, too.

We also recommend that you try to pay particular attention to keeping the skin folds clean. Sometimes, using powder or hydrocortisone cream can keep this condition under control.

Occasionally, intertrigo can be exacerbated by a fungus called *Candida albicans.* Diabetics with intertrigo are especially at risk for acquiring this fungal infection. If you develop a Candidal infection, your doctor may prescribe an antifungal cream or powder such as ketoconazole, clotrimazole, or miconazole. Always wear loose cotton underwear because cotton is less irritating to the skin and absorbs moisture better than other fabrics.

Herpes zoster, or shingles. *Herpes* is a skin infection that increases in incidence with advancing age and is most prevalent among those between the ages of 50 and 70. This *varicella zoster* viral infection lies dormant in the body for many years and then can become active again when one's immune system is not working well.

Approximately 80% of patients with herpes zoster have a rash on the trunk, neck, or abdomen for 10 to 14 days. The lesions begin as red bumps that within a day form clear blisters that eventually "weep" and crust over. Older people with herpes zoster infection can also experience severe nerve pain, which can begin a few days before the lesions appear and sometimes may last for as long as a year or more. Ice packs surrounding the affected area often help to reduce pain.

If you have this type of infection, your doctor or dermatologist may prescribe an antiviral drug called acyclovir. If you have developed a bacterial infection on top of your viral herpes infection, you may also need to take antibiotics.

Pressure ulcers, or bed sores. These common ulcers can occur because of the unrelieved pressure or rubbing of one's skin against another surface, such as a bed or wheelchair. These sores can begin as mild reddened areas on the skin. Unrecognized and untreated, they can progress to become serious, deep craters that can eventually penetrate as far down as the tendons and bones.

This is how pressure ulcers develop: When bones press down on tissue and skin that are pressed against another surface, the small blood vessels that feed the skin with oxygen and nutrients become squeezed. Eventually, the skin is starved, the tissue dies, and pressure ulcers can form.

More than 95% of pressure ulcers develop below the waist. In patients who are bedridden, these ulcers can form on the hips, the heels, and a part of the lower back called the sacrum. Other sites include the knees, ankles, back of the head, shoulder blades, and spine. Our colleague Gary Brandeis noted that a person's risk of developing pressure ulcers increases if he or she is incontinent, does not eat a balanced diet, has malnutrition, or is unable to move without assistance.

To prevent pressure ulcers, try the following:

- Inspect your skin, or have a friend, family member, or health care worker check your skin every day.
- Stay as clean as possible. Remember to use warm, rather than hot water and a mild soap when you bathe or shower, and follow up with a moisturizer.
- If necessary, use pads or absorbent underwear to keep moisture due to fecal or urinary incontinence away from your skin.
- Change positions often. If you are in bed, change your position every two hours. If you are sitting in a chair, shift your own weight every 15 minutes; if you need assistance, someone should help you to change positions every hour.
- If someone is helping you to change positions while you are in bed, make sure that he or she lifts you, rather than inadvertently drags or pulls you from one position to another, because the friction that can result from just rubbing briefly against the bed sheets can cause "sheet burn" and can damage your skin.
- Consider purchasing a mattress that is made of foam, gel, water, or air to help prevent bed sores. Some of these support surfaces can regularly alternate air currents in order to redistribute the pressure. Although studies have not shown that any one of these products is definitely superior to the others, your doctor may recommend a particular type, depending on your condition.
- Don't raise the head of your bed more than 30 degrees because doing so may cause you to slide down over the surface of the bed and may thereby increase your risk of developing friction-induced pressure ulcers.
- If you cannot move in bed, make sure that someone puts pillows underneath your legs just above your ankles (*not* under your knees) to keep your heels off the surface of the bed.
- When you are lying on your side, try not to lie directly on your hip bone for any length of time.
- Use a pillow or wedge to keep your ankles and knees from bumping into each other.
- Don't use donut-shaped cushions because such devices can lead to pressure ulcers.
- If you are a diabetic or have peripheral vascular disease, take any skin lesion seriously and contact your doctor promptly.
- Make sure you are eating a nutritious diet (see Chapter 2) that will help to keep your skin healthy. For new tissue growth, you need to consume enough total calories and protein, as well as vitamins C and E and the minerals magnesium, zinc, copper, and calcium.
- Wear comfortable, wide-width shoes, and alternate wearing at least two different pairs of shoes.

If, in spite of your good efforts to prevent pressure ulcers from forming, you do develop them, try to sit or lie in positions that do not put additional pressure on the ulcer. Your doctor can treat these sores by removing the affected tissue, cleansing the wound, and applying clean dressings. Sometimes antibiotic ointment may be helpful. He or she can also give you medicine for pain as needed.

CORNS AND BUNIONS. These lesions occur at pressure and friction points, often on the toes, from wearing ill-fitting shoes. Be careful in using over-the-counter solutions to treat corns because the chemicals can burn the skin. Read the directions carefully. See a podiatrist regularly.

ACTINIC KERATOSES. These sharply outlined, abnormal growths on the skin may appear in one's 50s, especially in fair-skinned people who have spent some time in the sun. If you've worked on a farm or spent a lot of time outdoors in your lifetime, you may have many of these red or flesh-colored lesions, especially on your face, hands, shoulders, upper back, and scalp. There is a small (1–5%) risk that these growths may become cancerous later, so if you have keratoses, you should see your dermatologist at least once a year.

HYPERTROPHIC ACTINIC KERATOSES. More advanced skin lesions than actinic keratoses, these thicker growths are associated with a slightly greater risk of skin cancer. If you have either of these types of lesions, we recommend that you stay out of the sun as much as possible, and that you use sunscreens and protective clothing when you must go out. Old lesions may gradually disappear, and the number of new lesions may diminish after you have begun to take such precautions.

Some physicians also treat keratoses by freezing them with liquid nitrogen cryotherapy, removing them with a procedure called *curettage,* or drying them out with a high-frequency electrical current (*electrodesiccation*). For more severe keratoses, your dermatologist may prescribe 5-fluorouracil (5-FU, or Efudex) cream or tretinoin cream.

LENTIGO MALIGNA. This form of melanoma, or tumor, is caused by exposure to the sun. Although this type of lesion may take decades to develop, it generally is recognized in people who are in their 70s or older. These lesions can be bigger than 5 centimeters in diameter and may have irregularly shaped borders. Treatment may involve surgical removal of the lesion and the skin surrounding it, freezing (cryosurgery), or laser surgery.

BULLOUS PEMPHIGOID. This autoimmune disorder increases in incidence by approximately tenfold after age 65. Itching and blistering skin lesions may appear, sometimes in the mouth. If this occurs, prompt medical attention should be sought. The treatment for this condition may be drug therapy with corticosteroids. Bullous pemphigoid needs to be evaluated carefully and treated promptly by your doctor.

PSORIASIS. Psoriasis is a chronic condition in which the skin becomes inflamed, thickened, and red. Sometimes the patches of red skin have a silverish, scaly appearance. Treatment may include steroid creams, vitamins A and D, and sometimes ultraviolet light.

DERMATITIS, OR ECZEMA. This inflammation of the skin is caused by allergies or other irritants. Often, in older people, there may be no identifiable cause for this disorder. Itching, red, and swollen skin can lead to blisters that ooze and crust over.

When a cause (such as a particular type of laundry detergent or body soap) can be identified, avoidance of that irritant is usually the first step in resolving the dermatitis. Lotions used after bathing or showering can help to keep the skin moist and less prone to irritation. Corticosteroid ointments also are sometimes applied. For severe cases, antihistamines may be recommended.

There are many forms of dermatitis:

- *Stasis dermatitis* causes itching, redness, and sometimes swelling of the lower legs. This disorder is related to insufficiency of the veins. People with this type of condition need to be especially careful about injuring their lower legs because cuts or bruises in this area can take a long time to heal. If you develop stasis dermatitis, elevating your legs and wearing support stockings can help. Applying an ointment containing hydrocortisone can alleviate the itching and inflammation.
- *Seborrheic dermatitis* generally affects the scalp, face, eyebrows, eyelids, and trunk. The treatment for this form of dermatitis may include special shampoos for the affected scalp, as well as hydrocortisone cream for the face and trunk.
- *Allergic contact dermatitis* is caused by sensitivity to various irritants, such as lanolin (a wool fat that is found in many creams and lotions), nickel (which is found in some jewelry), and medicines, including certain antibiotics and anesthetics that are applied to the skin.

A dermatologist or allergist can help you to determine which irritant is causing your dermatitis by performing a "patch test" that involves exposure to many typical culprit allergens. If the irritant is identified, you should take steps to avoid it. You should also let your primary care doctor know if you turn out to be allergic to any medicines, including anesthetics or antibiotics, so that you won't be given these agents in the future. To relieve the itching and discomfort of your allergic contact dermatitis, your physician may recommend special lotions or prescribe topical corticosteroid creams.

SKIN CANCER. The most common malignancies in older people are non-melanoma skin cancers. These lesions, which usually are caused or exacerbated by sun exposure, include basal cell and squamous cell carcinomas. Both of these types of cancer increase in incidence through the age of 80.

The sooner these cancers are diagnosed, the better one's chances of overcoming them. Fortunately, both of these types of cancer are highly treatable by local surgical removal when they are identified at an early stage.

- Pay attention to your skin. If you see that a mole has changed in appearance, or if you develop a new lesion, see your primary care doctor or dermatologist. Don't forget to check between your toes, on the soles of your feet, and on your scalp.

- Contact your doctor if you have a mole that changes in color, size, or shape, or if the mole begins to ooze, bleed, or crust over.

- Especially if you are fair-skinned, you should have a doctor check your skin every year as part of a normal physical examination.

Detecting Skin Cancer

A *basal cell carcinoma* looks like a clear bump that is surrounded by red spiderlike veins. It usually appears on a part of the body that has been exposed to the sun, such as the face, shoulders, or arms. These growths usually don't cause symptoms, and they hardly ever spread to vital organs. Occasionally they can bleed, however, and they can grow and affect the areas immediately surrounding them, so they should be treated. Surgery, freezing (cryosurgery), and radiation are very effective therapeutic options.

Squamous cell carcinomas, like basal cell carcinomas, may be caused by the sun. These lesions, which look like scaly red bumps, can also be related to scar tissue and to radiation treatment. Smoking may increase one's risk of developing a squamous cell carcinoma on the lower lip. Squamous cell carcinomas are less common than basal cell carcinomas, but they may be more dangerous because they can grow and spread more quickly to other organs. Surgery, cryotherapy, and radiation are available treatment options.

Malignant melanoma is the most serious type of skin cancer. It may appear as a new mole, or as a change in the color or shape of an old mole. If you notice either of these changes in your skin, you should see your doctor. If this type of cancer has *metastasized* (spread), one's prognosis may not be as good as it might be with other forms of skin cancer. It's thus very important to diagnose these tumors early, when they may be removed surgically. Sometimes, chemotherapy or immunotherapy may be recommended for advanced melanoma.

Cosmetic Solutions to Aging Skin

Some people feel perfectly comfortable with the character that time brings to their faces. Others are interested in finding ways to look younger. Dermatologists and plastic surgeons have several new methods of smoothing the lines and tone of older skin. If you're interested in pursuing these options, make sure that you are working with a skin specialist who is board-certified (see Chapter 3), and ask about the associated costs up front, because most of these cosmetic procedures are not covered by insurance.

BOTOX. Botulinum toxin (Botox) is a substance that has been found to take away crow's-feet and frown lines when it's injected into the muscles of the forehead and around the eyes. This treatment lasts for approximately six months.

PEELS. Chemical peels work by removing old skin cells so that healthier new cells can take their place. *Micropeels* smooth out skin by removing damaged skin cells with glycolic-acid-based products.

After the glycolic acid is applied, dry ice is used to shrink the skin pores and to make facial color more even. This process, which usually is performed on an outpatient basis, may need to be repeated every few months.

Power peels involve a short (approximately 20-minute) treatment to eliminate fine lines around the eyes, lips, and neck. These treatments can also lighten age spots and scars from acne. Ask your dermatologist for more information about these treatments.

LASER TREATMENTS. Just as with micropeels, laser treatments work by removing old, damaged skin cells so that new, healthy skin cells can be stimulated. This method employs laser energy to destroy the old cells, which then can be wiped off with a cloth. Laser treatments also vaporize wrinkles, zap red or brown liver spots and spider veins (collections of tiny blood vessels just under the skin), and remove tattoos and unwanted hair (by destroying hair follicles). This procedure usually does not leave a scar.

FACE LIFTS. The medical name for a face lift is *rhytidectomy*. This procedure, which is usually performed on an outpatient basis, involves taking years away from the face by removing wrinkled skin from both the patient's forehead and the areas near the mouth and eyes. After the patient has received anesthesia, the surgeon makes incisions from the temples to the ears. Excess skin is then separated from the underlying structures of the face and is pulled back toward the ear. This procedure is becoming increasingly popular.

EYELID TUCKS. *Blepharoplasty* is the medical name for removing extra skin and fat from the eyelids. This procedure, which is performed in an operating room while the patient is under anesthesia, involves the use of lasers to cut off tiny blood vessels in the eyelids.

Your Hair

"You are old, Father William," the young man said,

"And your hair has become very white;

And yet you incessantly stand on your head—

Do you think, at your age, it is right?"

Lewis Carroll (1832–1898)

What he hath scanted men in hair, he hath given them in wit.

William Shakespeare, (1564–1616), *The Comedy of Errors,* II, ii, 83

How Your Hair Changes as You Age

A father was explaining to his young child that the reason he was starting to get gray hair was because sometimes the child did things that made him sad or unhappy. The young child then asked, "So why is Grandma's hair all gray?" Half of us begin to have gray hair by the time we're 50. This is because we may lose the dark brown or black pigment called melanin from our hair follicles as we age. Our hair does not grow as quickly when we're older, and hair loss can occur in both older men and women (although it occurs more commonly and sooner in men, compared to women, and in certain individuals more than others). In men, *male-pattern hair loss* begins in the 20s and 30s and by age 70, 80% of men are quite bald. This occurs partly because of genes and partly because of changes in levels of male sex hormones. Conditions such as iron deficiency, hypothyroidism, and chronic kidney failure can exacerbate this condition.

Conversely, too much hair, or *hirsutism,* can occur after one turns 50. Men may find that they have more hair than they used to in their eyebrows, ears, and nose. Women can discover that they are developing a "beard" or "mustache."

HAIR LOSS. If your doctor determines that you're losing hair because of an underlying nutritional or other health problem, he or she can help you to treat that condition, and in many cases, the hair will grow back.

If, however, your hair loss is related to your years, he or she may recommend a drug called minoxidil or finasteride to stimulate the growth of new hair. If this solution is applied to bald areas every day, approximately one fourth of patients who try this remedy will experience hair growth. It's common, however, for patients to lose their hair again within 12 months of starting this treatment.

Hair transplants are another cosmetic solution to hair loss.

EXCESS HAIR. If you have too much hair in unwanted places, it can be removed by cutting, shaving, or plucking. Sometimes hair-removing cream may be helpful. A more permanent solution is a method called *electrolysis,* which involves the use of an electrical current to destroy the hair roots.

What You Can Do about These Changes

Like our skin, our fingernails and toenails can become dry and brittle with age. They may also become slightly yellow or gray. Sometimes, the nails become quite thick; in medical terminology this is called *onychogryphosis.*

Your Nails

How Your Nails Change as You Age

There really is no cure for these changes, but you can take some steps to protect your nails from breaking. For instance, keep your nails short, and don't use drying chemicals such as nail-polish remover. Wear rubber gloves when you are washing the dishes or doing other housework that involves scrubbing.

For problems such as ingrown toenails, you should see a foot doctor, or podiatrist, to evaluate your feet. Our colleague John Giurini notes that older people have a greater susceptibility to fungal infections than younger people do, so it's important to pay attention to good foot care and to visit your doctor if you develop any problems.

What You Can Do about These Changes

A strong body makes the mind strong. . . . It is of little consequence to store the mind with science if the body be permitted to become debilitated. If the body be feeble, the mind will not be strong.

Thomas Jefferson (1743–1826)

My 83-year-old mother fell a few months ago and fractured her hip. What a wake-up call! I had no idea before I witnessed her recovery firsthand how painful this kind of injury could be, or how long it could take to heal. My mother has been unable to get around the house easily, let alone go outside. She has always been a very independent person and I can see how hard it is for her to ask for other people's help.

After I went through menopause, I took estrogen for a while, but then I stopped taking it because I don't like to take pills unnecessarily. I've read that estrogen can lower a person's risk of developing osteoporosis, though, so I'm going to talk with my doctor about taking it again.

Cynthia, age 56

Changes with Age

Your Muscles

Your muscles are most robust when you are in your 20s; after that, their size and strength are determined primarily by your activity level. People who have physically demanding jobs or who often exercise tend to maintain the bulk and vigor of their muscles longer than those who are not active. After age 60, though, even physically fit individuals may lose some of their muscle tissue, and fatty tissue may take its place. This age-related loss in muscle mass is called *sarcopenia.*

Your Bones

Like muscles, our bones are not static substances; rather, they have the capacity to shrink and expand according to age, diet, and level of physical fitness. One usually reaches optimal bone mass at around age 30 to 35—a bit later than when one reaches the best muscle condition.

It's especially important to build strong bones when you're young because eventually you will start to lose more bone than your body can replace. Because of this diminishing bone density, one's risk of developing *osteoporosis,* or thin, weak bones, increases with age. This risk is especially high in women because of changing hormone levels and a substantial loss of calcium after menopause. In fact, one of two women over age 50 may experience a fracture related to brittle bones. In older women, the risk of a hip fracture is equal to the combined risks of uterine, ovarian, and breast cancer.

Although osteoporosis isn't just a disease of women, older men are far less likely to develop brittle bones. Perhaps this is because men tend to have larger builds than women, so most have more bone mass to begin with. Also, male sex hormones called *androgens* can maintain bone mass. As a result, fewer men than women lose balance and fall, and only one out of every eight men over age 50 has an osteoporosis-related fracture.

Do you worry about falling and breaking a hip? Have you at times given up certain activities or hesitated to venture out because you are afraid of falling? While we don't recommend that you take unnecessary risks, we don't think that avoidance of activity is the best way to prevent injury, either. Actually, inactivity puts you at even greater risk of broken bones because a sedentary lifestyle allows the muscles and bones to atrophy and weaken further.

In this chapter, we discuss treatments available for various musculoskeletal problems that you may already be experiencing or that you may encounter as you get older. First, though, we tell you about the many steps you can take to stay strong, limit your risk of falling, and prevent potentially debilitating bone fractures.

Keeping Your Musculoskeletal System Healthy

Estrogen is a natural hormone that may be important for preventing osteoporosis and fractures of the hip and of the column of small bones (vertebrae) in your back that surround and protect your spinal cord. Some studies have shown that estrogen may also protect people from heart disease, stroke, Alzheimer's disease, and possibly depression.

The Role of Estrogen

Physicians sometimes prescribe hormone replacement therapy (HRT) to replace the natural estrogen that is lost during and after menopause. Before deciding about whether to begin estrogen therapy, talk over the pros and cons with your doctor. Some women may experience side effects such as weight gain, breast tenderness, pelvic discomfort, and mood changes while taking this type of therapy. If you have breast cancer or a family history of breast cancer or endometrial cancer, you may not wish to take estrogen. Likewise, be aware that taking estrogen *may* increase your risk of developing endometrial cancer, breast cancer, and vaginal bleeding (see Chapter 5).

Recent research has shown that women who take calcium and vitamin D, in addition to estrogen therapy, can usually take a lower dose of these replacement hormones and still experience the same health benefits. Also, research is currently underway to test estrogen-like compounds called selective estrogen receptor modulators (SERMs) that will selectively prevent osteoporosis but not increase breast or endometrial cancer risk. Stay tuned for further developments.

Preventing Fractures

You don't have to fall down in order to experience a major bone fracture. Indeed, hip fractures can happen when a person is walking or standing on level ground! One study showed that a woman's risk of developing osteoporosis is highest if she had a mother, aunt, or grandmother who fractured a bone with *minimal trauma*. Thus, preventing falls is just one important aspect of preventing fractures. This section suggests some other things that you can do to protect yourself.

DO STRENGTHENING EXERCISES. Jogging, walking, swimming, and playing tennis are excellent exercises to prevent bone loss and to build up bone strength. Step aerobics, running on a treadmill, and aquatic exercise therapy are other good activities. It doesn't matter so much what you choose to do—just find something that you enjoy and keep doing it! Remember that you will continue to lose bone mass if you don't get active.

Some of our patients have derived a great deal of enjoyment from learning tai chi chuan, an ancient form of Chinese exercise. The slow, graceful movements of this shadow-boxing exercise can reduce your risk of falling by improving your flexibility and balance. Studies have also shown that this form of exercise can lower blood pressure.

GET ENOUGH CALCIUM. Much of the calcium that we consume is stored in our bones. If we don't consume as much calcium as the cells in our bodies need, our bodies will literally draw this nutrient right out of our bones. Between the ages of 25 and 65, both men and women need 1,000 milligrams (mg) of calcium every day. After menopause, women need even more calcium: a total of 1,500 mg every day. After age 65, all elders should take 1,500 mg of calcium per day, in divided doses.

Try to consume as much calcium as possible by eating calcium-rich foods. In addition to milk and milk products (such as cheese and yogurt), calcium is found in canned fish such as salmon and sardines, dark green vegetables such as broccoli and kale, calcium-fortified orange juice, and some breads.

We also advise our patients to take calcium supplements every day, especially if they are allergic to or intolerant of milk products or if they take certain medicines (such as corticosteroids, certain anticonvulsants, and antacids that contain aluminum) that may interfere with the absorption of calcium.

Calcium supplements come in several forms, including calcium carbonate, which is taken with meals, and calcium citrate, which may be taken with or without food. Calcium gluconate, calcium lactate, and calcium phosphate are other forms of calcium supplements. The ones to avoid are dolomite and bone meal because they are not always well absorbed. A good test of bioavailability is to place a calcium tablet in 4 ounces of white-wine vinegar. If it has not dissolved after 30 minutes, it probably will not be a good source of calcium and should not be used. You can talk with your doctor about which one would be most appropriate for you.

GET ENOUGH VITAMIN D. To absorb calcium, our bodies need vitamin D. Studies have shown that taking this vitamin can reduce the risk of hip fractures in older, frail women by as much as 40%. You can usually get enough of this important vitamin by drinking fortified milk and eating certain cereals. Your doctor may also recommend a vitamin D supplement (usually 400–800 international units per day) for you.

GET ENOUGH PROTEIN. Skeletal muscle serves as a storage place for protein in the body. In addition to drinking milk for its calcium and added vitamin D, you can drink milk and consume dairy products for protein value, too. If you don't tolerate milk or milk products, there are a number of equally nutritious alternatives, including soy milk and soy products.

TALK WITH YOUR DOCTOR ABOUT NEW METHODS OF PROTECTION. Scientists are constantly exploring new ways to prevent osteoporotic fractures of the hip, spine, and long bones. For example, our colleague Wilson Hayes and his workers have developed a hip-padding system, which can be worn as a girdlelike undergarment to protect the hip from fracture when one falls to the side. Also, researchers are now working to develop floor tiles that can spring back in response to high-impact stimuli such as a fall and can cushion the fall and prevent fractures.

TAKE STEPS TO PREVENT FALLS. Even if you've never lost your balance or tripped and fallen, simply being afraid of falling can affect your quality of life by making you less confident, more depressed, and even more isolated from others. In addition to the proactive steps that we've just mentioned, be aware of all of the factors that may lead to a fall (see the sidebar below), and do what you can to prevent them.

Preventing Falls

- See your physician regularly to have your vision and hearing tested (and corrected, if necessary).

- Talk with your doctor or pharmacist about the side effects of the medications you are taking. Do any of them affect your coordination or balance? Is there anything that you can do to limit these side effects? It may be possible to take a lower dosage, or to take your medicine before bedtime rather than in the morning, for instance.

- Reduce your alcohol consumption, which can affect your balance and reflexes.

- Stop smoking. Smoking nearly doubles your risk of a hip fracture because it robs your body of calcium.

- After eating a meal, lying down, or resting, you need to remember to get up very slowly. Sometimes, a drop in blood pressure associated with these activities can result in dizziness or falls.

- Check the nighttime temperature in your home. It should be at least 65 degrees F. If your body is exposed to cold temperatures for several hours, your body temperature can drop and make you dizzy.
- If you sometimes feel unsteady on your feet, use a cane, walking stick, or walker to help you maintain your balance.
- Be careful when you walk outdoors on wet or icy pavement.
- Wear low-heeled shoes with rubber soles.
- Keep your home safe and easy to navigate (see Chapter 18 for a list of suggestions).

Preventing Back Pain

In addition to fractured bones, backaches are another common affliction of older people. Once again, exercise can keep your muscles in good condition and can reduce your risk of back problems. Learn to bend down by bending your knees, not your back. Another back-saving tip is to always carry objects close to your body. Don't lift objects while you are bending forward, reaching, or twisting. Sleep on a firm (but not hard) mattress for good back support, and try not to fall asleep while sitting partially reclined in a chair. Finally, as your grandmother always told you, sit up straight, and don't wear high-heeled shoes.

Problems That May Occur

Osteoporosis

As we have just mentioned, *osteoporosis* is a progressive thinning of the bones, which usually occurs over many years. This disease can weaken your bones—especially in the spine, hip, and wrist—so much that you may hear of people who have experienced a fracture because of simple movements, even without falling. In addition to creating a risk of bone fractures, osteoporosis may also affect your breathing. That's because as bones lose calcium, the cartilage and ligaments of the ribs and spine are apt to become calcified and less elastic, limiting lung function and respiratory-muscle efficiency.

Finally, if you seem to be getting shorter, it may be because the *intervertebral space* (the distances between every two vertebrae of the spine) may become narrowed by a significant amount. The arch of your back may start to curve forward as your back becomes less straight and more hunched over. In addition to these common age-related changes, osteoporosis may be weakening your vertebrae so much that it may be causing compression fractures, which then further shorten the spine. This disease can cause some women to lose as much as four inches of their adult height! As your spine may be increasingly curving forward (this is known as dowager's hump, or *kyphosis*), spinal osteoporosis may cause further degeneration of the fibrous discs located between the vertebrae.

RISK FACTORS FOR OSTEOPOROSIS. Osteoporosis can occur in older women because of lower levels of estrogen after menopause. Insufficient exercise, a diet that does not contain enough calcium, early menopause (before the age of 45), and other conditions (such as anorexia, bulimia, diabetes, hyperthyroidism, and surgical removal of the ovaries) that lower hormone levels are additional risk factors for osteoporosis. Our colleague Harold Rosen explains that women with the highest chance of developing osteoporosis have a family history of this disease (some studies have shown that 70–80% of osteoporosis may be inherited) and a slender build, and they are Caucasian. Smoking, drinking three or more cups of coffee per day, and daily alcohol intake are also contributing factors.

How osteoporosis is diagnosed. Generally, there is no discomfort associated with the gradual thinning of bones, and you may not realize that you have this disorder until you fall and break or fracture a bone. If you fracture your spine, however, you may experience severe back pain without falling.

Our colleague Susan Greenspan and others have reported that very low bone density of the hip may be an important predictor of hip fractures in older individuals. Doctors can do *bone densitometry tests* to measure the density of the bones in your hip, lower spine, and wrists (Table 9.1). These radiological tests can be useful if you are a woman who is younger than 65, and you and your doctor are considering whether you should take drugs that may reduce your rate of bone loss. These scans may also be helpful in evaluating how effective a treatment for osteoporosis is after some time. Some doctors may recommend universal bone-density testing in all women over age 65 because most women will have low bone densities by that time. Bone densitometry may especially be helpful in patients who are taking steroids, anticonvulsant medicines, or thyroid hormone, as well as those with spinal abnormalities or other endocrine problems such as hyperparathyroidism or Cushing's disease.

How osteoporosis is treated. Doctors sometimes treat bone loss with the following medications:

- *Calcitonin* is a hormone that prevents bone loss in the spine and also helps to relieve the pain associated with fractures. This naturally occurring hormone may be injected or inhaled (the nasal spray is called *Miacalcin*).

Table 9.1 **Radiological Tests to Measure Bone Density**

Test	Description
Quantitative computed tomography (QCT)	Can sometimes detect signs of bone loss, especially of the spine and hip, but uses a higher dose of radiation than DEXA (described later)
Single photon absorptiometry (SPA)	Uses a low level of radiation and is helpful for measuring the bone density of the ulna, radius, or heel
Dual energy photon absorptiometry (DPA)	Can be used to measure the bone density of the femur and vertebrae, but the test may take longer than other methods (20–45 minutes); it is not used as often for older people because it may be less accurate in this age group
Dual energy x-ray absorptiometry (DEXA)	Uses a beam of x-rays (with a very low dose of radiation) to create an image of the bone and to measure bone mass throughout the body; is brief (usually 5–10 minutes) and more precise than other tests

- Drugs called *bisphosphonates* prevent bone loss by blocking bone resorption, increase bone density at the spine and hip, and have been reported to decrease spine, hip, and wrist fractures by 50% over three years. The medicine needs to be taken 30 minutes before breakfast, on an empty stomach, with a full glass of water, and the person should remain upright.
- *Alendronate (Fosamax)* is a bisphosphonate drug that increases bone mass at the spine and hip and prevents bone loss in women after menopause.
- *Etidronate (Didronel)* is a bisphosphonate drug that soon may be approved by the U.S. FDA for the treatment of osteoporosis. Tests have shown that it may prevent bone loss and can reduce the risk of vertebral fractures.
- *Raloxifene* is a drug called a *selective estrogen receptor modulator (SERM),* which may increase bone mass in the hip and spine. In 1999, scientists reported that it is effective for the prevention of osteoporosis. It also decreases cholesterol, and it may reduce the risk for endometrial cancer and breast cancer. Whether it may have other beneficial effects (such as protection from coronary heart disease) remains to be established.
- Other drug therapy under investigation includes the use of *parathyroid hormone* and *slow-release sodium fluoride* to treat bone loss.

Hip Fractures If, despite the precautions mentioned earlier, you experience a fracture, you may have only vague symptoms such as minor hip pain, or you may not be able to bear weight at all. He or she may recommend an assistive device (see Table 9.2). Therefore, if you have pain in your hip, you should see your doctor.

Paget's Disease of Bone After osteoporosis, the second most common metabolic disease that affects older people is called Paget's disease of bone. This disease affects 3% of people over age 50 and 10% of people over age 80.

Paget's disease appears to be an inherited condition; 30% of patients with this condition have a relative who was also affected by this disease. Researchers

Table 9.2 Devices That Can Make You More Mobile

The following assistive devices can be helpful for people with various musculoskeletal disorders. Talk with your physician about whether he or she recommends any of these types of medical equipment for you. If so, make sure that you use equipment that fits you properly.

Assistive device	Used for
Cane or walking stick	Relief of weight-bearing discomfort or increased stability
Walker	Increased stability and support
Wheelchair	Those who cannot walk or who tire quickly
Motorized carts	Those with severe disability and immobility

say that it is also possible that in certain cases, there may be a viral component to Paget's disease. More studies need to be conducted.

This condition can lead to bone deformity that can affect the joints, causing pain and arthritis. Rarely, Paget's disease can lead to a breakdown of skeletal lesions that can turn cancerous. When this happens, surgical removal of the affected bone may be required. Other complications of Paget's disease may include deafness and congestive heart failure. Some scholars suggest that Beethoven may have had Paget's disease.

HOW PAGET'S DISEASE IS DIAGNOSED. If you have Paget's disease, you may have joint and bone pain, or you may have no symptoms at all. A blood test to measure the amount of an enzyme called alkaline phosphatase can help to provide a clue to the presence of this disease. X-ray films of the skeleton, bone scans, and possibly biopsies may help to confirm the diagnosis.

HOW PAGET'S DISEASE IS TREATED. If you are diagnosed with Paget's disease, your physician may recommend that you take pain relievers and possibly other medicines for bone pain and arthritis. Sometimes, Paget's disease causes joint damage that can only be treated by complete replacement of the joint. Three types of medicine are currently used to treat Paget's disease:

- *Calcitonin,* a hormone that is given to relieve bone pain
- *Etidronate,* which slows down the rate of bone resorption
- *Plicamycin (Mithracin),* which is sometimes given for advanced disease

Finally, your physician may refer you to a physical therapist for strengthening exercises or to an orthopedic surgeon for total joint replacement surgery if severe arthritis of the hip or knee develops.

Backaches and Back Pain

Most people do experience backaches at some point in their lives. This pain may occur suddenly, or it may be gradual in onset. Although back pain may be quite uncomfortable, usually this problem is not dangerous.

Your backbone (spine) is composed of vertebrae that are separated from each other by cushions called *discs.* Nerves branch away from the spinal cord, exiting the spinal canal through the spaces that separate the vertebrae. Muscles and ligaments surround the vertebrae and hold them in place. Most of your weight is centered in the lower part of your back, and the bones, muscles, and ligaments there can be strained and cause pain when one changes position. Back discomfort can also be affected by emotional stress and by inactivity. Back problems that may occur include joint problems, muscle spasms, and a sprained back.

If you engage in heavy physical labor (for example, lifting) or strenuous exercise that puts stress on your back, you may also develop disc problems because of pressure on the intervertebral disc. Sometimes, a disc can pinch a nerve at the site of exit from the spinal canal. The resulting pain, called *sciatica,* if it is in the lower back, may be sharp and may shoot from the back and buttocks down the leg to below the knee. A slipped disc can also cause tingling, weakness, and even numbness in the legs.

Self-Help

What should you do if you develop a back problem? If your lower back pain is not severe, it may go away on its own within a few days. You should see your doctor, though, if the pain is severe enough to interfere with your everyday activities, or if it doesn't go away on its own within a couple of days. Moreover, if your leg becomes weak, if you have numbness in the groin or rectal area, or if you lose control of your bladder or bowels, you should seek medical assistance immediately.

Until your back pain has disappeared, be sure to avoid heavy lifting, sitting for long periods of time, or twisting.

Medical Help

What can your physician do? If you go to see your doctor because of an aching back, he or she will take your medical history (including any prescription and nonprescription medicines that you may be taking) and will perform a physical examination. There are several treatment options available to manage back pain, but no single approach is appropriate for everyone, and more than one approach may be considered.

MEDICATIONS. Your doctor may recommend medication for your back pain. For minor back pain, aspirin, acetaminophen, or ibuprofen may be helpful. For more severe pain, your physician may prescribe something stronger for pain relief, a muscle relaxant, or both.

BEDREST. For severe discomfort, your doctor may advise you to rest in bed for a day or two. Remaining on bedrest for a longer period of time may be counterproductive, though, because your muscles may actually weaken while you are not active. In most cases, it's better to keep moving in order to speed your recovery.

COLD AND HEAT. Another therapeutic option for back pain is to apply a cold pack to the affected area intermittently for 5 to 10 minutes every 4 to 6 hours for 48 hours. If the pain persists for more than two days, you may want to either continue with cold treatment or try a heating pad or a hot bath or shower.

SPINAL MANIPULATION. Some patients also visit a *chiropractor*, who can manipulate the spine and provide some relief. Spinal manipulation can be effective in relieving pain, but occasionally serious injuries including spinal cord injury and fractures have resulted. You should first consult your doctor before undergoing spinal manipulation. If the pain persists for a month or more after you have tried this remedy, however, see your primary care doctor.

PHYSICAL THERAPY. Physical therapy for back pain may involve stretching exercises, massage, or the use of a device called a transcutaneous electrical nerve stimulation (TENS) unit. This small, low-frequency electrical device generally is applied in several brief sessions per day to the affected area. By stimulating the muscles, a TENS device may be helpful in alleviating chronic back pain.

OTHER TREATMENT OPTIONS. If medications, cold or hot packs, or spinal adjustments do not relieve your pain, other treatment options, including acupuncture, biofeedback, massage, and injections of steroids, may be considered. A pain management center affiliated with your local hospital or health care clinic may offer these treatments, as well as more information. Although such measures may temporarily relieve the discomfort, they might not necessarily make your recovery much faster.

We also advise our patients with back pain to take the following steps:

- Sit in a chair that has good lower-back support. While sitting, try to keep your feet on the floor or slightly elevated on a low stool.
- Don't sleep on your stomach or your back.
- Sleep on your side, with one leg flexed and a supporting pillow beneath the flexed knee. This will help take the pressure off the spine.
- While standing for long periods of time, rest one of your feet on a low stool. Some patients also find that shoe lifts help to alleviate lower back pain, especially if it is necessary to stand for long periods of time (talk with your doctor about whether this would work for you).
- Keep a pillow or a folded-up towel behind your lower back while you are driving.
- Wear low-heeled shoes.
- Take short walks, swim, or use a stationary bicycle to strengthen your back.
- If you have weakness or a loss of sensation in your legs, or loss of bladder or bowel function, see your doctor immediately.

BACK SURGERY. If medical treatment and other options are not successful and there is severe compression of nerve roots or severe spinal stenosis, surgery may be recommended. Your physician will refer you to a neurosurgeon. In some cases, spinal surgery can be extremely successful. A 76-year-old woman who recently underwent surgery said, "I am a new woman after the back surgery. For the first time in 3 years I am free of pain, and I can now walk with my body upright. I feel 30 years younger!"

Fortunately, surgery is usually not necessary to treat lower back pain, and most back discomfort goes away within a short time. Nonetheless, some people who recover from an episode of acute lower back pain may experience a similar episode within a few years.

Arthritis

Arthritis is a condition that can increase your risk of falling by altering the function of your joints and influencing your perception of your body in space. This condition occurs more frequently in older people, although more often than not, it affects people who are younger than age 65 (and it can also affect children). The three most common kinds of arthritis are rheumatoid arthritis, osteoarthritis, and gout.

Types of Arthritis

Rheumatoid Arthritis. *Rheumatoid arthritis* is an autoimmune disorder that causes painful inflammation of the joints, and this inflammation can lead to cartilage and bone damage. Our colleague Lea Sewell notes that approximately 10% of cases of rheumatoid arthritis occur in people who are older then age 60. Rheumatoid arthritis can affect both men and women.

Osteoarthritis. Cartilage, like muscle and bone, changes as we age. Inflammation of the cartilage can lead to a condition called *osteoarthritis,* in which cartilage breaks down at the tips of bones in joints that are weight-bearing (such as the hips and knees). Osteoarthritis can also affect the hands and feet. The primary symptoms of this form of arthritis are pain after activity and morning stiffness. The joint discomfort generally improves after rest.

More women than men develop osteoarthritis. There may be a genetic component to this disease, but it usually skips generations. Previous trauma to the joints can also increase one's risk of developing it.

Gout. The joint swelling of this form of arthritis is caused by elevated uric acid levels in the body. This swelling most commonly occurs in the big toe, knees, wrists, hands, and elbows. It is usually treated with nonsteroidal anti-inflammatory agents, corticosteroids, and sometimes a drug called colchicine.

Pseudogout. *Pseudogout* is a form of arthritis that is more common in older people than in younger ones. One's risk of developing this disorder is higher if he or she has a thyroid disorder. Pseudogout most often causes inflammation in the knee, shoulder, wrist, hip, and elbow.

Symptoms and Treatment

Symptoms of Arthritis. These symptoms include pain due to stiff joints in the morning, which gradually gets better as the day goes on; joint swelling or discomfort; a joint that is hot or red; and sometimes joint discomfort accompanied by a fever of 100 degrees F. or more.

Control of Arthritis. There is no definitive cure for arthritis, but with local heat or ice, weight loss, strengthening and aerobic exercises, assistive devices for walking, and sometimes medications, its related discomfort can be alleviated. Some reports suggest that eating foods that are high in omega-3 fatty acids (such as salmon, cod, and tuna) may reduce inflammation.

Acetaminophen (e.g., Tylenol) is usually the first medication that patients with arthritis are given. If the joint pain and inflammation continue, your doctor may recommend *nonsteroidal anti-inflammatory drugs* (NSAIDs) such as aspirin, ibuprofen, naproxen sodium, or ketoprofen. In 1998, the U.S. FDA approved a new drug called celecoxib (Celebrex) to alleviate the discomfort of arthritis without irritating the stomach or causing gastrointestinal hemorrhage, as aspirin can. It may be better tolerated in most people and may have fewer side effects than aspirin. *Steroids* are sometimes administered, especially to patients with rheumatoid arthritis. *Other medicines* such as methotrexate also may be used in more severe cases of rheumatoid arthritis.

Some patients find that pain relievers in *sprays, creams,* and *ointments* can also be helpful. These topical preparations may contain *capsaicin* (which is derived from chili peppers), menthol, or camphor. Newer treatments for rheumatoid arthritis include a drug called etanercept (Enbrel). Also, an agent called infliximib may be used as an alternative to methotrexate in the future.

For more advanced arthritis, your doctor may recommend drugs such as Synvisc or Hyalgan, which are injected to supplement or replace the lubricant that your body naturally supplies for your joints. Joint surgery is also sometimes advised for people with very severe arthritis. Loose cartilage and bone fragments can be removed via *arthroscopic surgery,* and the joint can be realigned or replaced by a procedure called *osteotomy.*

If you have gout, an anti-inflammatory drug called colchicine and drugs such as probenecid and allopurinol, which help to lower uric acid levels in the body, may be helpful. In addition, indomethacin and ibuprofen also may help. Finally, if you have gout, you may want to eliminate foods such as wine, liver, and anchovies from your diet because these foods contain high levels of a chemical called *purine,* which may be relatively difficult for your body to excrete.

Polymyalgia Rheumatica

Polymyalgia rheumatica (PMR), a syndrome that causes joint and muscle pain, is a common problem in people over age 50. The incidence of this autoimmune problem increases dramatically in people over age 70. It is characterized by stiffness that tends to last half an hour or more, especially in the morning.

If you find that you have a difficult time rolling over in bed at night, and you experience neck, upper arm, or groin discomfort when you wake up in the morning, you may have PMR. If your doctor determines that you do, he or she may prescribe a drug called prednisone for you. You may need to take this medication for a year or two, but it tends to be quite effective in alleviating the symptoms of PMR.

Lupus Erythematosus

Lupus erythematosus is an autoimmune disorder that tends to occur more often in younger persons than in older persons and in women more often than in men. However, it can be a disease of older persons. An 80-year-old former accountant recently was diagnosed with it and he responded extremely well to steroid treatment.

Bursitis

A *bursa* is a sac or pouch located between a tendon and a bone. *Bursitis,* which is inflammation of such an area, can sometimes lead to shoulder and arm discomfort, for example. There may be severe tenderness at sites where bursas are located; there may be pain on motion and rest; occasionally the regional active motion may be limited; and there may be appreciable swelling when bursitis occurs close to the body surface (for example, over a bunion or over a knee).

Trochanteric bursitis can cause an aching or tingling feeling over the hip; this discomfort can be exacerbated by activity or by sitting cross-legged. Anserine bursitis may lead to knee discomfort that is especially noticeable at night.

If you develop any of these forms of bursitis, your physician may prescribe antibiotics to treat potential infection, corticosteroids to reduce the swelling, and/or aspirin or nonsteroidal anti-inflammatory agents to relieve your discomfort. He or she may also recommend that you do some mild exercises to keep the affected area limber. Also, if you have anserine bursitis, you may be advised to keep a pillow between your knees while you're sleeping.

Tendinitis   An inflamed tendon is called *tendinitis*. This common condition can cause tenderness in the shoulders, the fingers and wrists, the elbow ("tennis elbow"), the back, the knees, and the feet.

Like bursitis, treatment of tendinitis may involve gentle exercises, nonsteroidal anti-inflammatory agents, and in some cases injections of corticosteroids into the affected area. Regular treatment with ice (10–15 minutes, 4–6 times per day) can be very effective in relieving pain. Weight loss may also be helpful to relieve stress on the injured soft tissues.

CHAPTER 10
YOUR BREASTS

Hope springs eternal in the human breast.

Alexander Pope (1688–1744)

In addition to the many progressive and sometimes intriguing transformations that our bodies go through in our later years, our breasts almost certainly will also evolve into a different version of their former selves. After menopause, most women's breasts tend to become smaller, although about 1 in 10 women find that their breasts may have grown larger. Also, because older women's breasts no longer need to be ready to make milk at nine months' notice, the breast tissue usually shrinks, and its composition becomes less dense and glandular. Fatty tissue may increase, and the breasts may become more flaccid and in some cases slightly droopy.

How Your Breasts Change as You Age

If you're taking hormone replacement therapy, though, your body may still be under the impression that menopause hasn't occurred yet, so your breast tissue may remain as dense and firm as it was before.

If you are like most people, breast cancer may be the first thing that comes to mind when you think of breast problems in an aging body. Indeed, approximately 48% of cases of breast cancer and 56% of breast cancer deaths occur in women who are age 65 or older. One's risk of breast cancer keeps climbing until about age 85 years. Breast cancer can affect men, too, but extremely rarely: Less than 1% of malignancies in men are due to breast cancer.

Keeping Your Breasts Healthy

The encouraging news is this: In both women and men, 9 out of 10 cases of breast cancer can be treated successfully if the cancer is detected early, before it has spread to other parts of the body. In this chapter, we focus on what you can do to reduce your risk of developing breast cancer and, if it occurs, how you can discover it in its most treatable stages.

Diet The role of good nutrition is the same in keeping your breasts healthy as it is in taking care of the rest of your body. Your diet should be low in fat and high in fruits and vegetables, especially those such as carrots and broccoli, which contain antioxidants (vitamin A, C, and E), chemicals that can disarm certain unstable oxygen molecules called *free radicals*. Without sufficient antioxidant control, the free radicals can interact with other molecules in the cell, making them ineffective and causing damage in the process.

Researchers have also found that women tend to have a lower risk of developing breast cancer if they live in those parts of the world where a lot of soy protein is consumed. You may want to try to include some soy products such as tofu in your diet whenever possible.

Finally, some studies have shown that drinking alcohol, consuming red meat, or both can significantly increase one's chances of developing breast cancer. For this reason, and for the health of your whole body, we advise moderation in consuming alcohol and red meat.

Exercise Scientists have also determined that physical activity may protect against breast cancer. Although researchers are not sure exactly why this is so, young girls and adolescents who exercise regularly may experience certain hormonal changes that can protect them from developing this type of cancer later on in life. Therefore, it's a good idea to encourage your daughters and granddaughters to stay fit, and of course, it's never too late for you to enjoy the benefits of exercise, too.

Preventive Drug Therapies Three drugs—tamoxifen, raloxiphene, and 4-hydroxyphenylretinamide—have shown promise in preventing breast cancer in women who are at risk for developing this disease (see Chapter 5). Tamoxifen, in particular, has been proven to effectively prevent this form of cancer in animals and may greatly reduce one's risk of developing cancer in the second breast if cancer has been detected in one. This drug has a few side effects, including an increased thickness of the endometrial lining and possibly a slightly increased risk of endometrial cancer. There is a low risk of hot flashes in women who take tamoxifen after menopause.

4-hydroxyphenylretinamide is a vitamin A–like substance that is currently being studied for the possible prevention of breast cancer in humans. Talk with your doctor about whether you would be a good candidate to take this or other drugs.

Screening for Breast Cancer There are three primary ways to detect breast cancer in its early stages: by performing a breast examination by yourself, by having such an examination at your primary care doctor's or gynecologist's office, and by having a mammogram. All three forms of screening are important, and for your best chance of finding breast cancer early, you should make it a habit to have all three types of exams on a regular basis. The American Geriatric Society recommends screening for breast cancer until age 85.

BREAST SELF-EXAMINATION. Every month, you should examine your breasts to look for unusual lumps, knots, thickened breast tissue, dimpling of the skin, discharge from the nipples, or any changes in the size, shape, or color of your breasts. Your doctor, nurse, or other health-care worker can show you how to do this visual and manual exam (Figure 10.1). In addition to your breasts, you can also examine your armpits for the presence of any lumps or knots. If you are taking progestins as part of hormone replacement therapy (HRT), you should do your breast self-examination the week after you have taken your last dose of this hormone.

Figure 10.1
Breast Self-Exam

Source: American Cancer Society

EXAMINATION IN A DOCTOR'S OFFICE. In addition to breast self-examination, you should see your health care provider once a year for an exam at a doctor's office or community health facility.

MAMMOGRAPHY. Although examination of your breasts by yourself and a health care worker are extremely important, your best chance of detecting a lump in your breast is by undergoing a mammogram, a type of x-ray test that involves a low dose of radiation. Some studies have reported that these tests can sometimes find a mass up to two years before one can feel it! The loss in breast-tissue density that occurs with menopause makes a mammogram an especially good test for detecting breast tumors in older women.

This doesn't mean, however, that you should simply have a mammogram and skip manual exams, because not all tumors that can be felt can be detected on mammography. We recommend that you have a mammogram every one to two years at least until age 70 years, and also perform breast self-examination regularly.

What is the test itself like? Your doctor or nurse practitioner may ask that you not wear any deodorant, powders, or creams when you come in for this brief (15- to 30-minute) procedure (that's because these substances can look like spots on the x-ray film, and creams can make your breasts slippery). You will be asked to take your clothes off above your waist, and you will be given a gown to wear. Then, while you are standing, your breast will be placed on an x-ray plate and pressed against another plate while the x-ray is taken. There may be some discomfort while your breast is being squeezed between these plates, and your doctor may recommend that you take a nonsteroidal anti-inflammatory medication before the procedure to minimize this discomfort.

Mammography facilities are required to be certified by the U.S. FDA. If you are unsure whether the FDA has approved the procedures, equipment, and technicians of a certain facility, you can find out by calling the National Cancer Institute's Cancer Information Service at 1-(800)-4-CANCER.

Breast Cancer

Breast cancer has the highest associated mortality rate of any cancer that affects women between the ages of 55 and 74. Each year, 180,000 new cases of breast cancer are diagnosed and more than 80% of them occur in women over age 50 years. One's risk of developing this form of cancer is increased by the following factors:

- Giving birth to children after age 30 or not giving birth at all
- The use of birth control pills or estrogen replacement therapy
- A family history of breast cancer (increases the risk by about 50%). Two genes, BRCA1 and BRCA2, have been associated with an increased risk of breast cancer. Women with a first-degree relative (such as a mother or a sister) with premenopausal breast cancer may wish to be tested for BRCA1 and BRCA2. Since up to 80% of BRCA1-positive women later may develop breast cancer, they should see their doctors regularly and discuss their options.
- Prior history of cancer (especially in the other breast, thyroid, colon, or ovary)
- Early menstruation (before age 12)
- Late menopause (after age 55)
- Consumption of two or more drinks of alcohol every day
- Exposure to air pollution, pesticides, or chemical food additives
- Advancing age

Although being aware of these risk factors is certainly important, keep in mind that 7 out of 10 women who have breast cancer have no apparent risk factors other than age. Breast cancer is very uncommon in men. Although the diagnosis and treatment options for breast cancer are the same in men as they are in women, breast cancer is generally diagnosed later in men than in women. Also, breast cancer can affect men in other profound ways because of the psychological impact of having what generally is thought of as a woman's disease.

Myths about Breast Cancer

Myth: I probably don't have breast cancer because I don't have symptoms.

Fact: Most cases of breast cancer do not cause pain or other recognizable symptoms.

Myth: I'm too old to get breast cancer.

Fact: Your risk of developing breast cancer increases with every passing year. In fact, most women who have breast cancer are over age 50.

Myth: There's no breast cancer in my family, so I'm not at risk.

Fact: Eight out of 10 women who get breast cancer do not have a family history of the disease.

You probably will have no symptoms if you have breast cancer. Your doctor may only discover a tumor through a mammogram, or you or your doctor may discover it through an examination of your breasts. Sometimes, there may be discharge from the nipple. If there are any sores, pimples, or open wounds on your breasts, see your doctor promptly.

Symptoms

Diagnosis

Why Are You Avoiding Breast Exams?

I'm afraid of what I (or my doctor) might find.

If you or your doctor do find a tumor, your chance of surviving it is as high as 92% *if it's detected early.*

I don't want my doctor to touch me in that way.

Talk with your doctor about having a nurse in the room.

It's too expensive.

Medicare covers most of the cost. Some community clinics also offer screening for very low (or no) fees.

I can't get to the mammography lab.

Call your local office on aging to arrange transportation and to find out whether a mobile mammography unit (in a van) is available in your community. Sometimes, these units provide screenings at shopping malls, office buildings, and community centers.

What if a lump is found? If a mass is found in your breast, either through self-examination or on a mammogram, you should see your doctor right away. He or she will probably examine your breast and then may recommend a *biopsy* for you. A biopsy is a medical procedure that involves removing a tiny piece of tissue for examination under a microscope.

Your primary care physician or gynecologist will probably refer you to a surgeon at this point. The biopsy procedure will allow your physician to make a definitive diagnosis. There are different types of biopsies:

- *Fine-needle biopsy.* During this safe and simple test, the breast surgeon will anesthetize the breast before inserting a needle (that is attached to a syringe) into the breast lump. He or she will then draw out a sample of cells that will be looked at under a microscope.
- *Core biopsy.* This nonsurgical type of biopsy involves the use of a larger needle to procure a small core of tissue (rather than just a sampling of cells) from a breast lump.
- *Incisional biopsy.* An incisional biopsy involves removing a larger mass of tissue from the breast lump.
- *Excisional biopsy (lumpectomy).* This type of biopsy involves removal of the entire lump, as well as the healthy tissue that surrounds it. The pathologist may draw a black line around the outside of the biopsy specimen. This is

called the "margin." The tissue is then tested to determine whether cancer cells are present in the margin area. If so, further breast surgery may be required.

The biopsy may show that the growth is benign, or there may be some cancerous cells. If it is breast cancer, your doctor will discuss with you the possible next steps, and he or she may refer you to an oncologist (a cancer specialist).

How Widespread Is Your Breast Cancer? What Type of Breast Cancer Do You Have?

There are several different kinds of breast cancer. Most are called *adenocarcinomas*, cancers that form in a gland. In addition to telling you the type of cancer, your doctor will be able to answer the following questions:

- How big is the tumor?
- Did the pathologist assign a grade to this tumor after he or she examined the biopsy specimen under the microscope? Doctors usually use the "TNM" system to stage cancer. "T" stands for the size of the tumor. "N" stands for the involvement of the lymph nodes, and "M" stands for metastasis, or spread to other parts of the body.
- Did the tumor invade the blood vessels or lymph nodes?

The progression of your disease and your treatment options will depend on the answers to these questions. The treatment also will depend on whether your tumor may respond to hormones (i.e., whether it tests positive for estrogen receptors).

Treatment

The goals of breast cancer treatment are to remove cancerous areas, alleviate symptoms, prevent relapse, preserve quality of life, and improve the likelihood of survival. Your doctor may recommend a particular course of treatment for your breast cancer, but the final decision about which method to use is up to you. Feel free to ask your doctor for a referral to an oncologist to discuss your treatment options.

LUMPECTOMY. A *lumpectomy,* or partial mastectomy, involves removal of just part of the breast. This form of treatment is generally not recommended for patients who have large tumors. In addition to being a diagnostic biopsy procedure, a lumpectomy sometimes has a therapeutic role also, especially if no cancer cells are present in the margin area. A partial mastectomy often is followed by radiation and hormonal therapy to destroy any remaining cancer cells and to prevent recurrence of the cancer.

MASTECTOMY. Total mastectomy involves the removal of the entire breast, as well as some of the lymph nodes from underneath the arm. This operation is performed while the patient is under some form of anesthesia. You will probably meet with the anesthesiologist before your operation to discuss the type of anesthesia that you will have and its potential side effects.

Talk with your physician and any friends who have experienced it ahead of time to learn as much as you can about this operation and what you can expect in terms of your recovery afterward. Not only can this procedure leave you somewhat physically exhausted, but it may present you with some emotional issues, as well. Your family, friends, hospital social worker, or other counselor may be able to help you through this time.

RADIATION. Radiation therapy may be used after mastectomy to get rid of remaining cancer cells. It works by aiming cell-destroying radioactive particles at a small area. Radiation is also very effective in managing pain related to the spread (metastasis) of the cancer to the bones. If you are unsure whether you should undergo radiation therapy, ask your primary care physician for a referral to a *radiation oncologist*—a cancer specialist who has expertise in this form of treatment.

If you decide to proceed with this therapy, you will be given a small dose of radiation every day over several weeks. Side effects of radiation therapy may include swelling, redness, darkened pigmentation, and red spiderlike veins in the treated area. Often, patients also experience fatigue following their treatments.

HORMONAL THERAPY. Most breast tumors in older women are responsive to hormonal therapy. In fact, hormone therapy with a drug called tamoxifen, an oral drug that has been used to treat breast cancer since the 1970s, is most effective in patients who are over age 50. As we mentioned at the beginning of this chapter, treatment with tamoxifen has been found to decrease the risk of developing breast cancer in the other, unaffected breast. Like estrogen, tamoxifen also protects against osteoporosis. If your oncologist recommends that you take tamoxifen, you may take it for many years. If you are postmenopausal, it can decrease your risk of cancer relapse by approximately 30%.

This agent is well tolerated in most older women, although some experience mild hot flashes, and there may be a small associated risk of possibly developing endometrial cancer. Also, while you are taking this drug, you should see your ophthalmologist regularly because some patients have experienced retinal problems after taking tamoxifen for long periods of time.

HER-2/neu is a monoclonal antibody that in 1998 was approved for treating metastatic breast cancer. It may be very effective in 20–30% of breast cancers that have increased levels of this protein.

Megestrol is another form of hormonal therapy. Although it may be effective, it can cause some retention of fluid and ankle swelling.

CHEMOTHERAPY. This form of therapy involves the use of single drugs or combinations of drugs to treat large tumors or advanced breast cancer. Chemotherapy may also be administered when hormonal therapy is not effective, and it's sometimes used to reduce a person's risk of breast cancer recurrence. Common chemotherapy drugs include cyclophosphamide, methotrexate, 5-fluorouracil, doxorubicin, and mitoxantrone. Each of these drugs has associated benefits and side effects, so talk with your doctor about his or her recommendations; get a second opinion, if you wish, from an oncologist; and carefully weigh the pros and cons of each drug before making your decision.

Follow-up Care

Long-term care of older women with breast cancer involves routine visits to the primary care doctor, usually every 3 months for the first 18 months, then every 4–6 months. At these follow-up appointments, your doctor will give you a physical exam and will check routine blood tests. Be sure to tell your doctor if you experience *any* new symptoms, including urinary incontinence, back pain, or low energy.

If you've had a lumpectomy, you'll need to have a mammogram of both breasts every year. (Some doctors advise their patients who have had breast cancer to have these exams every six months initially.) If you've had a mastectomy, your doctor will probably advise you to have a mammogram of the remaining breast every year.

Other Problems That May Occur

Breast Pain

There are many causes of breast discomfort, and fortunately many of them are benign.

BREAST PAIN DUE TO HORMONES. Hormonal variations that occur with the menstrual cycle can cause slight breast pain in younger women. After menopause, this side effect of menstruation generally disappears unless a woman is taking estrogen, in which case her body may believe that she is still premenopausal, and this cyclic breast discomfort may continue. If your physician determines that your breast pain is related to hormones, he or she may recommend a low-fat diet and perhaps medication.

BREAST PAIN CAUSED BY TRAUMA. Occasionally, women develop breast discomfort after they have bumped into something, had a mammogram, or had a breast biopsy. This type of breast pain is usually short-lived. If it persists, see your doctor for further evaluation and advice.

DUCT ECTASIA. This disease occurs in older women and affects the ducts that are located below the areola. In addition to a burning sensation, swelling, and itching, there may be a discharge from the nipple. If you experience this constellation of symptoms, your doctor will probably have you undergo a biopsy of the area. Duct ectasia can be treated by removing the affected ducts.

Cysts

Cysts are less common in people over age 60 than they are in younger people. Fibrocystic breast disease, in which the breasts are marked by fibrous tissue, as well as cysts, rarely occurs in women after menopause.

Paget's Disease of the Breast

Paget's disease of the breast is a form of breast cancer that may begin as a rash that affects the nipple and then spreads outward to the skin of the breast. The underlying cancer looks like a pimple or skin disease but is actually cancerous. So any rash, pimple, or sore on the breast or nipple should not be ignored, but should be evaluated promptly by your doctor.

CHAPTER 11
YOUR URINARY SYSTEM

What is man, when you come to think upon him,
but a minutely set, ingenious machine for turning with infinite
artfulness, the red wine of Shiraz into urine?

Isak Dinesen [Karen Blixen] (1885–1962)

Mr. Smith is an independent 83-year-old man who lives at home with his wife. About 11 years ago, he had surgery for the removal of his prostate because of cancer. Over the next 10 years, he lived with worsening urinary incontinence.

Incontinence proved to be a powerful force over Mr. Smith's life: It brought social isolation because he was embarrassed about potentially leaking urine in public, and his wife was afraid that their friends would notice that his pants were wet or that he smelled of urine. He gave up his weekly golf game with his favorite foursome of over seven years. This shutting down of outside social contacts caused his wife, who had always been very socially engaged, to become severely depressed.

In an attempt to gain some control over his condition, Mr. Smith began to drink less fluid so that he would not need to urinate as often. Although his doctors told him not to reduce his fluid intake because it could lead to dehydration, Mr. Smith persisted. On one occasion, he became so weak that he fell and could not get up again. His wife, a petite woman who could not lift him up off the floor, called 911. When the rescue squad arrived, they told Mrs. Smith that her husband needed to be taken to the hospital. There, he was given intravenous fluids because he was so dehydrated.

Not long after that, Mr. Smith went to a urologist who specializes in the treatment of incontinence. He received a urinary sphincter, a device that was inserted into his scrotum to allow him better control over his urination. Now, when he feels the urge to urinate, he simply presses the device to prevent leakage.

This solution markedly improved the couple's social life and restored for both of them the freedom that they had previously enjoyed.

The biggest hurdles to overcome in addressing urinary problems—whether they are your own or those of your loved ones—are the misconceptions about the effect of aging on the urinary tract. Aggressive marketing of products that keep your clothes dry (and your dignity intact) when you experience urinary incontinence would lead you to believe that we are all destined to end our lives as we started them—in diapers.

It is true that about 10 million Americans have some degree of urinary incontinence, but many of these people, particularly the elderly, are suffering in silence. They are too embarrassed to speak with a doctor about the problem, and they are not aware that many causes of incontinence are treatable with behavioral techniques, medication, and surgery. In fact, less than half of those experiencing incontinence consult their physician about the problem!

In this chapter, we hope to change your perceptions about urinary incontinence and to encourage you to seek treatment from a physician—not endure it as part of getting old. We also address other problems that sometimes arise because of the changes in the urinary tract that occur in later life, including dehydration; *nocturia,* the interruption of sleep by the need to urinate; and urinary tract infections.

How Your Urinary System Changes as You Age

As with many organs, the functional effectiveness and strength of those that compose the urinary tract may decline with normal aging. The urinary organs (see Figure 11.1) include the *urethra,* which connects the bladder to the outside of the body; the *bladder,* which holds urine before it is excreted; the *ureters,* which connect the kidneys to the bladder; and the *kidneys,* which filter impurities from the blood.

Organ Changes

The kidneys tend to decrease slightly in size and weight during the later years, as does the effective surface that serves to filter urine. Blood flow through the kidneys may also progressively decrease slightly. The kidneys usually

Figure 11.1 *The Anatomy of the Urinary Tract*

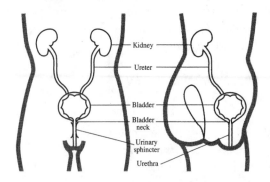

Woman

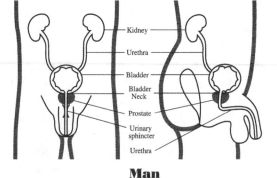

Man

become more susceptible to any kind of injury or insult with advancing age. This is due to the slight to moderate age-related reduction in kidney function and reserve capacity that occurs in most older persons. As a result of this decline, the dosage of certain medications that are excreted by the kidneys needs to be modified carefully and adjusted to a lower dose range and perhaps also a longer interdose interval. Such adjustments may help to avoid both further damage to the kidneys and any unnecessary side effects due to accumulation of the drug to excessive levels in the bloodstream.

The urinary bladder may also undergo changes in the bladder wall and in its emptying ability, as part of the natural decline in function with age. Our colleague Neil Resnick explains that after one empties one's bladder, the size of the empty bladder increases slightly, while the rapidity of emptying may decrease with age in both sexes. There may also be a decrease in the maximal voiding muscle contraction in women. In addition, we know from clinical experience, as well as from scientific studies that provide specific data, that the bladder's holding capacity and our ability to postpone urination tend to decline to some degree with age in both men and women.

Thirst and Water Balance

Those of us who care for older patients have long noted—and scientific studies have proven—that the sense of thirst in our patients declines with aging. Younger people can count on their sense of thirst to help them take in the amount of fluid they need to properly regulate the body's balance of sodium and water. When you're older, however, you may not feel thirsty when you should. In addition, when the aging body is deprived of water, its capacity to respond to the situation by conserving fluid and concentrating the urine is impaired. Such a situation can become more complicated if you're sick from any kind of illness. It may even cause dehydration.

Problems That May Occur

Dehydration

Dehydration is the most common fluid disturbance in older people. This problem may be difficult for even experienced health care professionals to detect early, but when it goes untreated, it causes severe illness and can have grave results in as many as half of dehydrated patients.

There are many causes of increased fluid loss in older people:

- Fever and illness (such as diabetes, vomiting, diarrhea, or swallowing disorders)
- Medications (diuretics, laxatives, and stimulants such as methylphenidate)
- A warm environment
- Diminished hormonal compensation in response to a loss of fluids from the body
- Difficulty gaining access to fluids because of immobility

How can you tell whether you or your loved one is becoming dehydrated? Transient feelings of dizziness, "haziness in the head," or weakness that are associated with getting up from a lying down or sitting position may be a sign of low blood pressure, which can occur with dehydration. Dryness of the mucous membranes is another feature. In those individuals who are taking a fluid pill to control their blood pressure, this can happen if the intake of oral fluids has not kept up with the fluid loss.

Encouraging oral fluid intake (not just water), especially fluids with some salt (such as tomato juice), may help to prevent dehydration, especially during warm weather.

If you or someone you love becomes severely dehydrated, fluid can be replaced orally (by drinking water or electrolyte solutions) or intravenously in the hospital.

Some Symptoms of Urinary Disorders

Nocturia

Nocturia is the interruption of sleep by the need to urinate. This problem is especially common among older people, who tend to urinate more at night than during the daytime. Usually, nocturia is caused by too much urine output (because of normal age-related changes, the intake of too much fluid right before bedtime, or health conditions such as congestive heart failure, which can lead to excess fluid), insomnia and other sleep disorders (see Chapter 6), or bladder dysfunction.

When you go to see your doctor because of a problem with nocturia, he or she will probably ask you how often you are experiencing this disruption of your sleep and will ask you about any other related problems that you may have, such as having to strain to urinate or feeling discomfort in the perineal area. He or she will probably ask you about all drugs that you may be taking (both prescription and nonprescription medicines) and will give you a full physical examination to identify any other medical problems that you may have. Then your doctor may take some blood and urine samples.

Your physician will probably recommend that you reduce your consumption of coffee, tea, and alcohol, and that you don't drink fluids shortly before you go to bed at night. He or she may also review the medications that you are taking and may prescribe for you a smaller dose of some drugs or recommend that you take certain medications (such as diuretics) at earlier times in the day.

Dysuria

Dysuria is painful urination. Just as with nocturia, if you experience this symptom, your physician will ask you several questions about the pattern of your discomfort and then will perform a physical examination. He or she will probably also do some laboratory tests, including a urinalysis to check for blood or for signs of bladder infection.

Hematuria

Hematuria (blood in the urine) has three main causes: bladder infection, kidney stones, or trauma; or very rarely, tumors.

Urinary Frequency

If you find that you're urinating more than six or seven times every day, you may be suffering from urinary frequency. There are many causes of this problem, including overflow incontinence (described later in this chapter), too much urine production because of a condition such as diabetes, consumption of a lot of fluids (which might be fine), or other health issues such as a bladder tumor (benign or malignant), bladder infection, or depression.

Urinary Urgency

Urinary urgency is an inability to keep from urinating once the urge to urinate is felt. Along with a physical examination and urinalysis, your physician will ask you several questions about the pattern and frequency of your urinary urgency. Do you experience this problem most often at night or during the day? Is it a constant problem or one that comes and goes?

Urinary Tract Infections

One evening, when Mr. and Mrs. Linden were getting dressed to go out for dinner, Mrs. Linden became very lethargic and couldn't stand up on her own. She told her husband that she felt very weak and didn't have the energy to go out with their friends to the restaurant. Mr. Linden called the doctor, who said that Mrs. Linden should rest and call him in the morning if she continued to feel so lethargic. That night, she became weaker and weaker.

In the morning, Mr. Linden called the doctor again. The doctor said that he should bring his wife into the doctor's office that day. They went and were sent home because the doctor said that he couldn't find anything wrong with Mrs. Linden "other than getting older."

Later that evening, Mrs. Linden was unable to walk on her own. Again, Mr. Linden called the doctor, who said that she should come back the following day for more tests. Mr. Linden became very fearful during the night when his wife seemed somewhat confused, and he called the emergency medical service, which transported Mrs. Linden to the hospital. After extensive tests, the resident said that she had a urinary tract infection. Mrs. Linden was given antibiotics intravenously for several days before being discharged from the hospital.

Mrs. Linden continued to be lethargic over the next few weeks. She returned to the doctor and was told that a dipstick test for a urinary infection was negative.

Mrs. Linden became progressively more lethargic and got out of bed less and less. Often, she spent the entire day in her pajamas resting in bed. She returned to her doctor, who performed a full urinalysis. It showed that Mrs. Linden still had a urinary tract infection.

When Mrs. Linden was found to have another urinary infection, she was prescribed an antibiotic at a low dose on a long-term basis to prevent the recurrence of future urinary tract infections. She felt much improved after that.

Age-related changes in the body can predispose both men and women to urinary tract infections (UTIs). In fact, UTIs are the most common bacterial infections among older people. UTIs result from overgrowth of bacteria in all or part of the urinary tract, from the urethra (*urethritis*) to the kidneys (*pyelonephritis*). Infection involving the bladder is called *cystitis.*

The most common symptom of a UTI is discomfort during urination. Other symptoms may include fever, abdominal pain, and back pain. Confusion, loss of appetite, and listlessness or lethargy are other symptoms.

Women of all ages are more susceptible to UTIs than are men, partly because of the short length of the female urethra, which allows bacteria to spread easily from the anus into the urinary tract. In addition, certain actions, such as wearing tight pants, riding a bike, using a douche, and having sexual intercourse, can promote the spread of bacteria and cause UTIs. Thus, for some older women, the incidence of what's commonly called "honeymoon cystitis" may decline as their level of sexual activity decreases. Sometimes, voiding soon after sexual intercourse may help to reduce the incidence of UTIs.

The estrogen deficiency in some postmenopausal women can cause conditions that predispose them to UTIs. These conditions include the loss of vaginal and uterine muscle tone, which in certain cases may result in partial extrusion, or prolapse. Estrogen deficiency also results in decreased resistance of the mucous membranes of the urinary tract to invading bacteria that cause infections.

As men age, their risk of experiencing a UTI also increases. UTIs in men may be caused by both benign enlargement of the prostate and prostate cancer.

In both men and women, neurological disorders such as dystonic bladder or autonomic neuropathy and diabetes can also predispose to UTIs. Older people who are hospitalized or living in nursing homes have an increased chance of having a UTI if they have an indwelling catheter in the bladder.

To diagnose a UTI, a urinalysis is often performed. Doctors also commonly perform blood tests to look for *bacteremia,* the presence of bacteria in the blood. The goal for treating UTIs is to suppress the bacteria causing the infection and to prevent chronic infection and scarring. Usually, a short course of an oral antibiotic for 4 days will be effective. If the infection persists, then a second course of antibiotics for a longer period (10 days) will probably be effective.

If the infection still remains, then further evaluation and testing are warranted. Sometimes, when two or more UTIs recur within a short period of time (a few months), then chronic UTI prevention with a low dose of an oral antibiotic pill two or three times per week (as was prescribed for Mrs. Linden) might be effective in preventing further recurrences.

Urinary Incontinence

Urinary incontinence, the involuntary leak or loss of urine, affects 10 million Americans, most of whom are older. According to our colleagues Neil Resnick and Catherine Dubeau, many of these people could be successfully treated by a physician if they would simply seek treatment and follow the doctor's instructions. Too many people assume that incontinence is a *normal* part of aging rather than an abnormality that can be corrected, and they use one of the many absorbent products on the market as a way to live with the problem. Also, some people are just too embarrassed to discuss it with anyone.

If your loved one is or will be in a nursing home, you should be assertive in finding out how the medical staff addresses and treats incontinence in their patients. At least half of all nursing home residents are incontinent, and some of them needlessly so. Incontinence does not and should not have to be a part of nursing home life.

Transient versus Established Incontinence

TRANSIENT INCONTINENCE. Several circumstances can set the stage for an aging person to develop urinary incontinence:

- Disease or other medical condition outside the urinary tract—for example, bladder infection, delirium, endocrine or metabolic disorders that cause increased urine production, stool impaction, or severe depression
- Restricted mobility, such as that caused by poor eyesight or Parkinson's disease
- Atrophic urethritis or vaginitis in older women, which can be treated with estrogen therapy
- Medications for other conditions, such as sedatives, antihistamines, antidepressants, and antispasmodics; drugs such as narcotics and calcium channel blockers, which can interfere with the bladder's ability to contract; alcohol, diuretics, and psychotropic drugs (such as haloperidol), which can affect one's mobility and cause confusion, thereby contributing to incontinence

We call incontinence that is caused by any of these circumstances *transient incontinence,* which means there's a very good chance that once the problem behind the incontinence is addressed by a clinician, the incontinence problem will be promptly resolved. Thus, the first step we take in evaluating a patient who comes to us concerned about incontinence is determining whether the incontinence is transient or established.

ESTABLISHED INCONTINENCE. Incontinence that cannot be resolved through the treatment of its underlying cause is considered to be "established." There are several types of established incontinence, and a person may experience more than one type at a time (this is called mixed incontinence).

Urge Incontinence

Urge incontinence, the most common type of incontinence in older persons, is caused by increased bladder muscle contraction. It is often characterized by a sudden urge to urinate and not enough time to reach the toilet. The causes of urge incontinence may include damage to the central nervous system due to a stroke, Alzheimer's disease, or Parkinson's disease, or a problem in the urinary tract, such as a bladder tumor, which decreases the brain's ability to control the bladder.

Stress Incontinence

Stress incontinence is the second most common type of incontinence in older women. (It only occurs in some men who have had surgical removal of the prostate or some types of radiation therapy.) Its hallmark is leakage during physical activities such as lifting, sneezing, coughing, laughing, or exercise. The most common causes of stress incontinence are childbirth (during which the ring of muscle around the urethra is stretched) and the hormonal changes that follow menopause.

Overflow Incontinence

Men with enlarged prostates often experience *overflow incontinence*. Because of the prostate's increased size, the urethra may be blocked, causing incomplete emptying of the bladder and dribbling of urine. If left untreated, this long-term retention of urine can dilate and damage the upper urinary tract. Women also can have this problem if they have bladder tumors or bladder outlet obstruction.

Prostate Problems

The *prostate* is a gland located at the base of the male *urethra* (the channel that carries urine away from the bladder). It produces an alkaline substance that is the major component of ejaculatory fluid. In young men, this gland is about as large as a golf ball. As men get older, the prostate usually gets bigger. As a result, the bladder wall grows thicker, and the bladder neck can become obstructed, leading to a diseased prostate (prostatism).

Acute prostatitis is acute inflammation of the prostate, sometimes accompanied by a bacterial infection that can make it difficult or painful to urinate. *Chronic prostatitis* is a recurring prostate infection.

Benign prostatic hypertrophy (BPH) is another term for an enlarged prostate. This occurs in more than half of men in their 60s. BPH may make it difficult to urinate and may lead to dribbling after urination. Some men also experience an urge to urinate often, especially at night.

Treatment includes:

1. *Watchful waiting* is by far the most common option. If you choose to go this route, we recommend that you try to relax during urination, avoid caffeine, avoid drinking anything at bedtime, and talk with your doctor about reducing the dosage or discontinuing your use of certain drugs such as diuretics.

2. *Medical treatment* may include (a) alpha-adrenergic blockers (such as prazosin [Minipress], terazosin [Hytrin], and doxazosin [Cardura]), which work by relaxing the *urinary sphincter* (the muscle that controls the flow of urine); or (b) 5α-reductase inhibitors (e.g., finasteride [Proscar]), which can shrink the prostate and provide modest improvement of symptoms over the course of several months.

3. *Surgery* may involve *transurethral resection (removal) of the prostate (TURP)*. In this procedure, the prostate is removed by means of a device called a *cystoscope,* which is passed through the urethra. This procedure generally is performed in a hospital while the patient is under spinal anesthesia. Most patients who undergo TURP experience relief from symptoms of BPH. Other surgical options include (a) prostate incision (for men who have symptoms of BPH but have a small prostate gland), which can be as effective as TURP and can be performed while the patient is under local anesthesia; (b) urethral stents, which can be effective for frail men who should not undergo general anesthesia or who suffer from urinary retention; or (c) cryotherapy, which may be administered on an outpatient basis—an area of active study, about which more information will become available in the near future.

Prostate cancer is discussed in Chapter 5.

Treatment of Incontinence

There are three main ways of addressing the problem of incontinence: with behavioral techniques, medication, and surgery. Sometimes, a combination of these therapies is recommended. Next, we look at each of these forms of treatment.

Behavioral Techniques. Behavioral techniques for treating incontinence are the least risky and can be quite effective, especially if you are motivated and receive proper training and support from your physician. There are several kinds of behavioral techniques:

1. *Bladder training:* In a bladder training program, which may take several months, you will be taught to resist the urge to urinate and instead to urinate according to a set schedule.
2. *Habit training*: A habit training (or timed voiding) program differs from a bladder training program, in that the patient is not encouraged to resist urinating. You will be instructed, however, to urinate according to a planned schedule.
3. *Prompted voiding:* A prompted voiding program is most often used for nursing home patients who are incontinent. The program involves monitoring the person for dryness, reminding him or her to urinate regularly, and praising him or her for staying dry and using the toilet.
4. *Pelvic muscle (Kegel) exercises:* Kegel exercises strengthen the periurethral and pelvic muscles to give you better urinary control. You will be taught how to contract the muscles and will perform the exercises 30 to 80 times a day for at least 6 weeks. Kegel exercises can be combined with other therapies. Behavioral therapy has been shown to be equally as effective as medication in reducing urinary incontinence.

Dave, a 71-year-old retired medical worker, was suffering from an enlarged prostate that was causing him to have nocturia. Wishing to avoid surgery or the use of medication, he began experimenting at home to try to ensure that as much urine as possible was voided before he went to bed at night. In addition to cutting back on his evening intake of fluids, Dave began to apply external pressure to his lower abdomen, compressing the bladder with both hands, while urinating sitting down each night.

His initial results were slightly disappointing. Dale was able to reduce the number of times he woke up at night, but he was still getting up to go to the bathroom a few times each night. He persevered, however, and learned how to relax his abdominal muscles to the point where he could press his fingers into his lower abdomen far enough to push his bladder until it did empty nearly completely.

Dave's results since then have been impressive. He has been able to go for weeks before having a single episode of awaking at night, and the number of times he is awakened to urinate during these rare occasions has decreased to a maximum of one.

Before trying such an experiment on your own, please speak with your health care provider. He or she can assess your problem and explain any possible risks and can show you how to use your hands to press on your lower abdomen to enable you to more completely empty your bladder.

Medication. Medication can be used to treat an infection that may be an indirect cause of urinary incontinence. Medication can also help to stop abnormal bladder contractions or help to tighten the bladder sphincter. Anticholinergic agents such as propantheline may help with overcontraction of the bladder. Alpha-adrenergic drugs, such as phenylpropanolamine, are used to treat stress incontinence because of their effects on the urethral sphincter. Estrogen therapy may also be used to improve the tone of the urethral tissue. Combination muscle relaxant/anticholinergic agents (such as oxybutynin, dicyclomine, toterodine, and hyoscyamine) may also be helpful.

Surgery. If behavioral techniques and medication fail to improve your urinary incontinence, your doctor may recommend other options, including surgery. Surgical procedures may be used to return the bladder neck to its proper position in certain women with stress incontinence, to remove a urethral blockage, or to replace or provide support for very weak pelvic floor muscles.

Kidney Problems

Sometimes kidney function can become impaired suddenly (*acute renal insufficiency*) or progressively (*chronic renal insufficiency*). Causes of acute renal failure include a large drop in blood pressure with insufficient blood flow to the kidneys; kidney stones; blood clots in the kidney circulation; drug toxicity; and infection or inflammatory conditions of the kidneys. In many cases the kidney failure will reverse with treatment if the injury was not severe. However, if the injury was severe, there may be permanent damage, resulting in chronic renal insufficiency, which may range from mild to severe. Another common cause of chronic renal insufficiency is diabetes mellitus (see Chapter 14). When chronic renal insufficiency progresses to severe impairment, it is called *chronic renal failure.*

Options for treating chronic renal failure may include dialysis or kidney transplantation. In the year 2000, it is estimated that about 60% of the dialysis patients in the United States are over age 65. The preferred method of dialysis in older persons is in-hospital hemodialysis. *Hemodialysis* is a method whereby the blood is cleared of the body's metabolic waste products and toxins artificially. The process takes about 4 to 5 hours and is usually done 3 to 4 times per week. In *peritoneal dialysis,* the body is rid of waste products by exchange of fluid in the abdominal cavity (also called the peritoneal cavity).

As with any chronic illness, the management of chronic renal failure and hemodialysis is complex. However, many people with this condition are still able to lead active lives. If you have chronic renal failure, it is important to discuss these issues with your doctor and to learn as much as possible about the management of kidney disease. For more information, contact the American Kidney Foundation at 1-800-622-9010, or the National Institute of Diabetes and Digestive and Kidney Diseases Internet site at http://www. niddk.nih.gov.

CHAPTER 12

YOUR RESPIRATORY SYSTEM

This Being of mine, whatever it really is, consists of a little flesh,
a little breath, and the part which governs.

Marcus Aurelius (121–180)

How Your Lungs Change as You Age

These muscles have a voluntary and an involuntary movement . . . the lung
opens like a pair of bellows, draws in the air in order to fill the space.

Leonardo da Vinci (1452–1519)

Do viral respiratory infections seem to take the wind out of your sails more quickly and more dramatically than they did when you were younger? Have you or your loved one ever stayed in a hospital to recover from one ailment, only to come down with another illness, such as pneumonia? Part of the reason that we may encounter these common problems is that aging itself can influence somewhat the function of our lungs and may in some cases slightly impair their ability to fend off infections.

This is usually what happens: Sometime after age 55, the muscles that help us to inhale and exhale, including the diaphragm, may begin to show a slight decline in strength. At the same time, our chest wall—composed of the ribs, the muscles between the ribs, and the connective tissue—becomes stiffer. These changes may slightly reduce our total lung capacity, which means that we may move a bit less air than we used to with each breath. Thus, even if we are reasonably healthy in other respects, these mild changes could mean that in some circumstances, we may respond less well to certain respiratory illnesses that come our way.

More subtle changes may occur in our respiratory system, too. For example, the *cilia,* tiny hairs that line our lungs, may not be as effective in keeping our airways clear of secretions as they formerly did, and we may not be able to cough as vigorously or to bring up phlegm as well as we did when we were younger. Sometimes, the use of certain medications such as sedatives or the intake of alcohol may further weaken the cough reflex, also.

Another reason why the ability to fight respiratory infections may decline slightly for some of us is because our lungs may produce somewhat less secretions than they once did, as is the case for the other organs in the body, and the reduced secretions in turn mean a less effective protective barrier against invasion by germs. In certain individuals, a lifetime of repeated insults to our lungs by cigarette smoking, exposure to smoke, dust and pollution in the environment, or illnesses that inflame our lungs may begin to take their cumulative toll. Finally, if we have heart disease, our respiratory function could be compromised, as well. Conversely, chronic changes that some of us may have in our airways increase our risk of death from heart disease (as well as our risk of developing lung cancer).

In this chapter, we discuss the important things that you can do to slow down your loss of lung capacity, strengthen your "functional reserves," and resist respiratory illnesses.

Keeping Your Lungs Healthy

EXERCISE. Regular exercise might not completely reverse all the effects of aging on your lungs or the lung muscles, but it can potentially restore and strengthen them somewhat, and possibly also somewhat slow down their progressive decline. It can also help your body cope better with certain illnesses. If you find that you're short of breath because of asthma or emphysema, for instance, doing exercises to strengthen your diaphragm can lessen the fatigue that is caused by insufficient airflow. Talk with your doctor about the types of activities that are most appropriate for your particular situation.

HAVE FLU SHOTS REGULARLY. Every autumn, you should get a flu shot to prevent infection with the influenza virus (the "flu"). It's especially important to be immunized if you are over age 65 or if you have a chronic illness such as congestive heart failure, kidney disease, anemia, or chronic lung disease. The vaccine is about 70% effective.

If you have an allergy to eggs, let your doctor know because you may not be able to take the flu vaccine, which is cultured in an egg medium. Other than that precaution, there are few risks associated with this vaccination, and it's usually quite effective. Some people may be concerned that the immunization itself may produce illness, but in truth, taking the vaccine will not cause you to get the flu or any other type of viral infection.

Finally, if you're reading this book in the wintertime and you realize that you forgot to get your flu shot last fall, it's still not too late to roll up your sleeve. You can be vaccinated safely and effectively at any time during the winter flu season.

MAKE SURE THAT YOU'VE RECEIVED THE PNEUMOCOCCAL VACCINE. A type of bacteria called *Streptococcus pneumoniae* is responsible for more than 80% of all cases of pneumonia that are caused by bacteria. A very effective vaccine is available to prevent infection with this type of bacteria, and if you are over age 65, you should receive it—especially if you have any other respiratory problems. You only need to get the vaccine every 6–10 years.

In some states (for example, New Jersey, Delaware, and South Dakota), the state law mandates that all residents of long-term health facilities and adult day care centers who are over age 65 should receive this vaccine.

TAKE OTHER STEPS TO PREVENT INFECTIONS. Although the flu shot is often effective, some people may still become ill, albeit with usually a milder case of the flu, even after being effectively immunized. Thus, it's important to wash your hands well and often, especially after you've had contact with people who are ill. Also, during the winter months, try to avoid crowded, poorly ventilated areas.

STOP SMOKING, DEFINITELY. Smoking can lead to all kinds of respiratory problems because it literally destroys our lungs' reserve capacity. Yet research has shown that whenever a person stops smoking, his or her lung function can begin to improve and the rate of decline in lung capacity can slow down and return toward normal.

Of course, quitting this habit is easier said than done. However, it is the single most important thing that a smoker can do to improve his or her health and the health of others. We suggest that you seriously choose a date in the near future to stop smoking, then make a sincere commitment to do so with the support of your physician or other health care worker, your family, friends, and possibly an organized smoking-cessation program. Many practice groups and clinics offer smoking-cessation programs (see also Chapter 2). You may wish to talk with your doctor about nicotine replacement therapy to help you manage the symptoms of cigarette withdrawal. Sometimes, physicians may prescribe other medicines for the same purpose.

Finally, if you're struggling to stop smoking, remember that this decision is best not only for your health but also for the health of those around you, including your children and grandchildren. Even passive exposure to cigarette smoke can affect children's lungs and have severely negative long-term consequences.

EAT WELL. Staying well nourished is an important way to keep your respiratory muscles strong and your immune system in good shape so that you can fight off pulmonary infections. Staying well hydrated is essential, too, because this enables you to maintain adequate production of secretions.

If your respiratory system is not functioning well and you're finding that you're fatigued because of the hard work of breathing, it might be good for you to get some help with food preparation and to rest just before meals so that you won't be too tired to eat. Also, try eating several small, nutritious meals every day.

Problems That May Occur

If you do develop a respiratory infection or illness, your primary care physician may oversee your treatment, or he or she may refer you to another doctor called a *pulmonary specialist,* who has training in disorders of the lung and chest. A pulmonary specialist can help you to manage the respiratory problems that we describe next.

Bronchitis

As we have just mentioned, our lungs may become more susceptible to certain respiratory infections and to developing complications from them. Bronchitis is one such illness. This condition occurs when the bronchial tubes (the two branches of the trachea that lead to the lungs) become infected and inflamed.

Acute Bronchitis

Acute bronchitis involves a cough that is *productive*—that is, there is a lot of phlegm. This problem, which may occur as a complication of the flu (see pp. 178–179), is usually short lived.

Chronic Bronchitis

If you have a productive cough that lasts day after day for at least three months of the year, and you develop this long-lasting cough year after year, you may have chronic bronchitis. Other symptoms include wheezing and shortness of breath. Doctors may treat bronchitis with drugs called steroids, as well as with devices called *bronchodilators,* which are used to clear the airways.

Pneumonia

Pneumonia is the fourth leading cause of death in older people. When autopsies are performed, this very common bacterial or viral infection of the lung is found in one fourth to one half of older patients. One's risk of contracting this infection is especially high during hospitalization or during stays in long-term care facilities.

What exactly is pneumonia? It's a lung disease brought about by an inflammatory reaction to infestation by various microorganisms. Some of the culprit microbes that you may be familiar with include influenza, or the "flu" virus, and strep and staph bacteria. Many types of bacteria that cause pneumonia (such as *Legionella,* the bacteria that causes "Legionnaires' disease") thrive in water; these pathogens sometimes can be spread through air conditioners and shower heads.

Symptoms. If you have pneumonia, you may have a fever or cough, feel weak, or have uncomfortable breathing.

Diagnosis. If your doctor suspects that you may have pneumonia, he or she will probably have you get a chest x-ray to look for signs of changes consistent with pneumonia. Your physician will also probably try to determine which organism caused your infection because your treatment options may depend on the cause of your illness.

Treatment. Fortunately, there are many effective medicines (antibiotics) to treat pneumonia. Some of the most common ones that are currently prescribed for older people are levofloxacin and amoxicillin. Other, equally effective medicines may also be prescribed.

Bill and Susan Johnson were at the annual accountants' convention that they had attended for many years. Bill, age 83, had experienced a mild cough prior to going but made the trip with little difficulty. Once at the convention, Bill became weak and developed a mild fever. When they were ready to go to one of the evening dinners, Bill fell to the floor, and Susan, age 79, couldn't get him up. After she received help in lifting her husband off the floor, she consulted a doctor, who recommended that Bill see his physician upon returning home.

Bill's physician hospitalized him immediately with a diagnosis of viral pneumonia. After several days of hospitalization, Bill's doctor told the family that his condition was progressively worsening, his lungs were failing to clear, and the prognosis did not look good.

Bill's daughter Elaine consulted a friend and colleague who was a geriatrician with training as an infectious-disease specialist. After listening to the array of symptoms and Bill's lack of improvement, the infectious-disease expert recommended that the doctor test for Legionnaires' disease, a bacterial pneumonia that would require a different treatment than the one that Bill was then receiving. Based on the advice from the infectious-disease specialist, Bill's doctor ordered erythromycin and a sputum test. After several days on erythromycin, Bill's lungs slowly began to clear until he recovered completely. Six months later, the sputum sample came back with a positive result for Legionnaires' disease.

Influenza　*Influenza* is a perennial problem all over the world, and outbreaks continue to occur year after year because the virus frequently changes form into a variant form that most people have less resistance against. This virus tends to affect people over age 70 four times more often than it affects those who are younger than 40. Moreover, 9 out of 10 deaths from the flu occur in people who are over age 65.

There are two types of influenza to be aware of: influenza A and influenza B. The first type is the most common and the most serious; the second may also be serious in older people, although it is less so in younger people. The flu shot usually is effective against both types of viruses.

How does one contract the flu? This virus could be in the air around us. It may be in our nasal passages, or it may travel through the air in minute water droplets that can be aerosolized and spread when one sneezes or coughs. The contagious microorganism then may be inhaled by another person.

One of the reasons why the flu can be a more serious illness in older adults is that after about age 50, our immune system may become slightly less effective and can allow several complications of the flu, such as bronchitis and pneumonia, to occur more easily.

Symptoms. You probably know what the flu feels like already: a fever that usually comes on quickly, muscle aches and pains, headache, fatigue, and loss of appetite. Your eyes may hurt and may be watery. You may have a cough, a sore throat, and a clear, runny nose that may stay with you for two weeks or longer.

Diagnosis. Your physician may make the diagnosis based on symptoms alone, or he or she may take a nose or throat culture to determine whether you have the flu.

Treatment. In addition to bedrest, plenty of fluids, and pain and fever relief with aspirin or acetaminophen, two antiviral drugs—amantadine and rimantadine—may be given to treat influenza A. (These drugs usually are not as effective for treating the influenza B virus.) Amantadine and rimantadine are also sometimes prescribed for family members of persons who are ill with the flu or for people who appear to be getting the flu even though they've had a flu shot.

If your doctor prescribes amantadine for you, you should be aware that there are some common side effects associated with this drug, including dizziness and insomnia. There appear to be fewer side effects associated with rimantadine, so it is being prescribed more often, even though it is more expensive than amantadine.

A new drug that became available in 1999 is zanamivir. It has been reported to be effective for treating both influenza A and B, and has been well tolerated. You may wish to ask your doctor about it.

Tuberculosis

As is the case with the flu, tuberculosis is an infectious disease, but in this case, it is caused by a type of bacteria. Since the start of the twentieth century, deaths from tuberculosis infections have fallen dramatically. However, outbreaks do occur, and in the United States, the incidence of tuberculosis is on the rise again, partly because of drug-resistant strains of bacteria, acquired immune deficiency syndrome (AIDS), and demographic changes in the American population. Unfortunately, there is no effective vaccine available yet to prevent infection from this pathogen.

Many new cases of tuberculosis occur in people who are over age 65. This is because of a decline of immunity, a reactivation of a tuberculosis infection acquired decades before (this may happen when one's immune system is weakened), and an exposure to other people who have the infection in communities such as long-term care facilities.

Symptoms. Tuberculosis often appears in older people as other respiratory problems do: with a cough, weakness, a low-grade fever, and sometimes weight loss.

Diagnosis. To determine whether you have tuberculosis or another type of infection, your physician will have you get a chest x-ray, a skin test to detect the presence of antibody to tuberculosis bacteria, and a sputum culture for tuberculosis.

Treatment. Four different drugs are generally available to treat tuberculosis: isoniazid, rifampin, pyrazinamide, and ethambutol. Treatment usually lasts for approximately six months. If you are found to be infected with a strain of bacteria that may be resistant to certain drugs, you may be given one or more other drugs for one and a half years or longer. Finally, if you are diagnosed with tuberculosis, your family or household members may also be given isoniazid to protect them from infection.

Chronic Obstructive Pulmonary Disease

The condition known as *chronic obstructive pulmonary disease (COPD)* is not one type of illness, but rather represents a combination of respiratory conditions that can make breathing somewhat difficult. Emphysema, chronic bronchitis, asthma, and small airway disease all may be contributing factors to the development or progression of COPD.

COPD is a major health problem and 1 of the 10 leading causes of death in the United States. The incidence of COPD apparently is growing, especially among older people. In 8 out of 10 instances, COPD is attributable at least in part to cigarette smoking, which can cause the airways and lungs to become damaged. Other risk factors for COPD are:

- Passive exposure to cigarette smoke in childhood
- Male gender
- Exposure to air pollution and industrial fumes and dust (especially coal dust)
- Alpha$_1$-anti-trypsin deficiency, an inherited disorder that primarily affects whites of Northern European descent

Conditions That Can Lead to COPD

Emphysema. The word *emphysema* comes from the Greek word *emphysan,* which means "to inflate." This disease involves permanent, abnormal enlargement of the air spaces of the lung.

Chronic bronchitis. This productive cough lasts for three months or more, year after year. It is associated with sputum production and in most cases responds well to antibiotic treatment.

Asthma. This disease may be associated with inflammation and a narrowing of the airways under certain circumstances. It may cause shortness of breath, wheezing, tightness in the chest, and a cough that can be especially pronounced early in the morning and at night. Coughing, rather than wheezing, is often the predominant symptom of asthma in older adults. The number of cases of asthma in the United States is growing at an astounding rate, perhaps because of environmental factors. Although many people think of asthma as being an illness that affects children, it can also occur for the first time in older adults.

Education is the key to the treatment and prevention of asthmatic episodes. You should ask your doctor for instructions in the use of a peak expiratory flow meter, which can help you to monitor your breathing capacity and alert you to the need for extra medication or a visit to the clinic or emergency room.

Small airway disease. This disease leads to a condition called *bronchospasm,* or constriction of the lung's air passages by spasmodic contraction of the bronchial muscles.

Symptoms. Shortness of breath, cough, wheezing (especially when one is lying down), and increased amounts of sputum production are usually the common symptoms of COPD. Men more than women occasionally may experience severe shortness of breath. The cough may be minor or it may be severe enough to fracture a rib, especially in older women with osteoporosis. COPD also can cause chest tightness and discomfort that can feel like angina. During acute flare-ups, the impaired breathing can cause one to have difficulty concentrating and possibly even cause acute confusion. Some of the symptoms also may herald heart disease such as angina or congestive heart failure. A visit to the doctor's office may be helpful for appropriate diagnosis.

Diagnosis. Your physician will certainly do a physical exam and may perform a test called respiratory spirometry to see whether your airway is affected. He or she may check your arterial blood-gas levels to measure the amount of oxygen in your blood, and he or she may also have you get a chest x-ray to exclude other causes of your breathing difficulty.

Because your airflow obstruction may vary from day to day, once a diagnosis of COPD is made, your doctor may show you how to use a device called a "peak expiratory flow monitor" to assess its severity. You may sometimes need to use this device in the morning and evening.

Treatment. Treatment options include prevention, exercise, medication, oxygen therapy, and surgery.

PREVENTION. Indoor mold is a common cause of asthma throughout the world, and if you have this component of COPD, your doctor can advise you about ways to reduce your exposure to this allergen. Smoking cessation is another important preventive measure.

EXERCISE. While your airway is acutely compromised, as during a flare-up, your doctor may encourage you *not* to exercise or engage in other strenuous activities for that short time. However, in most instances, when you are back at your baseline, gentle exercise (walking, ascending stairs) is encouraged.

MEDICATIONS. Drug therapy for COPD may include:

- *Beta-agonists* such as albuterol, metaproterenol, salmeterol, and bitolterol. These drugs are generally inhaled. They work by opening up the constricted airways, thereby easing your ability to breathe.
- Corticosteroids to reduce inflammation in the lungs are especially helpful for patients who have bronchitis. They may be taken orally or inhaled via a device called a metered dose inhaler (MDI). There are several different types of MDIs, and you may need to use more than one. If so, make sure that you know how each one works and what it is for. The effect of this medication is

cumulative, so you may not notice any results for several weeks. Also, the common side effects from steroid therapy are skin thinning and bruising, voice strain, high blood pressure, reduced bone mineral density (which can increase your risk of a bone fracture), and sometimes glaucoma. Talk with your doctor about which side effects to watch for and what you can do to prevent or manage them.

- Other medications such as *ipratropium,* an inhaled drug that may slow the progression of the disease, and *theophylline,* a drug to improve breathing, are generally prescribed in addition to other drugs for COPD.

OXYGEN THERAPY. This type of therapy is sometimes recommended to supplement the oxygen from room air. At home, an oxygen concentrator device may be used for this purpose. This electrical machine works by drawing oxygen out of the air and sending it through a tube (called a *cannula*) that is inserted into the nose. These devices, which weigh about 35 pounds, are plugged into a wall outlet.

A portable version of this device is a tank that contains compressed or liquid oxygen. This device can be carried in a bag that has a shoulder strap. Some of these units may provide oxygen for up to eight hours.

Your physician can help you to determine which type of supplemental oxygen delivery device is best suited to your needs. Oxygen tanks vary in terms of cost, weight, portability, and need for maintenance and refilling. Remember that all of these units present a fire hazard, so you and your friends and family must refrain from smoking around them. For the same reason, be sure to store them away from sources of heat.

Oxygen therapy may also be required if you have COPD and you need to travel by plane. Most airlines are equipped to provide oxygen, but always contact the airline at least a day before your flight to make arrangements.

SURGERY. For severe cases of COPD, especially when emphysema is involved, surgery is sometimes advised. *Lung-volume reduction surgery,* a technique that has been used with some success, entails removal of diseased parts of the lungs to enhance the breathing capacity of the remaining healthy portions. Lung transplants are also sometimes recommended for very advanced cases of COPD. However, this operation is seldom performed for patients who are over age 60, due to reduced success rates.

Pulmonary Embolism

An *embolus* is any type of material that can block a blood vessel. In the lung, a blood clot—and much less commonly, tumor cells, fat, or even bone marrow—occasionally can obstruct a blood vessel and lead to compromised breathing. Blood clots that travel to the lungs generally begin their journey in a vein in the legs or the pelvis, although they may also get started in the heart or in other major veins in the body. One's risk of experiencing a pulmonary embolism is heightened by a prior history of blood clots in veins, the use of estrogen (in some persons), immobility, and various health problems, including obesity, hip fracture, certain cancers, and heart failure.

Symptoms. If you have a pulmonary embolism, you may have no symptoms, or you may experience shortness of breath, chest discomfort, leg pain or swelling, fainting, or anxiety. You may or may not develop a fever, rapid heart-beat, rapid breathing, cough, and shortness of breath.

Diagnosis. Your doctor will perform a physical exam and will have you get a chest x-ray, an electrocardiogram (ECG), and perhaps a lung scan. Sometimes a test called *pulmonary angiography* may also be used to view the blood vessels of the lung.

Treatment. If a pulmonary embolism is found, you may receive supplemental oxygen and pain medication for discomfort, as needed. Your doctor will also probably prescribe treatment with anticoagulant drugs such as heparin and warfarin. If blood-thinning medicines have been tried and are not effective, the placement of a small filter in the major vein to prevent another pulmonary embolism may be recommended.

The leading cause of cancer deaths in the United States is lung cancer, and more than half of people who die because of lung cancer are over age 65. Most of these deaths are caused by cigarette smoking. Although smoking for many years increases one's risk of developing this form of cancer, this risk can be reduced dramatically by giving up this addiction *at any age.*

Lung Cancer

There are four major types of lung cancer:

- *Squamous cell carcinoma* is the most common type of lung tumor in the elderly. Fortunately, these tumors grow more slowly than the others.
- *Adenocarcinoma,* the second most common type of lung cancer experienced by older adults, may have a less positive prognosis than squamous cell carcinoma.
- *Small-cell carcinoma* grows more quickly than other forms of lung cancer, but it responds to chemotherapy better than the other types do.
- *Large-cell carcinoma* is the least common form of lung cancer that affects the elderly.
- *Mesothelioma,* malignant tumors of the lining around the lungs, is usually associated with prior exposure to asbestos. Treatment includes surgery, local radiation, and chemotherapy.

Symptoms. It's easy to mistake symptoms of lung cancer for symptoms of other respiratory problems. Cough, shortness of breath, chest discomfort, weight loss, wheezing, fever, and sometimes hoarseness are among the common indications of this disease.

Diagnosis. A physician may use various types of scans (CT, MRI) to determine the diagnosis and spread of a person's lung cancer. Bronchoscopy is also frequently used.

Treatment. The treatment of lung cancer depends on the type of cancer, the extent of the disease, and other health problems that one may have. For most cases of lung cancer (other than small-cell lung cancer), surgical removal of part of the lung may be effective. Most people with these types of lung cancer can also benefit from chemotherapy and sometimes radiation treatment.

For small-cell lung cancer, treatment options depend on the extent of the cancer spread.

CHAPTER 13

YOUR GASTROINTESTINAL SYSTEM

A great step towards independence is a good-humored stomach.

Seneca (4 B.C.–65 A.D.)

I eat to live, to serve, and also, if it so happens, to enjoy,
but I do not eat for the sake of enjoyment.

Mahatma Gandhi (1869–1948)

Our gastrointestinal (GI) systems do not change dramatically as we age, but illnesses that are more common later in life (such as diabetes and heart failure), a buildup of fatty deposits in the blood vessels, and an increased use of medicines can all have a negative effect on the GI tract.

In this chapter, we talk about several things that you can do to keep your GI system in good working order. Then we review some of the GI problems that you may encounter as you grow older. We start at the top, with swallowing disorders, and continue down the foodpipe (esophagus) to the stomach, duodenum, small intestine, bowel, colon, and rectum, followed by the pancreas, liver, and gallbladder.

A little in the morning, nothing at noon and a light supper
doth make to live long.

Old Proverb

Keeping Your GI System in Good Shape

Diet

You've been hearing about what constitutes a healthy diet for years now: Eat more fiber (whole-grain breads and nuts), fruits, and vegetables, and cut back on red meats and processed foods (such as bacon and lunch meats) and fried, fatty foods. You should also limit your intake of alcohol because it can cause problems for your stomach, liver, and pancreas.

What you may not think of right away when you consider good nutrition is whether you are eating regular, well-balanced meals. If you live alone, you may not be interested in cooking just for yourself. Consider getting together with friends several times each week so that you can take turns cooking for each other. Even if you're just cooking for yourself, don't hesitate to prepare a large meal—you can eat part of it the day that you make it and refrigerate or freeze the rest (divided into meal-sized portions) to enjoy at another time.

If trips to the grocery store are becoming difficult for you, see whether your store will deliver food to you, or contact your local council on aging about programs such as Meals on Wheels, which will deliver nutritious meals right to your door.

Exercise   *Kegel exercises,* which involve squeezing the pelvic muscles together as if to hold back the flow of urine, can do wonders not just for urinary incontinence (see Chapter 11) but also for strengthening the abdomen because they lift and strengthen the entire pelvic-floor musculature. Other exercises, such as leg raises and sit-ups, are important for building muscle tone in the lower and mid abdomen.

Whatever form of exercise you choose to engage in, though, the most important thing is to simply get moving. A lack of physical activity can certainly affect your GI health. In fact, inactivity has been implicated as being an important risk factor for developing colon cancer. Studies also suggest that inactivity is a risk for diabetes. So the message is clear: Exercise.

Aspirin   Although blood-thinning (anticoagulant) drugs such as aspirin and warfarin (Coumadin) can help to prevent strokes and heart attacks, these medicines can also sometimes cause GI bleeding. If your physician has recommended that you take a blood thinner for your heart health, talk with him or her about whether you should take a new drug called a COX2 inhibitor (such as Celebrex) instead, because these medicines have a much lower associated incidence of GI bleeds. Regardless of which anticoagulant you may take, try to drink very little, if any, alcohol because it can irritate your stomach, and always see your physician if you notice that you have blood in your stool.

Stress Reduction   The feelings that we experience during times of transition (such as retirement) or loss (such as the death of a loved one) can have a direct effect on our GI system, and these emotions may exacerbate conditions such as irritable bowel syndrome. The lack of interest in eating that sometimes accompanies these emotional upsets doesn't help matters. If you are feeling low because you are going through a stressful period of transition, or because of other health problems, try talking to a friend first, then with a doctor, a member of the clergy, or another counselor who can help you to cope both emotionally and physically.

Screening   One of the most important things that we can do to keep our GI system healthy is to see our doctors regularly for checkups and to screen for potential problems. We should talk with our doctors about our diet, and every year, we should undergo a rectal examination and a stool test. Beginning at age 50, we should also undergo a diagnostic test called a *sigmoidoscopy* to screen for bowel cancer every three to five years.

If you do develop a GI problem, your primary care physician may refer you to a *gastroenterologist,* a specialist in disorders of the stomach and intestines, or a *hepatologist,* a specialist in disorders of the liver.

Swallowing and the Esophagus

How Swallowing Changes as You Age

Problems That You May Encounter

You never may have given swallowing much thought, but this process involves an extremely complex set of reflexes, muscles, and nerves. As you grow older, you lose lean muscle mass, which may make chewing and swallowing more difficult. It's also possible that the wavelike contraction of your foodpipe (esophagus), which moves food down to your stomach, may not function as well as it did when you were younger. There may be some discoordination in the contraction, which may result in pain or discomfort.

Esophageal Motility Disorders. Discoordinated movement of food down the esophagus is a very common problem among older people. This disorder may be caused by another health problem, such as diabetes or benign ulcers of the esophagus. Esophagitis, or inflammation of the esophagus, may cause difficulty swallowing and chest discomfort. If you have an esophageal motility disorder, your doctor may recommend that you lose weight, sleep with the head of your bed elevated, and try not to eat anything in the evening shortly before going to bed. Medicines such as antacids may also be helpful.

Heartburn (Gastroesophageal Reflux Disease, or GERD). As its name suggests, heartburn is a hot feeling caused by a reflux (backing up) of the gastric contents into the esophagus, and this problem also may cause chest discomfort. *Dyspepsia* (which comes from the Greek words *dys* and *pepsis,* which mean "bad digestion") is another term for this condition, which affects at least one third of older people, especially after age 50. Heartburn occurs most often after eating and laying down when you are full.

Milk and antacids such as cimetidine, ranitidine, famotodine, and nizatidine usually help, although antacids may cause side effects such as diarrhea, constipation, and malabsorption of other medicines. *Proton pump inhibitors* (which contain the drugs omeprazole and lansoprazole) can be very effective and well tolerated. They work by inhibiting gastric acid secretion. Some patients may be weaned off after eight weeks of therapy, but a longer duration of therapy is usually needed for patients with *erosive gastritis,* acute inflammation of the lining of the stomach, which is caused by a corrosive substance such as aspirin or an infectious organism or food poisoning.

Your doctor may refer you for a test called an "upper endoscopy" if you have both dyspepsia and other symptoms such as vomiting, anemia, weight loss, or bleeding.

- Raise the head of your bed.
- Eat smaller meals in the evening.
- If you are overweight, try to lose weight (this is extremely important).
- In the evening, do not drink caffeinated or alcoholic drinks or juice, and do not eat acid or tomato products or fatty foods (such as chocolate or pizza).
- Don't smoke.
- Talk with your doctor about changing the types or dosages of medications that may lead to heartburn; these include anticholinergics (such as dicyclomine, or Bentyl), calcium channel blockers and beta blockers for heart conditions, and sedatives such as benzodiazepines.
- Your physician may recommend antacid medications.

Difficulty Swallowing (*Dysphagia*) and Painful Swallowing (*Odynophagia*). Many conditions can lead to swallowing disorders, including strokes, Parkinson's disease, and thyroid disorders (both hypothyroidism and hyperthyroidism). The treatment of this problem usually depends on its cause. For instance, if the problem has been caused by food that is lodged in the esophagus, simply drinking a lot of liquids may help the food to go down. If the dysphagia worsens, surgical dilation of the esophagus may be necessary.

"Pill Esophagitis." Sometimes, when we take capsules or pills, especially if we take them while we are lying down, they can get lodged in our foodpipe, where they cause irritation and even ulcers. We may not even be aware that these medications have not "gone down" the esophagus until we find that it is painful to swallow. Common offending medicines include antibiotics, ferrous sulfate, nonsteroidal anti-inflammatory drugs (NSAIDS), and potassium chloride.

To prevent this from happening, be sure to chase medicines with lots of water, and, if possible, do not take medicines right before you go to bed at night because your body does not produce as much saliva while you are resting, and the motor activity of your foodpipe slows down while you are asleep.

Esophageal Tumors. Less than 4% of all GI cancers originate in the esophagus. A *leiomyoma* is the most common benign esophageal tumor. These tumors usually do not produce symptoms; if a person does have symptoms (such as difficulty swallowing or bleeding), surgery may be recommended.

Malignant tumors of the esophagus are most common among men between 50 and 70 years and among smokers. These types of cancer usually include adenocarcinoma and squamous cell carcinoma. Once these tumors have been diagnosed by endoscopy and possibly biopsy, treatment may include radiotherapy, chemotherapy, and surgery.

The amount of acid that your stomach produces to break down the food you eat may decrease as you get older. This decline in acidity in the stomach may lead to increased production of a hormone called *gastrin,* which increases the amount of gastric juices (digestive fluids) in your stomach. There may also be some thinning of the mucous membranes that line the stomach.

The Stomach and Duodenum

Achlorhydria. *Achlorhydria* is decreased hydrochloric-acid secretion. This decrease can lead to one problem after another: There may be increased production of *gastrin,* which can lead to an increase in digestive fluids in your stomach. This imbalance could potentially allow coliform bacteria to thrive in your stomach and the upper part of your small intestine, and this colonization, in turn, can make you slightly more susceptible to infection with (gram-negative) pneumonia.

Problems That You May Encounter

Peptic Ulcer Disease. Peptic ulcer disease in older people includes *gastric ulcers* (that is, ulcers in the stomach) and, less commonly, *duodenal ulcers* (ulcers in the *duodenum,* the upper part of the small intestine). If you have an ulcer, you may have no symptoms, or you may experience weight loss, discomfort after eating, or mild to severe abdominal discomfort. Peptic ulcers are the most common causes of upper GI bleeding, and an ulcer may cause internal bleeding even if you don't have any symptoms. If your ulcer has been undiagnosed, you may experience vomiting of what looks like coffee grounds and possibly dark, tarry stools as indicators of active internal bleeding.

At least half of the world's population is infected with *Helicobacter pylori* bacteria, which may cause gastroduodenal ulcers. The use of steroids or NSAIDs such as ibuprofen may also contribute to the development of ulcers. Stress and cigarette smoking have also been implicated.

Gastric ulcers. Gastric ulcers are probably due to a breakdown of the stomach's mucosal barrier. These types of ulcers generally result from continued inflammation and damage. Symptoms may include pain on eating and weight loss or weakness.

Duodenal ulcers. Duodenal ulcers, which are more common among older men than older women, may cause pain and bleeding. Giant duodenal ulcers (those that are bigger than 2 cm in diameter) may cause upper abdominal discomfort that radiates to the back. Surgery may be required to address this problem if medical treatment is not successful.

A radiological test called computed tomographic (CT) scanning may be used to diagnose ulcers. A physician should also evaluate them by examining them with a device called an endoscope. If *Helicobacter pylori* is found to be the cause of your ulcer, you may be treated with antibiotics and acid-suppressing drugs. If NSAIDs are found to be the cause, your physician will probably recommend that you stop taking these pain relievers and that you use acetaminophen (Tylenol) instead. He or she may also prescribe antibiotics (to prevent infection) and antacids to neutralize acids, an H2 blocker to suppress acid secretion, or a proton pump inhibitor to prevent acid production. These medicines may need to be continued for 2 to 3 weeks to allow for appropriate healing and to strengthen the lining of your stomach.

Stomach Tumors. The incidence of both benign and malignant stomach tumors increases with age, and although the incidence of this disease is gradually declining in the United States, it remains a common problem, especially among white men. *Benign* (nonspreading) tumors of the stomach occur as different varieties: leiomyoma, fibromas, lipomas, and carcinoids. These tumors usually do not cause symptoms and are often discovered during examinations for other conditions. These lesions may be removed in an endoscopic procedure, or more extensive surgery may be warranted.

Malignant (spreading) tumors of the stomach are predominantly found in men and are more common in blacks than in whites. Gastric cancer is the second most common cause of cancer death in the world. The majority of these tumors are *adenocarcinomas* (that is, they are glandular); less than 5% are *lymphomas*, or tumors that affect the lymph tissue. In 1994 the International Agency for Research on Cancer declared a type of bacteria called *H. pylori* to be a risk factor for gastric adenocarcinoma. *H. pylori* may also be a risk factor for gastric lymphoma. In the early stages of these malignancies, symptoms may be absent or mild (abdominal discomfort). In later stages, there may be loss of appetite, nausea, depression, and weight loss. In more advanced disease, these symptoms may become more severe, and liver dysfunction may occur.

Surgery followed by radiation therapy may be recommended for both adenocarcinoma and lymphomas. Chemotherapy may also be helpful for gastric lymphoma.

The Small Intestine

How Your Small Intestine Changes As You Age

The ability of your smooth muscles in your intestines to contract and thereby move the contents forward may be unchanged or increased as you get older, but the supply of nerves to the small intestine tends to decrease. Also, while fat-soluble vitamins (such as vitamin A, E, and K) may be absorbed more readily through this part of our bodies as some of us age, the absorption of vitamin D and of calcium and iron tend to decrease.

Our small intestines are lined with small, finger-shaped *villi* that help our bodies to absorb nutrients. As we age, these villi become shortened and clublike, so that it may become more difficult for our bodies to absorb carbohydrates. Certain imbalances can also lead to bacterial overgrowth in the intestines, which may predispose us to develop infections.

Problems That You May Encounter

Bacterial Overgrowth. Bacterial overgrowth in the small intestine may occur when the secretion of gastric acid—which destroys these microorganisms—is impaired. This gastric-acid impairment may be due to inflammation or infection (gastritis), or ingestion of antacids, or it may follow surgery for peptic ulcer disease. When bacterial overgrowth occurs, the risk of malabsorption of nutrients and lactose intolerance increases. An examination of the small bowel may help your doctor to diagnose this problem. If it is discovered, he or she may prescribe antibiotics.

Decreased Absorption. Problems of absorption and digestion of nutrients in older people are generally related to lactose intolerance or to diseases such as celiac disease, pancreatic insufficiency, and certain types of tumors.

CELIAC DISEASE. This inherited disease may lead to weight loss, diarrhea, excess fat secretion, and mild malnutrition. Treatment is a *gluten-free diet* (that is, a diet that does not contain any barley, wheat, or rye) and extra vitamins and minerals. Your doctor may also prescribe extra vitamin D to strengthen your bones.

PANCREATIC INSUFFICIENCY. Sudden, frequent bowel movements that are oily (and may be difficult to flush) may be caused by a lack of pancreatic enzymes. If your physician diagnoses this problem (through blood tests, x-ray, ultrasound, or CT scan), he or she may prescribe an enzyme supplement such as Pancrease. He or she will probably also recommend that you stop drinking alcohol.

Tumors of the Small Intestine. Less than 5% of all GI tumors are benign tumors of the small intestine. Usually, these tumors do not cause symptoms. If they do cause abdominal discomfort, bleeding, or blockage, they can be removed surgically.

Malignant tumors of the small intestine are more common. These include carcinoid tumors, adenocarcinoma, lymphoma, and leiomyosarcoma. Usually, these tumors do not cause symptoms, although patients with late-stage disease may experience abdominal discomfort, bleeding, and possibly malabsorption, diarrhea, and weight loss. Surgical removal of these lesions is generally recommended. Radiation and chemotherapy may also be helpful for people with lymphoma.

Our bowels may not be as well lubricated in our later years as they were when we were younger, and atrophy and weakening of our abdominal muscles may make elimination more problematic. Inactivity can further exacerbate this difficulty. It is good to remember that "movement begets movement."

Inflammatory Bowel Disease. Inflammatory bowel disease may describe both Crohn's disease and ulcerative colitis. Both of these diseases may appear in early adulthood (in the 20s) or much later, between the ages of 50 and 80 years.

CROHN'S DISEASE. This disease causes inflammation and ulceration (most often of the lower part of the small intestine and colon), but it generally does not involve the rectum. Older patients with Crohn's disease are usually women. Symptoms of Crohn's disease include abdominal discomfort, diarrhea, weight loss, and fever.

Your physician or gastroenterologist can diagnose Crohn's disease by tests called colonoscopy, double-contrast barium x-ray study, ultrasound, and CT

The Bowels

How Your Bowels Change As You Age

Problems That You May Encounter

scan of the abdomen (see Table 13.1). Sometimes, biopsies of the colon are also performed.

If your doctor diagnoses Crohn's disease, he or she will prescribe medicines for you according to the severity of your disease. Generally, patients with Crohn's disease are prescribed anti-inflammatory drugs such as prednisone, immunosuppressive agents such as imuran, and antidiarrheal drugs such as diphenoxylate hydrochloride (Lomotil) to allow the colon to rest. Infliximib is the latest drug in the treatment of Crohn's. Antibiotics also may be prescribed to prevent infection.

Surgery will not cure Crohn's disease, but it may be necessary if medicines are not helpful.

ULCERATIVE COLITIS. This disease, which is more common than Crohn's disease, is similar to Crohn's disease, except that it also generally involves the colon and rectum. Most people with ulcerative colitis have chronic diarrhea, and bleeding may occur easily. To diagnose this condition, your doctor or specialist may take x-ray films of your abdomen and a stool sample. He or she may also recommend a sigmoidoscopy (see Table 13.1).

Drug therapy for patients with ulcerative colitis is similar to that for patients with Crohn's disease. For both conditions, it is also important to eat several small meals per day. Surgery may be recommended if medical therapy is not helpful. Because your risk of developing colorectal cancer is increased if you

Table 13.1   Tests That Are Commonly Performed to Assess Gastrointestinal Disorders

Test	Description
Esophagogastroduodenoscopy (upper GI endoscopy)	To view the entire upper GI tract
Colonoscopy (lower GI endoscopy)	To view the entire colon
Sigmoidoscopy	To view the inside of the large bowel
Barium x-ray studies	To view the esophagus, stomach, duodenum, and jejunum, and to detect blockages and strictures
Proctosigmoidoscopy	To view the colon, rectum, and anal canal
Proctography	To measure rectal diameter and to assess defecation
Anorectal manometry	To view the rectal area
Endoscopic retrograde cholangiopancreatography (ERCP)	To determine the cause of jaundice and to look for blockages in the common bile duct

have ulcerative colitis, your doctor will probably recommend that you have a yearly colonoscopy with a biopsy to screen for this type of cancer.

"Pseudomembranous" Colitis. Sometimes, diarrhea and inflammation of the colon may be caused by chemotherapy or antibiotic use, which may lead to overgrowth of a bacteria called *Clostridium difficile.* This infection may be spread from person to person, so hygiene and handwashing are keys to prevention. Symptoms of this type of infection include abdominal discomfort, fever, and sometimes diarrhea streaked with blood. Tests for this type of colitis include stool cultures, endoscopy, and occasionally sigmoidoscopy (see Table 13.1). Treatment may include cessation of the antibiotic that led to the bacterial overgrowth. Other antibiotics such as flagyl may be used to destroy the *Clostridium* bacteria. As you are recovering from this type of infection, you will need to restore the fluids and electrolytes that your body has lost. Research efforts are underway to better understand why older persons are more susceptible to *C. difficile* infections.

Ischemic Bowel Disease. *Ischemia,* or insufficient blood supply to the small bowel and colon, may cause inflammation and swelling. This common cause of lower GI bleeding may also cause abdominal cramping and bloody diarrhea.

Your doctor may recommend a colonoscopy or barium enema test to diagnose ischemic bowel disease. To treat this condition, he or she may recommend intravenous fluids and antibiotics. In severe instances, surgery may be required.

Vascular Ectasias (Arteriovenous Malformations or Angiodysplasia). These degenerative tangles of dilated vessels, which arise from normal blood vessels supplying the small intestine and colon, occur most often in people who are older than 70 years. Your doctor can diagnose vascular ectasias through a procedure called colonoscopy or, if the bleeding is heavy, via angiography, a radiological test to assess the site of bleeding from the blood vessels.

Usually, vascular ectasias do not cause symptoms except for blood loss, which may resolve on its own. If it doesn't, your doctor or specialist has many therapeutic options, including replacement of the iron and blood that you have lost, laser coagulation, and infusion of the bleeding area with a drug called vasopressin.

The Colon

How Your Colon Changes as You Age

Ordinarily, the colon does not change much with time, aside from some thinning of the muscle layers and a decrease in the secretion of mucus, which keeps the colon lubricated. These changes may affect the transit time of waste matter through this part of the large intestine. The weakening of the muscles of the colon may also lead to an increased incidence of abnormal pouches called *diverticula* that form off the intestines.

More important than any age-related changes in this part of our bodies are our lifelong dietary and excretory habits. Many North Americans eat too many refined foods and not enough fiber, and they use laxatives that can irritate the colon.

Diverticulosis. *Diverticulosis,* a condition in which tiny pouchlike herniations protrude through the muscular layer of the colon, occurs in about one third to two thirds of both men and women over age 60. This condition is sometimes associated with the use of NSAIDs such as ibuprofen. Most cases of diverticulosis are asymptomatic; however, related infection (diverticulitis), perforation, or bleeding of these herniations may cause constipation, diarrhea, abdominal pain distention, weight loss, steatorrhea, and occasionally bloody stools.

A sigmoidoscopy test (see Table 13.1) may be performed to look inside your colon. If your doctor diagnoses diverticular disease, he or she may suggest that you change the amount of fiber in your diet. He or she also may prescribe antibiotics to prevent infection. Surgery is occasionally necessary to tie off or remove the affected portion of the bowel.

Constipation. About one third of women and one fourth of men over age 65 complain of constipation. This problem is even more common among those who live in nursing homes, perhaps because of other health problems, inactivity, and use of medications. If you are constipated, you may experience straining on defecation and hard stools, and fewer bowel movements than usual. Anything from three defecations per day to three per week is normal, though most people have a regular bowel movement nearly every day.

This condition may be caused by eating too little fiber; depression; immobility; other health problems such as hypothyroidism, Parkinson's disease, or stroke; and use of drugs such as pain relievers, sedatives or tranquilizers, medicines for high blood pressure, and iron or calcium supplements.

The accompanying sidebar lists some suggestions for reducing or clearing up constipation. For occasional constipation, your doctor may recommend laxatives. We don't recommend the use of mineral oil as a treatment for constipation, however, because it can hurt the gut. In some cases, it also can lead to a condition called aspiration pneumonitis. Enemas are occasionally necessary.

*Some
Antidotes to
Constipation*

- Allow yourself enough privacy and comfort in the bathroom—don't rush.
- Try defecating 15 to 30 minutes after you eat breakfast; a suppository or enema may be helpful (ask your doctor).
- Ask your doctor whether you can change the dosage or type of medication that may be causing your constipation.
- Get regular exercise.
- Drink lots of fluids, especially in the summertime.
- Eat plenty of fiber (such as whole-wheat bread, apples, grapes, figs, broccoli, carrots, and bran and shredded-wheat cereals). Avoid cheese.
- Treat your hemorrhoids, if you have them (see p. 196).
- Elevate your legs (with a footstool) while you are sitting on the toilet.

Diarrhea. *Diarrhea,* or frequent defecation (more than three stools per day), is at the other end of the spectrum from constipation. There are many types of diarrhea and many causes, including bacteria, viruses, and other disorders that affect the GI system, such as ulcerative colitis and Crohn's disease. Rarely, dilation of the aorta, or an abdominal aortic aneurysm, causes diarrhea in older people. Also, the organism *Clostridium difficile* can cause not only diarrhea, but also inflammation of the colon and associated complications such as an abnormally enlarged or dilated colon (megacolon). If you develop diarrhea, you should rest. If you are in bed, change your position frequently to prevent the development of pressure sores (see Chapter 8).

The loss of fluids because of diarrhea can create further problems for you, so during the first day of your illness, you should take in lots of clear fluids (ginger ale, decaffeinated tea and cola, Gatorade, gelatin, and broth). On the second day, you may add bland foods such as rice, bread, crackers, and applesauce to your diet (but avoid spicy or fried foods or high-fiber items such as fruits, vegetables, and foods that contain bran). You will probably be able to return to your usual diet after a few days. If you have pain, fever, bloody diarrhea, or if your diarrhea continues, see your doctor promptly. You may be asked to give a stool sample. If you have diarrhea due to *C. difficile* infection, you will likely be given a course of antibiotics such as metronidazole and/or vancomycin. Prevention includes frequent handwashing and personal hygiene.

Irritable Bowel Syndrome. If you have this motility disorder, you may suffer from constipation (with or without diarrhea), excessive gas, and abdominal discomfort and distention. This very common problem, which you may first experience in your 60s or 70s, occurs more often in women than in men. It generally does *not* lead to more serious health problems.

When you visit your doctor because of symptoms related to this disorder, he or she will probably take some common blood tests and may have you undergo a sigmoidoscopy (see Table 13.1) to view the inside of your lower GI tract.

Your physician will probably recommend that you try increasing the amount of fiber in your diet, getting more exercise, and defecating soon after you eat your first meal of the day.

Colorectal Tumors. Both benign and malignant tumors of the colon and rectum are common in the United States. Benign tumors of the colon are generally *polyps,* protruding growths of tissue. More than half of all people over age 60 may have the most common of these tumors, which are called *adenomatous polyps.* Fortunately, the chance that these tumors will become malignant is extremely low (roughly 1%). Usually, these benign polyps do not cause symptoms, although occasionally they may cause bleeding from the rectum. They are sometimes surgically removed.

Malignant tumors or cancers of the colon are very common in people over age 40. Most of these cancers are adenocarcinomas; others include lymphoma, leiomyosarcoma, and carcinoid tumors. Two to six percent of adenocarcinomas are hereditary and are due to gene mutations. If you have any close family members who have had this cancer and it has been diagnosed in more than one generation of your family, then you should be diligent about having yearly medical examinations and regular colonoscopies. In the early stages, colon cancer generally does not cause symptoms, so regular screening for this cancer (through a sigmoidoscopy and fecal blood testing) is very important. Surgical removal of these tumors is often recommended. Chemotherapy and radiation therapy are also sometimes helpful.

The Rectum

How Your Rectum Changes as You Age

The muscle wall of the rectum and anus may become less elastic as we age; this change may in rare instances lead to occasional fecal incontinence. In some people the nerve supply to the rectum may also decrease. Finally, the rectum's capacity for storing feces tends to increase, so that fecal impaction may become more likely.

Problems That You May Encounter

Rectal Prolapse. *Rectal prolapse* involves a portion of the rectum that has bulged through the pelvic floor into the vagina or outside the body. This condition can lead to fecal incontinence. Surgery is sometimes performed to repair this problem.

Hemorrhoids. Hemorrhoids are clusters of dilated varicose veins that may protrude from the opening of the anus or may be located internally, just inside the anal opening. These veins may cause bright red blood in the stool. This common condition may be exacerbated by other conditions such as constipation, heart failure, or cirrhosis.

If constipation is the cause, treatment of that problem, as discussed previously, will alleviate the pressure on the anal area. Occasionally, doctors also recommend topical anesthetics, cold packs, or warm baths to relieve the discomfort.

For hemorrhoids that are not relieved by these methods, surgical procedures such as sclerotherapy or *rubber band ligation* (in which the hemorrhoids are "tied off"), *cryosurgery* (in which the area is frozen), *hemorrhoidectomy* (in which the hemorrhoids are removed), or laser surgery may be recommended.

Fecal Incontinence. Although fecal incontinence is less common than urinary incontinence, it can be just as embarrassing. This condition can be a consequence of severe constipation, and it is a common concern, especially among patients who are in long-term care facilities. A variety of other causes may lead to this unpleasant problem, including diabetes, rectal prolapse, anal surgery, and stroke.

After examining your rectum and performing other tests, your physician may recommend a mild laxative (such as milk of magnesia) or stool softeners. Bowel training, which involves attempting to have a bowel movement every day after breakfast, may also be helpful. If defecation does not occur naturally, a suppository and/or an enema may be used to stimulate this process. After several days, the gastrocolic reflex may operate automatically. Electrical stimulation via a device that emits electrical impulses when the anal sphincter contracts can also be helpful.

Our livers usually experience mild changes as we age. This organ may lose weight, and there may be a decrease in the total number of liver cells (*hepatocytes*). There may also be less blood flow through this important organ. It's also possible that after injury (because of infection or a disease process that leads to scarring, or cirrhosis) the liver does not regenerate as well as it did when we were younger. Our livers may also be more sensitive to injury from medicines such as antibiotics, acetaminophen, and anesthetics.

The Liver

How Your
Liver Changes
as You Age

Hepatitis. There are many causes of liver inflammation, or *hepatitis*. Among them are infection with the hepatitis A, B, or C virus (and rarely with hepatitis D or E), and alcohol and other drugs, such as acetaminophen. Any type of hepatitis may cause you to lose weight, have abdominal discomfort, and lose your appetite. Your doctor or specialist may be able to diagnose viral hepatitis with a simple blood test.

Problems
That You May
Encounter

Cirrhosis. *Cirrhosis,* liver scarring, sometimes occurs as a result of hepatitis infection, drug toxicity, or alcohol consumption. In the latter case, abstinence from alcohol is very important to prevent further liver damage.

There are several complications of cirrhosis. One of the most serious complications involves engorged veins in the esophagus (foodpipe) known as "esophageal varices." If these varices rupture and bleed, it could be a life-threatening emergency. Therefore, if you are diagnosed with cirrhosis, your physician or specialist may consider a barium swallow or possibly an endoscopic examination to look for varices in your esophagus. If these dilated veins are found, you may be given drugs called beta blockers to reduce the risk of bleeding.

A fluid-filled abdomen (*ascites*) may also complicate cirrhosis of the liver. If this fluid becomes infected, you may develop a condition known as *spontaneous bacterial peritonitis*. Your doctor can prescribe an antibiotic to treat this condition. Treatment of the ascites itself may involve removal of the ascitic fluid either with diuretics or, sometimes, if needed, by using a catheter (large-volume abdominal paracentesis). Surgical treatment is also an option.

Finally, another complication of cirrhosis may be *hepatic encephalopathy,* an alteration in mental status ranging from confusion to coma. A drug called lactulose and a low-protein diet may be prescribed to prevent this condition from occurring.

Primary Biliary Cirrhosis. Primary biliary cirrhosis (PBC) is not caused by a viral infection or alcohol consumption, but rather is an *autoimmune condition* (that is, the body produces antibodies to fight against its own tissues). Quite often, people with PBC may also have other autoimmune disorders such as thyroid disease (hypothyroidism or hyperthyroidism), dry glands (sicca, or Sjögren's syndrome), or rheumatoid arthritis. If you have this disease, which occurs most commonly in middle-aged and older women, you may have no symptoms, or you may feel unwell, have upper abdominal pain, itching, or jaundice.

Your physician may recommend a drug called ursodeoxycholic acid (Actigall) to slow the course of PBC, as well as a medicine called cholestyramine to relieve the itching that may accompany this disease. In severe cases, a transvenous intra-abdominal portal venous shunt (TIPS) procedure may be recommended. Alternatively, a liver transplant may be considered, although these operations are not very common for people over age 70 because of the presence of other medical problems that may preclude such a major procedure.

Hemochromatosis. *Hemochromatosis* is an inherited disorder associated with excessive deposits of iron in the liver and heart. This disorder generally is not related to excessive consumption of iron-rich foods; rather, it involves a genetic problem that leads to excessive absorption of this trace mineral from the gut. This disorder is found most commonly in individuals of Celtic ancestry.

If you have this "iron overload" disorder, you may experience weakness, lethargy, and abdominal discomfort. Joint pain, symptoms of diabetes (such as increased thirst), and loss of libido or impotence may also be associated with this disorder. In more advanced cases, you may develop liver failure, cirrhosis, and possibly primary liver cancer. Congestive heart failure may also occur.

The treatment for hemochromatosis is *phlebotomy,* or regular blood drawing to reduce the amount of iron in your blood. Once your iron level is within a normal range, you will probably need to have follow-up phlebotomy a few times per year to prevent the reaccumulation of excess iron in your body.

Liver Cancer. Cancer that originates in another part of the body and spreads to the liver is more common in older people than cancer that originates in the liver. Cancer that has spread to the liver is generally managed by a cancer specialist (*oncologist*).

Hepatocellular cancer, cancer that arises from within the liver, is often associated with liver scarring (cirrhosis) or with hepatitis B or C viral infection. A liver specialist (*hepatologist*) can diagnose and manage this disease. Patients who develop hepatocellular cancer may have any of the complications of cirrhosis: esophageal varices, ascites, or hepatic encephalopathy. Because of the link between cirrhosis and this type of cancer, patients with cirrhosis should be screened regularly with a blood test called alpha-fetoprotein and with ultrasound scanning to look for early evidence of liver tumors. If a tumor is found, the treatment may include *hepatectomy* (excision of part of the liver) or chemotherapy.

The pancreas is an important gland that secretes digestive enzymes, as well as the hormones insulin and glucagon. The function of our pancreas does not change much as we get older, but some disorders of the pancreas can be of concern in older people.

Pancreatic disorders common in older people include *pancreatitis*, inflammation of the pancreas; pancreatic enzyme insufficiency; and pancreatic cancer.

Pancreatitis. Inflammation of the pancreas may be *acute*—that is, it may come on suddenly—or it may be chronic. This problem may be caused by excessive alcohol consumption or by another problem (such as gallstones) in the gallbladder and biliary area. Symptoms of pancreatitis usually include abdominal pain that may radiate to the back or lower chest; this discomfort may be accompanied by nausea, vomiting, and confusion.

Physicians use blood tests, chest x-rays, ECG, and abdominal ultrasound tests to diagnose pancreatitis. If you are found to have this disorder, your doctor will probably give you medicine to control pain, possibly an antibiotic to prevent infection, and extra fluids and electrolytes to replace the fluids that you have lost. If gallstones are determined to be the cause of your pancreatitis, they may need to be surgically removed.

Pancreatic Enzyme Insufficiency. The pancreas is responsible for releasing several important enzymes, such as *amylase* (which is essential for the breakdown of carbohydrates), *lipase* (which is used in the breakdown of fats), and *proteases* (which are necessary for the conversion of proteins into amino acids). If this gland is not releasing these enzymes sufficiently, enzyme replacement therapy (with Pancrease) can be very helpful.

Pancreatic Cancer. A high percentage of people with pancreatic cancer are between 60 and 80 years old. Risk factors for this disease may include cigarette smoking, a high-fat diet, and alcohol consumption. The primary symptoms of pancreatic cancer may include abdominal discomfort, weight loss, back pain, depression, and diarrhea. A person with this disease may also have *jaundice* (yellowing of the skin and of the whites of the eyes).

Doctors use ultrasound, CT scanning, angiography, and laparoscopy to diagnose pancreatic cancer. Most patients with this disease undergo surgery to remove the affected areas.

The gallbladder is a tiny sac in which bile from the liver is stored. The development of stones (made of cholesterol and bile pigment) in this sac is a very common disorder among people who are older than 50 years.

Gallstones (Cholelithiasis). Approximately one third of older women have gallstones, and they are common in older men, as well. Gallstones may be caused by cirrhosis, inflammatory bowel disease (Crohn's disease or ulcerative colitis), or weight loss, or they may form for no apparent reason.

Most gallstones do not cause symptoms, and if you have no symptoms of gallstones, surgery may not be necessary. However, if you do have symptoms (including abdominal discomfort and jaundice), you have a one-in-four chance of developing complications such as inflammation or blockage of the bile ducts, so surgery may be indicated.

If your doctor suspects that you have gallstones, he or she may give you an ultrasound exam to look for them. Other tests that are commonly used to diagnose gallstones include endoscopic retrograde cholangiopancreatography (ERCP) and endoscopic retrograde catheterization of the gallbladder (ERCG).

Treatment options for gallstones include dissolution of the stones with solvents or removal of the stones with surgical procedures such as endoscopic sphincterotomy and laparoscopic cholecystectomy. Sometimes, small tubes called *stents* are placed in the bile ducts to keep them open following surgery for stone removal.

Inflammation of the Gallbladder (Cholecystitis). People who have gallstones or who are overweight may develop inflammation of the wall of the gallbladder, or cholecystitis, which is usually caused by the blockage of a duct by a gallstone. Abdominal discomfort, nausea, vomiting, and a fever are all symptoms of cholecystitis. Your doctor can confirm this diagnosis with an ultrasound test or an abdominal x-ray. If the presence of this disorder is confirmed, you may be treated with antibiotics. Sometimes, a surgical procedure called cholecystectomy is performed to drain the gallbladder.

Cancer of the Gallbladder. Gallbladder cancer is rare. Gallstones are associated with both benign and malignant tumors of the gallbladder. If such an abnormal growth of cells is identified on ultrasound, regular ultrasound examinations will be necessary in order to rule out a change in the lesion's size. If the lesions have spread, there may be abdominal discomfort, weight loss, and jaundice. Removal of the gallbladder may be necessary.

The Appendix

Inflammation of the appendix, a 3- to 4-inch tube attached to the lower, right-hand section of the abdomen (the cecum), is rare in older people. This is because the appendix generally shrinks as we age. However, appendicitis does occasionally occur in seniors, and when it does, it can be quite severe.

The symptoms of appendicitis at any age may include abdominal discomfort, nausea and vomiting, and sometimes constipation or diarrhea. When appendicitis is diagnosed, removal of the appendix (appendectomy) is required, followed by antibiotics to prevent infection.

Persons who are naturally very fat are apt to die earlier than those who are slender.

Hippocrates (460?–377? B.C.)

When doctors talk about the endocrine system, they are referring to certain glands that secrete substances (such as hormones) that then are distributed to other parts of the body via the bloodstream. These substances can affect all the other systems in the body, including our reproductive system, our metabolism, and our growth and repair process, as well as many other processes. In Chapter 5, we talked about the hormonal changes that can lead to enlargement of the prostate gland in older men and to reduced levels of natural estrogen (the hormone that stimulates the production and release of eggs) in older women. In this chapter, we discuss some of the other major endocrinological changes that we may encounter as older adults.

Hormonal changes that tend to occur with aging may have profound effects on the whole body. For example, the levels of growth hormone and androgens (the male sex hormones such as testosterone) begin to fall. A reduction in the amount of growth hormone, which is secreted by the pituitary gland, may have negative effects on our muscle mass.

How Your Endocrine System Changes as You Age

Another significant change that can happen is that our blood sugar (*glucose*) levels may rise, probably in part because of increased body weight, decreased physical activity, and changes in diet that may occur in later life. Hormones such as glucagon and insulin, which are secreted by an important endocrine engine—the pancreas—enable the body to convert glucose into energy that it needs. Diabetes is a disorder that can develop when this conversion doesn't happen properly. Diabetes affects approximately 18% of people over age 65. Far more people—20–40%—over age 80 have glucose intolerance and perhaps only half of them realize that they have this condition.

Another important endocrine processor—the thyroid gland—may sometimes undergo mild changes in later life. It may shrink slightly and may develop some scar tissue (fibrosis). Occasionally, small *nodules,* tiny growths of tissue, may develop; for the most part, these tiny growths are not cancerous. Later in this chapter, we discuss conditions such as hypothyroidism, which may occur when the thyroid's production of certain hormones is altered.

Problems That May Occur

Diabetes

When you eat food, your body usually converts the starches and sugars into *glucose,* a type of fuel that your body needs for energy. This process is made possible by a hormone called insulin. In diabetes mellitus (literally "honey-sweet diabetes"), this process becomes deficient, either because the body is producing insufficient amounts of insulin or because the insulin is not working effectively. As a result, glucose begins to accumulate in unhealthy, excessive amounts in the bloodstream, and, if the condition goes untreated, infection, dehydration, peripheral vascular disease, stroke, and heart, kidney, nerve, and eye problems can ensue.

Type 1 (Insulin-Dependent) Diabetes
With Type 1 diabetes, which can develop rather quickly (within a few days or weeks), one's body virtually stops producing insulin. Daily injections of replacement insulin are needed to maintain the glucose conversion process. This form of diabetes is most common in children and young adults, although in rare instances it can affect older adults also. In total, it constitutes less than 10% of all cases of diabetes. Type 1 diabetes is usually more severe than Type 2 diabetes.

Type 2 (Non-Insulin-Dependent) Diabetes
If you have Type 2 diabetes, your body can produce insulin, but it may be making insufficient amounts or an unusable form of this hormone. Sometimes, a good diet and regular exercise are all that are needed to remedy this problem. In other instances, medication or injection of insulin may also be needed.

Nine out of 10 cases of diabetes fall within this Type 2 category. This form of diabetes, which develops gradually, was once called "adult-onset diabetes" because it tends to affect people who are over age 40, but it may affect younger people also. Being overweight and having a family history of this disease are two of the most important risk factors for developing it.

Risk Factors for Type 2 Diabetes

- Excessive body weight (more than 120% of one's desirable body weight)
- A family history of diabetes
- Nonwhite (African, Asian, or Native American, or Hispanic) ancestry
- A history of gestational diabetes (that is, a history of having developed diabetes during pregnancy)
- A history of having delivered a baby weighing nine pounds or more
- High blood pressure

Symptoms. The common symptoms of Type 1 diabetes are weight loss, increased hunger or thirst, blurred vision, fatigue, and frequent urination. You may or may not have any symptoms if you have Type 2 diabetes. Symptoms of this form of the disease may include increased thirst, hunger, or fatigue; unexplained weight loss, even when one is eating more than usual; blurred vision; frequent urination (especially at night); frequent infections; dry, itchy skin, skin infections, or wounds that don't heal easily. Too often, people don't pay attention to these symptoms because they mistakenly think that they are just part of the natural aging process.

If diabetes is allowed to advance without treatment, other, more serious symptoms may occur. These may include deep, rapid breathing, nausea and vomiting, severe dehydration, and potentially even loss of consciousness or coma. A coma is a signal that your brain is not getting the glucose it needs to function, and it has shut down. Prompt treatment is required. The treatment of diabetes is also essential in order to prevent other problems that sometimes accompany this disease; these problems include high blood pressure, heart or kidney disease, and loss of sight due to tiny hemorrhages in the eye.

Diagnosis. If you don't have any symptoms of diabetes, your doctor may detect it while doing a routine test to measure sugar in the urine or blood. If you go to see your doctor because of any of the aforementioned symptoms, he or she will probably take your medical history, perform a physical exam, and do some routine laboratory tests to confirm the diagnosis.

For one of these tests, called a *glucose tolerance test,* you may be asked to forgo eating or drinking anything except water for about 12 hours ahead of time. Then, during the test, you will be given a sugary liquid, and your doctor will monitor your blood for the level of glucose.

The normal range for a fasting blood sugar is below 110 milligrams (mg) per deciliter (dl). A level of more than 126 mg/dl is indicative of diabetes. Once

What Do the Symptoms of Diabetes Mean?

Symptom	What It Means
Increased thirst	The body is trying to dilute the excess amount of sugar in the blood.
Frequent urination	The kidneys are working overtime to purge the blood of excess sugar.
Frequent or persistent infections	The immune system is weakened.
Fatigue	Glucose is not finding its way into the cells, which need this form of blood sugar to function.
Blurred vision	The blood vessels in the back of the eyes may be undergoing changes.

diabetes is diagnosed, your physician may refer you to an *endocrinologist,* a doctor who specializes in managing diseases of the endocrine system.

The American Diabetes Association (ADA) advises that if you are over age 45, you should be tested for diabetes every three years. If you have any risk factors for diabetes, you should be tested every year.

Treatment. There is no definite cure for diabetes, but there are many steps that you can take to control it.

EAT WELL. Eating right may be the best answer. In fact, quite often, patients find that their diabetes comes under control just a few weeks after they have embarked on a new diet. Eating several small, regular, nutritious meals per day (rather than three large ones) will help to regulate your glucose levels. It may be worthwhile to see a dietitian to help you plan meals. In general, the ADA recommends that diabetics consume

1. Approximately 55% of total calories from carbohydrates such as breads and pasta
2. Approximately 15% of total calories from protein sources such as meat, fish, eggs, and dairy products
3. Less than 30% of total calories from fat, with an emphasis on choosing unsaturated fats such as olive oils, canola oil, and some safflower and sunflower oils, or using low-fat salad dressings

Finally, eating plenty of foods that contain a lot of fiber will help to keep your blood sugar levels under control.

GET EXERCISE. Exercise is important, too, because it can help you take off excess weight, burn off extra amounts of glucose that your body doesn't need, and enable the insulin to work better in your body. Try to exercise at least two or three times a week.

Be sure to eat something before you work out, so that your blood sugar does not fall too low (this is called *hypoglycemia*), and take a snack or glucose tablets along. You should also keep an ID card with you when you exercise (and at all other times), which says that you have diabetes.

Drink plenty of fluids to prevent dehydration. Stop exercising if you feel dizzy during strenuous physical activity because diabetes can make you prone to fluid loss and can affect the nerves that maintain your blood pressure when you are standing. These conditions may predispose you to developing *hypotension,* or low blood pressure, when you stand.

Wear comfortable, well-fitting footwear while you are exercising to prevent sores that can become infected more easily and may heal more slowly if you have diabetes. Also, you'll need to monitor your blood glucose level both before and after you exercise. This can be done with a device called a blood glucose monitor.

How often should I monitor my blood sugar level?

Check with your doctor. Most diabetics need to check their glucose level at least once per day. If you are taking insulin, you should check your glucose level three or four times each day—before each meal and before a bedtime snack. Also, always monitor this level if you begin to take a new medication or if you are ill.

Blood Glucose Monitoring

What types of monitors are available?

There are two types: Chemstrips and a finger-puncture device. *Chemstrips* can provide a rough estimate of your blood sugar level. You simply wipe a drop of blood onto the strip and then compare the strip to a color chart that shows blood glucose values.

Using a finger-puncture device involves pricking your finger and placing a drop of blood onto a strip of paper. Just as with Chemstrips, you then may compare the color of the strip to a chart that indicates the blood glucose value, or your glucose measurement kit may provide a glucose meter that does this job for you when you insert the strip.

What should I do with these test results?

You'll find that these tests will help you to keep your blood glucose level in a normal range; for instance, you'll see the cause and effect of eating foods that contain a lot of carbohydrates. In time, you'll be able to make the necessary changes to your diet, exercise level, or stress level to keep your glucose level in balance.

These results can also help your doctor to guide your treatment. Keep a log of the results, and take the log with you when you see your physician.

Finally, we advise our patients not to do strenuous exercise just before bedtime because doing so may cause their blood sugar to drop during the night.

TAKE CARE OF YOUR SKIN. Diabetes can reduce your body's ability to fight infection, so be sure to keep your skin clean and moisturized to prevent cracking and other problems associated with dry skin. Also, treat minor cuts and bruises promptly, to prevent delayed healing or infections.

HAVE REGULAR CHECKUPS. See your primary care doctor, your eye doctor, your dentist, and your foot doctor (podiatrist), if necessary, for regular checkups. Diabetes can limit the blood supply to your feet and can affect feeling in your lower extremities, so it's especially important to see your primary care physician or your podiatrist promptly if you notice any blisters, possibly infected areas, or sores on your feet.

TAKE PRESCRIBED MEDICATION. For Type 2 diabetes, several kinds of medications are available. Generally, medications are prescribed only after dietary changes and exercise have not brought the blood sugar level into optimal balance. These drugs may be prescribed alone or in various combinations with each other.

Sulfonylureas work by stimulating the secretion of insulin from the pancreas and by helping a person's own insulin to work more effectively. These drugs, which are taken as oral medications, rather than injections, are prescribed for people whose bodies are producing some amount of insulin. Commonly used sulfonylureas include acetohexamide (Dymelor), chlorpropamide (Diabenese), and tolbutamide (Orinase). These drugs are generally effective and have few side effects, although some people may experience weight gain and possibly low blood sugar (hypoglycemia) while taking them.

Biguanides (such as metformin, or Glucophage) also work by lowering blood sugar levels. They do so by preventing the liver from forming and releasing glucose. Many people lose an average of 5 pounds while taking biguanides, and these drugs can cause diarrhea. They're not prescribed for patients who have liver or kidney problems, or for people who drink alcohol. It's best not to drink alcohol except very occasionally, anyway, even if you're not taking this medication, because alcohol can damage your liver and pancreas, as well as other organs (see Chapters 4 and 6).

Alpha-glucoside inhibitors (such as acarbose, or Precose, and miglitol) lower blood sugar levels (especially after eating) by slowing down the absorption of carbohydrates by the gastrointestinal tract. This type of medication can cause gas and diarrhea, so doctors often prescribe a low dosage initially and then increase the dosage over several weeks while the body adjusts to this drug.

Thiazolidinediones (such as troglitazone, or Rezulin) are known to work by helping the cells of the body to take in insulin. Such drugs are given to patients who are taking insulin, and sometimes their insulin dosages may be reduced or even stopped altogether with these agents. If you take thiazolidinediones, you will need to have regular blood tests to check your liver function before you start treatment, then monthly for eight months to ensure that no liver problems develop (this is a *rare* complication). Be sure to discuss this possibility with your doctor.

Insulin is prescribed when the aforementioned medications do not succeed in bringing blood sugar down to an appropriate level. Insulin may also be added to therapy with other drugs such as sulfonylureas. There are several types of insulin, and the duration of their effectiveness varies, depending on whether they are fast-acting or long-acting. All currently are given by injection, although scientists are developing oral and inhaled forms of insulin, and they may be available for use in the near future.

If your doctor prescribes insulin for you, he or she (or a nurse) will teach you how to inject it. You will need to rotate these injection sites frequently to prevent scar tissue from forming.

You will also need to learn to dispose of used needles properly. Used syringes (which are called "sharps") should be placed in a glass container or a special box designed just for syringe disposal. You may be able to return used syringes to a pharmacy or dispose of them with the rest of your trash—contact your trash collection company or your local health department if you take your trash to a local landfill.

Types of Insulin

Type of Insulin	Brand Name
Very fast acting (15 minutes)	Humalog
Fast-acting	Regular, Semi-Lente
Intermediate-acting	Neutral protamine Hagedorn (NPH), Lente
Long-acting	Ultralente
Combination insulin preparations	70% NPH, 30% regular 50% NPH, 50% regular

WATCH FOR COMPLICATIONS. If your blood glucose level drops too low because you've missed a meal, your blood glucose monitor is not reliable, or insulin is being absorbed too fast in your bloodstream, you may develop a complication of diabetes called *hypoglycemia,* or low blood sugar. If you have kidney or liver problems in addition to your diabetes, you may be especially susceptible to developing this complication. Also, large doses of drugs such as propanolol or atenolol (often prescribed for high blood pressure, coronary heart disease, or irregular heart rhythm) and excessively large amounts of aspirin can be associated with hypoglycemia.

How will you know whether you are developing hypoglycemia? You may experience any of the following symptoms: nervousness, shakiness, sweating, palpitations, chest discomfort, hunger, nausea, or tingling or numbness, particularly around the mouth.

If your hypoglycemia advances without treatment, you may experience confusion or trouble with memory, headache and/or dizziness, difficulty speaking or seeing, sudden fatigue, weakness, or feelings of coldness. In addition, your friends or family members may notice that you are sweating, pale, irritable, shaky, drowsy, uncoordinated, and acting differently.

If you are conscious, you should try (and your loved ones can help you) to consume small amounts of fast-acting carbohydrates, such as fruit juice, candy, table sugar, glucose tablets, milk, or cola drinks. (Because it's not always easy to predict when you may become quickly hypoglycemic, if you have diabetes, you should always keep such carbohydrates with you for use if necessary.) If you have lost consciousness, someone such as your friend, neighbor, or family member should call 911.

Sometimes, it's not low blood sugar, but the opposite problem—very high blood sugar (*severe hypergylcemia*)—that causes illness. This serious condition, called *hyperglycemic hyperosmolar nonketotic syndrome (HHNS),* results from a lack of effective insulin in the body, and it is often more dangerous for older adults, who may be taking medications for heart or kidney conditions that can exacerbate the hyperglycemia. Dehydration, which is common in older people because of a diminished thirst sensation, can contribute to the development of HHNS also.

Symptoms of HHNS mirror those of diabetes; they can include thirst, frequent urination, weakness, blurred vision, confusion, and possibly leg cramps. If you or your family members recognize that you are experiencing these indications of HHNS, you should go to a hospital emergency room for prompt treatment. In the hospital, you will be given fluid, insulin, and potassium replacement therapy.

The most common long-term complication of diabetes is a degenerative disease of the nervous system called *neuropathy*. The legs and feet may be affected by a loss of sensation to heat or light touch or by intense sensitivity to the same. There sometimes may be a pins-and-needles sensation, or occasionally, shooting, knifelike discomfort may occur in the legs. In advanced stages of this condition, one may have severely reduced or sometimes absence of sensation in the feet.

If you start to develop this complication of diabetes, it will be especially important for you to pay attention to your legs and feet, and to watch for the development of any cuts, cracks, or calluses that you may not be able to feel. Be especially careful with hot liquids because you may not be able to feel a burning sensation. Likewise, be sure to check the temperature of your bath or shower water with your hand, your elbow, or a thermometer before you stand in the bath or shower. Make sure that your shoes fit properly and comfortably. Some people find that shaking their shoes out before putting them on helps to get rid of small objects such as stones or sand that can irritate the feet.

To prevent your feet from feeling cold, it's good to wear socks, but try not to use heating pads or hot water bottles, which can burn you. If your feet and legs are most uncomfortable with cramps at night, try wearing warm pajama pants and socks, drinking a glass of milk, and walking a little just before bedtime. Your doctor could also prescribe a pain reliever for you, if needed.

Eye problems may also develop as a complication of diabetes, so it's very important for you to visit an ophthalmologist regularly, at least once per year, to have a dilated-eye examination. Eye disease that is caused by diabetes may have no warning signs, but if detected and treated early, blindness can be prevented.

Kidney disease is another serious complication of diabetes; in fact, diabetes is the leading cause of end-stage renal disease. Your doctor will monitor you often and can prescribe medicines to help you avoid this problem.

Heart disease is a serious concern for diabetics. If you have diabetes, your risk of developing heart disease is higher than it is for people who don't have diabetes. To minimize your risk, you should not smoke. Exercise often, take medicines as prescribed to control high blood pressure, and try to limit the fat and cholesterol content in your diet (see Chapter 4).

To learn more about diabetes, call the ADA (1-800-342-2383).

The *thyroid* is an endocrine gland located at the base of the neck. It is shaped like a small bow tie, and sits about where a real bow tie would sit. Its primary function is to produce two important and related hormones: thyroxine (also called T_4) and triiodothyronine (also called T_3).

Thyroid Problems

The symptoms and signs of thyroid problems in older people differ considerably from those of younger people. Just as with diabetes, the symptoms of thyroid problems in later life may resemble other health problems, and some people may delay seeking treatment because they mistakenly associate these health problems with old age itself.

Hypothyroidism

Deficient activity of the thyroid gland, or *hypothyroidism,* increases in incidence with age, and it affects approximately 2–7% of older people. The incidence of hypothyroidism is higher among older women than men. The slower function of the thyroid gland leads to a lower metabolic rate in the body and may result in a feeling of loss of energy.

The most common cause of hypothyroidism in the elderly is called *autoimmune thyroid failure* (or *Hashimoto's thyroiditis*). An *autoimmune condition* means that your body is treating part of itself like a foreign entity and is creating antibodies to attack it.

Hypothyroidism is also sometimes caused by drugs such as iodine and lithium. The use of radioiodine or radiation therapy for a condition called Grave's disease can lead to hypothyroidism, too.

Symptoms of an inactive thyroid gland in older people may include changes in weight (gain or loss), falls, incontinence, chest or muscular discomfort, intolerance to cold, fatigue, dry skin, depression, weakness, and confusion. Just as with diabetes, if hypothyroidism is untreated, it can lead to impaired function and confusion.

Hypothyroidism is easily diagnosed by a simple blood test that measures thyroid-stimulating hormone (TSH). Usually, a drug called L-thyroxin (levothyroxine, or Levoxyl) is used to correct this hormone imbalance. The dosage may sometimes need to be adjusted, so see your physician for follow-up blood tests.

Hyperthyroidism

The incidence of excessive activity of the thyroid gland, or *hyperthyroidism,* remains fairly constant with age, and it affects an estimated 2% of the elderly. With this condition, the thyroid gland gets larger and produces excessive amounts of thyroid hormones. As a result, the body's metabolic rate can increase, the blood pressure can rise, and the heart rate can accelerate.

In older people, symptoms of this disorder may include heart (such as chest discomfort and heart failure), gastrointestinal (e.g., weight loss, diarrhea, and constipation), and other problems, such as confusion and depression.

Just as with hypothyroidism, hyperthyroidism is easily diagnosed by a simple blood test that measures TSH in the blood.

Radioiodine (I^{131}) is the most common treatment for hyperthyroidism. So-called antithyroid drugs, such as propylthiouracil and methimazole, can also be given to reduce the amount of thyroid hormones in the thyroid gland.

Thyroid Nodules and Thyroid Cancer
Thyroid cancer accounts for less than 1% of all cancer deaths in the United States. It is usually readily treatable, especially if diagnosed promptly.

Lipoprotein Problems   For information about cholesterol metabolism, please see Chapter 4.

Salt Metabolism Problems   For information about common problems with salt metabolism, see Chapter 11.

CHAPTER 15

YOUR IMMUNE SYSTEM

*Healing is a matter of time, but it is sometimes also
a matter of opportunity.*

Hippocrates (c. 460–400 B.C.)

*It seems like lately I'm picking up one "bug" after another. I can't seem to
shake a common cold as quickly as I used to, and sometimes I get diarrhea that
will go away only after my doctor has prescribed an antibiotic for it. What can
I do to help my body to fight off these infections?*

Tony, age 81

Our body's ability to resist infection stems from a complex system comprising
our spleen, liver, thymus gland, tonsils, lymph nodes, bone marrow, and white
blood cells. In this chapter, we briefly discuss how this system operates, as well
as some of the problems that can develop when it's not working as well as it
might. We also review some suggestions for how to prevent infections from getting out of hand.

How Your Immune System Works

Like a sentry, your immune system stands guard to identify and protect you
from foreign invaders—pathogens such as viruses and bacteria—that try to
wreak havoc with your health. When such invaders are recognized, one team of
white blood cells produces proteins called *antibodies,* which travel through your
body, tagging various pathogens to prepare them for consumption by other
white blood cells.

Many of our white blood cells live for a long time, and they carry the memory of the prior invaders that they have encountered. That's key to the whole
immune process—it's how, for example, our bodies may continue to be immune
to measles, even though we may have had measles as a child, a number of
decades earlier.

Physical Changes

As you grow older, your immune responses may become slightly lower and less adaptable, compared to those of young adults. Many of these changes are in cell-mediated immunity, and the number and quality of antibodies produced in your body may also decline. Your *thymus gland,* located in the upper part of your chest, tends to shrink progressively as the years go by, in turn producing less of the important infection-fighting white blood cells called T cells. T cells that are destroyed by trauma (such as burns) can also take longer to be replaced. In some people over age 80, there is thus a slightly reduced immune reserve. Furthermore, certain physiological changes, such as thinning of the skin, can also diminish our natural barriers to infection.

Because of this potential loss of reserve and the resulting ability of pathogens to gain a foothold in the body, an older person may take longer than a younger person to recover from an infectious illness. Even in cases in which we may have the same number of white blood cells as a younger person, and even when these cells are just as effective at disarming and engulfing unwanted microorganisms, these infection fighters may have a slightly slower reaction time, so the illness-causing pathogens can have a greater opportunity to cause harm.

Factors That Can Inhibit Your Ability to Fight Infection

Common Illnesses. In addition to having potentially less effective white blood cells, you may have any of a number of diseases that are more common late in life. Many of these disorders, such as diabetes and chronic obstructive pulmonary disease (see Chapter 12), can weaken your immune system and increase your risk of acquiring infections. Likewise, you may find that you are more susceptible to infections because you have a condition such as heart disease, which can interfere with blood flow; this disruption can affect your body's natural ability to defend itself against infection, as well as its ability to heal.

Exposure to Tenacious Pathogens. Being exposed to various microbes in hospitals and long-term care facilities also increases the risk of developing an infection with drug-resistant pathogens or ones that are not easy to treat. Nevertheless, hospital infection teams are very vigilant about identifying these microorganisms and keeping them under control. Scientists are also working hard to create new antibiotics to fight some of these persistent pathogens.

A Weaker Response to Vaccines. Although many effective vaccines are available to protect against illnesses such as influenza, pneumococcal pneumonia, and tetanus, studies have shown that these vaccines can be far less effective in older adults because the immune response itself may not be as vigorous as it once was. This doesn't mean that you shouldn't be immunized, however; to the contrary, such protection is as important as ever. See Chapter 2 for a discussion of vaccines and recommendations for how often you should receive them.

Older people tend to experience more instances of autoimmune disorders, which may be likened to "friendly fire": Antibodies go on the defensive against the body's own healthy proteins, creating, in the process, disorders such as some forms of hypothyroidism, lupus, and arthritis. Women appear to be more vulnerable than men to these conditions, which are described in Chapters 9 and 14.

As we discussed in Chapter 12, pneumonia is a common infection among older individuals, especially among those who reside in long-term care facilities. The influenza virus is the most common illness that predisposes older people to developing pneumonia. Making sure that you are immunized with the flu vaccine can lower your risk of developing this complication.

Other illnesses such as cancer, congestive heart failure, and diabetes can also affect one's respiratory muscle strength and ability to cough effectively, so these conditions may be predisposing factors also. It's thus especially important, if you have a condition that affects your respiratory health, that you be aware of your risk of developing pneumonia and that you contact your physician promptly if you develop a fever, a slight cough, or shortness of breath.

The incidence of urinary tract infections is also higher in both men and women who are 65 years old or older than it is in younger people. The increased risk of developing this type of infection is associated with an enlarged prostate in men, uterine prolapse in women, and catheterization in both men and women. The symptoms, diagnosis, and treatment of urinary tract infections are discussed in Chapter 11.

Problems That May Occur

Autoimmune Disorders

Pneumonia

Urinary Tract Infections

If you do develop an infection, your doctor can prescribe something for you to clear it up. It's very important that you only take the medicine that your care provider prescribes for the infection that you have. Even if you have some left-over antibiotics in your medicine cabinet, which you took for a previous illness, taking it for this new infection could do more harm than good because there are many different kinds of antibiotics, and they're not equally effective against every microorganism.

Here are some of the terms that you may encounter if your care provider prescribes an infection-fighting medicine for you:

Medicines to Fight Infections: Some Terms You Might Encounter

Antibiotic

An *antibiotic,* which literally means "against life," is a useful drug for fighting bacterial infections. A *broad-spectrum antibiotic* means that the drug is effective in fighting a wide range of different bacterial organisms.

There are several different types of antibiotics, such as the penicillins, cephalosporins, and sulfonamides, and these drugs have very specific applications, so be sure to take only the medicine that your physician has prescribed for you (don't borrow medicines or use leftover medicines from previous infections).

Also, the side effects of these drugs may vary according to their type, so talk with your health care provider about which, if any, side effects you should be aware of.

Antifungal

Antifungal agents (such as amphotericin B, nystatin, ketoconazole, and fluconazole), are used specifically for infections (such as "athlete's foot") that are caused by a fungus.

Antiviral

An antiviral drug works by destroying a virus or inhibiting its ability to replicate. Such medicines include acyclovir for the treatment of the herpes zoster virus (the virus that causes shingles). Other antiviral drugs, amantadine and rimantidine, are sometimes used for the treatment of influenza A, and zanimivir is used for the treatment of influenza A and influenza B viral infections in older people.

Infections in the Extremities

As mentioned earlier, as older persons, our skin barrier may not be as robust as it is in younger people. We may thus develop a localized infection if we stub our toe, scrape our shin, or cut our fingers accidentally. These abrasions may also take longer to heal. If you have such a wound, and the area around it turns red, gets slightly swollen, or causes discomfort, see your doctor. A short course of antibiotics may be helpful. Also, your physician can check to ensure that you're up-to-date on your tetanus shots (see Chapter 2).

If you have diabetes, you need to be especially careful about any injuries to your hands, toes, arms, or legs. Diabetes can slightly or moderately reduce the blood supply to the extremities (especially the legs and feet), so be extra vigilant to make sure that an infection hasn't developed. For this reason, we recommend that patients with diabetes have regular visits to the foot doctor (podiatrist). For more information, see Chapter 14.

Human Immuno-deficiency Virus

The human immunodeficiency virus (HIV) and the acquired immune deficiency syndrome (AIDS) can strike older adults with ferocity because the immune system may already be slightly compromised in an older body stressed by other chronic conditions. Also, unfortunately, HIV is often not diagnosed right away in older people because the symptoms of this infection can mimic other conditions that are common in late life, such as fatigue, pneumonia, and chronic gastrointestinal problems. For more information regarding the prevention and treatment of HIV, see Chapter 5.

Gastrointestinal Infections

Bacterial infections that affect the gastrointestinal tract may be more severe and may have a more prolonged course in older adults than in younger people. Our colleague Lorraine Kyne explains that one form of bacteria, *Clostridium difficile,* causes an especially opportunistic infection that may take hold while a person is taking an antibiotic for something else (such as pneumonia).

Why is it that one sometimes develops another infection while taking an antibiotic? Why doesn't the antibiotic prevent this from occurring? As we said earlier, not all antibiotics are equally effective in fighting all pathogens. Furthermore, antibiotics work by destroying certain forms of bacteria in the body. In doing so, they may destroy not only the bad bacteria that have caused an illness, but also some of the good bacteria that normally reside in our gastrointestinal tract. Thus, it's possible to develop diarrhea a few days after starting antibiotic therapy for one illness, and an additional course of a different antibiotic may be necessary to treat it.

Endocarditis is an infection that can travel through your bloodstream and may sometimes affect the heart valves. This infection is most prevalent among older people, especially among those whose immune system is slightly compromised. To protect yourself from developing this type of infection, talk with your doctor about whether he or she wishes to prescribe an antibiotic for you before you undergo certain procedures (such as dental work). Also, make sure that you have good mouth care. For more information about endocarditis, see Chapter 4.

Endocarditis

Rarely, an infection that involves the brain and spinal column may occur in some older persons. This infection, which causes a fever, headache, and stiffness and discomfort in the neck, requires prompt attention. If you have these symptoms, you don't necessarily have meningitis, but it's a good idea to see your doctor, especially if these problems come on suddenly.

Meningitis

We're fortunate today to have available both vaccines to prevent and antibiotics to treat many of the infections that may come our way. Antibiotics can have an especially important role for some older individuals, whose weakened immune systems may need some extra help in holding down and destroying harmful viruses and bacteria.

On the other hand, some people believe that the problem of *drug-resistant microorganisms* (that is, pathogens that aren't suppressed by antibiotics) may be in part caused by some patients' insistence that their doctors give them antibiotics for illnesses for which such drugs are not required. So, our advice to you is this: If you are ill, feel free to talk with your doctor about your medical options, but don't be disappointed if he or she doesn't prescribe antibiotics for you, or if he or she prescribes a shorter course of antibiotics than you might expect. There certainly are instances when it's necessary to take antibiotics, but sometimes they're not necessary, and in those instances you may be better off not taking them. It's important to keep in mind that before the discovery of antibiotics, people often recovered quite well on their own from various illnesses that are now routinely treated with these drugs.

Last, we answer the question posed at the beginning of this chapter: What can you do to help your body to fight off infections in the first place? As we've mentioned throughout this book, the best way to stay healthy and to nurture your natural immunity is to eat well and take additional nutritional supplements, such as zinc and vitamins. You should also exercise well, rest well, and see your doctor both for regular physical exams and whenever your immune system doesn't seem to respond sufficiently.

CHAPTER 16
YOUR MOUTH

Is not old wine wholesomest, old pippins toothsomest, old wood burn
brightest, old linen wash whitest? Old soldiers, sweethearts, are surest,
and old lovers are soundest.

John Webster (c. 1580–1625)

Today, most people are able to remain toothy, if not toothsome (attractive) in their later years, probably because of fluoride (the compound that prevents tooth decay) that is present in public water supplies, toothpaste, and in treatments in the dentist's office. In fact, these days, 6 or more out of 10 older Americans have their own teeth, whereas far less than half did just 30 years ago.

Of course, our concern with good dental health isn't really so much with cosmetic beauty as it is with functional ability, for we need our teeth to eat well and to speak clearly. Although more of us are keeping our teeth in later life, the older we get, the more cavities we may have, and the greater our risk of infection and periodontal disease. In this chapter, we discuss ways to reduce your risk of dental problems and what you can expect if they occur in spite of your best efforts to keep your mouth healthy.

One of the most obvious changes that may happen as you age is the slight yellowing or coloration of your teeth. This may occur in part because enamel, the hard surface of the tooth, wears down somewhat and makes it possible for the darker color of the next layer—the dentin—to show through.

How Your Mouth Changes as You Age

As we get older, we may also experience a decrease in our ability to control the muscles that enable us to chew well. This difficulty can lead to impaired nutrition if we're not careful. It could also increase our risk of choking because we may tend to swallow pieces of food that are too large or incompletely chewed. Some of us may lose some muscle tone, so that we may find it difficult to completely close our lips. Drooling and dribbling of food and drink from the mouth can result from this incomplete closure. Finally, although people may associate the loss of teeth with aging, it is the increased incidence of tooth decay and periodontal disease—not the number of years that one has lived—that can cause tooth loss.

Keeping Your Mouth Healthy

See Your Dentist

You should have regular, annual or semiannual visits to the dentist, even if you wear dentures. Dentists may carry the title of either "doctor of dental surgery" (D.D.S.) or "doctor of dental medicine" (D.M.D.). You may also be able to find a dentist with special training in geriatric dentistry. All types of dentists can provide regular preventive care, which may include cleaning the teeth, filling cavities, and providing dentures. Dentists are also qualified to treat gum disease and tooth decay with medicine, if necessary, and sometimes with surgery.

For certain conditions, your dentist may refer you to other dental specialists. These include an *oral surgeon,* who can remove teeth and perform surgery on the jaw; an *endodontist,* who has expertise in performing root canals; and a *periodontist,* who specializes in treating gum disease. If you have difficulty with chewing or closing your mouth completely, a *speech language pathologist* or a *specialist in rehabilitative medicine* may be able to help.

If you're concerned about the expense associated with visits to the dentist (most are not covered by Medicare), look into discount programs sponsored by your local dental society or low-fee care that may be available through a local dental school or public health center. Your local council on aging may also be able to direct you to dentists in your area who provide reduced-fee services to elders.

HOW TO MAKE THE BEST OF DENTAL APPOINTMENTS. Just as with your visits to your primary care physician, it helps to be prepared when you see the dentist. Bring along a list of all of the prescription and nonprescription drugs that you're taking, or just open your medicine cabinet and put all of these drugs into a paper bag to take with you.

THINK OF DENTAL CARE AS BEING PART OF YOUR WHOLE HEALTH CARE. Be sure to let your dentist know if you have any other health conditions (especially heart problems) that would require you to take antibiotics before certain dental procedures (see p. 219). To prevent oral infections that may develop after radiation therapy, you should also see your dentist before you undergo this type of treatment. Ideally, your dentist and your primary care physician will work together to share this important information. You should ask your dentist to call your physician (provide the telephone number), and vice versa.

ASK QUESTIONS, AND BE HONEST. If your dentist advises you to brush your teeth more often, do you wish to do so but you're embarrassed to admit that you have a hard time squeezing the toothpaste out of the tube? Does your arthritis make it difficult to hold your arm, hand, and wrist in the right position for brushing your teeth? Helpful products such as toothpaste squeezers and holders are available, and your dentist is the ideal person to help you find them, but you'll have to let him or her know what your needs are.

Also, are your dentures uncomfortable? Perhaps they don't fit properly (this sometimes happens if one has lost weight). By all means, let your dentist know because ill-fitting dentures can lead to mouth sores and other forms of mouth trauma that are easily preventable.

Do You Need to Take Antibiotics Before You Have Dental Procedures?

You may need to take antibiotics before you have dental work if you have any of the following conditions (or if you have had them in the past):

- Bacterial endocarditis (inflammation of the lining of the heart and its valves) (see Chapter 4)
- Rheumatic heart disease
- Prosthetic cardiac valves
- Prosthetic joints (such as knees, hips, or shoulders)
- Hypertrophic cardiomyopathy (see Chapter 4)
- Mitral valve prolapse (see Chapter 4)

Brush and Floss

We advise our patients to brush their teeth at least two or three times per day if possible with a toothpaste that contains fluoride and to use dental floss to clean between the teeth. Be sure to brush not just your teeth, but also your tongue, the inside of your cheeks, and the roof of your mouth. Doing so will help to wipe out some of the bacteria that can lead to bad breath.

If you have difficulty holding the toothbrush because of arthritis or other conditions that affect your arms, hands, and fingers, you may try attaching your toothbrush to a long straw or a wooden spoon to make it easier to handle. Also, talk with your dentist about whether an electric toothbrush would be a good option for you.

Eat Well

Studies have shown that a lack of nutrients such as vitamin C, calcium, and zinc can lead to an increased risk of periodontal disease. A deficiency of iron and vitamin B can cause redness and a sensation of burning on the tongue. Try to eat a balanced diet, and talk with your physician about whether you should be taking a multivitamin.

We also recommend that you try to minimize snacks between meals—especially snacks that contain refined sugars—because such foods can lead to tooth decay. Last, if you have health problems that require you to eat a diet of soft foods that are easy to chew, you'll need to pay particular attention to keeping your teeth clean because these types of foods can predispose you to tooth decay. Smoking can increase your risk of developing oral diseases, too.

Problems That May Occur

Tooth Decay

You may be surprised to learn that most people experience more tooth decay, or caries, after age 65 than ever before. This progressive breakdown of the root surface and the crown of the teeth is often due to disorders of the salivary glands, which, when working properly, provide not only essential fluids for digestion but also protective lubrication and proteins for the oral cavity. If you have tooth decay, you should see a dentist as soon as possible because delays in treatment can lead to tooth loss and the need for tooth extraction or even a root canal procedure.

Gingivitis

Gingiva is another name for the gums, and *gingivitis* is inflammation of the gums that occurs when bacteria accumulate on and around the teeth and invade the gum tissues that support the teeth. Untreated, gum disease can lead to tooth loss. How can you tell whether you have gingivitis? If your gums bleed when you brush your teeth, or your gums become swollen, you may have gum disease.

In older people, there is a greater tendency for the gums to recede, and the gums can become inflamed more easily, especially in patients with diabetes, which may make healing of damaged gum tissues occur more slowly. Drugs that are commonly used by older people—such as cyclosporine, phenytoin, and nifedipine—can irritate the gums also. Other medicines can inhibit the production of saliva, which is necessary to protect our mouths from infection.

What should you do if you have gum disease? See your dentist promptly. Brush and floss your teeth well. A mouthwash that contains an ingredient called chlorhexidine can be helpful in killing the bacteria that cause and aggravate this condition. For advanced gingivitis, your dentist may prescribe antibiotics for a few weeks.

Dry Mouth (Xerostomia)

Are you having difficulty swallowing dry foods such as crackers? Does the dryness in your mouth make it difficult to speak for long periods of time? Is your dry mouth becoming irritated and uncomfortable when you wear dentures?

The composition and flow of saliva don't usually change with age, but we may experience a loss of this fluid because of medicine, surgery, radiation therapy, or a condition called Sjögren's syndrome. A good amount of saliva is important for keeping our teeth clean and for helping us to break down food when we eat. It also keeps the oral environment healthy by cleansing the mouth with antifungal and antimicrobial substances. Next, we look at the important factors that can lead to a dry mouth and what we can do about this condition.

Medicines That Cause Dry Mouth (Xerostomia). A dry mouth is not usually a normal consequence of aging; rather, it is a common side effect of hundreds of different medications that are commonly taken by older adults. These drugs include medicines for high blood pressure, antihistamines for allergies, drugs for Parkinson's disease, decongestants, diuretics, tranquilizers, and analgesics. Talk with your doctor about changing the dosage or the type of medication that you are taking to minimize this side effect. He or she may also be able to help you with your medicine-taking schedule, so that this side effect occurs at meal-times, when eating will help to stimulate your salivary glands and keep your mouth moist.

Radiation or Surgery. Radiation or surgery for head or neck tumors can also lead to a decline in saliva production, and unfortunately, this type of damage to the salivary glands is usually not reversible. However, a drug called pilocarpine may be helpful in relieving dryness in the mouth due to radiation therapy.

Sjögren's Syndrome. Another cause of dryness in the mouth is *Sjögren's syndrome,* an autoimmune condition that can be harmful to the salivary glands and the *lacrimal glands* (which produce tears). This condition affects women more often than men, and it tends to occur in those who are middle-aged or older.

An oral surgeon can test for this syndrome by doing a biopsy (i.e., removing a small sample of tissue from the salivary glands for examination under the microscope). If a diagnosis of Sjögren's syndrome is confirmed, your doctor may prescribe pilocarpine to stimulate the salivary glands. The sidebar below lists other suggestions for keeping your mouth moist.

What to Do If Your Mouth Is Dry

- Try sugarless gum or candies.
- Saliva is composed mainly of water, so drink as much water (or other drinks that do not contain caffeine or sugar) as possible.
- Whereas drinking fluids can help your body to produce the saliva that it needs, products called salivary substitutes provide only temporary relief. These products generally are in the form of a gel that one puts into the mouth before bedtime to prevent dryness.
- Use moisturizing lip balm or lipstick to prevent your lips from chapping.
- Use only mouthwashes that do not contain alcohol.
- Avoid alcohol and caffeine—both can dry your mouth further.
- Choose a toothpaste that contains fluoride and has a mild flavor (some tooth-pastes that are made for children have flavors that are less irritating to a sensitive mouth).
- A dry mouth can lead to increased tooth decay, so ask your dentist about a fluoride gel that you can use at home to help you prevent this problem.
- See your dentist regularly to have your teeth cleaned.

Bad Breath (Halitosis)

Just as certain medications can cause your mouth to become dry, others can lead to bad breath. Some illnesses can, too. There are several steps that you can take to solve this problem, though. First of all, keep your mouth as clean as possible. Brush and floss your teeth often, paying particular care to brush all around the inside of your mouth. Brush your tongue, too.

Gargling may be helpful in clearing up some of the bacteria that congregate at the back of your throat. Mouthwash may also be helpful. Last, breath mints can freshen your breath temporarily, although they won't do anything to solve the underlying problem.

Mouth Sores If you have a dry mouth or if you have broken teeth or dentures that do not fit properly, you may develop uncomfortable lesions inside your mouth. Diabetes, radiation therapy, or an immune-deficiency illness can make one more susceptible to developing these sores. In addition to drugs for some specific causes of mouth sores, which we describe next, your dentist can prescribe a medicated rinse or a soothing topical medicine to help them heal. You should eliminate spicy foods from your diet until this healing occurs.

Candidiasis. If you have dentures, if you take certain drugs (such as antibiotics, steroids, chemotherapy agents, or immunosuppressants) for a long period of time, or if you have a dry mouth, you may develop a fungal infection called *oral candidiasis* (also called *thrush* or *monolithiasis*). People who have diabetes mellitus (see Chapter 14) or infection with the human immunodeficiency virus (HIV) are quite susceptible to this type of infection also. The fungus that causes this problem, *Candida albicans,* is present in the mouth and many other parts of the body in most healthy people. Sometimes the use of certain medications, however, allows overgrowth of such organisms so that they can cause problems.
    Candida infection appears as white, curd-like flakes on the inner surfaces of the mouth and on the tongue. Affected areas of the mouth can have a burning sensation. If you develop thrush, your doctor may prescribe an oral antifungal medicine called nystatin or chlortrimazole lozenges. These medicines may need to be taken for at least two weeks.

Lichen Planus. This autoimmune disorder causes chronic inflammation and sores within the mouth. Stress, the use of certain medications, a family tendency to develop this illness, and a viral or bacterial infection can bring about this problem, too. These sores, which usually appear on the gums and tongue (but rarely on the lips), often are surrounded by white, lacelike lines. The treatment for lichen planus may include a steroid medicine that is applied to the lesions after meals and at bedtime. See your physician or dentist for instructions.

Disorders of the Salivary Glands In addition to Sjögren's syndrome, a disease of the salivary gland that can cause a dry mouth, other salivary gland problems may emerge as we age:

Bacterial Infection. A swollen, uncomfortable salivary gland (especially while eating), along with a fever and possibly a headache, can signal the presence of an infected salivary gland. If your doctor determines that you have this type of infection, he or she may prescribe antibiotics for you and will probably suggest that you drink as many noncaffeinated and non-alcohol-containing liquids as possible in order to stimulate salivary flow.

Sialolithiasis. *Sialoliths* are calcium stones in the salivary glands that may develop when a person is inactive. These stones can cause irritation and swelling, and chewing can be uncomfortable because of the blockage of the salivary gland. These stones can be removed by a minor surgical procedure.

Mucoceles. A *mucocele* is an enlarged cavity in which mucus accumulates. Like bacterial infections and stones in the salivary gland, a mucocele generally causes swelling. As with sialoliths, surgery is often required to remove the affected gland.

Temporomandibular Joint (TMJ) Disorders

The incidence of diseases that involve the temporomandibular joint (TMJ) rises with age. This joint is located between the skull and the mandible (the jaw), and it affects the muscles that help us chew. A TMJ disorder can cause popping or clicking sounds, pain in the ear and neck, and even a sense of pain in the teeth. If you have this condition, you may find it difficult to open your mouth completely. TMJ problems may be exacerbated if one does not have teeth or if one has dentures.

If your doctor suspects that you have a TMJ disorder, he or she may have you undergo certain radiologic imaging tests such as magnetic resonance imaging (MRI). Once the diagnosis is confirmed, he or she may recommend that you see a specialist who has experience in treating TMJ disorders, a physical therapist, and perhaps a psychologist. Your doctor may also advise you to eat a soft diet and to use moist heat and perhaps nonsteroidal anti-inflammatory drugs or muscle relaxants to ease the discomfort associated with this condition. Physical therapy and the use of special devices may also be helpful.

Oral Cancers

The incidence of oral cancers becomes more prevalent in old age, and most cancerous lesions of the mouth are diagnosed in people in their early 60s. Oral cancers are twice as common in men as in women. Most cancerous lesions appear on the floor of the mouth, beneath the tongue and behind the last molar teeth, although they can also appear on the other inner surfaces of the mouth and on the tongue, lips, and pharynx. In women, most oral cancers are located on the gums.

Risk factors for oral cancers include the use of tobacco (chewing tobacco, cigarettes, cigars, and pipes) and alcohol. Exposure to the sun can also lead to cancerous lesions on the lips.

An early symptom of oral cancer is bleeding or sores in the mouth that last for two weeks or more. White or red spots or ulcers in the mouth that last for this amount of time are also of concern. Usually, oral cancer does not cause pain.

If your doctor determines that you have oral cancer, he or she will check your mouth, pharynx, larynx, esophagus, and lungs for other possible cancerous lesions. Small (less than 1 cm in diameter) oral cancers can be treated by local surgical removal and possibly radiation or chemotherapy. If the lesions have spread to the lymph nodes, radiation therapy or chemotherapy, or both, will probably be recommended.

If you have a tumor of the salivary gland, the gland may have to be removed, and radiation treatment may be needed.

PART THREE

ADAPTING TO LIFE'S TRANSITIONS

CHAPTER 17

RETIREMENT

It's not by muscle, speed, or physical dexterity
that great things are achieved,
but by reflection, force of character, and judgment;
in these qualities old age is usually not only not poorer,
but is even richer.

Cicero (106–43 B.C.)

What do you think of when you hear the word "retirement"? Do you picture yourself bored and lonely, maybe staring blankly at the TV? Longing for the comfort and familiarity of the office, the morning commute, and the paycheck?

Or do you envision yourself making the most of retirement by experiencing new activities and spending precious time with loved ones? In short, do you see yourself doing everything you've wanted to do all these years if only you hadn't had to work every day?

In some ways, *retirement* is a misnomer for this important transition. Think about it—why should you have to withdraw from an active life or view yourself as being no longer useful just because you aren't racing around the hamster wheel as you may have in the past? Really, just the opposite is true. After years of hard work, you can shake off the restraints of business obligations and embrace a creative time of endless opportunities.

Another way to look at this transition is to compare it with other major changes in your life. For instance, you may have retired from the U.S. Navy decades ago, but that didn't mean that you had to stop sailing. You just left the restrictions and regimentation of military life and enjoyed the freedom to float your own boat wherever and whenever you wanted to.

Likewise, you wouldn't say that you've retired from parenthood just because your children no longer live at home. Rather, your role has evolved, and you're doing other important things. Your children may need you in a different way, but your grandchildren and other younger persons need you and would benefit from your company just as surely as your children and other children did (and still do).

Once you've stopped working, you'll have even more energy to pursue your own interests and to give even more to your family. You'll also have the time to reach beyond your family circle and contribute to your community and world in ways that you never have before. "Retired"? No. "Untired" at last? Most definitely.

In this chapter, we discuss ways to make the liberating role shift from employee to retiree. We start by looking at the different issues that you may be facing if you're still working, and then we explore the major transition that retirement involves. Finally, we address some of the many opportunities that await you once you've broken free of the working world.

Before Retirement

Changes in the Workplace

THE LOSS OF THE "COMPANY MAN." If you're still working, and you hope or expect to continue doing so for years to come, you know that the modern job market has changed dramatically. It used to be that newcomers to the workforce could expect to spend their careers within the safe and secure confines of a single company, ideally becoming more productive and more valued through the years.

Today, however, company loyalty is largely a thing of the past. Many people advance their careers themselves by leaving one firm and joining another that is bigger or offers more attractive opportunities. Nowadays, in fact, each American works at an average of eight different places throughout her or his adult life and most people now enjoy more than one type of occupation or career during their lifetime.

DOWNSIZING. The flip side of this loyalty issue is that employers no longer expect employees to sign on forever. In some businesses, *downsizing* (reducing the number of employees) is practically par for the course. In order to stay competitive in a tough global marketplace, many corporations are forced to reduce their workforces by laying off employees or offering older employees incentives to retire early. More and more, pension plans are becoming a thing of the past.

NEW TOOLS. Also, workers today must keep abreast of technological advances in order to perform and keep their jobs. If you started working long before new, fast-paced information technologies were introduced, you may have had to take a training course or two—and you're not alone. Just about everyone is being forced to retool at least every few years just to keep up with the latest systems.

THE NATURE OF THE WORKFORCE. Who is working has also changed. Since the late 1960s, more women are working than staying home. Also, the general population has increased, and the number of workers has swelled commensurately.

These changes don't necessarily mean that the workplace is or will be too crowded to accommodate people who want to continue working late in life, though. In fact, the size of the workforce is already beginning to decline. The last of the "baby boomers" went to work in the mid-1980s, and the generation of newcomers that follows them is much smaller, so there should be an abundance of job openings available in the years to come.

THE CRUCIAL ROLE OF SENIORS. In today's workplace, while some prejudices about older workers may be on the wane, they still exist. Antidiscrimination legislation is now in place to ensure that you can't be fired (or denied a new job) for being too old. (See sidebar below on age discrimination.)

Moreover, attitudes are gradually changing for the better, and the contributions of seniors are finally starting to be valued as they should be. In the rapidly changing business world, there is growing respect for the strong, consistent work ethic and experience of many older adults.

Other qualities that come with experience and maturity—such as reliability, professionalism, and commitment to doing a good job—can also work in your favor. These qualities, as well as your ability to be a good role model for younger employees, can make you a valuable asset to your employer. So, if you want to continue working, you should do so, and you should feel confident that you have a great deal to offer. Now we talk about ways to make the most of your continued employment.

Thanks to the Age Discrimination in Employment Act (ADEA), discrimination due to a person's age is now prohibited in the United States. The 1978 amendment to this act effectively changed the mandatory age of retirement from 65 to 70. In certain professions, the mandatory age of retirement has now been abolished.

Age Discrimination

What do these laws really mean? An employer is not allowed to consider your age when he or she is hiring you, training or retraining you, paying you, or letting you go. The law also forbids employment agencies from discriminating against job hunters because of age.

If you have questions about the ADEA or want to file a complaint, contact the Equal Employment Opportunity Commission (EEOC) toll-free at 1-800-USA-EEOC.

ATTITUDE COUNTS. Are you wistful for the way your business used to be run in the good old days? The chances are that many things may have been better then, but as with most things, if your company didn't change and grow, it probably wouldn't have survived.

Keeping the Job You Have

Instead of becoming discouraged, try to think of your many years of experience and the perspective you've gained as powerful tools that you can employ to make unequaled contributions to your company. If you add to these tools a positive and open mind, your employer and employees will value your efforts more than ever.

PLAY IT SAFE. You may feel that younger people are anxious for you to move on so that they can take your place. You may also fear that you'll be edged out of your position by forced retirement or downsizing. It may sound obvious, but if you want your job to last, you should be a model employee. In addition to the experience that you have to offer, punctuality, reliability, and loyalty are qualities that will always work in your favor.

LEARN NEW SKILLS. You can also increase your value to the company by keeping your skills up-to-date. To do so, take advantage of all the retraining programs and seminars that are relevant to your job. Show your willingness to take on new tasks and responsibilities and to learn new things.

SET AN EXAMPLE. Emphasize your value as an older employee by acting as a role model to young people in the company. For example, look into pioneering a mentoring program. You have a great deal to offer, so share your know-how in any way possible.

What If You're "Let Go" Anyway?

Regardless of all your good efforts and the laws that protect you, it's always possible that you may lose your job. No amount of planning can prepare you for a retirement that happens sooner than you expected. Losing this job doesn't mean that you have to accept early retirement if you're not ready to, though. If you need or want to continue working, talk with your human resources department about flexible retirement options, such as a shift from full-time to part-time work. The sidebar below lists some of the alternatives that you may want to consider.

You'll also have more options if you can find ways to stay involved in your industry. *Networking* is one of the best ways to do this: List all of the people you know in your profession who could help you find gainful work; contact them, and let them know what you're doing and what your interests are.

Also, consider consulting, on a paid or volunteer basis. It may lead to a permanent position or help you begin a second, independent career.

Outside the Daily Grind

Henry always worked every day throughout his adult life. He never had a single moment to spare. When he retired after 35 years of service, he was presented with a watch. Some people might find it ironic to receive a watch when one retires, but Henry took it in a positive light. He planned to be just as busy as before with his diverse creative interests and neighborhood activities.

Retirement is no longer all or nothing. Maybe you still enjoy your job, but you'd like more free time for leisure activities, or you need time off to care for an ailing relative or spouse. Perhaps your company forced you into retirement, but you're just not ready to give up working for good.

In today's workforce, there are many in-between options. One of these may be just right for you:

- *Leave of absence.* If you need a breather from work, but you're not sure you want a permanent break, you may be a candidate for a paid or unpaid leave of absence, also known as a *sabbatical.* Many employers now encourage workers to take breaks if they can give sound reasons for wanting to do so.

- *Flexible time and job sharing.* Look into whether your company offers flextime or part-time work schedules. You may be able to cut your work week from five days to three, or switch to just mornings, for a reduction in pay. Maybe you and another employee could devise a way to share one full-time job. *Job sharing,* as this practice is called, is becoming more popular all the time.

- *Part-time work.* Maybe you could change your status from a full-time employee to a part-time one. If your company doesn't hire part-time, you may want to look around for a company that does.

- *Gradual retirement.* Investigate working fewer hours while keeping your retirement benefits. Retiring gradually instead of suddenly can make the transition easier for everyone and can provide you with time to pass on your experience to a successor.

- *Temporary work.* If you lose your job, or your company is demanding more than you want to give at this point, you might consider temporary work. Signing on with a temp agency allows you to work full- or part-time for a variety of companies, get paid, and keep on top of your industry—all without making a long-term commitment that you may no longer want to make.

Looking for Work

If you're looking for a new job, you may have already come across people with misconceptions about stereotypical older workers who are unwilling to learn new things. The best way to counter such misperceptions is to convey an image that shatters that stereotype. Share your work record, and express your desire to learn and grow with the company. Make people's low expectations work to your advantage—they'll be pleased and surprised when they realize what you can do for them.

If you feel daunted by the technology that a prospective job requires, remember that all employees, regardless of age, are faced with the same challenge. With technology changing so rapidly in most industries, nearly everyone is required to be retrained every five years or so. You are not alone, so long as you are always open to learning and relearning new skills and techniques.

There are many examples of creativity and productivity long after retirement. For example, former U.S. Senator John Glenn at the age of 76 went up in a space shuttle. This not only fulfilled his dream, but also made a valuable contribution to the study of older persons in zero-gravity conditions. Former U.S.

President George Bush enjoyed sky-diving at the age of 72. Please do not let age deter you. It is true that not everyone has the opportunity to sky-dive or go up in space, but remaining socially active and following your interests will be very beneficial for you and others. You have much to contribute.

Retirement Planning

Whenever and however you stop working, will you be ready for life as a retiree? A successful retirement depends on two things: a positive attitude and careful planning. Your personal agenda will change as retirement grows closer. Therefore, the best retirement plans are formed slowly and revised as necessary.

It's never too early to start planning for your retirement. That's old tried-and-true advice, so it's quite astonishing how few people actually follow it. Many people think retirement is too far off; they can't plan for the future. The majority of Americans today retire well before they expected to, however, due to downsizing and forced retirement. Also, most retired people will tell you that they wish they'd spent more time doing careful planning in advance.

Why do so many of us put off this important type of planning? Some people just don't want to think about the day when their paychecks will stop and life on a fixed income will begin. Others may think—wrongly—that retirement planning is about finances alone, and they don't want to deal with their grim financial status until they have to.

There's more to consider about retirement than mere money, though. There is the effect of retirement on your spouse, the prospect of moving away from home, the abundance of free time that awaits you.

In spite of these serious considerations, retirement planning doesn't have to be fraught with pain or anxiety. You don't have to sit down with a group of professional advisors and make decisions that are irreversible. Retirement planning simply means thinking long and hard about the sort of lifestyle you see for yourself once you're no longer working—and figuring out how to make it happen.

As you begin to work out your own retirement plan, there are lots of resources available to you. Many employers offer retirement-planning workshops. Adult education and community programs do, too. In any case, it's up to you to make the first move.

Try starting with the basics. Picture yourself in your postwork life. Then consider your feelings regarding factors such as your new role and the effect of your retirement on your family and your time, and your plan for the future will be under way.

Your Role

Right now you're an employee, a worker, a wage earner, possibly a breadwinner. Once you're none of these things, what will your new role be? If you can't envision an answer and the question leaves you feeling a bit unsettled, you may find yourself feeling somewhat bereft after retirement. These feelings are common and natural. Anticipating them will help you to accept and deal with them.

In our very work-oriented society, the first question you ask or are asked by a new acquaintance is probably, "What do you do?" Think about how you will feel when your answer to that question is, "I don't work anymore. I'm retired."

Many couples report that retirement (usually the husband's retirement) can cause marital rifts. It's difficult for a woman who's kept house for many years to suddenly have underfoot a man with little to do. She may miss her old routine or be annoyed by her husband's opinions about how she spends her day. Happily, these problems usually correct themselves in time, and most marriages remain as they were before retirement. If you and your spouse lived in harmony before, you should continue to do so after a short adjustment period.

Your Family

Retirement may be difficult when children still live at home or when elderly parents are part of the household. All of a sudden, you are privy to everything that goes on in your house throughout the day—things you may never have seen before, and of which you may not approve.

How will retirement affect *your* family? You may be afraid that your spouse and your kids will see you in a different light. They will. All at once, you'll be a stay-at-homer, not a go-to-worker. They may view you as aging for the first time. Talking to them about your feelings and theirs before the change happens, rather than after, will help ensure the smoothest transition.

Some people occupy themselves so naturally when they retire that they actually feel they had more free time when they were working. Others cannot wait for the sun to set on another seemingly long day. People are different and respond differently to life changes. Some can adapt more easily than others.

Your Time

People who typically have trouble adjusting to retirement life are those who always worked long hours, brought work home with them, and had few leisure activities. If this description applies to you, consider how you'll feel once you can no longer fill your hours with work tasks.

You've spent all your life perfecting your job performance—it's what you do. After retirement, you're not going to do it any more. How does that make you feel?

Your Talents

In today's highly flexible job market, you may find many ways to continue working even after you retire. Your company might hire you as a consultant, for instance, or on a part-time basis. These arrangements are quite common.

A 1999 report suggested that men tend to be more satisfied when they go back to work after retirement. Even if you don't go back to work, you don't have to let your skills lie fallow. A bit later in this chapter, we talk about ways to apply your skills in other ways, such as for a volunteer organization.

When you picture your retired self, where are you? Have you relocated to Florida or Cape Cod or Arizona, or somewhere else that's closer to your children? Have you sold your house and bought or rented a smaller, less expensive one? Have you moved to a retirement community where you'll be surrounded by other retirees, and chores such as cutting the grass and fixing a leaky faucet will be somebody else's responsibility?

Your Home

The possibilities are endless, and you certainly may change your mind as time passes and your situation changes. Whatever your situation is, you and your spouse or partner should discuss this matter as soon and as openly as possible. Where to live after retirement is a major source of disagreement for couples. Typically, one wishes to stay put and the other wants to move. Fair and even communication now may spare you arguments and disappointments later. We talk more about different housing options in the next chapter.

Your Health   It's an indisputable fact that healthy retirees are much happier than unhealthy retirees. If you're not in great shape, there are steps you can take now to make your retirement life more comfortable and enjoyable. You probably know the rest. If you smoke, see your doctor and figure out a way to stop. It will never get any easier than it is today. If you drink, do so in moderation. Eat a balanced, low-fat diet, rich in fruits, vegetables, and whole grains. Also, get some aerobic exercise—walking, jogging, swimming, cycling—a minimum of three times a week for at least 20 to 30 minutes at a time. Don't fool yourself into thinking you can put off good health habits until retirement. The time to start is now.

Your Money   How much do you think you'll need to earn before you're secure enough to retire? Financial planners can help you settle on a reasonable amount, but if you're like many people, you'll want to squirrel away a massive nest egg before you give up your paycheck forever.

Financial security is a wonderful thing, but also be realistic. Working long hours for many years at the expense of enjoying family, friends, and leisure activities might not necessarily lead to a happy retirement. More importantly, you need to do what you enjoy doing.

You may always have thought that when it comes to retirement, money is everything. As the adage says, however, it can't buy happiness. Reflect on your emotional as well as financial net worth, and celebrate it.

The Stress of Retirement   For years, people have considered retirement one of life's top stress-inducing events, right up there with divorce or the loss of one's home. Recent research suggests that retirement may not be so stressful after all, however. In fact, the majority of retirees make a smooth transition from work life to retirement life, and most people are quite content once they settle into nonworking life.

Still, retirement is stressful for about 30% of the retired population. That percentage basically represents those who retire unexpectedly. Either they were forced into retirement by their employers, or they had to quit because of an illness or disability. It's hard to be content with retirement under those circumstances. Financial worries and marital or family problems also inject stress into retirement. People with a history of depression may have trouble adjusting, too.

Once again, the best advice is to be prepared. If you're at risk because of any of the factors we have just described, expect that some stress may find its way into your postwork life. Anticipating that stress beforehand will help you manage it once it's upon you.

Leaving your job doesn't mean that your life must grind to a halt. Quite the opposite is true. There are countless opportunities available for retired seniors today. Whether you choose to retire or you are downsized into it, look at retirement as a golden opportunity for a deservedly bright future.

Once you retire, you'll find that there is no shortage of activities available to people who want to stay involved in the world around them. Following is a general sampling, but contact your local agency on aging for a list of what's happening in your town.

After Retirement

We've already discussed ways to keep active by working part-time or consulting, but maybe earning an income is no longer a priority for you. If so, volunteering may be the answer.

One study showed that 26% of older people volunteer for organizations, 29% informally help the sick and disabled, and about one third of seniors help their grandchildren. Moreover, our colleague John Rowe has reported that volunteering can be a positive predictor of successful aging.

There are hundreds of organizations across the country that welcome senior volunteers. Through some—at nursing homes and senior centers, for example—you will assist other elders. Maybe you prefer to work with children or with small businesses in need of help. You may want to devote your efforts to the sick, the homeless, the abused, or others in need.

Decide how you'd like to invest your volunteer hours, choose an organization that interests you, and call for more information. You may wish to contact one of the following clearinghouses that place senior volunteers nationwide.

Volunteer Work

Retired Senior Volunteer Program (RSVP). This program places volunteer retirees in community-based organizations. Contact your local council on aging for the chapter in your community.

Time Dollar Program. One model program in New York enlists younger elders to help older elders with tasks such as grocery shopping. In doing so, the younger elders build up credits that they can cash in when they are older and need assistance, too. This type of program is a wonderful way to help yourself and your community at the same time.

Service Corps of Retired Executives (SCORE). Volunteers offer management advice to small businesses and community organizations. Contact your local chapter of the Small Business Administration (SBA).

Volunteers in Service to America (VISTA). VISTA volunteers are people of all ages who serve in programs that deal with hunger, child abuse, illiteracy, and drug abuse. Call your local VISTA office.

Going back to school is one of the most difficult things to do while you're working or raising a family, so your retirement years may be your best opportunity ever to expand your education. Is there something you've always wanted to

Continuing Education

study? Maybe you're interested in landscape gardening, or architecture, or the Internet. Perhaps you've always wanted to improve your high-school French. Colleges and universities welcome senior citizens in both regular classes and continuing education programs. Also, check out the adult education program in your community. Seniors usually enjoy tuition discounts. For more information, talk to your librarian, or contact your local agency on aging.

Elderhostel   Following in the tradition of the youth hostels of Europe, the national Elderhostel program was designed specifically for elders who want to travel, socialize, and learn new things. If you go on a trip with this program, you'll travel with other elders to spend a week at a college or university, where you may hear lectures and discuss topics ranging from computers to cinema to research in geriatric medicine. As you learn, you'll take field trips, share meals, and make friends. Discounts are usually available. For more information on finding an Elderhostel that appeals to your specific interests, write to Elderhostel; 75 Federal Street; Boston, MA 02110-1941.

It's never easy to give up what we're used to, and you may well have been working all of your adult life. Still, try to think of retirement as a beginning, not an end. Work as long as you like, or as long as you must, or as long as you are able. Then close that chapter and look toward the next. Not working for pay can be a wonderful thing! Now you should do what you like to do. If you want to continue to learn, or to help people, or both, all the better.

CHAPTER 18

YOUR HOME

Should we have stayed at home,
wherever that may be?

Elizabeth Bishop (1911–1979)

Most of us crave stability; permanence brings peace of mind. Is it any wonder that the majority of us wish to stay right where we are?

A 1996 survey conducted by the American Association of Retired Persons (AARP) found that more than 80% of people over age 50 would like to remain in their current homes for the rest of their lives.

Fortunately, thanks to home health care professionals and a wide variety of services designed especially for the fast-growing elder population, most of us will be able to make this wish a reality because many needed services can be brought straight to our door.

Nevertheless, it's a good idea to prepare yourself for any eventuality, no matter how unlikely it may seem now. Even people who are perfectly healthy and capable of maintaining their homes can unexpectedly injure themselves or become seriously ill or disabled.

What would you do in such a situation? Can you afford in-home care, or have you explored other alternatives? Today we have a wider array of housing choices than any generation before us, from senior apartments to assisted-living facilities. Have you talked with your children or other loved ones about your preferences? It's a good idea to talk with them now so that they can help you, if need be, with arrangements later on.

In this chapter, we discuss the variety of resources available to make staying in your own home a safe and workable option. We also explore other housing alternatives that you may want to consider someday.

Staying Home

I've lived alone since my husband Bill died 15 years ago, and I'm comfortable living this way, with my own routines and my familiar surroundings. My two daughters live nearby and they visit me every few days. However, my eyesight isn't as good as it used to be and so I never use my front steps because I'm afraid of falling. I'm terrified that if I fall and my children find out, they will make me move to a nursing home.

Shirley, age 75

Do you want to stay in your own home no matter what? If so, is your house or apartment a safe place to be, or does it need some repairs or improvements to minimize your risk of falling or getting hurt in some other way? Also, if keeping up with cooking, housework, and getting around town are becoming real challenges, have you looked into community resources for help with meals, cleaning, and transportation?

What about contact with others? If you live alone, do you get lonely? Do your friends, relatives, and priest, rabbi, or clergy visit you at home? Do you get out to social gatherings at your local senior center? Next, we talk about ways to stay well, independent, and happy while remaining in your own home.

Making Your Home Accident-Proof

If you love your house or apartment but have been avoiding certain danger zones, such as your treacherous front steps, perhaps it's time to do a safety survey. The sidebar below contains a room-by-room checklist that you can use to determine which areas need particular attention. If you're concerned about slipping in the shower, for instance, "grab" bars can be helpful. How about the lighting in your kitchen? Is it bright enough there to cook safely? Are you concerned about falling out of bed? Side rails are easy to install.

If you don't have anyone to help with safety renovations, ask your local council on aging for the name of a carpenter or handyperson. Many offer senior discounts. (You can locate the agency in your community by calling the Eldercare Locator at 1-800-677-1116, or call your state agency, listed in Appendix A on pp. 333–338.)

Tips for Accident-Proofing Your Home

In General

- Are your telephone number and address written clearly so that they're easy to read, and is this information placed next to each telephone in your house? In an emergency, it's sometimes difficult to remember such information. Also, next to the phone you should post the telephone numbers of the fire department, police, and a neighbor or a close friend who lives nearby, in case you need to reach them in a hurry.

- Can you see the numbers on your telephone clearly? Consider purchasing a push-button telephone with large numbers.

- To prevent falls, don't use area rugs. If you have carpets, make sure that the edges are held down securely with double-sided carpet tape or tacks (you can buy these at most hardware and drug stores).

- Are your smoke detectors in good working order? Do you have one in every room? Can you reach them to change the batteries when necessary?
- Are the stairs both inside and outside your home safe and well lit? Are they free of clutter? Do they have handrails on both sides? Inside your house, are there light switches at both the top and bottom of the stairs?
- Can you unlock your doors easily? If you have several locks on one door, consider replacing them with one very good lock.
- If you have a doorbell, does it work? Can you hear it when it rings?
- Can you get to your mailbox easily?
- Are all electrical, telephone, and extension cords located where you won't trip over them? Check them regularly to make sure that none are frayed.
- Is your hot-water thermostat set below 120 degrees to prevent scalding?
- Have you had your chimney cleaned recently?
- Are your windows easy to open?
- Are you using lightbulbs with the right wattage for your lamps and light fixtures?
- Can you turn on the lights with a switch in every room so that you never have to walk through darkness to reach a light?

In Your Kitchen

- Can you reach items from high shelves and cabinets without standing on a chair?
- Are your cabinets easy to open?
- Do you have good lighting over your stove and sink?
- Are all of your electrical appliances located away from the sink and the stove?
- Is the exhaust system on your stove working properly?

In Your Living Room

- Can you sit down and get up from your favorite chair easily?
- Are there any unstable pieces of furniture that could tip over and cause you to fall?
- Have you removed throw rugs and other seemingly harmless items that may actually be hazardous? These may include small magazine racks or electrical cords that you could trip over.

In Your Bedroom

- Are the nightlight, light switch, and telephone located near your bed?

- Is your bed low enough so that your feet can easily reach the floor when you get up in the morning? Do you worry about falling out of bed? Side rails may be helpful.
- Are there any obstacles between your bed and the bathroom that need to be removed, so that you don't bump into them when you get up at night?
- Is the floor around your bed carpeted? Even a large area rug (held down well with carpet tacks or tape so that it can't move) can provide warmth and some protection in case you fall.

In Your Bathroom

- Are there rails beside the toilet and in the shower to grab onto?
- Are your bath mats or rugs held down securely?
- Is there a nonskid surface in your bathtub?
- Do you have a shower-hose extension for more flexibility?
- Is there a fold-up bench or chair in your shower?

Finding Help with Everyday Activities

Even if you've been living alone for years, certain tasks may become more difficult or even impossible over time. Perhaps arthritis occasionally makes it harder to prepare a meal, or possibly you've recently lost a spouse who always cooked or sorted out the taxes for you. Perhaps hip surgery has made it more difficult for you to bathe yourself or to perform certain household chores. Possibly you can manage at home, but you're less able to drive now.

If any of the preceding conditions applies to you, don't worry. These conditions are very common, and you can find help. Your local council on aging can assist you to find the household help, meal delivery, transportation, and other aids that you may need. Some community-based programs are free of charge or are available at a discounted rate for seniors. Services vary among communities, but the following are the most common ones:

Meal Delivery. Through free programs such as Meals on Wheels, which are staffed and run by volunteers in your community, you can receive free hot meals delivered straight to your kitchen.

Grocery Delivery. If you prefer to cook for yourself but find it difficult to get to the market, many grocery stores now offer shopping and delivery services for a reasonable service charge. You can call (or use e-mail) to submit your order, and your food, cleaning supplies, and even nonprescription pharmacy items will probably arrive several hours later.

Home Shopping. Likewise, if you no longer drive and don't want to depend on friends or relatives to get you to the store, you may want to use catalogs to shop by telephone or mail, or look at some shopping sites on the Internet. You may even be able to save money by buying things this way because you can comparison shop through different catalogs and websites—all in the comfort of your own home. The key thing to remember when shopping in this manner, though, is that it's only safe to give out your credit card number if *you* initiate the phone call. Never give this information out if someone calls you and asks for it.

Dry Cleaning and Laundry Services. Have you been putting off having those heavy curtains, bedspreads, and winter coats cleaned because the thought of hauling them to the cleaners is so daunting? Check your local yellow pages to see which dry cleaners offer pickup and delivery services.

Do you worry about falling down the basement stairs with a basket of dirty clothes in your arms? Talk with a repairer, maintenance person, or your landlord about moving your washer and dryer to the main floor of your home, or consider contacting a laundromat that will collect your dirty laundry and return it to you washed, folded, and even ironed. A less expensive option may be to find a person in your town who does laundry for a living; such services may be listed in the classified section of your local newspaper.

House Cleaning. If you're finding that you're less able to keep up the hard work of heavy cleaning, you may want to hire a cleaning service to give your home a good sprucing up once every week or two, or even just once a month. Consider this expense a good investment in your good health and your good spirits!

Financial Services. Have you recently lost a spouse who always handled the bills, bank account, and taxes? Even if you have always been the one who managed your family's dollars and cents, are you finding it increasingly difficult to keep up with the constant ups and downs in the stock market and changes to the tax laws? It may be time to make use of the services of a certified public accountant (CPA) or other money specialist. Be sure to check the credentials of any CPA or financial planner that you use, though. Chapter 19 details ways to minimize the risks of white-collar crime.

You may also want to talk with someone at your local bank about telebanking options that you can use to manage your bill payment and money transfers over the telephone, without unnecessary trips to the bank or the post office.

Transportation. If you don't drive, or you don't feel confident about driving at night or in inclement weather, your local council on aging may be able to connect you with volunteers who can pick you up at home and drive you to and from doctor's appointments, supermarkets, and other important destinations.

Other Services. Some beauticians are happy to pay house calls, and your local newspaper is probably full of listings by handypersons looking for a room to paint, a lawn to mow, or a driveway to plow or shovel. You can also hire companions or find volunteers to perform a variety of other tasks, such as reading aloud, paying bills, or writing letters.

Getting Good Health Care at Home

In addition to all of the other services that have been mentioned, today many types of health care professionals will come directly to your home. Your local hospital or senior center can help to put you in touch with professionals in your area. Medicare and Medicaid may cover some or all of the costs involved. Here are a few home health care professionals and the services they provide:

- *Nurses* can administer medication.
- *Certified nurses aides (CNAs)* cannot administer drugs, but they can provide many other nursing services.
- *Home health aides* perform grooming and bathing tasks and light house-keeping chores.
- *Geriatric care managers* will arrange for and supervise every aspect of your home care.
- *Respite care workers* visit for several hours to give your regular caregiver some time off.
- *Other helpers* may include home-care professionals who can give you a hand with miscellaneous tasks such as shopping, bills, and yardwork.

Staying Connected with the Outside World While Living on Your Own

In addition to maintaining a safe environment and making sure that you have clean clothes, a clean home, and warm food on the table, the other very important part of living independently is making sure that you stay in contact with others.

If you have children, do they live far away? Is your nearest neighbor two miles down a country road? Do you want to stay in your own home but you worry that you may faint or fall and no one will find you for many days? If so, here are some ways to stay secure and to overcome isolation:

Personal Emergency Response System. If you live alone and you have a condition that may make urgent medical attention necessary at some point in the future, you may want to rent a *personal emergency response system*. Although it has a rather unwieldy name, this device is really very simple. You wear it around your neck like a necklace, and if you fall or need help and cannot get to the phone, you simply push a button on this device. An operator then will call you on the telephone to see whether you need assistance. If you cannot answer the telephone, the operator will call 911 and perhaps a neighbor to make sure that you're okay.

Telephone Reassurance. You may also want to contact your local council on aging to see whether a volunteer is available to call or to visit you on a regular basis to check on your health and well-being. Although such a visitation is less high-tech than your own emergency response system (and not necessarily geared for emergencies), it does provide a way to ensure frequent contact with the outside world.

Visiting Groups. If you're not homebound, you and your friends should make an effort to get together about once a week, and you should take turns visiting each other's homes regularly.

Visits from Clergy. If you're finding it more difficult to get to your church, synagogue, or other place of worship the way you used to, don't hesitate to contact a fellow congregant or parishioner to assist you with transportation. Also, don't hesitate to ask the priest, rabbi, or other spiritual leader to visit you at home. Studies have shown that people who continue to practice their religion as they age tend to do better not only spiritually, but also physically, mentally, and emotionally.

Senior Center. If your community has a senior citizens center, you ought to use it as a private club (just for people who are 55 and older!) to socialize, participate in classes and activities, and learn more about the elder services available in your town.

Adult Day Care. As people are being discharged to home from hospitals and rehabilitation centers earlier and earlier, the adult day care centers are growing in popularity. These centers may be the perfect place to spend the day if you are still recovering from a setback due to an illness or injury, or if you need help with everyday tasks. Remember that full recovery from an acute illness involving the heart, lungs, brain, muscle, or bone can sometimes take up to nine months to a year, so don't feel discouraged.

Day care centers offer contact with health professionals who understand your condition, your needs, and your limitations. When you join, the staff will work with you to map out a goal-oriented program. In some cases, you'll be helped to acquire the skills you need to recover the ability to perform simple tasks, such as dressing and feeding yourself.

Just as importantly, such centers can be a fun place to meet people and to do interesting things during the day. Most centers offer meals, activities, and social functions, and some feature outings and day trips to shopping malls and local attractions.

Finally, these centers should also provide a beneficial link with the community. Staff members may help to connect you with local services that suit your special needs.

Finding the Right Adult Day Care Center

Before you choose a center, consider your own needs. Will you require rehabilitative or other types of therapies, or are you more interested in social programs? Once you've determined what you're looking for, visit several centers in your area. Participate in some of the activities, eat a meal in the cafeteria, and talk to clients and staff members. Finally, ask the administrators these important questions:

1. Does the center focus on health services or social services?

2. Will the staff develop a goal-oriented therapy program for me? How will it be set up, and by whom?

3. Who is on the staff? Most centers have at least one care provider for every six

clients. How many nurses and social workers are available? Is there an activities director?

4. Does the center maintain links with local schools and civic organizations?

5. What are the center's hours of operation?

6. Is transportation provided?

7. Which meals are served? What about snacks? Is there flexibility regarding food service? Can I bring food from home?

8. How much does the center cost? Is it government subsidized?

9. Will I have opportunities to exercise and enjoy the outdoors?

When an Adult Child Moves Back in with You

Until now we've talked about successful ways to live well in your own home. A little later on, we talk about the issues that you may need to consider if at some point you move in with a relative. More and more, though, adult children are moving back in, at least temporarily, with their parents, and this situation can present its own set of issues.

Your adult "child"—and he or she will always be your child, at any age—may be returning because he or she is available to help you manage your needs while you're recovering from an illness. Maybe your child is returning because he or she is going through a divorce or is having financial or personal difficulty. Perhaps this is a temporary arrangement while your son or daughter is saving up a down payment for a house of his or her own.

Regardless of why you're sharing your home with your child again, there are a few important items to consider:

You don't own your child's problems. We all love our children, no matter how old they are. They are who they are, though, and especially once they're adults, we can't hold ourselves accountable if they haven't quite turned out as we hoped they would. Does your son have a drinking problem? Does your daughter have trouble keeping a job? Are there financial difficulties? These are serious issues, but don't assume responsibility for situations that you did not create. Of course you should continue to give advice and be patient. Don't feel guilty about your child's problems, though. Talk with your friends and physicians about your concerns, and seek their advice.

This is still your home. If you own your own home, you (and, if you are or were married, your spouse) worked hard for many years to make the down payment on your house, then you worked hard for many more years to meet those mortgage installments every month. You had the place fixed when it needed fixing, you maintained and kept your home in good repair.

If you rent your place, you've also made considerable investments. You bought the furniture, paid the rent, and kept your home clean and relatively orderly. Through many years and many seasons, you've always taken pride in your home and the fine state in which you've kept it.

Perhaps your arthritis has made the upkeep of your home more difficult lately, or maybe you could use a hand this year in taking care of the gutters. If your child is living with you and paying you little or no rent, you should not hesitate to ask for his or her help in caring for your home. Don't let anyone make you feel as if you're burdening them—especially under your own roof.

Aside from potential disagreements regarding household responsibilities, the atmosphere in your home may be unpleasant for other reasons. Your grown child may be making you feel that your opinions and decisions don't count for much anymore. You may even be feeling like an outsider in your own house. Keep in mind that *your home is still your home,* regardless of who is sharing it with you now. If you don't want people to smoke in your living room, for instance, it's your right to say so. Remember that the house rules are yours to make—which leads us to the next point: respect.

YOU DESERVE TO BE RESPECTED AND TREATED WELL, ESPECIALLY IN YOUR OWN HOME. Is your adult child always asking you for money? Is your food disappearing and not being replaced? If you no longer drive, do you feel especially powerless and dependent on your child, who does drive? Do you worry that if you speak up about these concerns you will be ridiculed, abandoned, or even hurt?

If you feel that you are being mistreated, don't suffer in silence. Share your concerns with others. Talk to someone you trust: a friend, a neighbor, a clergy member, a health care provider, or even a police officer. Don't hesitate to seek advice as soon as possible—and definitely don't wait too long to do so. No matter how much you love your child, you *don't* deserve to be taken advantage of or harmed in any way. In Chapter 19, we talk more about your rights and how you can assert them.

Finding a Home in Your Own Community

If you're like most of your peers, your first choice is to stay in your own home, and your second is to find another housing arrangement in your own community. There are many options to choose from; the right choice for you will depend on your social and health needs and your budget.

Two friends in Virginia have found a solution that works for them. After retiring from careers in the military and teaching, they sold their house and moved to a nearby facility called "Green Village." They recently sent the following Christmas letter:

Dear Friends and Family,

It's time for an end-of-year letter as we celebrate two years in Green Village.

Today, December 2, the weather is glorious, almost 70 degrees, after a beautiful fall. The weather since we moved here has been very comfortable.

Our apartment is truly lovely. We have our own furniture, two screened porches, and a bay window that opens to the west to enjoy eagles soaring and dazzling sunsets. In our compact but efficient kitchen we can do anything we want to, and we relax and socialize at dinner downstairs in the dining room. Not only are we comfortable in our apartment, but the meals and services are excellent.

Jack's computer activities give him much pleasure. Betty has gotten involved in editing the Green Village newsletter. Our social, church, and other activities keep us busy and happy. We have enjoyed having time to tour the historic homes along the Southern River, go to the Oyster Festival along the Eastern Shore, and visit other attractions nearby.

In July, Jack had surgery for an aneurysm on the aorta. The operation went well, though he's still healing and regaining strength. We are pleased with the local hospital and the doctors involved.

The best part of living here is the wonderful camaraderie among our "150 best friends," mostly military and government retirees. There are many hobbies, games, and interest groups that have been formed; two vans transport us wherever we want to go.

Our children and grandchildren (Lily is 12, Eric is 9, and Gail is 6 months) enjoy visiting us here, especially for the heated pool and the elegant dining.

We hope this year has been kind to you. Come and see us, and God Bless.

Betty and Jack

Health problems, financial limitations, or simply a desire to be free of the responsibilities of home ownership may make you decide to move sooner or later. As Jack and Betty have found, relocation can make life easier and more enjoyable. A move can bring you companionship, proximity to stores and services, and many other pluses. Like Jack and Betty, you may choose to live in something called a *continuing care retirement community* (see pp. 248–249), or you may opt for one of the many other housing arrangements available today.

Shared Housing

Shared housing is exactly as it sounds: Two or more people live together in a house or apartment. Arrangements vary widely, but typical participants are individuals who are on their own but don't want to live alone; they desire the companionship of other persons. Shared housing can also pair older and younger roommates. In many cases, younger tenants exchange assistance with household chores for full or partial rent.

Basically, shared housing is a roommate situation. If you still own your home and have the space available, you might seek one or two tenants to move in and share with you expenses and housekeeping duties. If you're looking for a place to move to, you might (through your local senior center or council on aging, a newspaper ad, or other means) find someone who is also looking for a roommate. Perhaps you already know some friend(s) with whom you'd like to set up housekeeping.

It's crucial that you and your prospective roommates have an open and honest discourse before moving day. Well in advance, you should discuss issues such as pets, chores, and finances. Be sure that each person is clear about how meals will be paid for, purchased, and prepared. Chart out which chores need to be done, and get agreement on who is to do them, or how the duties will be rotated. Discuss how household bills will be split and who will pay them. Such thoroughness may seem a bit much in the beginning, but it will save you and your roommates many headaches down the road.

Like shared housing, *congregate housing* is a catchall term that encompasses a wide variety of situations. It's designed for people who want to live independently but would like to have some extra services. Housekeeping and transportation as well as social activities are usually available. Congregate housing differs from shared housing in the same way that life in a college dorm may differ from that in an off-campus apartment. Congregate-housing residents have their own rooms, usually in a large house or apartment complex, but they share meals prepared in a common cafeteria. There may be other shared living space, too, such as a TV room or a recreation room. In recent years, congregate housing has become more popular, but it's usually more expensive than shared housing. Congregate housing facilities are usually not licensed.

Congregate Housing

Senior apartment buildings are created for and cater to an elderly clientele. They may be houses with just a few apartments or may be huge buildings with several hundred apartments. There are usually no stairs, everything is wheelchair accessible, and the buildings are generally safe and secure. Most senior apartments offer a wide range of activities and services.

Does it sound too good to be true? The catch is that senior apartment buildings are generally expensive. Some are subsidized, however, and therefore may be more affordable, but the waiting lists for admittance to these buildings are usually long. Also, most buildings do not accept residents who have major health problems. Be sure to inquire about the building's policies before you consider moving in.

Senior Apartments

I knew that when I could no longer live in an apartment by myself I would still prefer to stay in my neighborhood. I've lived here all my life and I'm not interested in moving to a brand-new place at the age of 84!

My daughter helped me to look into some senior housing complexes that are located within a few blocks of my old apartment, and I found one that gives me three good meals a day. Now I'm sharing a room with a wonderful new friend named Adelaide, and I can still see "my" part of town when I look out the window, and stay near to my old friends.

Mary, age 84

Board and Care Homes

Board and care homes are essentially boarding houses that provide services designed just for elders. They offer rooms, meals, and various kinds of assistance. If you live in a board and care home, you will probably share a room with one or more residents. You will eat your meals cafeteria-style. If need be, aides will assist you with bathing, dressing, and other daily tasks. Although this is not a nursing home, staff members will supervise your medications. Linens are usually provided, and your clothes will be laundered.

As with other senior housing options, board and care homes vary widely by definition. Many are privately owned by families or individuals. Some are not-for-profit or government-subsidized. Nonetheless, all offer services that you would not find in a shared or congregate housing arrangement, and none offer the type of medical attention you would receive in a nursing home. Because these facilities are not always licensed or inspected by the state, as nursing homes are, you should do a careful inspection of your own before moving into one.

Assisted Living

Assisted living combines private residences with nursing supervision and personal assistance. Medication reminders and help with dressing, feeding, and bathing may be provided. Assisted-living facilities are similar to studio apartments. The apartments are usually small and are designed for one person or a couple. Some residents choose to have a roommate to defray costs. Most assisted-living homes contain some kitchen facilities, and all include a full bath.

Residents pay for assisted living with private funds plus supplemental security income (SSI) or long-term care insurance. In some instances, Medicaid patients may be eligible for such facilities.

Assisted living is often one level in a continuing care retirement community—the type of facility that Jack and Betty chose. It bridges the gap between residential and nursing home life.

Continuing Care Retirement Communities

Continuing care retirement communities, which are becoming more and more common, help create an "aging-in-place" lifestyle. These communities are highly attractive to older people who wish to make just one more move in their lifetimes. Here's what happens: You pay a fixed price when you enter the community, or "life center," as they are sometimes called. No matter what befalls you from that point forward, you will be cared for.

Let's say that you are healthy and ready to move into a continuing care retirement community. You will move into a private apartment designed for independent living, complete with kitchen and bath facilities and safety features. The center usually plans senior-oriented activities and social functions just for you and your peers in good health.

In time, you may become ill, suffer a disability, or grow frail. Then you may be eligible to move into an assisted-living unit. You'll retain your privacy, but you'll also have staff available to provide health care and personal assistance. If your health becomes such that you need around-the-clock nursing supervision, you will be eligible to move into the community's skilled-nursing facility.

Continuing care communities are appealing because they offer residents security and stability. You don't have to worry about what might happen if you can no longer care for yourself or if you can't participate in planning your future.

Such communities are usually expensive and may require a major initial investment. Costs vary, and payment plans differ among communities. Be sure that you or your children thoroughly research any community that you are considering.

Moving to a foster home—another increasingly popular housing option—involves paying a monthly sum to a family or an individual to take you into that residence and help with your care. In some places, foster care is covered in part by Medicaid and other state funds.

Foster Homes

Generally, no more than three senior citizens live in a foster home at a time, so you may or may not share a room with another elder. You will be provided with meals and given help with laundry. If you need nursing care, a home health care worker may visit your foster home just as he or she would do if you lived in your own home. If you need full-time nursing care, though, a foster home is probably not the best option for you.

Although foster home–like arrangements have been around for centuries, state oversight of foster care for senior citizens in the United States is a relatively new phenomenon. The idea started to become more popular in the late 1970s, and currently, a little more than half of the states run foster care programs. Not all states that have such programs regulate them carefully, though, so if you pursue this housing option, you will need to be especially careful about visiting the home before you move in and making sure, as best as you are able, that this is a place where you will be comfortable, well cared for, and happy. In a successful arrangement, you will become part of the family, much as you would if you moved in with your own relatives.

To find out more about available foster homes in your area, contact your state's elder affairs bureau. They can put you in touch with the staff that run the local foster home program in your community. Generally, these programs identify and screen potential caregivers and their homes, match caregivers with residents, and then make periodic visits to the foster home to ensure that the situation is working out well for everyone.

If this housing option appeals to you, one of the factors that you may need to consider is the effect that your decision will have on your own family. Will your family support your decision to become a foster resident? Will this be a successful way to remain close to your children while preserving some independence, or will your family feel guilty or jealous? As with every housing alternative that you consider, it's key to have good communication and frank discussions, if possible, with your relatives about the choices that you face.

Suppose you've made the decision to put your house on the market or to move out of the apartment that you've rented for many years. Next comes . . . the great cleanup! Certainly this is the perfect time to part with many of your household belongings and lighten up so that your mobility and transition to a new home can be as manageable as possible.

A Few Words about "Downsizing"

The problem is, this is usually much easier said than done. Our consumer-oriented society values acquiring possessions far more than paring them down. Also, it's difficult to look at the material things that you've lived with for years without associating those things with a thousand memories: the book that your dear wife used as a gardening reference before she went outside to transplant her favorite irises, the bed that your son slept in from the age of five until he graduated from high school, the platter your family always used for the Thanksgiving turkey.

To ease some of the pain of parting with these items, you ought to look at this scaling-down process positively, as an excellent opportunity to give gifts to your friends and loved ones. Once you begin the process, it really will ring true that "it's better to give than to receive," and you will enjoy more and more the idea of sharing your valued treasures, and of helping others.

You may also want to think of the work that you are doing now—the sorting, the giving away, and the trips to Goodwill or the Salvation Army—as a gift to your family because you'll be sparing them the equally difficult task of sifting through all of your possessions some time in the future.

Even if you choose to remain in your home or apartment, you can do your loved ones a favor by periodically going through your closets and drawers, as well as your attic and basement, and finding a new home for those things that you no longer use or need.

Moving to a New Community

More and more people are choosing to move to another state or even country to be closer to their children, friends, or a warm beach year-round. In addition to these considerations, costs can also be a factor for some of us. For example, the costs of in-home skilled-nursing care and nursing home care in the Northeast are somewhat higher than they are elsewhere in the United States. You may also decide to move to a particular area to have access to certain medical specialists or facilities.

Moving in with a Relative

Ruth and Steve retired, moved to New Hampshire, and were enjoying their unhurried life together. In time, though, Ruth became ill with a long debilitating illness and died. Steve had a terrible time adjusting to being alone. He lost 40 pounds and developed his own physical problems, including a stroke and arthritis.

Steve (now 81) recently moved in with his son, Ian, who was divorced and had grown children; he considered himself to be an "empty nester." Both Steve and Ian had mixed feelings about this arrangement at first. Both father and son had to give up a certain amount of independence and privacy that they were used to at this stage in their lives in order to gain a new kind of companionship that actually turned out to be quite therapeutic for both.

Steve is now doing well. He has gained weight and strength and has gotten involved in the senior group at a nearby church. Ian has adjusted to sharing his home with his father, although Steve now has such an active social life that they only have dinner together a few nights a week.

At one time, you may have vowed that you'd never move in with your children. Perhaps you don't want to be a burden, or maybe you can't bear the idea of adapting to the routine of somebody else's household. If your spouse or companion has died, and your place is too big for one person now, though, or you and some of your family members may do better financially by combining your two households, don't rule out the idea of a short- or long-term living arrangement with your sister or brother, one of your children, or even your grandchild.

Blending lifestyles may not be easy. In fact, it's almost guaranteed to be difficult for everyone on some level. With honest communication and patience on both sides, however, moving in with a relative can work out to the benefit of everyone.

If you've decided to move into a spare bedroom in your son or daughter's (or other relative's) house, there are a few things to keep in mind:

Becoming Part of the Family

You're Not a Burden. You have so much to offer this family with whom you are sharing a home. You may be the only one at home in the afternoon to read your granddaughter a story, for instance. You're certainly likely to be one of the few, if not the only one who can share some memories of the Depression and give others your perspective when the conversation around the dinner table turns to the economy. Even more important, this is an opportunity for the family to benefit from your wisdom and experience directly, and for you to get to know each other in a way that probably would not happen otherwise.

You're Not Responsible. As enjoyable as this time may be with your family, you're bound to disagree with some of their habits some of the time. Does it irk you to find that your daughter-in-law serves her family take-out food four nights a week? Are you appalled that your grandson stays up late and watches TV for more than three hours each and every night when he should be doing homework or sleeping? Your reaction is certainly understandable. Remind yourself, however, that the family was living in this manner when you arrived, and you are not responsible for them.

Instead of allowing these lifestyle differences to eat away at your relationships with your relatives, be thankful that the burden of providing well-balanced meals and overseeing schoolwork no longer falls on your shoulders. If they are your children, be proud that you've already raised your family to the best of your abilities. Now you can simply enjoy your role as a friend and counselor—not as a third parent—to the young children in the family.

Also, now that you are free of the many stresses and responsibilities that go along with parenting young children, you can direct more attention to influencing your grandchildren in subtle and positive ways. For example, you may be the only adult in the home who has time to entice your grandson away from the TV with a more constructive offer. Chances are, he'd love to play cards or a board game with you instead.

Family Life Can Be a Spectator Sport! Your son and daughter-in-law are arguing again. Your grandson is talking disrespectfully to his mother. Your nephew broke his curfew. What should you do? Feel free to excuse yourself, go to your room, and close your door. Disengage. These are not your problems.

Though you can certainly discuss any issues that bother you with your relatives, if their disputes do not concern you, don't jump in. You can assume the role of outsider and let them fight their own battles. Then, when the tension passes, you'll be valued more than ever for being the uninvolved party with whom everyone can feel comfortable.

Living with a Family Member While Living on Your Own

If sharing a room in a family member's house feels "too close for comfort" to you, there are two other options that you may want to consider. Both accessory apartments and "ECHO" housing would allow you to live close to, but remain separate from, your family.

Accessory Apartments. An accessory apartment, also known as an "in-law suite," is an ideal place for a relatively healthy older person to set up housekeeping. These apartments—usually contained within a single-family home or attached later as a separate wing—let you keep your privacy while you live close enough so that your children can look out for you, provide assistance when necessary, and vice versa. Typically, these apartments include a bedroom, bathroom, and kitchen, and possibly a living area.

Few people, however, are fortunate enough to have a willing son or daughter with an extra unoccupied apartment that is available to move into at any time, so an apartment may have to be constructed or renovated, usually in the basement, the attic, or a newly built addition. This can be very expensive.

Before you or your children embark on a major project, however, call your local zoning board and housing authority. Some communities do not allow accessory apartments in a neighborhood that is designated for single-family homes. On the other hand, you may find that there's a tax break or other assistance for people who are constructing living space for the elderly.

ECHO Housing. Another option to think about is an ECHO home. An ECHO (which stands for elder cottage housing opportunity) is a modular home set up on the property of an existing home. These homes are created especially for aging people who are moving closer to relatives.

Many different construction companies can build an ECHO home, but they must adhere to the ECHO standards published by the AARP. Most are about 500 square feet and cost approximately $50,000 to $80,000. Again, your local zoning board can tell you whether your community allows this type of structure.

Shared Housing

What it is: Two or more similarly aged persons may choose to live as roommates, or an older person may choose to live with a younger roommate or roommates.

Pros: If you are the home owner, your roommates can help you to cover the mortgage and expenses. If you are renting, you can gain companionship and save on living costs.

Cons: This choice requires some thought and adjustment all the way around. Roommates of all ages sometimes find living together more difficult than they had anticipated.

Congregate Housing

What it is: Elders may choose this dorm-style living.

Pros: You can enjoy the privacy of your own room but share meals and social time with others.

Cons: Sometimes the private rooms in such homes are small.

Senior Apartments

What it is: These houses and apartment buildings rent exclusively to elders.

Pros: These are generally safe and sometimes offer social opportunities.

Cons: Waiting lists can be long, and these apartments may be expensive. You should ask what the policy is if you become ill.

Board and Care Housing

What it is: This living situation provides a room, meals, supervision, and assistance.

Pros: All of your social needs will be tended to by the staff.

Cons: You may have to share a room with one or more people. You should ask what the policy is if you become ill.

Assisted Living

What it is: This private apartment offers nursing staff and personal grooming assistance.

Pros: You (and possibly a roommate or spouse) have your own apartment, complete with kitchen and bath.

Cons: This option may not be right for people who need constant care or have serious medical problems.

Continuing Care Retirement Communities

What it is: In this "life center," you can stay as long as you like, regardless of how your health care needs change.

Housing Options in Your Community

Pros: You achieve peace of mind because you know that you will be taken care of, and you will never have to move again.

Cons: This option is often prohibitively expensive.

Foster Home

What it is: Some people choose to pay a family (not their own) to house and feed them and help with their care.

Pros: This may be a wonderful way to build strong, enriching relationships with a second family.

Cons: Your own family may find your choice somewhat difficult and may feel guilty about not taking you into their own home.

Accessory Apartment or ECHO Housing

What it is: This type of apartment (or suite) is inside, attached to, or on the property of your family member's home.

Pros: You can retain your privacy, yet still have your family nearby.

Cons: Sometimes the construction that may be required to make this sort of space possible can be expensive and may be prohibited because of space constraints or local zoning laws. Check with the town's building inspector.

Long-term Care Homes

I'm in my early 70s and my mother is 99. She has lived with us in our home for 20 years and has done well. We promised to always take care of her here, but her increasing health problems are becoming almost impossible for us to manage. What can my husband and I do to plan ahead so that we won't put our own children in this situation someday?

June, age 72

Even if you're in good health now, someday you may need constant medical attention beyond what a home health care worker can provide. Although some of the other housing situations that we have just described may provide some nursing care, only a long-term care facility, or nursing home, can provide round-the-clock medical assistance.

While referred to as long-term facilities, more people than ever before are receiving nursing care in these centers for a little while and then going back home. In all, the limited use of these facilities may surprise you: Less than 5% of people over age 65 and less than 20% of people over age 80 are in long-term care facilities at any given time.

Planning Ahead

Many people who enter a nursing home do so in a time of crisis. In most cases, they've just been released from the hospital after a disabling illness or injury. They require more care than they would be able to receive in their own homes or apartments, so they enter a nursing home. Unfortunately, they've had no time to prepare or to research their options.

You can increase your chances of finding a satisfactory long-term care home if you or your children shop around before you find yourself in this situation. In the following pages, we talk about how to choose a nursing home that can best suit your needs. We also take a look at what you can expect when you are admitted, and we address how you and your family can best manage any difficulties that arise once you're at home in a long-term care facility.

What Are Your Needs?

Might you require 24-hour medical attention? Might your condition demand the constant availability of a staff member to get you through the day and night? Are you a private person who prefers to be alone rather than be surrounded by other residents, or would you prefer a long roster of activities and plenty of opportunities to socialize? Do you have family and friends who will want to visit you frequently? If so, how far away from them is too far? Once you know and understand what you might need, you're ready to start calling and visiting nursing homes.

Site Visit

If possible, visit any home that you're considering moving into—and we don't mean just a quick meeting with an administrator. Tour the facility at odd hours; see several occupied rooms; eat a meal in the dining hall. Talk to the residents and their families, and find out what they like and don't like about the place. Bring along a list of your needs and desires, and then determine whether the nursing home will fulfill them.

Touring and visiting various homes can be tiring and confusing, though. Ask a family member or friend to come along to offer moral support and a second opinion. You may also want to keep a running list of pros and cons for the different facilities that you see.

Figuring Out the Finances

Costs may vary substantially, depending on the type of facility, geographic location, and number of Medicare versus Medicaid beds. A year in a nursing home costs approximately $30,000 to $70,000 in United States. Basically, there are four ways to pay for nursing-home residency:

1. With your own money
2. Through Medicaid or Medicare
3. Through an HMO or other managed care plan
4. Through private long-term care insurance, which may be very expensive to purchase if you are very old or very ill

Medicaid. Many people gain admission to a nursing home and begin making payments with their own income and savings. When their private funds are depleted, they apply for state and federal health assistance called Medicaid. If you don't have any funds of your own, you may have a hard time getting accepted right away because many homes limit the number of Medicaid residents they will accept. That's because Medicaid residents pay lower rates than private residents. If it's a Medicaid home, though (about 80% of nursing homes are), they must let you stay once your own money is spent and you are switched to Medicaid status.

Medicaid pays about half the nursing home costs in this country. It's available to people with low incomes and to nursing home residents who have run out of their own resources.

Medicaid nursing homes are monitored and inspected at least once per year by state regulators. If you are a resident in a Medicaid home, you are entitled to a long list of civil rights under the law.

Check with your state council on aging for more information about your state's Medicaid program, and about your own eligibility for coverage. If you feel that you have been denied admission to a nursing home because you are on Medicaid, contact your state's long-term care ombudsman (see Appendix B, pp. 339–343), whose job it is to investigate nursing home complaints.

Medicare. Medicare, which is different from Medicaid, is a health insurance program that was started in the 1960s for people who are disabled or over age 65 (see Chapter 3). As with other insurance programs, you will still have to pay some portion of your medical expenses out of pocket, but you may end up paying less for Medicare than you would for other coverage options. In these matters, it always pays to read the fine print very carefully!

If you are a Medicare recipient, you are entitled to 20 days of professional nursing care in a Medicare-certified home. Medicare will then pay for a percentage of your care for the next 80 days. (This coverage ends sooner if you have improved and no longer require professional nursing attention.) Your public assistance office, local council on aging, or Social Security office should be able to tell you more about how Medicaid and Medicare benefits work in your state.

Managed Care Plans. If it's run properly, a managed care plan (also sometimes referred to as a health maintenance organization, or HMO) can have a lot to offer. These prepaid (as opposed to "fee-for-service") health plans may encourage you to stay healthy by paying for most of the cost of enrollment in a fitness center, for example. They may also promote early screening and intervention to detect and treat many different kinds of illnesses.

HMOs can also be good for seniors because they tend to provide a broad network of services, so they may offer special programs to help you manage concerns such as bereavement and depression. They can also do a good job of involving and coordinating your family and various caregivers and doctors when it's necessary to make decisions about the best course of treatment for you.

All of these pluses, of course, stem from the idea that preventive medicine ultimately will keep health costs down. The downside is that if the managed care program is run improperly, you may end up without adequate coverage for your medical needs.

There are two types of managed care programs: for profit and not for profit. They differ in the way the finances of the HMO organization are structured.

Nursing Home Residents' Bill of Rights

Nursing Home Reform Amendments were enacted by Congress on December 22, 1987, as part of PL 100-203, the Omnibus Budget Reconciliation Act. The law directed the U.S. Department of Health and Human Services (HHS) to incorporate Residents' Rights provisions into regulations that every nursing home must meet in order to participate in Medicare or Medicaid.

Quality of Life

The law requires each nursing facility to "care for its residents in such a manner and in such an environment as will promote maintenance or enhancement of the quality of life of each resident." This principle places emphasis on dignity, choice and self-determination for nursing home residents.

Providing Services and Activities

The law requires each nursing facility to "provide services and activities to attain or maintain the highest practicable physical, mental, and psychosocial well-being of each resident in accordance with a written plan of care which . . . is initially prepared, with participation to the extent practicable of the resident or the resident's family or legal representative."

Participation in Facility Administration

The law emphasizes the importance of "resident and advocate participation" as criteria for good facility administration.

Specific Rights

Each nursing facility must "protect and promote the rights of each resident" including:

Rights to Self Determination

Nursing home residents have the right to:

- Choose their personal physicians;
- Full information, in advance, and participation in initial and ongoing planning for their care and treatment;
- Receive reasonable accommodation by the facility of individual needs and preferences;
- Choose activities, schedules, and health care consistent with interests, abilities and needs;
- Make choices about significant aspects of life in the facility;
- Voice grievances about care or treatment they do or do not receive, without fear of discrimination or reprisal, and to receive a prompt response from the facility; and
- Organize and participate in resident groups in the facility. (Families have the right to organize family groups.)

Personal and Privacy Rights

Nursing home residents have the right to:

- Participate in social, religious, and community activities as they choose;
- Privacy in medical treatment, accommodations, personal visits, written and telephone communications, and meetings of resident and family groups; and
- Confidentiality of personal and clinical records.

Abuse and Restraint Rights

Nursing home residents have the right to:

- Be free from physical or mental abuse, corporal punishment, involuntary seclusion, or disciplinary use of restraints;

(continued)

- Be free of chemical and physical restraints used for the convenience of staff rather than the well-being of residents;

- Have restraints used only under written physician's orders to treat their medical symptoms. Residents have the right to refuse treatment, including restraints;

- Be given psychopharmacologic medication only as ordered by a physician as part of a written plan of care for a specific medical symptom, with an annual review for appropriateness by an independent, external expert.

Rights to Information

Nursing homes must:

- Provide residents with the latest inspection results and any plan of correction submitted by the facility;

- Notify residents in advance of any plans to change their rooms or roommate;

- Inform residents of their rights at admission and upon request, provide a written copy of the rights, including their rights regarding personal funds and their right to file a complaint with the state licensing agency;

- Inform residents in writing, at admission and throughout their stay, of the services available under the basic rate and of any extra charges for extra services, including, for Medicaid residents, a list of services covered by Medicaid and those for which there is an extra charge;

- Prominently display and provide written and oral information for residents about how to apply for and use Medicaid benefits and how to receive a refund for previous private payments that Medicaid will pay for retroactively.

Rights to Visits

The nursing home must permit:

- Immediate visits by resident's personal physician and by representatives from the licensing and certification agency and the ombudsman program;

- Immediate visits by the resident's relatives with the resident's consent;

- Visits "subject to reasonable restriction" for others who visit with the resident's consent;

- Reasonable visits by organizations or individuals providing health, social, legal, or other services, subject to a resident's consent;

- Ombudsmen to review resident's clinical records if a resident grants permission.

Transfer and Discharge Rights

Reasons for transfer—Nursing homes "must permit each resident to remain in the facility and must not transfer or discharge the resident" unless the transfer:

- is necessary to meet the resident's welfare which cannot be met by this facility;

- is appropriate because the resident's health has improved such that the resident no longer needs nursing home care;

- the health or safety of other residents is endangered; or

- The resident has failed, after reasonable notice, to pay an allowable facility charge for an item or service provided upon the resident's request.

(continued)

Notice Before Transfer

A notice to residents and their representatives must address the following:

Timing—In advance, or as soon as possible if changes in health require a more immediate transfer;

Content—Reasons for transfer; the resident's right to appeal the transfer; and the name, address, and phone number of the ombudsman program and protection and advocacy programs for mentally ill and developmentally disabled persons;

Returning to the Facility—The right to request that a resident's bed be held, including information about how many days Medicaid will pay for the bed to be held and the facility's bedhold policies, and the right to return to the next available bed if Medicaid bedhold coverage lapses.

Orientation—A facility must prepare and orient residents to ensure safe and orderly transfer from the facility.

Protection of Personal Funds

A nursing facility must:

- not require residents to deposit their personal funds with the facility;
- if, however, it accepts written responsibility for resident's funds, it must:
  - keep funds over $50 in an interest bearing account, separate from the facility account;
  - keep other funds available in a separate account or petty cash fund;
  - keep a complete and separate accounting of each resident's funds, with a written record of all transactions, available for review by the resident and his or her representative;
  - notify Medicaid residents when their balances come within $200 of the Medicaid limit and notify them of the effect of this on their Medicaid eligibility;
  - upon the residents' death, turn funds over to the resident's trustee;
  - purchase a surety bond to secure resident's funds in its keeping;
  - not charge a resident for any item or service covered by Medicaid, specifically including routine personal hygiene items and services.

Protection Against Medicaid Discrimination

Nursing homes must:

- Establish and maintain identical policies and practices regarding transfer, discharge, and the provision of services required under Medicaid for all individuals regardless of source of payment;
- Not require residents to waive their rights to Medicaid;
- Provide information about how to apply for Medicaid;
- Not require a third party to guarantee payment as a condition of admission or continued stay;
- Not "charge, solicit, accept or receive" gifts, money, donations or "other considerations" as a precondition for admission or continued stay for persons eligible for Medicaid.

From *Nursing Home Life,* American Association of Retired Persons, 1997. Reprinted with permission.

In a not-for-profit program, for example, any revenues that exceed the program's costs are redistributed into the company or given to charitable organizations. In contrast, as their name suggests, for-profit HMOs are money-making ventures.

For-profit HMOs may offer fewer services in order to contain costs. They may also be less willing to serve disadvantaged individuals. Be especially wary of for-profit plans that try to entice you with lower monthly premiums than you would pay for Medicare, free membership in a health club, and other appealing bonuses for signing on. None of these seeming extras will do you an ounce of good if ultimately you won't have the coverage that you need.

To protect yourself from enrolling in a less-than-adequate plan, always ask the company representative the following questions:

- Will the coverage that I would obtain through this plan be adequate for my needs?
- Will I be able to see the doctors and specialists that I have been seeing, or will I have to go to other providers?
- Will I have the option to disenroll and go back to Medicare coverage if I want to?
- Is this a not-for-profit plan?

Once you've answered these four important questions, be sure to take your time, read the fine print, and have a trusted advisor go over all documents before you sign anything. If you've enrolled in a managed care program and you're not satisfied, feel free to disenroll and pick up Medicare coverage again instead—you aren't obligated to stay with a plan that's not meeting your needs.

Long-term Care Insurance. The costs associated with long-term care homes can also be covered by certain long-term care insurance policies. These private insurance policies have varying costs and benefits.

Many of these plans have not been around all that long, so you'll need to be especially careful in reviewing their terms and limitations. For example, it will be important to find out whether benefit rates are fixed or whether they will increase with inflation. These policies may also be quite expensive, and some companies may not sell you one if you have serious medical conditions.

Medigap Plans. *Medigap plans* can also be purchased to cover costs (for instance, doctor visits, hospitalization costs, or prescription drugs) that Medicare may not completely cover. These plans also vary widely, and you should review their costs and benefits carefully before buying this type of coverage.

Policies   In addition to the financial arrangements, it's important to find out what kinds of policies each long-term care facility has regarding whether you can continue to see your own doctor or what will happen if you have to go to the hospital. Will the home save your space until you return?

You'll also want to find out about the center's programs including activities, visiting hours, and rules concerning menus, meal plans, and the availability of snacks between meals. It's also important to know about policies regarding roommates (and whether you can switch if you're unhappy with yours), spending money, personal phone calls, and the security of any personal items that you bring with you.

No two homes are run the same way, so always request a list of rules and regulations. Be sure to ask whether policies are strictly adhered to or the home has a more flexible approach.

Signing Up

You will be asked to sign a contract before you are admitted. This document protects you as well as the nursing home. It's a good idea to review the contract with your lawyer or local ombudsman to ensure that everything is as it should be. The contract will state the cost of your residency, the services that are included, and the home's legal responsibilities regarding your care.

Watch out for clauses that exempt the nursing home from responsibility for property losses and damage or personal injuries. If you are eligible for Medicaid, a nursing home is not allowed to ask for contributions as a condition of admission. Similarly, the home may not ask for the name of a responsible party to cover your bills if you cannot pay.

The nursing home is obligated to discuss with you what will happen if you become mentally unable to make decisions about your care. The facility administrators are also legally bound to ask you for your living will or other legal documents, such as a power of attorney. If you don't have such documents, now is a good time to consider seeing your lawyer or ombudsman to draw some up. In this book, you'll find a useful listing of such documents in Chapter 20.

What You Should Expect

If you are a Medicaid patient, federal law entitles you to basic care. That means you get a semiprivate room (for you and a roommate), meals and dietary services, personal care (having your hair shampooed, for example), nursing care, activities, and social services. You'll also receive any needed dental, pharmaceutical, rehabilitative, or mental-health services. Private-pay residents have to be more careful, as they can be billed for many unforeseeable expenses. Before you sign your contract, find out exactly what is and is not included in the daily rate that you are paying.

Your rights under the law aside, you should learn as much as you can about what your daily routine will be like. Questions are often more easily asked and answered before moving day. The head nurse or a supervisor should be able to answer most questions: Who will plan your schedule? Who will oversee your care? How often will you be bathed? When will your hair and nails be trimmed? You should also ask about your meals. Will you be given a choice each day, or is the menu fixed? Does the dietary staff take special requests? What activities and programs does the home offer? Choose a few that interest you, and ask how frequently they take place. Meet the activity director to discuss specifics.

Laundry is also important to many residents. Find out how frequently your clothes will be washed. Should you label your things to protect against loss and theft? Speaking of that, ask the administrator about the home's record of petty crime. It is a problem in many facilities. Nursing homes hire new people every week, and a large and changing workforce can have its disadvantages. If theft is a problem, ask what measures are taken to curtail and stop it.

Before moving day, discuss with the nurse or supervisor any routines or activities of your day-to-day life that you intend to maintain. These include religious observances, wake-up and sleep times, bathing schedules, visits from family and friends, and whatever else is important to you. In most cases, staff members will accommodate you whenever they can. Making you happy is truly in their best interest.

Making the Transition to Nursing Home Life

It's hard to imagine that a move into a long-term care home can be pleasant, even if you are moving there from a hospital bed. Many residents say they feel dejected and cast aside when their families and physicians decide that this is the best that they can do for them.

Such feelings are understandable. So are the feelings of guilt and anger that your children may be experiencing at this time. It may not be easy, but try to talk to your children about your feelings and their feelings. If you think they've let you down, say so. Don't keep it bottled up inside. Then they can tell you how they see the situation. You will probably find that this decision was as difficult for them as it was for you. They are probably doing the very best they can do with whatever resources they have. In the end, that is all you can ask of anyone.

Reassure yourself that you are moving to a place where you will be cared for around the clock, a place full of people who are specially trained to meet your needs. You will be living with people who are in your same situation. They will understand exactly what you are going through because they are going through it themselves.

Make a list, either on paper or in your mind, of what you'll miss most about your former life. Don't worry about how trivial the items on your list seem; if they're important to you, that's all that counts. Maybe your afternoon cup of tea is something you can't bear to give up, nor should you have to. The same is true of your weekly worship service, or hair-styling appointment, or favorite TV program.

Then talk to the staff. It's entirely possible that you can keep many elements of your routine just as they were. Tea and hairdos are not all that hard to arrange, as long as you make your wishes known.

Group Living

For many people, the toughest thing about adjusting to life in a nursing home is having to share your world with everybody else's. Before now, you probably lived an existence in which you had control over when you wanted to be alone or in the company of others. Now, all at once, you're never alone. You look across the room, and there is your roommate. At mealtimes, you're surrounded by dozens of others. Even though you retain your right to privacy when you enter a long-term care home, communal life is never truly private.

Try to deal with this problem by making the space you do have all your own. Decorate your half of the room with treasured possessions—a favorite print, house plants, artwork from your grandchildren. At mealtimes, arrange to sit with people whose company you enjoy. If you have a difficult time doing so, speak to a supervisor. Remember that you have a right to live as comfortably as possible.

How well you get along with the aides, nurses, and social workers who are responsible for your care can make all the difference in your experience as a resident. Don't expect to love every staff member you meet, and don't expect every staff member to love you. Their jobs are demanding, and you are one of many people they are caring for.

Dealing with Staff

At the same time, you are a human being, and you deserve respect, dignity, and fairness. If anyone is keeping you from getting those things, you must let the proper authority know.

In 1987, Congress passed the Nursing Home Reform Amendments of the Omnibus Budget Reconciliation Act (OBRA). These measures guaranteed nursing home residents "the right to be free from physical and chemical restraints." Since then, nursing homes have reduced the use of restraints and continue to seek and find alternative practices.

Restraints

Restraints involve binding residents to their beds or wheelchairs. Years ago they were used routinely to prevent falls or other injuries. Chemical restraints—antipsychotic drugs—are also illegal except in *rare* cases when they are deemed absolutely necessary (if, for example, a resident is endangering himself or herself, other residents, or staff members by hitting, pushing, or being sexually abusive).

We have found that when chemical restraints are used, they are generally used only temporarily. Nowadays, behavioral alternatives to restraints are much more common. Instead of restraining residents to keep them from falling, staff members may arrange exercise programs to help residents become stronger and less likely to fall. In the past, a resident may have been medicated if she or he became combative or threatened the safety of others. Today, that resident may be taken for a walk in the yard or given a calming bath.

If a problem arises, you should certainly face it and do what you can to have it resolved (though you may feel more comfortable having your children intervene for you). Remember the old adage: You catch more flies with honey. Always be polite when approaching staff members with complaints. It is not easy to work in a place where people are unloading grievances on you all day long. Temper your words with kindness, and you should see results.

Problems and Solutions

Some situations are particularly difficult. Maybe you cannot bear living with your roommate. It could be that his or her health problems are more than you can take, or perhaps your personalities just clash. Try to be patient. After a period of adjustment, you may find that the two of you are quite compatible. If a month or two passes, however, and you are still uncomfortable with each other, it's time to speak to the head nurse about arranging a change.

Often, problems arise when a resident keeps valuables, cash, or personal treasures in his or her room. Wanting to keep your most beloved possessions nearby is a natural impulse, especially if you feel that you've already forsaken many things that were part of your former life. Still, you're better off leaving valuable items safe with family members. If that's not possible, see whether you can arrange to have a locked cabinet in your room for safekeeping.

It's also important to remember that as a resident of a long-term care facility, you have civil rights that are protected by federal and state laws. Nursing homes are required to be carefully monitored and regularly inspected by state licensing agencies. If you feel that your rights are not being respected, speak up! Don't be afraid to tell someone you trust, such as a family member or a clergyperson. Also, don't hesitate to contact your ombudsman (through your state division on aging). That's what he or she is there for.

In Conclusion

As you embark on this new stage in life, try to focus on the positive and keep an open mind, particularly during the early weeks. From now on, as always, "home is where the heart is." You bring a lifetime of experience and inner resources to this new opportunity, and you may find that you'll like this caring environment. With proper treatment, you may relearn skills that you thought you had lost forever. With luck, you may also form meaningful friendships.

Long-term Care Home Checklist

When choosing a nursing home, first locate ones in your desired area. Then visit as many as you can. If possible, bring a friend or family member along for a second opinion. As you're talking with staff members, administrators, and residents, keep the following questions in mind:

Quality of Life

1. Do the residents seem relatively calm and content?

2. Do they seem comfortable with the staff?

3. Does the staff treat the residents with respect? Do they refer to each resident by his or her proper name?

4. How quickly do staff members respond to a resident's request for help?

5. How are roommates paired? What happens if a roommate arrangement is not working out?

6. Is there a designated group of residents that meets with the staff regularly to discuss general concerns and complaints?

Activities and Outside Interests

1. What sort of activities are available to residents? Ask to see a current calendar of events.

2. Do many residents participate in the home's activities? If not, why not?

3. Are there links between the home and the community?

4. Is there organized religious worship?

5. Are residents allowed or encouraged to leave the grounds?

6. Is there an exercise room, a library, and a TV room?

Visitors

1. What are the home's visiting hours?

2. Is there a comfortable place to receive visitors? Will you have privacy when your spouse visits?

3. Are children allowed?

4. Will you have a telephone in your room?

Food

1. Sample a meal. Is the food tasty and attractively presented?

2. Is there a dietitian on staff who will accommodate special needs?

3. Are the menus varied and interesting?

4. Will the chef take special requests? Will your personal and cultural tastes be satisfied?

5. Can you choose your dining companions?

6. Are snacks available between meals?

7. Are residents allowed to keep their own food? Is a refrigerator available to them?

8. Will staff members assist residents who need help feeding themselves?

9. How clean is the kitchen?

Health Care

1. Who evaluates each resident's medical needs?

2. Will you and your family be involved in planning your health care program?

3. Is rehabilitative therapy available?

4. What is the home's policy on physical and chemical restraints?

5. Are there special-care units for patients with dementia, respiratory problems, and so on?

6. Are there registered nurses and doctors on staff? Will you be allowed to see your personal physician?

7. Is the home affiliated with a hospital? Will the home hold a place for you if you need to be hospitalized for any length of time?

Costs

1. Does the home accept Medicare and Medicaid? What happens when residents are forced to go on Medicaid after they have been living in the home for some time?

2. Will you be informed if your fees increase? Have the home's fees increased significantly in the recent past? Are they expected to go up in the future?

3. What does the basic rate include, and what are considered extras?

4. What is the home's refund policy?

5. Ask to see annual reports for the past few years.

Facilities

1. Is the home clean and odor free?

2. Are there safety features, such as handrails and grab bars, in residents' rooms and hallways?

3. Are toilets convenient?

4. Is the home unnecessarily noisy?

5. Is there ample community living space?

6. Is the home entirely wheelchair accessible?

7. Do residents keep personal belongings? Is there a safe place where personal items may be stored?

8. Are the rooms furnished in a pleasing fashion?

9. Is the facility either too hot or too cold?

Grounds

1. Are there walkways or yards outside where residents may enjoy good weather?

2. Are the grounds well tended?

Community Standing

1. Can the home provide a list of references?

2. Does the home enjoy a good reputation?

3. Does the local ombudsman visit regularly?

I uphold my own rights and therefore
I also recognize the rights of others.

Rudolph Virchow (1821–1902)

Crime and abuse are a part of life, and they continue to present risks to us in later life just as they did when we were younger. We know that these problems can occur no matter how rich or poor we may be and no matter where we live. Being harmed or taken advantage of by others can be more subtle now, though. If a person who is supposed to be taking care of us isolates us from others and threatens to leave us alone for days on end, that's a form of emotional maltreatment with the threat of abandonment. If he or she fails to have our prescription drugs filled or doesn't help us to get to necessary medical appointments, that's also a form of neglect or maltreatment. Although we may feel slightly more vulnerable now, we should not let these realities rob us of our basic rights of life, liberty, and the pursuit of happiness. Just as with matters related to our health and where we live, we can and should stay in control and have the right to take steps to stay safe and secure, no matter how old we are.

Crime comes in many forms, from the overt and impersonal (such as robbery on the street) to the more subtle and personal (such as theft of a person's savings by someone whom he or she entrusted to manage his or her financial affairs). In this section, we talk about the various forms of infringements on your rights that may occur, and we suggest ways to correct and prevent them.

Crime

If, in spite of your attempts to stay safe, you are affected by a crime, it's very important to always report it to the police so that someone can help you. The National Organization for Victim Assistance (NOVA) (1-800-TRY-NOVA) may also be of some help.

Burglary   The thought of someone breaking into and entering our homes is one of the worst violations that most of us can imagine. Not only the potential theft of our possessions, but also the risk of harm to ourselves can be psychologically very traumatic. That said, we don't have to barricade ourselves in our homes and live with debilitating fear—we simply need to do all that we can to ensure that our living space is as safe as it can be. Here are some suggestions:

- Don't open your door to strangers. Before you open your door, find out who is there. (Have a peephole installed into your door if you don't have one already). If it's someone you don't know, ask for some identification. Keep your door locked and chained if you are concerned even after the person has identified himself or herself.
- Check the locks on your doors and windows, and make sure that they are secure.
- Keep the shrubbery beneath your windows trimmed to make it more difficult for a thief to gain access to your second floor or your roof.
- Make sure that there is enough lighting outside your house (and above your garage door, if you have one) to prevent burglars from approaching unseen. Keep a good lock on your garage to prevent car theft.
- Consider purchasing an alarm system. It is likely to be well worth the investment.
- Place deadbolt locks on all outside doors, but make sure that you can open these locks easily in case of fire or other emergency. Also, make sure that you have locks on all of your windows.
- Don't hide your door key outside your house or apartment in a place that may be easy for people to find—such as under the doormat.
- Never leave a note on your door saying that you've gone out.
- Talk with an officer at your local police station about ways to keep your home safer.
- Make a list of your valuables (some people also photograph them to make identification easier in case they are stolen). Store this list in a safe place, such as a safe-deposit box or a safe. Talk with the police about engraving identifying information on expensive items. Have your valuables insured.
- Don't tell someone you don't know too well that you live by yourself or that you're planning to go away on vacation. If you have a telephone answering machine, don't leave a message indicating that you live alone.
- When you go away on vacation, use timers on your lights, or ask a neighbor to turn lights on for you. Have your mail held at the post office, and cancel newspaper delivery.
- Consider starting or joining a neighborhood-watch program to look out for vandalism or other crimes in your neighborhood.

Robbery   Theft that may occur while we are out and about can be just as dangerous as a break-in. How many of the following precautions do you take?

- Try to always walk with a friend, and avoid walking in dark places.
- Don't carry much money. Don't wear much jewelry. Try to keep money, your checkbook, and credit cards in a pocket in your clothing that cannot be easily reached by a would-be robber. Avoid carrying a purse if you can. Carry traveler's checks when you are on vacation.
- Never open the door to someone you don't know when you are in a hotel room. Keep the doors and windows of your hotel room locked, and keep your room door locked and chained.
- If you are threatened by a robber, give him or her whatever cash you have. Your life is far more valuable than anything you might have to turn over.
- Keep your car doors locked when you are driving, and be alert to anyone who might approach your car while you are stopped in traffic or at a red light.
- Don't leave your car unlocked or your keys in the ignition when you leave your car—even for a few minutes. In fact, you may want to consider purchasing a steering-wheel lock if you live in an area where there is a lot of car theft.
- If you are transporting valuable possessions, keep them locked in the trunk of the car, out of sight.

We've all read about dishonest individuals who steal other people's credit card numbers and then use the account for their own benefit. There are many steps you can take to prevent this from happening to you:

Credit Card Fraud

- Keep your credit-card bills and other information related to those accounts in a safe place.
- Sign your credit cards as soon as you receive them in the mail.
- If you have a PIN, memorize it—never write it down.
- Treat credit cards as if they were cash—never leave them unattended. If you won't be needing them for a while, lock them away in a safe place.
- Tear up receipt carbons and credit cards that have expired.
- Examine your credit-card bills carefully every month, and contact the issuing company (both by telephone and in writing) right away if you see any suspicious or incorrect activity.
- Never lend your credit card to anyone.
- When you sign a credit card receipt, cross out any blank spaces above the total. Never sign a blank credit-card receipt.

If you do discover that your credit card has been stolen (or lost), or if you suspect that someone is using your credit card without your consent, call the card issuer right away. Once you've reported it, you won't be held accountable for unauthorized charges made to your account (by law, you can only be charged $50 per credit card in such an instance).

Finally, if you need further assistance, contact the Consumer Response Center of the Federal Trade Commission (1-202-FTC-HELP). You can write them at Consumer Response Center, Federal Trade Commission, Washington, DC 20580.

Financial Abuse by People You Know

Unfortunately, sometimes people whom we have trusted to help us manage our finances take advantage of that privilege. We may find that money is missing from bank accounts to which he or she may have access, or that bills that we thought he or she had paid are not being paid at all. The many forms of financial exploitation can be mild—charging you too much for rent or care, for example—or extreme, such as forging your signature on checks, stealing your checks, or forcing you to change your will or to turn over ownership of your home, bonds, stocks, bank accounts, or other titles or deeds.

A family member may also misuse an elder's assets to pay for his or her own wants and needs. If you have an arrangement with a friend or family member whereby you turn over certain assets in exchange for care (shelter, food, assistance with transportation, etc.), and he or she doesn't hold up his or her end of the bargain, what can you do? There are steps you can take to protect yourself from this form of crime:

ASK MORE THAN ONE PERSON TO HELP YOU WITH YOUR FINANCES. In addition to a financial advisor, ask a few people whom you trust to help you oversee your financial matters. Also, try to maintain contacts with your friends, neighbors, and loved ones, so that you don't become isolated and thereby more vulnerable to financial abuse by any one individual. This also enables your helpers to monitor each other and allows them and you to identify fraud more easily.

ASK FOR AN ACCOUNTING. If one person has power of attorney, or the legal authority to make financial or legal decisions on your behalf, ask him or her to provide a regular accounting of your books to a lawyer or a financial planner. It's always good to have some accounting regularly.

Set up automatic check deposits and bill payments. Have your Social Security and pension check deposited directly into your bank account, and have regular bills (such as your telephone bill, for example) paid for directly out of your checking or savings account.

HIRE A THIRD PARTY TO PAY YOUR BILLS. A bill-paying service will take this task out of the hands of your caregiver or caregivers and will provide you with a regular accounting of your cash flow. Of course, just as with other financial helpers, always check references thoroughly. If you are concerned about the qualifications and legitimacy of a financial advisor or a securities broker, you can contact the Securities and Exchange Commission (SEC) at 1-800-732-0330 or the National Association of Securities Dealers at 1-301-590-6500.

TALK WITH A BANK EMPLOYEE. If you are concerned about unusual withdrawals or activity concerning your accounts, speak with someone about your concerns.

Con Games and Insurance Scams

Many scams are successful because they take advantage of our good intentions, our trust in others, and our optimism. To protect yourself from ill-intentioned individuals, never give out any financial information that is asked of you over the telephone (such as a credit-card number or bank account number), unless you initiated the call to buy something from a catalog. Other guidelines are listed in the sidebar on page 271.

1. Beware of people who may try to take advantage of your desire to remain healthy or your less than perfect health by selling you miracle cures for arthritis or other conditions. Never purchase such items without talking with your physician first.

2. Never pay money up front for promising returns in the future.

3. If someone you don't know says that he or she works for the bank and while you're at the bank asks you to withdraw money to help in training a new bank teller, don't do it. This is *not* the way that banks teach their employees.

4. If you find that your automatic teller machine (ATM) card is missing, and someone calls you on the telephone and claims to work for your bank, do not give him or her your password "to see if any money has been stolen from your account."

5. Beware of work-at-home schemes that promise that you'll get rich quick.

6. Don't enter contests or sweepstakes or accept prizes that require you to send money up front.

7. Always confirm that a charity is legitimate before you make a contribution.

8. Never make a down payment on a retirement property without checking out the legitimacy of the selling organization.

9. Look out for home-repair scams. Ask for advice from neighbors.

If you are not sure whether a business is legitimate, contact your local Better Business Bureau, the consumer protection office of your local government, your local police department (which may have a fraud unit), the U.S. Postal Inspection Service, or the National Fraud Information Center (1-800-876-7060).

Finally, you should report aggressive telemarketers or telephone solicitors whom you feel may be fraudulent to the Telemarketing Fraud Hotline at the National Consumers League (1-800-876-7060), to protect others from similar potential frauds.

Maltreatment or Abuse

If young, healthy adults can find it difficult to escape from abusive situations, it can be even harder for older people. Perhaps you've had difficult times with your husband or wife, child, or grandchild through the years. If he or she has developed a problem with drugs such as alcohol, or if he or she suffers from a mental illness, you may be at risk for emotional or physical injury or financial exploitation.

If this type of abuse is already occurring, do you worry about being placed in a nursing home if you tell someone? Are you concerned about being separated from your family? Getting help does not necessarily mean that you have to leave your home, or that your abusive loved one will go to jail. A social worker or other counselor may be able to work with you and your family. Perhaps you will be able to move in with a friend or another family member for a while.

Remember that if someone is hurting you, this is not a family problem to be taken lightly or to be hidden from the community at large. Nor is it your fault. Talk with your neighbor, your pastor, or your doctor—a person whom you trust. You don't have to and should not suffer in silence.

Finally, if you have a hired caregiver or companion, be sure that the agency through which you hired the person has conducted a thorough background check of his or her past employment and criminal record, if any.

Are You at Risk for Abuse?

- Are you alone much of the time at your home?
- Has anyone in your home ever hurt you in any way or thrown anything at you?
- Have you missed eating a number of meals? Why?
- Has anyone ever made you do things you really did not want to do?
- Has anyone ever touched you in your private areas without your permission?
- Has anyone ever yelled at you or threatened you in any way?
- Has anyone made you sign any documents that you did not understand or did not want to sign?
- Has anyone taken jewelry or items from your home without your permission?
- Are you afraid of anyone you know or anyone at home?
- Has anyone ever grabbed, shoved, or hit you in any way?
- Are you able to make or receive telephone calls or have visitors without first obtaining permission?
- Is your caregiver providing all the services that you need?

Source: Weinberg, Andrew D., and Wei, Jeanne Y., eds. *The Early Recognition of Elder Abuse: A Quick Reference Guide.* Bayside, NY: American Medical Publishing Co., Inc., 1995, p. 20. Used with permission.

Physical Abuse

Hitting, slapping, shaking, shoving, and sexual abuse are all forms of physical harm. You may want this abuse to stop, but you may want your relationship with the person who is hurting you to continue. You may be concerned that if you report this person's mistreatment of you, he or she may be sent to a psychiatric hospital, jail, or even end up homeless.

In all likelihood, the person who is hurting you needs some form of help, and help is available, if it is requested. He or she may have Alzheimer's disease, or perhaps he or she is mentally well but is simply overwhelmed with the responsibilities of life. If this is the case, this person may be very embarrassed about his or her treatment of you, and may be too ashamed to seek help on his or her own.

If you are in this situation, there are steps that you can take to protect yourself:

- Seek counseling from your doctor, lawyer, social worker, or clergy person.
- Call your state's elder abuse hotline through your local Area Agency on Aging, or call the Eldercare Locator (1-800-677-1116).
- Contact your state's adult protective services (APS) program. These programs can provide a case worker to assess the problem and often can provide counseling, substance abuse services, and legal services.
- Obtain a restraining order.
- Contact a battered women's shelter in your area if you need emergency, safe housing, or legal support.
- Try to find a support group for people who share these concerns, too.

Much as we'd like to believe otherwise, if someone has physically harmed us, there's a very great chance that he or she will do so again. A restraining, or protective, order can be put in place to make it illegal for an abusive person to contact the person whom he or she has abused. To get such protection, you will need to contact the police and possibly go to court, where such an order can be issued. If you are unable to do so, a guardian can be appointed to represent you in court.

How Do Restraining Orders Work?

Physical harm is the most obvious form of abuse that most of us can think of. Yet yelling, threatening to abandon you, and casting insults are serious forms of abuse, too—emotional and psychological abuse. Silence can also be injurious if it means that someone is intentionally ignoring you.

Emotional or Psychological Abuse and Neglect

Another silent form of harm is intentionally separating you from others so that you feel dependent on or more vulnerable to the person who is supposed to be caring for you. Isolating you from your friends, doctors, or lawyers can be just as injurious as many other forms of abuse.

Also, if the person who is supposed to be your caregiver is not providing you with food, water, or medications; is not helping you to bathe or otherwise take care of yourself; or is not providing you with the glasses, hearing aids, false teeth, or other aids that you need, then you are being neglected. More subtle forms of neglect include taking away the TV or radio or depriving you of light (by closing the window shades or keeping you confined in a dark room).

Again, don't suffer in silence. You don't have to be treated this way, and you don't deserve to be. Let someone know what's going on. Speak up for yourself. You are your own best advocate.

It is as natural to die as to be born.

(Sir) Francis Bacon (1561–1626)

Live as you will have wished to have lived when you are dying.

Christian Fuumlautrchtegott Gellert (1715–1769)

A good death does honor to a whole life.

Petrarch (Francesco Petrarca) (1304–1374)

If you were to become seriously ill or incapacitated, what measures would you wish—or not wish—for your doctor or other health care workers to take to keep you alive? Does your doctor know what your preferences are? Does your family know?

This is certainly not an easy subject, but fortunately there are some tools available to help us articulate the choices we have made. In any case, these should be our choices—not only are these decisions some of the last important ones that we can make in our lives, but also they can be wrenching for loved ones to make if we are no longer able to do so.

In this chapter, we discuss what the law says about end-of-life decisions and we try to clarify the array of options available. We also try to help you focus on what may be involved in getting your affairs in order, and finally, we talk about the important relationship between living well and dying well.

Clarifying Your Values

The decisions that you make regarding the type of care that you would like to receive at the end of your life should be guided by the values that are important to you. In order to begin focusing on the choices that coincide with your beliefs and wishes, consider the following questions:

- What does life mean to you? What do you value most? Your independence? Physical activity? Mental activity? Your garden? Being with your family?
- How do you view medical care? Specifically, do you believe that it should only relieve pain, heal the body, or improve your quality of life? How do you feel about medical treatment that itself may be painful, or that may only extend the length of your life without improving its quality?
- What are your religious beliefs about death and dying? If you are a Jehovah's witness, for instance, you may believe that receiving a blood transfusion will compromise your chance of achieving eternal salvation. In contrast, if you are Catholic, you may follow the direction of the National Conference of Catholic Bishops, who in 1995 stated that "a person has a moral obligation to use ordinary or proportionate means of preserving his or her life. Proportionate means are those that in the judgment of the patient offer a reasonable hope of benefit and do not entail an excessive burden or impose excessive expense on the family or the community." (An "excessive burden" might involve suffering or a loss of function that is caused by the treatment itself. A "reasonable hope of benefit" would include a longer life with improved well-being.)
- What are your cultural beliefs? How might they affect some of the important decisions that you need to make? In some cultures, for example, people believe that the family, rather than the individual, is the best decision maker regarding end-of-life choices.
- If you lost your decision-making ability, whom would you choose to make important decisions for you?
- How would your family and friends feel about the decisions you have made?
- Will your doctor follow your instructions? (Doctors are not obligated to follow them if they find them immoral or unethical).

If you are ill, you have a right to ask your doctor what your prognosis is, what the available treatments are, what their likelihood of success might be, and what the complications of those therapies might be. If your disease is progressive and irreversible (incurable), it's perfectly appropriate to ask about the types of physical and mental disabilities that you may face. Will your illness ultimately lead to a state of dependency on others for your care? Will the treatment plan that your doctor intends to use improve your quality of life by reducing discomfort, or will the planned intervention merely prolong your life without improving your condition? Is your health such that you will be able to tolerate the proposed treatment well, or might it lead to further disability?

Exercise Your Rights

Ask these questions until you receive the clear answers you need.

Keep in mind that you have a right to refuse medical treatment, and you also have a right to ask that treatment be discontinued if it is not working or if it is causing you to suffer.

Managing Pain

When many of us think of dying, it is potential pain that we fear more than letting go of life. Fortunately, we know more about pain control now than ever before, and we have many tools in our medical arsenal: drugs such as non-steroidal anti-inflammatory agents (such as acetaminophen) and narcotics (such as codeine and morphine), surgery, and "alternative," or nonmedical means, such as biofeedback, massage, and relaxation therapies.

When you're in pain, do you usually ask your doctor for something to relieve it? Sometimes people hesitate to ask for adequate pain relief. Also, individuals sometimes take pain medication, but when it begins to wear off or when the pain begins to break through and reappear, they don't want to complain or inconvenience anyone. Please remember that the goal is to make you feel better. Your doctor can prescribe pain medicines to keep you completely comfortable and to prevent pain.

You can also ask him or her whether patient-controlled analgesia (PCA) would be appropriate for you. If you are receiving pain medicines intravenously, a PCA can be set up so that you can get more of the drug simply by pushing a button when you begin to feel uncomfortable.

Some people are also hesitant to take narcotics to control discomfort because they fear that doing so can lead to addiction. In fact, addiction is rarely a problem unless a person already has a problem with drug abuse.

Your Plan for the Management of Pain

- Let your doctor know about your preference for pain management. Increasingly, hospitals are developing palliative-care teams to help people feel comfortable when they are in the hospital.

- Learn as much as you can about the different pain-relief measures (both drug and nondrug) that are available to you so that you can make informed decisions. Find out about both the benefits and the side effects or risks of each option.

- Think about whether you would rather be alert and in some discomfort, or less alert and pain-free.

- Tell your nurse or doctor when you are feeling discomfort (even if you are taking medication to control pain), and try to be specific if you can. Use a scale of 0 to 10, with "0" being no pain and "10" being extreme discomfort.

A Place for the End of Life

The decision regarding where one should be cared for at the end of one's life is not always an easy one, and the answer may change over time. You may wish to remain at home, yet your caregivers may not have the physical or emotional capacity or the time necessary to commit to caring for you around the clock. If you're currently at home and this arrangement seems to be working for now, it's still a good idea to consider where you would like to be cared for if your health begins to decline further.

Although many people are choosing to be cared for in a hospice center, in a nursing home, or in their own home if they have been diagnosed with a progressive, terminal illness, many people do spend their last days in hospitals. This arrangement shifts the responsibility for their care from family members to trained medical staff.

Hospitals

If you or your loved one are entering a hospital under these circumstances, there are some issues to consider:

- What are the hospital's options for patients with terminal illnesses? For instance, are visiting hours more flexible?
- Are your advance directives (see pp. 279–288) on file?
- What is the process for moving patients from the hospital to other facilities, such as to a nursing home or a hospice center?

If you are being cared for in a nursing home, you and your family should have the following information:

Nursing Homes

- Which staff member will be the key contact person to talk with you about your care?
- Are your advance directives on file? If you need to be transferred to a hospital, who will make sure that this information is transferred, too?
- Is the facility run by a specific religious organization? If you are of a different faith, will your beliefs and requests for important rituals (or lack thereof) be respected?

Chapter 18 provides more information about long-term care homes.

If you have been diagnosed with a terminal illness and you've decided that you want to go home to spend your last days among your family members and your familiar surroundings, what assistance might you need? Many insurance companies are willing to cover the cost of 24-hour nursing care because it's less expensive than hospitalization. Some plans also pay for the assistance of home health aides, hospice care (see the following section), and social services.

Staying at Home

Many health care plans will also cover the expense of renting equipment such as a commode, a wheelchair, or a hospital bed that may be more comfortable for you than a regular bed. Medical supply companies also sell special mattresses that may be more comfortable and may be better for your skin (see p. 136) than the mattress you are sleeping on now.

As you consider acquiring such equipment, you may also want to think about a new arrangement of your living space. What type of surroundings do you prefer now? Would you prefer a restful bedroom that is removed from the hustle and bustle of your family's life, or would you rather stay in the living room, where you can look outside at the changing weather and where you won't miss a minute of activity?

In addition to these practical considerations, you'll probably receive much-needed support from friends, neighbors, and loved ones at this time. In general, most people want to help when their loved ones are in need, but they don't always know how to help. You can make this time easier for them by being specific about what your needs are. Would you like a book from the library, or a gallon of milk from the store? Have you been craving a certain type of bagel from your favorite deli? These are not large requests, and the people around you will be happy to fulfill them for you.

Hospice   *Hospice care* (also called *terminal care* or *palliative care*) is another way to provide comfort and support for dying patients and their loved ones. This form of care has evolved in response to the dehumanization of health care that sometimes appears to be dominated by technology at the expense of the emotional and spiritual needs of the dying person. The medical care provided in a hospice program is directed at relieving pain and providing a peaceful transition to death, rather than attempting to cure the incurable, and its focus is on maintaining the best quality of life possible for all concerned.

Hospice care may be provided in a special facility, in the patient's home, or in the hospital. If you choose to remain at home, hospice nurses and home aides can visit regularly. In addition, spiritual counselors, social workers, and trained family caregivers may be sent by the hospice organization (see Figure 20.1), not

Figure 20.1   *Interdisciplinary Team for Palliative Home Care*

Attending Physician
Patients designate an attending physician to manage their care.

Hospice Medical Director
The medical director oversees the treatment by the hospice team and coordinates with the attending physician.

Hospice Nurse
Hospice nurses coordinate the individualized care plan and provide specialized palliative care services.

Social Worker
Hospice social workers offer emotional support, counseling, and community resource support services.

PATIENT AND FAMILY

Spiritual Care
The hospice spiritual care coordinator assists in identifying spiritual concerns.

Home Health Aide
Hospice home health aides assist with personal care and light housekeeping services.

Other Therapists
Physical, occupational, and speech therapists provide palliative care according to the individualized care plan.

Bereavement Coordinator
Bereavement care supports the person and family throughout the dying process and offers follow-up grief education and support.

Volunteer
Trained volunteers provide a variety of services, including companionship and respite care.

Adapted with permission from the Minnesota
Hospice Organization, "Hospice Care: A Physician's Guide," 1996.

only to help you, but also to help your loved ones who are caring for you. Volunteers play an important role in all hospice organizations. Hospice care also provides support with legal counseling, grief and bereavement issues, and sometimes funeral arrangements.

How does one pay for hospice care? Medicare will pay for hospice care if the patient has a life expectancy of six months or less, and if the patient chooses hospice care in place of curative care for the disease. This doesn't mean that you will never be allowed into a hospital once you have elected to have hospice care, though—you will be allowed short-term visits to manage severe symptoms or as part of respite care for those who are taking care of you.

Medicare covers the cost of hospice care for a total of three benefit periods. You may be admitted and readmitted to a hospice program as your condition worsens or improves. While you are enrolled in a hospice program, Medicare will cover the cost of nursing care, physical therapy or occupational therapy, a social worker, chaplain and bereavement counseling, medical supplies and equipment such as a wheelchair or hospital bed, drugs to control symptoms, and respite care for caregivers. Medicare will also pay for short-term hospital costs.

If you are considering hospice care, here are questions you may want to consider:

- Will hospice caregivers be available to you and your family around the clock?
- What type of spiritual counseling, practical assistance, and other services are available through this program?
- If you or your family decide at some point that you would prefer care in a hospital or other setting, how can that be arranged?
- Will you be able to continue to use the services of your own doctor, or will you be assigned a physician through the hospice program?

For more information about hospice programs available in your community, contact Hospicelink (1-800-331-1620) or the National Hospice Organization (1-800-658-8898).

Advance Directives

Another important aspect of end-of-life decision making involves recording your specific preferences regarding which health care measures you would or would not want if you were critically ill, and which person or persons you would elect to represent you in the event that you could not articulate these choices on your own. Now let's go over the various forms that you may wish to include in your permanent medical record.

Values History

The *values history* is a general questionnaire (see Figure 20.2) on which you can document your views on religion, medical intervention, and where you would prefer to die (e.g., at home or in the hospital). Unlike some of the forms that we describe next, this document does not cover specific treatment options for specific scenarios, but it's useful for helping to focus on the personal beliefs that should underlie such decisions.

Figure 20.2
Values
Questionnaire

The following questions can help you think about your values as they relate to medical care decisions. You may use the questions to discuss your views with your health care agent and health care team. (If you fill out this worksheet and want it to be part of your Durable Power of Attorney/Health Care form, sign it in the presence of witnesses and attach it to your DPA/HC form.)

1. What do you value most about your life (e.g., living a long life, living an active life, enjoying the company of family and friends)?

2. How do you feel about death and dying? (Do you fear death and dying? Have you experienced the loss of a loved one? Did that person's illness or medical treatment influence your thinking about death and dying?)

3. Do you believe that life should be preserved as long as possible?

4. If not, what kinds of mental or physical conditions would make you think that life-prolonging treatment should no longer be used?

   - being unaware of my life and surroundings
   - being unable to appreciate and continue the important relationships in my life
   - being unable to think well enough to make everyday decisions in severe pain
   - discomfort
   - other (describe)

5. Could you imagine reasons for temporarily accepting medical treatment for the conditions you have described? What might they be?

6. How much pain and risk would you be willing to accept if your chances of recovery from illness were good (e.g., 50/50 or better)?

7. What if your chances of recovery were poor (e.g., less than 1 in 10)?

8. Would your approach to accepting or rejecting care depend on how old you were at the time of treatment? Why?

9. Do you hold any religious or moral views about medicine or particular treatment? What are they?

10. Should financial considerations influence decisions about your medical care? Explain.

11. What other beliefs or values do you hold that should be considered by those making medical decisions for you if you become unable to speak for yourself?

12. Most people have heard of difficult end-of-life situations involving family members or people in the news. Have you any reaction to these situations? If so, describe.

Adapted with permission from Montpelier, VT: Vermont Ethics Network, "Taking Steps to Plan for Critical Health Care Decisions," fourth printing, 1997.

Another form, called a "health care proxy," "durable power of attorney for health care," or "medical power of attorney," is used to record whom you would appoint to be your "health care agent" if you should lose the ability to communicate. Your agent (also called a "surrogate," "attorney-in-fact," or "proxy") would act on your behalf to represent your choices, based on the documents that you have signed or the wishes that you have expressed. If you have not prepared such documents, he or she would try to determine which decision is in your best interest.

This person should be someone whom you trust, naturally. He or she may be a friend or family member, but not a doctor. (Your agent does *not* need to be a spouse or blood relative.) You may choose one primary agent and then designate other people to step in if your primary agent is not able to represent you when the time comes. You may also choose a group of agents who will need to consult with each other before making a decision on your behalf.

Talk with your chosen agent or agents about whether he, she, or they would be willing to assume this responsibility. If so, discuss your wishes and make sure that they are clear. Go over the documents that you have prepared, and give your agent or agents a copy of these forms. Your doctor should also have a copy.

Ask your lawyer about how these forms are prepared in your state. In some states, one or more adults will need to sign the proxy form as a witness or witnesses.

Generally, your proxy will be void if you have assigned your spouse to be your health care agent and you legally separate or divorce. Also, if you revise your proxy, your first proxy will automatically become invalid. You can orally nullify your proxy by notifying your doctor and agent that you no longer want it to remain in place.

What happens if you have not chosen a health care agent and you develop a medical problem that takes away your decision-making abilities? If your family cannot decide whether you should undergo a procedure that requires informed consent (such as certain types of invasive tests or surgery), your doctor may need to go to court to appoint a guardian *ad litem,* who will make such a decision for you.

Surrogate laws, which are similar to health care proxies, are valid in 20 states. These laws enable family members or other responsible individuals to decide about the aggressiveness of medical treatment for a patient who is no longer able to make such decisions for himself or herself but does not have an advance directive in place.

Unlike a health care proxy, a document called a "living will" does not formally designate a person to act as one's representative in the event that he or she can no longer make decisions regarding health care. Rather, a *living will* (also called a "medical directive to physicians" or a "health care declaration") states one's preferences about life-sustaining treatments in the case of terminal illness or a

Health Care Proxies

Health Care Surrogate Laws

Living Wills

loss of ability to communicate because of a stroke or serious head injury. (A living will should not be confused with a *last will and testament,* which is a different legal document, reflecting your intentions for the distribution of your property after your death.)

In 1990, the U.S. government enacted the Patient Self-Determination Act (PSDA), which allowed that a patient's wishes can dictate decisions about removal from life support. This act also requires nursing homes and hospitals that receive Medicare or Medicaid funding to talk with patients about these directives and to help them to create one if such a document is not already in place. The PSDA also requires such institutions to keep these directives in patients' files. They are not allowed to discriminate in any way among patients according to whether they have signed these forms.

When you fill out this type of document, you will be asked to consider your wishes in the event that you should develop any of these four conditions:

1. Severe dementia
2. Dementia and a terminal illness such as cancer
3. Comatose state with the possibility of recovery
4. Comatose state without the possibility of recovery

You will also be asked which, if any, of the medical interventions listed in the sidebar below you would like your health care team to provide for you if you were to develop any of the aforementioned conditions.

Commonly Used Medical Interventions

- Simple diagnostic tests (such as routine blood tests or a chest x-ray)
- Antibiotics
- Chemotherapy
- Blood products (such as blood plasma)
- Invasive diagnostic tests (such as cardiac catheterization)
- Minor operations (such as a feeding-tube placement)
- Major operations (such as cardiac surgery or bowel resection)
- Dialysis
- Artificial feeding and intravenous hydration
- Ventilators
- Cardiopulmonary resuscitation (CPR)

If you were to have a terminal illness, would you want doctors and nurses to keep you alive by taking "heroic measures," such as cardiopulmonary resuscitation (CPR), or by using life-support systems or artificial means such as respirators or tube feeding? These systems can sustain normal functioning of part of the body when that function has been temporarily or permanently impaired. Let's look at how some of these interventions work.

Respirators. Mechanical ventilators (respirators) are sometimes used to sustain lung function by forcing air into the lungs via a tube that is placed into the mouth or nose. This tube travels down into the trachea (windpipe). Respirators may be used if a patient has experienced short-term respiratory failure or if he or she requires long-term support in order to breathe.

If you have a terminal illness, a respirator will keep you breathing by supplying oxygen, but it will not help you to heal. If you would never be able to breathe on your own without a respirator, would you want one to be used?

Tube Feeding. "Tube" or "enteral" feeding provides nutrients and fluids, usually through a tube that is inserted into the stomach (a nasogastric tube) or into the intestine (gastrostomy or jejunostomy). Tube feeding that is given through a vein is called "parenteral" feeding. This may be a temporary measure to keep one's body nourished while one heals, or it may be a long-term arrangement for people with serious intestinal disorders that prevent them from eating, drinking, and digesting food normally.

Artificial feeding and hydration may also be used for people with irreversible illnesses. In such instances, these measures may not contribute to one's healing but may satiate the feeling of hunger. Would you want to have tube feeding under such circumstances?

In 1990, the U.S. Supreme Court decided that tube feeding is a medical treatment that patients have a right to refuse, even though it is considered to be "ordinary" care rather than an "extraordinary" or heroic measure.

Many people mistakenly fear that the withdrawal of tube feeding may lead to painful starvation. In truth, many people who are dying stop eating and drinking naturally in the late phases of their disease, and doing so triggers chemical changes in the body that can lessen feelings of anxiety and pain. Most people in this situation do not appear to need additional fluids in order to be comfortable; in fact, a dry mouth, which can be alleviated with good oral care, is generally the only side effect.

Cardiopulmonary Resuscitation (CPR). CPR is performed to try to get a person's breathing and heartbeat going again after it has stopped. This process may involve mouth-to-mouth breathing and pressing on the patient's chest to stimulate blood flow through his or her body. The use of an electrical device called a defibrillator and the administration of drugs (such as epinephrine) may also be used for this purpose.

CPR is sometimes used to restore breathing and heartbeats in healthy individuals who have drowned or experienced a sudden heart attack. For people with terminal illnesses, though, such measures may not have much success in reviving them. Under what circumstances would you want to receive CPR? If you would not wish to be resuscitated under certain circumstances, say so in your medical directive, and also ask your doctor to write a "do-not-resuscitate (DNR)" order on your chart.

Just as with a health care proxy, a living will is a legal form (Figure 20.3) that your lawyer can help you prepare. Such documents are regulated differently in all 50 states, so be sure to talk with your health care team and your lawyer about which ones are applicable where you live. In most states, the two witnesses to the signing of a living will cannot be related to the patient or in any way involved in his or her financial affairs or medical care. It is important to know that you can always change your advance directive or living will at any time. For more information about advance directives, you can go to the Internet site of the U.S. Health Care Finance Administration (www.hcfa.gov).

Do-Not-Resuscitate Order

A do-not-resuscitate (DNR) order instructs health-care providers not to perform cardiopulmonary resuscitation (CPR) for a patient if he or she goes into cardiac or respiratory arrest. A nonhospital DNR order carries the same instruction, but it's applicable to a patient who is at home. When such an order is in place, emergency workers may not perform CPR on such a person. (In such instances, the DNR order should be clearly posted in the patient's home in case 911 is called.) For each of these documents, a doctor must sign it in order for it to be valid.

In some hospitals, DNR orders are called "Do not *attempt* to resuscitate," because in some situations (particularly involving those who are terminally ill), resuscitation is nearly impossible. In fact, one study indicated that only 14% of all patients who are given CPR survive to leave the hospital. Sometimes, in those who do survive, CPR itself causes complications such as fractured ribs, a collapsed lung, and brain damage. For patients with serious end-stage illnesses, there may be so few precedents of patients surviving after CPR is administered that doctors consider this procedure to be futile and could choose not to perform it even if patients and their families were to request it.

We want to assure you that having a DNR order on file does not mean that your doctor will give up on you, or that you won't receive the best care possible to control your pain and relieve your other symptoms. If you have a DNR order and you or your loved ones call 911 because you are having trouble breathing, for instance, the rescue squad will still come and will provide oxygen, fluids, and transportation to the hospital, if necessary.

What about Euthanasia and Physician-Assisted Suicide?

Sometimes, people with end-stage diseases get to a point where their own pain and the suffering of their loved ones seem to be too much to bear. They may turn to health care workers, not to cure their disease but to put an end to their agony by helping them to die.

In *euthanasia,* which literally means "easy death," a physician administers a lethal medication to assist a terminally ill individual to die in a relatively painless manner. At present, such "mercy killing" is not legal.

Physician-assisted suicide differs from euthanasia, in that the patient himself

Figure 20.3
Modified Medical Directive

From Gillick, Muriel R., Hesse, Katherine, and Mazzapica, Nancy. "Medical technology at the end of life: What would physicians and nurses want for themselves?" *Arch Intern Med* 1993; 153:2544–2545. Used with permission. © 1993, American Medical Association.

Scenario 1

If I am in a coma or in a persistent vegetative state, and in the opinion of my physician and several consultants have no known hope of regaining awareness and higher mental functions no matter what is done, then my wishes regarding use of the following, if considered medically reasonable would be:

Scenario 2

If I am in a coma and I have a small likelihood of recovering fully, a slightly larger likelihood of surviving with permanent brain damage, and a much larger likelihood of dying, then my wishes regarding the use of the following, if considered medically reasonable, would be:

	I Want	I Do Not Want	I am Undecided	I Want a Trial: if no Clear Improvement Stop Treatment	I Want	I Do Not Want	I am Undecided	I Want a Trial: if no Clear Improvement Stop Treatment
(1) Cardiopulmonary Resuscitation If on the Point of Dying the Use of Drugs and Electric Shock to Start the Heart Beating and Artificial Breathing								
(2) Mechanical Breathing Breathing by a Machine								
(3) Artificial Nutrition Hydration Nutrition and Fluid Given Through a Tube in the Veins, Nose, or Stomach								
(4) Major Surgery Such as Removing the Gall Bladder or Part of the Intestines								
(5) Kidney Dialysis Cleaning of the Blood by Machine or by Fluid Passed Through the Belly								
(6) Chemotherapy Drugs to Fight Cancer								
(7) Minor Surgery Such as Removing Some Tissue From an Infected Toe								
(8) Invasive Diagnostic Tests Such as Using a Flexible Tube to Look into the Stomach								
(9) Blood or Blood Products								
(10) Antibiotics Drugs to Fight Infection								
(11) Simple Diagnostic Tests Such as Blood Tests or X-ray Films								
(12) Pain Medications, Even if They Dull Consciousness and Indirectly Shorten my Life								

(continued)

Figure 20.3
*Modified Medical
Directive (continued)*

Scenario 3

If I have brain damage or some brain disease which cannot be reversed and which makes me unable to recognize people, or to speak understandably, and I also have a terminal illness such as incurable cancer which will likely be the cause of my death, then my wishes regarding use of the following, if considered medically reasonable, would be:

Scenario 4

If I have brain damage or some brain disease which cannot be reversed and which makes me unable to recognize people, or to speak understandably, but I have no terminal illness, and I can live in this condition for a long time, then my wishes regarding use of the following, if considered medically reasonable, would be:

	I Want	I Do Not Want	I am Undecided	I Want a Trial: if no Clear Improvement Stop Treatment	I Want	I Do Not Want	I am Undecided	I Want a Trial: if no Clear Improvement Stop Treatment
(1) Cardiopulmonary Resuscitation If on the Point of Dying the Use of Drugs and Electric Shock to Start the Heart Beating and Artificial Breathing								
(2) Mechanical Breathing Breathing by a Machine								
(3) Artificial Nutrition Hydration Nutrition and Fluid Given Through a Tube in the Veins, Nose, or Stomach								
(4) Major Surgery Such as Removing the Gall Bladder or Part of the Intestines								
(5) Kidney Dialysis Cleaning of the Blood by Machine or by Fluid Passed Through the Belly								
(6) Chemotherapy Drugs to Fight Cancer								
(7) Minor Surgery Such as Removing Some Tissue From an Infected Toe								
(8) Invasive Diagnostic Tests Such as Using a Flexible Tube to Look into the Stomach								
(9) Blood or Blood Products								
(10) Antibiotics Drugs to Fight Infection								
(11) Simple Diagnostic Tests Such as Blood Tests or X-ray Films								
(12) Pain Medications, Even if They Dull Consciousness and Indirectly Shorten my Life								

(continued)

Figure 20.3
Modified Medical Directive (continued)

	Scenario 5			
	If I am over 85 years of age and was previously in good health, but am unable to indicate my wishes because of an acute medical problem rendering me at least temporarily incapable of rational decision making, my wishes regarding the use of the following, if considered medically reasonable, would be:			

	Scenario 6			
	If I am over 75, have multiple chronic medical problems that make me homebound and dependent on extensive support from family and community agencies, and am unable to indicate my wishes because of an acute medical problem, my wishes regarding use of the following, if considered medically reasonable, would be:			

	Scenario 5				Scenario 6			
	I Want	I Do Not Want	I am Undecided	I Want a Trial: if no Clear Improvement Stop Treatment	I Want	I Do Not Want	I am Undecided	I Want a Trial: if no Clear Improvement Stop Treatment
(1) **Cardiopulmonary Resuscitation** If on the Point of Dying the Use of Drugs and Electric Shock to Start the Heart Beating and Artificial Breathing								
(2) **Mechanical Breathing** Breathing by a Machine								
(3) **Artificial Nutrition Hydration** Nutrition and Fluid Given Through a Tube in the Veins, Nose, or Stomach								
(4) **Major Surgery** Such as Removing the Gall Bladder or Part of the Intestines								
(5) **Kidney Dialysis** Cleaning of the Blood by Machine or by Fluid Passed Through the Belly								
(6) **Chemotherapy** Drugs to Fight Cancer								
(7) **Minor Surgery** Such as Removing Some Tissue From an Infected Toe								
(8) **Invasive Diagnostic Tests** Such as Using a Flexible Tube to Look into the Stomach								
(9) **Blood or Blood Products**								
(10) **Antibiotics** Drugs to Fight Infection								
(11) **Simple Diagnostic Tests** Such as Blood Tests or X-ray Films								
(12) **Pain Medications,** Even if They Dull Consciousness and Indirectly Shorten my Life								

or herself takes the step to end his or her own life, but a health care worker is involved in supplying the fatal dose of the drug or other method of suicide. In 1997, the U.S. Supreme Court decided that physician-assisted suicide is not a constitutional right, nor must it be prohibited, according to the U.S. Constitution. The court allowed the individual states to authorize or ban it. As of this writing, only Oregon has passed a legalization statute (1998). There, a patient must undergo a psychiatric assessment and must wait for two weeks before obtaining a prescription from a physician for the purpose of committing suicide.

If you are in pain or depressed, you don't need to come to the conclusion that your only available solutions must be euthanasia or physician-assisted suicide. You may feel that making such a decision is a final act of control in a situation that otherwise has robbed your life of choices, but there are other brave choices that you can make, and there are other courageous ways to address the extreme feelings that you are experiencing.

You should not walk this last leg of your journey by yourself. If your illness has led to a sense of despair, talk with someone, and you will find comfort. Doctors and nurses can help you to manage pain and discomfort. Social workers, counselors, and psychiatrists can help you to manage depression and sleep problems. Your friends and family can provide you with the support and respect that you deserve. Your priest, rabbi, or minister can attend to your spiritual needs and help you find peace.

Putting Your Other Affairs in Order

If you have a terminal illness, you may feel overwhelmed not just by the emotional and physical distress of this phase of your life, but also by the number of things that you still want to take care of in the limited time that you have. You may need to refocus your goals to concentrate on the most essential ones, such as reconciliation with a loved one. Depending on your particular situation, you may have a number of other things to attend to also. These may include:

Practical Matters

- Making arrangements for children and pets with whom you may share a home
- Looking into care for your loved ones who are taking care of you
- Settling financial matters (If you have always paid the bills, who will do it now? Does your partner or another responsible person know where your records are kept? Does someone have access to your safe-deposit box? You may wish to speak with a financial advisor or to a financial counselor or caseworker at your hospice center or hospital to help you straighten out these matters. The sidebar on pages 289–290 lists essential information that you should keep in a safe place; a loved one should either have a copy of this information or have access to your copy.)
- Tying up loose ends with friends and family members
- Considering organ donation
- Helping your family to prepare for your death by making funeral arrangements in advance, a list of people to notify, and so on

Personal Information

Important Personal and Financial Information

- Your full name
- Your address
- Your date and place of birth
- Location of your birth certificate, citizenship papers, and marriage and/or divorce certificate
- Names and addresses of your spouse and children; if your spouse is deceased, date when you were widowed
- Your Social Security number
- Names of your parents, their birthdates, and place of burial, if they are deceased
- Branch and dates of your military service, rank, serial number, and veteran's claim number
- Education records
- Religious affiliation; name of church, mosque, or synagogue; name(s) of clergy or priest to be contacted
- List of your employers and dates of employment
- Membership in organizations and awards received
- Funeral prearrangements and burial plans (including name, location of cemetery lot, if you have one, and location of the deed to it)
- Names and addresses of close friends and relatives, as well as your attorney, financial adviser or accountant, banker, doctor, employer, funeral director, insurance agent, and estate executor
- Location of your will; name, address, and telephone number of attorney who helped you write it
- Location of your living will, if you have one

Financial Information

- List of checking and savings account numbers and banks and addresses; note which accounts are owned jointly with another person
- Name, address, and telephone number of a person who is authorized to sign your checks
- Location of safe-deposit box, location of keys to the box, and name of other individuals who have access to the box
- List of assets and income (from pension, interest, stocks, bonds, etc.)
- Medicare and Social Security information
- Life, health, and property insurance policy numbers and locations of policies; names, addresses, and telephone numbers of insurance brokers

- Copy of most recent tax return
- List of liabilities (what is owed to whom): Include mortgages, credit-card debts (list names and numbers of credit cards), and property taxes
- Location of deed(s) to real estate
- Location of valuables such as jewelry and savings bonds
- List of any legal matters that are pending

Writing a Will   Just as it's up to you to choose whether you would like doctors and nurses to use heroic measures to save your life, it's also up to you to decide where your belongings will go after your death, and if you have young children, who their legal guardian will be. Anyone over the age of 21 (in some states the age is 18) can make a *will,* a legal document that states these choices.

If you do not have a will (in legal terms, this is called being "intestate"), the state will decide how your property will be distributed after your death. If your spouse survives you, he or she will receive the property, followed by your children, your parents (if they are living), your siblings, and other relatives.

Think carefully about how you would like your assets to be distributed: Whom should they go to? When? In what amounts? Many people leave everything to their surviving spouse, and to their children if their spouse is no longer surviving. Some establish "trusts" to benefit their descendants—these can be set up so that income is paid to the children, grandchildren, and so forth as long as one would like. You may have special family needs to be considered: Will one child feel disappointed if certain items are left to another child? Will an enormous sum of money left to a young adult be handled responsibly?

Also, do you want to leave money to charities? This is a tax-free form of giving. Take some time to consider this type of legacy: What are your intentions in giving to certain organizations? Do you feel the need to pay something back for services that you may have received from this organization at one time? Do you wish to give something back because you have been so fortunate?

You should have your will prepared according to your state's laws in order for it to be legal and valid, although once you write a will in one state, it will automatically be legal in all others. A lawyer can help you with this.

Some legal arrangements can affect your eligibility for Medicaid in the event that you may need to enter a nursing home, so it's especially important to seek the advice of a lawyer who is familiar with the current rules regarding the creation of trusts and the transfer of property. Typically, a transfer of assets must take place at least two years prior to a nursing-home placement in order for a person to be eligible for Medicaid. An estate planner or attorney can also set up your estate so that there is less of a tax burden on your heirs.

Another thing to keep in mind is that if you have a life-insurance policy, the proceeds will be issued to your named beneficiary after your death, *regardless of whether he or she is the same as the person to whom you have left "every-*

thing" in your will. This is the time to clarify that such policies truly reflect your intentions.

You'll also need to decide whom you would like to appoint to administer your estate after you have died. This person may be a close relative or someone you know and trust but who is not emotionally involved with your family. Again, your lawyer may be able to guide you in this regard.

Once your will has been drafted, make sure that it is accessible to your loved ones, not locked away in a safe-deposit box that may not be available for a long time after you have died.

Estate is another term for your property, including your home and all of your possessions.

Probate is the legal process of transferring property from a person's estate to his or her beneficiaries. This process generally takes place within a year of a person's death and is carried out in the probate court that is located closest to the deceased person's final place of residence.

Revocable living (or inter vivos) trust is similar to probate, except that the estate can be transferred quickly to one's beneficiaries without having to go through a probate court. Lawyers generally charge more to write these documents than to write wills.

Tenancy at common means that the surviving tenant does not receive the deceased's share of the property—unless he or she is named as the beneficiary of the property in the will.

Joint tenants are generally couples who own property together. If one person dies, the surviving partner will automatically own the property of the other.

Writing a Will: Some Terms You May Encounter

Now that you have made arrangements for passing on your material possessions, have you considered the spiritual or ethical legacy that you will leave to your children and grandchildren? Such wills have roots in many religions. Judaism, Islam, and Christianity, for example, all contain traditions of handing down moral instructions and a commitment to God from one generation to the next.

Ethical Wills

What values do you wish to bequeath to your descendants? Do you want them to have a sense of their family history or your background in another country and your experience as an immigrant? Do you want your grandchildren to know of your experience during the Great Depression? These are gifts that you can hand down in equal measure to each of your children and grandchildren.

Consider writing a journal that records your values and beliefs, making notes on a family tree, or leaving letters to your loved ones. Photographs, audiotapes, and videotapes are other ways to record your messages to those who have been important to you. Such personal gifts can be very meaningful heirlooms.

Handing Down Cherished Possessions

In Chapter 18, we talked about the importance of purging our attics and closets regularly as a way of passing along possessions that we no longer need. Such giving is a gift to ourselves and to our loved ones, for in taking responsibility for our belongings in this way, we spare them from having to go through all of our things when they are grieving later on.

This may be a time to consider setting aside treasured family items, such as jewelry that you may have inherited from your own grandparents, to hand down to your grandchildren or to your nieces or nephews. Such items do not have to be of great monetary value to be treasured; sometimes photographs are the dearest gifts of all.

Spiritual Preparation

The end of life can be viewed as the end of a journey and a search for meaning. Many people have found their answers through religion or through a personal, philosophical set of beliefs. Some may find themselves still searching. Others may find peace through a life-review process, in which one tries to make sense of his or her life through careful exploration with a qualified counselor. Our colleague Margery Silver explains that through this process, one can come to understand memories in new ways and can find new meaning in one's life and the strength to cope with its challenges.

This is a time for reflection about what has been most important in your life, and it is a time to forgive yourself and others for perceived failures and problems that may have occurred. You may need to wrestle through some anger and work through some old hurts, as well as to grieve for the loss of your own future. Chaplains, religious leaders of your faith, counselors, and hospice volunteers may be able to help. If there are any religious rituals that are particularly meaningful to you, make sure that those around you are aware of them.

Dying Well

What does it mean to you to die with dignity? Ultimately, dying well means living well to the end, and for most of us, that means having the freedom to chart our course according to our own hopes and beliefs.

Now that you've had a chance to consider all of these end-of-life decisions in light of your own convictions, it's very important that you act on them. Prepare and sign the forms that reflect your choices and that are legal in your state. Make sure that if you have more than one form (for example, a living will, as well as a durable power of attorney document), they don't conflict with each other. Then distribute copies of these forms to where they need to go. Some should go in your medical record, some should go to your loved ones or to a trusted friend. Tell your doctor and loved ones whom you've appointed to be your health care agent, and let your family know where your important papers are kept.

A good death means more than simply having one's affairs in order and having time to make peace with your loved ones, however. It means different things to different people, as we've discussed in this chapter. For most people, a good death probably means leaving this Earth having found some love and purpose here and having felt that your life made an impact on those whom you loved.

CHAPTER 21
LOSS AND BEREAVEMENT

What is the worst of woes that wait on age?
What stamps the wrinkle deeper on the brow?
To view each loved one blotted from life's page.
And be alone on earth, as I am now.

Lord Byron (1788–1824)

The loss of a loved one is one of life's most stressful and heart-wrenching events. It affects us on many levels—psychologically, physically, socially, economically, and spiritually.

If you are able to anticipate the death of your parent or loved one, you are fortunate indeed. Although you may be heartsick in the weeks preceding the actual event, you will benefit later because you have probably had a chance to say good-bye and to learn how your loved one wants to leave this world.

Nobody enjoys talking about death, particularly with people we love who are ill and suffering. The dying are sometimes shushed or otherwise denied the chance to talk about their deaths. Those who love them may be told not to talk about such morbid or depressing topics.

Death is a normal and inevitable part of life, however, and we shouldn't approach it unprepared. It's never too early to discuss dying. In fact, looking forward toward death nearly always results in less suffering for family and friends in the long run.

If you are close to someone who is nearing death, ask what kind of funeral or memorial service he or she would like. What sort of music would she like played? Is there someone in particular whom he would like to deliver a eulogy? Is there certain prose or poetry that should be read? Are there old friends or acquaintances who should be contacted?

There are other considerations, too. What would he like to wear? Would she prefer a cremation to a traditional burial? Would your loved one prefer a closed casket or an open casket?

Discussing such topics won't be easy, but you will be grateful later on when you can plan the memorial according to your loved one's wishes.

Funerals and Memorial Services

Your loved one has died, and it's up to you to find a funeral home, contact the church or synagogue, deliver the sad news to all who will wish to attend, and perform countless other small tasks between now and the day of the service. It's all a bit overwhelming, but take heart. Keeping busy may be the best thing for you right now. Channel all the emotions you're currently experiencing into the job first at hand. It will be over soon, and then the real work of grieving can begin.

The Obituary

One of your first tasks will be to send an obituary to the local newspaper. The funeral home may offer to do this for you, but it is not as difficult as it sounds. You don't have to be a writer to supply information for an obituary. In fact, the newspaper will edit what you send them, so just write down the facts. These include

- The full name of the deceased (including maiden name)
- Current and former addresses
- Date and place of death
- Cause of death (some newspapers will not print it, though)
- Education
- The deceased's employment history, or list of accomplishments
- Memberships in organizations
- Names of survivors, including spouse, siblings, children, and grandchildren
- Information about the funeral and other services, such as a wake
- Where donations should be sent, if appropriate

You may also want to include some personal information ("he was an avid skier" or "she was happiest when caring for her grandchildren," for example), but realize that the newspaper will decide whether they wish to print it. Send a photo, too, if you'd like.

Be aware that some newspapers charge a fee for obituaries, and that fee may be calculated based on length. Find out before you submit a costly obituary.

Finding a Funeral Home

It's tempting to call the funeral home closest to you and to ask the director to arrange everything. You may be sorry later, however. Prices vary widely among funeral homes. Media exposés have shown that the traditional funeral can vary in price from $1,500 to $10,000, with no real difference in the services provided.

Federal law states that funeral homes must quote prices over the telephone, and they must itemize everything that you are paying for. The usual services that funeral homes provide are director's services, transportation of the body to the funeral home and to the burial place, embalming and dressing the body, and use of facilities for a wake or service. The director may also take care of miscellaneous tasks such as an obituary or flowers, for an extra charge.

Call an array of mortuaries in your area, or divide the list among friends. You can use an out-of-town mortuary if you hold the service in your church or synagogue—a practice that is becoming more and more common. If you don't attend church regularly, it's quite possible you can rent one for the occasion.

If you need help, call a local memorial society. This nonprofit group will provide you with a list of funeral homes in your area and can make some low-cost recommendations. Contact the Funeral and Memorial Societies of America at 1-800-765-0107 to find a society in your area.

Caskets

The casket will be your most expensive purchase. Investigations have shown that some disreputable mortuaries charge as much as ten times the wholesale price, so shop with caution. Remember that more expensive is not necessarily better.

Cremation

Cremation is a process that reduces a body to ashes, or bone fragments, by burning. It's a very personal decision, a wish that is usually expressed by the deceased beforehand. More people choose cremation today for a variety of reasons. It's a simpler process, and causes less damage to the environment. Also, it's now accepted by many different religions. Cremation is usually less expensive than a traditional embalming and burial, but that is not always the case.

If you choose to cremate, you can still hold a funeral or memorial service that is similar in all ways to traditional services. The ashes are usually contained in either a casket or an urn—required by most crematories and supplied by funeral homes.

Once the service is over, there are several ways to dispose of the remains. You can bury the urn in a regular gravesite or in a burial ground designated for urns rather than caskets, or you can have it entombed in a mausoleum (an above-ground cemetery that is usually very reasonably priced).

The best-known disposition of ashes, however, is scattering. Some cemeteries designate special lawns for this purpose. The ashes also may be scattered over a body of water or other place special to the deceased. (Remember that the law forbids scattering of ashes in certain places, so you may want to check with authorities before you dispose of them.)

While the scattering of ashes may seem a natural and fitting course of action, consider the long-term ramifications. Many family members find that they feel unfulfilled and empty later when they have no final resting place to visit their loved one, unless the place where the ashes were scattered has special meaning to them.

The Burial

There are three basic varieties of cemeteries: municipal, religious, and national. If the deceased is a veteran, he or she is entitled to a free burial in a national cemetery for the military. Spouses may be eligible, too.

Many people make plans for their burials prior to death. You can buy a single plot or a family plot, or reserve space in a mausoleum. Some cemeteries offer links to funeral homes and crematorium services. Cemetery directors may arrange for headstones or grave markers, as well, but these can be ordered after the service has taken place.

The Service   Think of a funeral or memorial service as a chance to say good-bye to the deceased, and for those left behind to begin their journey on the long road of bereavement. Many services are dictated and run according to the religion of the deceased. Nonetheless, there are many ways that a service can be personalized for your loved one. Include music or readings that were dear to the deceased or are especially commemorative of his or her life. Favorite flowers or special photos also lend a personal touch.

If the deceased shared his or her wishes for the service before death, certainly they should be honored whenever possible. Nowadays, people are finding creative ways to take part in their own services. For example, a singer might leave a recording of himself or herself performing a favorite song.

Usually, mourners gather after the service or burial for a meal and conversation about the deceased. This is an important occasion and particularly helpful for those most affected by the death. It typically takes place at someone's house, or in a rented hall or a restaurant.

After the Funeral   The service is over, but the paperwork is not. Following is a list of small but important tasks that should be taken care of as close to the death as possible:

- Get copies of the death certificate from the funeral director or your local health department. Organizations such as the insurance company, the IRS, and Social Security will probably need to see it. If you are the spouse, make copies of your marriage certificate, which will be necessary if you are collecting benefits.
- List assets and debts of the deceased.
- Find the will, or contact the deceased's lawyer. If you are the surviving spouse, you may have to revise your will if you listed the deceased as a beneficiary.
- Contact Social Security or the Veterans Affairs office about possible death benefits.
- Call former employers of the deceased to find out about pensions due.
- Locate a copy of the deceased's most recent tax return. You may have to file one for the current year on his or her behalf. There may also be federal taxes due on her or his estate. Contact the Internal Revenue Service for more information.
- Close all bank accounts in the deceased's name, and check for the existence of safe-deposit boxes.

Life

What is a person's life journey?
'Tis but a swan alighting on snow/mud,
Perchance, leaving a few prints.

Whence and whereto, the swan?
The mud knows not,
East or west.

Su Dong-Po (A.D. 1036–1107)

The funeral is over, the deceased has been buried. People stop dropping by to visit and offer food and comfort. You are alone with your loss. Everybody experiences loss in a different way. Some will emerge unscathed after a period of grieving; others will grieve for the rest of their lives.

In the following pages, we discuss ways to turn your bereavement into a less painful experience. Remember that a successful grieving period can and should be an opportunity to appreciate the life of the person who died, and to feel gratitude for having known her or him.

If you are living with the pain of grief, you may be asking, "When will it end?" It's an understandable question, but unfortunately, there is no reassuring answer. Survivors should not expect to manage grief in a quick or easy fashion. In fact, it's likely that you will endure a period of adjustment that may last anywhere from one to four years.

Time truly does tend to heal most wounds. The intense emotional pain you're feeling now will abate in time and will be replaced by different emotions that are not so detrimental to the requirements of daily living. Life as you knew it before this death, however, may well be changed forever.

We believe that understanding the bereavement process is key to weathering it successfully. In the following pages, we explain what you can expect when you lose a loved one and begin your own personal journey of bereavement, grief, and mourning.

What do these terms actually mean? *Bereavement* is loss. When you are bereft, you have lost something or someone dear to you. *Grief* comes afterward. Feelings surrounding grief include denial, anger, guilt, sorrow, and confusion. Grief causes suffering, but that suffering is necessary and healthy. *Mourning* is the way that you express your grief. It is often determined by your culture.

**What Loss
Means to
Older People**

In general, older people seem to deal with death better than their younger counterparts. Studies show that they do not fear dying as much, perhaps because they have had more experience with it or more time to contemplate it. Also, many of their peers are suffering similar losses, so the elderly often have friends with whom to share the experience of grieving.

Seniors are less likely than the younger generation to seek help, however. They are not accustomed to sharing their feelings and their grief. It's important to seek and accept support during this difficult time. A wide variety of resources are available today, so there is no reason to suffer alone or in silence.

For the elderly, the greatest and most difficult loss is probably the loss of a husband or wife. There's an old saying that goes like this: When a child dies, you lose your future, and when a parent dies, you lose your past. With your spouse's death, however, you've lost your present—the most immediate and jarring loss of all.

If your husband or wife dies after a long illness, chances are you've prepared for his or her death, and you may well have an easier time accepting it. That is not always the case, however. If you are the sole or main caregiver, the illness may have brought you and your spouse closer than ever. During the weeks or months or even years of caregiving, the two of you may have become isolated from others. Thus, the loss may leave you feeling more bereft than you would have if your partner had died suddenly or unexpectedly.

There are other considerations when you lose a spouse. In addition to losing your life partner, you may also lose regular income and face new financial difficulties. If your spouse was more outgoing and active than you, you may find that your opportunities for socializing are now limited. Maybe all of your friends are still married and the idea of being single makes you uncomfortable.

You may also experience new fears: fear of being alone in the house, fear of making bad decisions, fear of poverty. You may lose a sense of self or feel that you've lost your most important role in life. You've gone from being somebody's wife or husband to being somebody's widow or widower.

Factors Affecting Grief

Gender. Many studies have been done on how the bereavement process affects men (widowers) and women (widows) differently. Women, who tend to be more emotional and less focused, generally grieve longer. They find it more difficult to give up the role of being somebody's wife, and they experience anxiety over their ability to cope alone. Women also often grieve more successfully. That's because they more readily share their suffering with others, whereas men are apt to grieve in silence. While men usually return to work and other normal tasks sooner, they may be plagued from within by feelings of helplessness and guilt and displacement. Left unchecked, these feelings rarely disappear on their own.

Mortality among Widowers

There is a much higher incidence of mortality among men than women following the death of a spouse. This is especially true for men whose wives were their closest friends and companions, or men who slip away from their social circle after the death occurs. Sometimes they lose their will to live, and they stop taking care of themselves. Sleep and weight disorders often surface, as well as dependency on alcohol or other drugs.

For a man who's lost his closest bond in his wife, the best course is to create new emotional attachments. Forging new friendships or rekindling relationships with old friends or family members may help.

The Death Itself. Grief over a sudden or violent death is generally more difficult to endure than grief over an expected death. In most cases, having time to prepare for the death and to say good-bye makes the grieving process easier down the road.

Depression. Survivors who exhibit symptoms of severe depression early on, such as uncontrollable crying and a wish to die, are likely to suffer through a prolonged bereavement. Untreated depression is a roadblock to successful grieving.

Grieving is a long, involved process for everybody. For people who fall into certain categories, however, it's a grim state from which they may never emerge. It's important to determine whether you are what's known as an *at-risk survivor*—someone who's not likely to weather the bereavement process without professional help.

Hospice bereavement counselors, available through a hospice program, visit survivors after the patient dies. They are trained to look for various signs of trouble ahead. These include:

High-Risk Grieving

- An inability to express feelings or to cry
- Uncontrollable anger or rage
- Guilt or denial that doesn't let up
- Extreme weight loss or gain
- Dependency on alcohol or other drugs
- Pre-existing family problems
- Past history of other losses
- Clinical depression

If you are exhibiting some or all of these signs, it's probably wise for you to talk to a friend or see a therapist, and also for your whole family to consider going through counseling together. During the therapy process, you will learn that you're not alone, that thousands of people need help to deal with loss and get on with their lives successfully.

Self-esteem. People who are confident to begin with will usually cope with grief more effectively than those who are not. If you have trouble managing small daily hurdles, the bereavement process will probably prove extra difficult for you.

Relationship with the Deceased. Research shows that the more successful the marriage, the more painful the grieving. In other words, if you were very happy with your spouse, you will be very sad without. Console yourself with the fact that you were blessed with a happy union—a rare and wonderful thing indeed.

Social Support. It's no surprise that supportive friends and family make the grieving process easier to bear. Having people to share memories of the deceased and help commemorate his or her life can be a very healing. If you are not so fortunate, consider joining a bereavement support group (see p. 303).

Coping with the Four Phases of Grief

Much has been written about the various twists and turns that mark the journey through the bereavement process. Here we divide the process into four basic phases, and we offer suggestions on how to react to them.

1. Shock. Most people immediately react to the death of a loved one, even an expected death, with numb disbelief and denial. Feelings of guilt may also surface at this time.

What to Do. Focus on the reality of your loss. Your loved one is truly gone, and the sooner you can accept that fact, the sooner your grieving, and subsequent healing, will begin.

2. Grief. Grief usually sets in several weeks after the death and the funeral. At this point, you begin experiencing feelings of sadness, regret, anger, and a host of other emotions.

What to Do. Feel the pain. Don't try to shove your feelings aside, unpleasant as they may be. Grieving is crucial, so let the tears flow. Work through your feelings of anger toward the deceased.

3. Despair. Around the time that your grief symptoms abate, you will start feeling lonely and depressed. You may think your life no longer has meaning, that you have nowhere to turn.

What to Do. Realize that your life is entirely changed. Set small goals (clean out Tom's closet; sell Gina's car) that will help establish your new life.

4. Adjustment. It may be a year or more before you enter this phase. You're finally able to take care of yourself and to envision a future without your loved one. You probably still feel intense loss, but you now know that life truly goes on.

What to Do. Redirect your energy toward new friends and new activities. At the same time, tending to your loved one's grave or setting up a fund in his or her name can help you to maintain a connection to the person you have lost.

How to Grieve

We all grieve at our own pace. A lucky few manage grief effectively and get on with their lives in record time. For most of us, though, grief will become a part of our daily lives for the next few years. You have to let your grief wash over you and perhaps engulf you before you can swim through the often-wide sea of bereavement.

There are a number of ways that you can coax your grief to the surface. Here we suggest a few, but you may have your own ideas that suit your personality better.

Cry. Tears are surely one of the best antidotes to pain. Crying is essential to creating the emotional catharsis that will result in your ultimate healing. If you find yourself unable to cry, try seeing a sad movie or reading a book that will stimulate your tears.

Share with Friends. Unless you share your grief with others, you cannot end the bereavement process. Initially, you may find that people are uncomfortable talking with you about the person you lost. Encourage them to listen to your thoughts anyway. Once they realize you are at ease discussing the topic, most people will open up and lend a sympathetic ear.

Write a Poem. You don't have to be a great writer to benefit from the power of poetry. Writing a short verse about your loss can be wonderful therapy. You may wish to share your poetry with others, or prefer to keep it to yourself. Either way, poetry can help you speak from the heart.

Write a Letter. Often, people feel more bereft because they long for just one more opportunity to speak with their loved one. Some find it useful to write a letter to the deceased, saying everything they wish they had said. Just getting it down on paper can be an enormous comfort.

Listen to Music. It can be very therapeutic. Get in the habit of filling your home with soft music when you are alone. Select music that soothes and comforts you, or choose something that reminds you of your loved one—such as beloved Broadway show tunes or a favorite Mozart piece.

Remember. Don't avoid activities or places that were special to you and the person you have lost. Enjoying your old routine is a good way to live through your loved one and reminisce with joy and success.

Appreciate Your Loved One. Reflect on the blessing it was to have known the deceased and to have shared his or her life. You were enriched in many ways by your relationship—try listing them. This is an excellent way to commemorate his or her life.

If you have lost a loved one, you may experience some or all of the following physical symptoms. Among the elderly, these symptoms are often mistaken for signs of aging, when actually they are just part of the normal expression of grief.

Possible Physical Reactions to Loss

- You feel cold and empty.
- You cannot sleep.
- You are confused or moody.

- You lose your appetite.
- You experience shortness of breath.
- You are preoccupied with death.
- You lack energy.
- You experience headaches and chest pains.
- You feel exhausted.
- You are susceptible to illness.

About Drugs

If you are suffering symptoms of grief such as headaches and depression, it's tempting to take something to relieve the pain. Talk to your doctor, but remember that the feelings you're experiencing are normal and essential to the healing process. Numbing your grief through drugs is probably a mistake. You need a clear mind to successfully get through the bereavement process.

Making It through the Holidays

You've probably heard that the holidays are especially taxing for someone who is bereaved. Realizing that this will be a challenging time and planning accordingly will do much toward helping you make it to the New Year. Here are some other helpful tips, compiled by the AARP:

- **Create new traditions.** Maybe you can't bear the idea of trimming a Christmas tree without your spouse to string the lights and haul the old decorations from the attic. There's no law that says you must have a tree. Plan a different way to dress up your home. Maybe you'd like to share treasured tree ornaments with your children or other family members this holiday season, or even take part in their tree-trimming celebration.
- **Talk about the deceased.** Chances are that he or she will be on your mind more than ever. Bring up her or his name in conversation, and assure others that you really do enjoy talking about her or him. Having to suppress memories is stressful and painful.
- **Help someone in need.** Realize that you are not the only one suffering this holiday season. Find a way, through your senior center or area agency on aging, to offer assistance to someone whose needs are even greater than yours. The person who benefits most just might be you.
- **Treat yourself.** What is the one luxury you've never granted yourself: a special vacation, a piece of jewelry, or a new television? This holiday season, give yourself the gift of indulgence. You deserve a boost.
- **Revisit holiday memories.** If you wish, spend time canvassing your memories of holidays past. Your recollections are your most dear and true connection with your loved one, and the holidays may be more bearable if you conjure up the past to meet the present.

• **Avoid holiday hassles.** Bereavement aside, the holidays are tough. This year, don't let yourself get caught up in the hustle and bustle unless you want to. Limit your visiting, entertaining, and gift-giving, and be sure to allow yourself plenty of sleep and leisure time.

Bereavement Groups

During this time, you may find that well-meaning friends are urging you to "move on." Maybe they tell you "it's better this way," or suggest that "you'll feel better soon," when in fact you've never felt worse and aren't even sure you ever want to feel better. Perhaps they even hush your attempts to talk about your loved one in conversation. Try not to be offended. People are nervous around death, and they often say things that seem terribly inappropriate or insensitive.

How can you find support you need from others? One way is through a bereavement group. *Bereavement groups* consist of people who've suffered losses and are enduring grief, just like you. They want to talk about the way they feel and about what they've lost. Participants enjoy the family atmosphere and the chance to express feelings they may not be comfortable sharing with their own circle of friends and family. Being part of such a group can help you tremendously. You may find plain old comfort, or even a brand-new self-image as a survivor.

Some groups are led by professional counselors or hospice workers. Others are organized and run by the ordinary people who attend them. Some are specifically designated for seniors, others are open to everyone. There are also specific-need groups—for people who have lost a child, or lost a loved one to suicide, for example.

Many bereavement groups are free of charge. Others charge a membership fee, but your insurance company may cover it. Find out about groups meeting in your area by contacting your area agency on aging or senior center, or check with local hospitals, churches, or synagogues.

PART FOUR
ASSISTING AGING PARENTS

CHAPTER 22
HELPING YOUR AGING PARENTS

Can You Imagine

Can you imagine for just one moment with me;
How hard it is to see someone you love . . .
completely lose their dignity?
This loved one once so almost perfect in her ways;
So flawless in her character,
So loving every day.

Can you just try to imagine what happens in one's heart;
When this loved one changes so much—
how can this be?
I'd like you to STOP and just try to imagine with me . . .
I'm now the Mother . . . what's going on?
She is the daughter . . . something is wrong.
I'm now the mummy . . . She is the child . . .
She is the child . . . Can you imagine . . .
I can't describe . . .

I'm still the Mother . . .
She is my baby . . . and so she will stay . . .
Until the dear Lord takes her away.

Joan Mimi, caregiver, Cape Town, South Africa

It's a fact that people are powerfully and overwhelmingly inclined to care for their loved ones whenever possible. Ten million American elders currently require long-term care. For 90% of them, that care is provided by their families. Still, many people enter a caregiving situation with preconceived ideas about the hassles and heartaches of children caring for parents who can no longer care for themselves.

If you are a parent, you probably dread the prospect of burdening your family with your health care needs. You may also be concerned about relinquishing control of your daily living to your children. Perhaps your kids have always had trouble sorting things out among themselves, or maybe you and your child have had an unsatisfactory relationship. These issues will no doubt add to your worries.

If you are a child, you may fear that caring for your parent will affect your career, your spouse, and your children. You know that you will be forced to sacrifice at least some aspects of your previous lifestyle. Maybe you and your parent have a history of conflict, and maybe much of that conflict is unresolved. When a parent is neglectful or abusive toward a young child, it's common for that child to grow into an adult who feels he owes his parent little or nothing.

If you are both a parent with children at home, and the child of parents who require care, your conflicts multiply. You may feel torn between your parenting responsibilities and your caregiving responsibilities. It's wise to be aware of your feelings at this delicate time so that you and your family can face these conflicts and share in trying to resolve the issues surrounding them.

The good news is this: Although caregiving is difficult on many levels, it is often ultimately rewarding—much to the surprise of all involved. Caregiving allows people to discover many wonderful things about their parents, their children, and themselves—things that would have gone unrecognized without the forging of this intimate connection. It also offers children a chance to show parents their love and devotion, and to pay them back for the years of caring that they received as children.

There are many different caregiving scenarios, such as an elder parent who lives with a grown child who is his or her caregiver; an adult child who supervises a parent's care from a distance; several children sharing the care of one parent; or a child helping one parent to care for another.

This chapter is written especially for caregivers, but it's also useful for those receiving care. When both sides are aware of what everyone is facing as the parent-child caregiving relationship takes shape, the chance for success is optimal.

Who Is the Caregiver?

The typical caregiver is a woman in her mid to late 40s, but male caregivers are gradually becoming more common. People in their 50s and 60s are also finding themselves caring for elderly parents, as the senior population extends its life expectancy.

Most caregiving situations fall into five categories:

1. The *chosen caregiver* either volunteers for the job, is selected by his or her parent, or is selected by the family as a whole.
2. The *in-law caregiver* is usually the wife of the elderly person's son, probably the female relative who lives nearest.
3. The *caregiving team* is a combination of family members and friends who coordinate and provide long-term care with team members dividing up the responsibilities.
4. *Supervised caregiving* is when children take responsibility for the care of their parent, but hire other people and services to do the actual work.
5. *System caregiving* occurs when children take advantage of various caregiving options, such as adult day care, to form a system that doesn't burden a single person or strip the elder of his or her independence. (See Chapter 18 for more information on adult care options.)

Gender and Caregiving

Most caregivers are women, either the daughters or the daughters-in-law of elders in need of care. In general, women bring to the caregiving role a nurturing focus, with a sensitivity to relationships, feelings, and the effects of their behavior on others. Sometimes men may approach caregiving from a different angle. They tend to concentrate on taking charge: setting goals, performing tasks, and solving problems. In the best-case scenario, both men and women (possibly a husband-wife or a brother-sister team) share caregiving responsibilities.

Caregivers of both genders may find affirmation through support groups (both traditional and through computer networks), and they may find that respite services can provide the breaks that they need to keep giving.

The Primary Caregiver

When families begin planning a caregiving endeavor, it may be helpful to designate one person as the main, or primary, caregiver. In most cases, one family member ends up taking most of the responsibility on himself or herself, so it's best to make the primary caregiver's role clear from the beginning. This eliminates the problem of family squabbles.

In some families there is an obvious choice, such as an only child or the family's sole daughter. When the choice is not so apparent, other factors come into play. The primary caregiver may be chosen because she or he has the most free time, lives closest to Mom or Dad, or has a personality best suited for the job.

If your family does designate a primary caregiver, it's important for all to remember that the children should all share in their parents' care. Going it alone is difficult—in some cases even impossible—and breeds resentment among family members. Even though one of you is in charge, be sure that everyone offers assistance and provides the main caregiver with relief whenever possible.

At the same time, the main caregiver must resist the trap of martyrdom and learn to accept help whenever it is offered. It is helpful to seek information about the illness and medical problems of the person you are caring for. This knowledge will give you greater confidence and peace.

**What Is
Your
Family
History?**

No two families are alike, so there is no surefire method for dealing with sparks that may fly when crisis hits. All of a sudden, you're in a brand-new role. For maybe the first time ever, your parent needs you, not the other way around. You and your brothers and sisters are catapulted back into a family unit that may have begun dissolving decades earlier.

This coming-together can be great. The care of a parent sometimes brings families closer than ever. It creates an opportunity for adult siblings to renew their relationships and rediscover closeness that was lost due to time, distance, and other factors. Through caregiving, children often grow closer to their aging parents and experience genuine satisfaction from doing something that's really important for someone they love very much. It also enables grandchildren or great-grandchildren to connect with their heritage and their elder relatives.

This is a roller coaster ride. There's no question about it. The thing that has made it easy for us is that she laughs and we don't allow ourselves to get depressed. We've had a lot of good laughs with her. The things that she comes out with are hysterical. And somebody else would say, "Oh, isn't that sad that she's talking that way." Hey, we're having a laugh with her; we're all laughing. She's laughing. We're having a good time.

Jeff Adams, age 39

On an individual basis, caregiving helps certain people to grow up. Taking on the care of a parent in need may afford an adult the self-esteem that allows him or her to finally turn the corner from childhood to adulthood. Some so-called dysfunctional families find that caring for their parent helps them to tackle and achieve something as a unit, perhaps for the first time. That's because the adult children were able to put their family on the proverbial back burner while the parent was functioning independently. Thus, the aging parent's needs may actually keep the family together and going strong where otherwise it would have fallen apart.

On the other hand, the caregiving situation may cause ancient grievances to bubble up to the surface as everyone slides backward into childhood roles: the spoiled baby brother, the bossy older sister, the shy middle child who resists conflict. The grown-up siblings may not have had to deal with each other since they were kids. Any hope that old brother-sister conflicts have melted away over time are usually dashed at the first sign of trouble.

Then there are generational conflicts between the cared-for parent and the caregiving child or children. There's often disagreement on the best course of treatment and care, and unresolved problems from years past do nothing to help matters. If grandchildren are old enough to voice an opinion, they may disagree with their parents on how Grandma or Grandpa should be cared for.

Finally, divorce and remarriage create a new host of conflicts. Should an ex-wife play a role in the caregiving of her former mother-in-law? Maybe so, if the two remain close. What does that mean for the ex-husband, however, and maybe his new wife? What about the children involved?

These factors exist before caregiving begins. Once the caregiving system is in place, new issues typically arise. Someone is not pulling his or her weight; somebody else is too controlling. Nobody can agree on whether to sell off assets, whether to research nursing homes, whether to force Mom to stop driving. If the arguments rage unchecked, all-out war may ensue. This conflict hurts everybody, most of all the parent who is in need of care.

So what can a family do? First of all, stay focused on Mom or Dad. Call a family meeting, and encourage every sibling to attend. Depending on your situation, it may be helpful to ask a clergy member or other family friend to moderate. You can also hire a family counselor, social worker, or geriatric-care manager (see pp. 317–318) to run the meeting and help the family to follow an agenda.

Before the meeting, clearly list all aspects of your parent's care and the jobs to be filled. Examples included grocery shopping, doctor's appointments, pharmacy visits, exercise sessions, and housekeeping. Ask the doctor to indicate on paper your parent's current health care needs and any that he or she thinks may arise in the near future.

Everyone should be able to play some sort of role. Even siblings who live far away can contribute by planning periodic visits that will take pressure off regular caregivers. They can also research health care or housing options at their library or on the Internet. Family members who live out of town need to be especially sensitive to and supportive of their relative or relatives who are caring for the parent. Suggestions about how the caregiving might be improved must be considered carefully. The primary caregiver needs all of the appreciation and encouragement you can provide.

The Sandwich Generation

Adult children today spend more and more time caring for their parents. There are many reasons why: Seniors live longer; hospitals send sick patients home much earlier; professional outside care is often unaffordable because of cuts in Medicare and other health care system reimbursements. As a result, in 25% of all American families, a family member is serving as a health care worker.

The term *sandwich generation* was coined when it became common for women to care for young children and elderly parents at the same time. They were sandwiched between the young and the old, with both sides demanding constant attention. Today's caregivers may be even more surrounded. Not only are they caring for their children and their parents, but many of them have full-time jobs, as well. Some are also helping grown children by caring for grandchildren at the time they're called on to care for their parents. The caregiving sandwich can have many layers!

Assuming a variety of roles (including husband or wife, parent, employee, and caregiver) doesn't necessarily lead to stress and anxiety for everybody. In some cases, research shows, it creates for the caregiver a richer and more satisfying life.

It's more likely, however, that caregiving will make you feel—at least part of the time—overburdened, underappreciated, and hopelessly inadequate. These feelings are entirely normal.

Everything you do, you do for yourself and the other person. Every single thing. You go to the bathroom and you say, "I wonder if she went to the bathroom." So that, in time, your body can't be too good, you know, because your body is two bodies, and it's like three minds because you've got your own mind and her mind and the mind of everybody that comes in contact with her.

Ann O'Connor, age 50

Remember that you are only one person, and one person can only do so much. As your parent's demands increase, you may be forced to choose between your children and your parent. Should you help your son study for his spelling test or go visit your mother in the nursing home? If your children sense that they are no longer your main priority, they may act out. More responsibility may fall on your husband or wife, who may not be willing to accept it.

Once again, your best bet is to keep the lines of communication open. Explain to your spouse that the pressures of caring for both the children and your parent are overwhelming. That may seem obvious to you, but he or she cannot really know what you're going through unless you talk about it.

Then talk to your children honestly about their grandparent's situation. Explain that you miss spending your extra time with them, but that Grandma or Grandpa has special needs right now. They might surprise you by wanting to lend a hand. Moreover, remember that you are setting a wonderful example for your children.

When my grandmother moved in I was nine years old. At first, I really hated it. She complained and criticized all the time, and my mother seemed more on edge than ever. But over time, she stopped acting like a visitor and became one of the family. She still criticized, but it was less hurtful, more joking. My brother and sister and I learned to tease her right back, and she loved it. My mother relaxed, and started enjoying her mother again. Grandma told the best stories. She had been a real party girl once, and still loved music and dancing. There were sad stories, too, about her family. Our family. We really learned from her in a way I'm sure we wouldn't have if she hadn't moved in. It brought all of us much closer together.

Barbara, age 34

Caring for the Caregiver

If you are caring for a parent, chances are that you've experienced feelings of depression, stress, and fatigue. These feelings are common and natural. If your loved one has Alzheimer's disease or has experienced a debilitating stroke or other form of mental impairment, you may also be experiencing a form of grief that Pauline Boss, a professor of family social science at the University of Minnesota, has called an "ambiguous loss." Your parent is present physically, but the person you once knew may be absent. In a very real sense, you have lost your loved one, but you may be having trouble resolving your grief because your parent is still here. If you find yourself in this situation, a social worker or other counselor may be able to help you address your resulting grief and perhaps anger so that you can move forward.

People say, "She's not your mother anymore." What do you mean she's not my mother? She's still my mother. I can't detach myself from her like that. Maybe at some other point, I may, but I can't let go yet. So I still treat her as if she were . . . . a piece of her is my mother.

Miss Donius, 29

One of the worst things you can do when you are caring for a parent is to stop caring for yourself. You need your strength—both emotional and physical—more than ever. Researchers have found that caregivers who don't take time out for themselves can suffer long-term health problems caused by stress and depression.

Caring for an older loved one can be exhausting and very stressful. Try to find a stress-reduction activity that works for you, such as meditation, warm baths, or classical music. Also, be sure to get enough sleep. Eat right, and exercise regularly. Don't abandon hobbies that might help you relax, such as reading or playing sports.

Maybe you're saying, "How am I supposed to do that? I can barely give Mom the time she needs." That may be true, but you're not helping Mom if you allow yourself to burn out and become exhausted or ill yourself. Push away the damaging feelings of guilt that plague nearly every caregiving son or daughter. It's perfectly okay and even advisable for you to take breaks from your parent.

Appeal to other family members or friends to give you occasional breathers. If no one else is available, find a respite care worker or an adult day care center that can help take some pressure off you. Hire someone to help with housework or shopping, or to provide companionship. If you and your parent can't afford those options, check out volunteer programs for seniors in your community (see Chapter 18).

During this time, it's very important that you be aware of your own needs and limitations. Asking for help isn't always easy; neither is accepting help that others offer. You must learn to do it, however, for your sake and for the sake of your parent.

Take some time off of work if you can. The Family and Medical Leave Act provides up to 12 weeks of unpaid leave for employees of businesses that employ 50 or more workers. Your employer may be willing to let you extend your own paid sick time so that you can care for your loved one.

It's also advisable to learn as much as you can about your parent's health problems. Turn to the Internet or your local library for the information that will make you a more confident caregiver.

Some people find that keeping a journal or diary of the care they provide their parent is helpful. Just a few minutes of quiet writing time each day can give you a real boost and help keep you in touch with your feelings. Make sure you don't lose touch with friends during this tough time. It's always beneficial to have someone to talk to who really cares about you. Some people also turn to their religion as a source of strength.

My father and sister were away and I was trying to change her and we both landed on the floor. I was just yelling in frustration, "Jesus, what are you doing to me?" And getting good and pissed off. And then getting pissed off to God. But then at the same time getting in control again, and just saying, "Help me." It's a strength. And I think that it's carried through with how we deal with it.
                                                                Emma Mahoney, age 45

Finally, consider joining a support group for caregivers (see the sidebar below).

Starting a Support Group

If you're a caregiver, you may find strength in a support group with others who share your situation. It's a forum to discuss daily challenges and stresses and to exchange ideas for dealing with a wide variety of problems. Many hospitals or community agencies run support groups. If you cannot locate one in your area that suits your needs, consider starting one yourself. Here's how:

1. If you know of other families in your situation, contact them. If not, post notices at senior centers, grocery stores, or hospitals asking potential members to contact you.

2. Ask doctors, nurses, social workers, or other experts for their assistance. They can offer advice and may be persuaded to address the group. Having a professional speak at your first meeting will help get your support group started on a positive note.

3. Set a time, place, and agenda for your first meeting.

4. Garner free advertisements by sending a press release to the newspaper or writing a public-service announcement for the local radio station.

5. At your first meeting, discuss what everyone hopes to gain from belonging to the group. Also, set up regular times and dates for future meetings.

6. It's helpful to appoint somebody to lead the discussion at each meeting. This person might be a professional who works with elders or a caregiver who is dedicated to keeping the group going.

7. Brainstorm a list of possible agendas for future meetings. Delegate tasks such as contacting national agencies or searching the Internet for up-to-the-minute information on geriatric medicine and caregiving issues.

8. Once your group is under way, approach the newspaper about running a human-interest story. This will heighten awareness and help you to locate other potential members.

When you're old and disabled, once-simple activities sometimes become insurmountable hurdles. Bathroom faucets may become impossible to turn, for instance, or the formerly innocuous back-porch steps may turn into a deadly hazard. No caregiver can watch a senior at all times, nor can she be there every time Mom or Dad might require assistance with some household task. Nonetheless, there are many ways that you can make his or her home as safe as possible.

It's always helpful to get a mental picture of your parent's day. What are the biggest challenges: navigating the stairs, reading the knobs on the stovetop, buying groceries, getting dressed in the morning, or something else altogether?

There are lots of ways to help. Install an extra handrail on the staircase, for instance. Use masking tape and markers to label the stovetop knobs in bold, bright letters. Arrange to do your grocery shopping together, or hire a companion to accompany your parent to the store. Buy clothes with easy fasteners. (Turn back to Chapter 18 for more practical suggestions.)

Also, locate any and all resources available to elders in your community, and take advantage of them. Begin by telephoning the Eldercare Locator service toll-free at 1-800-677-1116. Provide your parent's zip code, describe the type of help that he or she needs, and someone will tell you what's out there.

Then talk to a variety of professionals in the area. Social workers, nurses, doctors, and clerics are often excellent resources for seniors. Also, consult neighbors or friends of your parent who have used local services themselves.

You may also want to ask for referrals from government agencies listed in the telephone directory. Local agencies on health care and the Social Security Administration can be very helpful, as can national organizations such as the United Way, Catholic Charities, Jewish Family Services, and Protestant Welfare Agencies.

For a list of typical community resources, see Chapter 18. In the appendices at the back of this book, you'll also find some useful listings for state and national organizations.

If you are the primary caregiver and you live far from your parent, you'll face a new host of challenges. Organization is the key to making a long-distance caregiving relationship work.

First, find out what kind of informal support your parent already enjoys. Are there family friends or neighbors who visit regularly? Does your parent belong to a church or synagogue whose members provide support? Is he or she a member of any social clubs or senior citizens' groups? If the answer to these questions is yes, compile a list of people who already offer your parent companionship or assistance. Then telephone them and explain your situation.

The Practical Side of Caregiving

Caring from a Long Distance

You may feel awkward at first, but remember that the people on your list have already shown that they care for your parent. You might say, for example, "I understand that you visit my dad every couple of weeks. Would you mind making it a regular thing?" Perhaps say to a neighbor who occasionally offers to pick up groceries for your mother, "I'd really appreciate it if you could give Mom a call whenever you're going to the supermarket." Most people who are naturally kind and generous with their time are happy to be even more helpful if they possibly can be.

In addition, ask the members of the support system whether you might telephone them regularly to inquire about your parent's well-being. Also make sure they have your number so they can contact you if any unforeseen changes or problems arise.

Be sure to thank these supportive individuals and tell them how much their help means to you and your parent. They can be the foundation of successful long-distance caregiving.

Many elders have no means of informal support. Maybe they don't get out much and are unlikely to go to religious services or join clubs. Take heart. Home companions are readily available. You should have no problem hiring someone to visit your parent regularly and perform simple household tasks or do some grocery shopping. Check with your local agency on aging for information about hiring a home companion, or inquire about volunteer visiting programs.

If you are far away, you may also be worried about safety and security issues. There are many ways to make the house safer for an elder who lives alone: Install an alarm system and a medical-alert system so your parent can call for help if needed. It's also wise to inform the local police that your parent is alone. They may agree to check on him or her from time to time.

Also, check out all available community services for seniors. A few hours a week at a day-care or senior center may squelch loneliness. You may also find some organized activity that he or she will enjoy.

It's crucial that you have copies (one set for you and another for your parent) of all the documents that you'll need if a crisis hits (see Chapter 20).

Important Documents to Have on Hand

Be sure that your parent tells you whether the following documents are in order, and where you can find them if need be (see Chapter 20):

A *valid will* to guarantee that his or her estate will be passed on as he or she wishes

A *durable power of attorney* to designate someone to make important decisions and control finances if he or she becomes incapacitated

Advance directives (also known as living wills) to articulate your parent's wishes regarding his or her health care and to designate someone to make medical choices if necessary

Other documents and information that you may need and should locate—these include insurance policies, Social Security cards, Medicare and Medicaid numbers, a list of all assets and debts, real estate deeds or rental contracts, and tax information

Make your visits count. Set up appointments with your parent's physicians, nurses, or therapists so they can offer a full report of his or her condition. Carefully assess your parent's daily activities. If his or her needs are growing, you'll have to rearrange the system you already have in place. You may want to consider alternative housing options, outlined in Chapter 18, if living alone doesn't seem to be working for your parent anymore.

When the stresses of long-distance caregiving become too much, you might be tempted to have your mother or father leave home and move in with you. Before you do anything rash, however, consider your motivation. Do you want your parent to move so that he or she will be happier and live a better life, or are you hoping to assuage your guilt and make your life easier?

Moving your mother away from friends or social contacts may be detrimental to her spiritual and physical well-being. If your father's health is deteriorating, remember that it will be much harder for him to meet new people or join new activities in a strange place, regardless of how outgoing he was before. Again, Chapter 18 explores ways to make living together or living apart work out for everyone. For more information, you may also contact the National Family Caregivers Association at 1-800-896-3650.

Geriatric-care managers are people who work privately to help caregivers and their families find and coordinate social services for elders. A good care manager is especially useful for people who live far from their parents. This is a new field, and it is not regulated, so it's important that you choose your parent's geriatric-care manager carefully.

Choosing a Geriatric-Care Manager

Care-management organizations—local and national—are usually listed in the Yellow Pages under "Social Services," "Aging Services," "Social Workers," "Senior Citizen Services," or "Home Health Organizations." For referrals, you also can call the National Association of Professional Geriatric-Care Managers at 602-881-8008 or send a stamped, self-addressed envelope to 1604 N. Country Club Road, Tucson, AZ 85716.

Various care managers work differently, but usually they will visit your parent's home for a paid consultation. Then they will evaluate your parent's situation, recommend and arrange for services, and keep your family informed at all stages of their client's care. Before you hire a manager, be sure to ask the following questions:

1. How will the manager assess your parent? What will the assessment cover?

2. Does the manager have good information about relevant services available in the community? Will she or he connect your parent to the right resources?

3. Will the manager help your parent fill out necessary medical forms—an application for Medicare, for example?

4. What kind of advice can she or he provide the patient and the family?

5. When and for how long will the manager visit your parent? During what hours is the manager available?

6. Can she or he arrange for or provide transportation? Will the manager accompany your parent to appointments if necessary?

7. Can she or he hire and supervise home-care staff?

8. If a move becomes necessary, will the manager help your parent find alternative housing?

9. When and how often will she or he communicate with you?

10. What is the cost for the initial consultation, and what will it include?

11. How are fees structured beyond the consultation—hourly, weekly, or by the services performed?

12. Is there a sliding-fee scale for low-income elders? Does your parent qualify?

13. What, approximately, should your parent expect to pay, based on the manager's initial assessment?

Mail-Order Products for Seniors

Elders are big business these days. Myriad products are now designed to make your parent's life easier and safer, and many are available through mail order. The National Rehabilitation Information Center (800-346-2742) and the Access Foundation (516-568-2715) are helpful sources of information about products for elders.

You may also want to order several catalogs of specialty products to get an idea of what's out there. Here are some of the most popular:

Access to Recreation (1-800-634-4351)

Adaptability (1-800-243-9232)

Basic American Medical Products (1-770-368-4700)

Bruce Medical Supply (1-800-225-8446)

Enrichments (1-800-323-5547)

HouseWorks (1-800-928-3393) (home adaptation equipment)

LS&S Group (1-800-468-4789) (vision aids)

Independent Living Aids (1-800-537-2118)

Sears Home Health Care (1-800-326-1750)

Smith & Nephew (1-800-558-8633) (rehabilitation)

The Lighthouse (1-800-346-9579) (vision aids)

USA Rehab (1-888-727-3422)

The following companies sell easy-to-wear clothing designed for elders who have trouble dressing themselves:

American Health Care Apparel (1-800-252-0584)

Buck & Buck (1-800-458-0600)

Fashion Ease, M&M Health Care Apparel (1-800-221-8929)

JC Penney Easy Dressing Fashions (1-800-222-6161)

Mature Wisdom (1-800-691-9222)

Wardrobe Wagon (1-800-992-2737)

Wishing Well (1-818-840-6919)

On the Road

If you think your parent should stop driving, and he or she thinks you should mind your own business, you're involved in a common debate between care-givers and the elders they love. First of all, your concerns are well-founded. Statistics show that senior citizens have more accidents per driving time than younger drivers, due mainly to limited vision and slower reflexes, as well as illness and medication. If your parent insists on driving, you probably can't stop him. Do, though, suggest that he enroll in a "driver refresher course." You may find that the local senior center or Division of Motor Vehicles offers the course. If not, contact the National Safety Council (1-800-621-6244) or the American Association of Retired Persons (1-800-424-3410) for more information.

There are other ways you can help your parent be a safer driver. For example, convince your mother to wear her seat belt properly at all times. Have your father's sight and hearing tested regularly. Be sure that your parent's car is serviced every three months. Also, discourage your parent from driving during rush hour, at night, in bad weather, or through unfamiliar areas.

If you decide that your parent should not drive under any circumstances, ask his doctor to speak to him about giving it up for good. Then find ways to arrange transportation so that he can keep his former routine.

Despite warnings, your parent may still insist on driving. You can ask his or her doctor for a referral to a clinic that tests reaction time and assesses whether continuing to drive is a risk. However, be cautious about their reports. Often, clinics, though well intentioned, are not really adequately prepared to conduct these tests. Even if your parent is told that he or she has the mind of a 45-year-old and can continue to drive safely (this happened once to an 86-year-old man with dementia), listen to yourself, and don't let a parent drive if your gut tells you that he or she shouldn't be behind the wheel. One helpful way to think about this dilemma is to consider, "Would you want your parent driving your small children to their soccer or piano lessons?"

You can also report your parent to the Department of Motor Vehicles or your state licensing agency, and your parent's license may be revoked. This will probably be a tough decision for you, but it may be a lifesaving one for your parent and for others who drive the same roads.

Money Matters

It's entirely possible that you and your parent have never discussed finances before. Now, however, it's crucial that his or her money is properly managed, especially with the spiraling costs of health care and the complicated webs of insurance and taxes.

Have an honest and open discussion with your parent. Find out what his or her assets are, and whether he or she has debts that are insurmountable. Be sure that bills are being paid and that nothing is going to waste.

If your parent resists your help or advice, arrange for him or her to speak with an accountant, lawyer, or financial planner. The local senior center or area agency on aging may be able to help you locate someone who will provide financial advice to elders free of charge.

The Rewards of Caregiving

We probably all hope for the opportunity to assist our aging parents in some way. After spending a long weekend tending to her elderly father's physical and mental needs, a colleague said that although it was difficult and tiring to care for her father, who was unsteady on his feet, incontinent, and moderately cognitively impaired, doing so was a gift that she would always have to cherish long after her father was gone. No matter how challenging your situation may be, remember that caring for your older loved one is one of the most meaningful opportunities that life presents.

PART FIVE

THE LATEST ON ANTI-AGING THERAPIES

CHAPTER 23

"HEALTHY AGING" RESEARCH AND POTENTIAL THERAPIES

*To gather knowledge and to find out new knowledge is the noblest
occupation of the physician. To apply that knowledge . . . with
sympathy born of understanding, to the relief of human suffering,
is [his/her] loveliest occupation.*

Edward Archibald (1872–1945)

Aging is a phenomenon that is familiar to all of us, and yet research on aging has gained popularity only relatively recently, especially since the early 1990s. This gain in interest and recognition is due partly to revolutionary scientific breakthroughs and partly to the demands of society and its growing population of older persons (of which those age 85 years and older are the most rapidly growing group).

Older persons often suffer from a multitude of age-related conditions and disorders, the care for which costs a disproportionately large and rising portion of health care dollars. These demographic changes help to explain why new discoveries in aging seem to attract so much press coverage nowadays.

In this chapter, we highlight some of the latest research and potential therapies that are being explored, and we share with you some of what science has taught us about healthy aging.

How long can we possibly live? The longest that humans have lived is probably somewhere between 120 and 130 years. There are several theories about why some people are able to live this long, and most researchers adhere to more than one of these hypotheses. Probably, longevity is linked to both "programmed" factors, such as our genes, and "nonprogrammed factors," such as our environment. Just as with child development, nature and nurture both appear to be important during aging. Next, we look briefly at some of the different ways that theorists approach the aging process.

How Scientists View the Aging Process

Internal **Endocrine System Theory.** As we discussed in Chapter 14, the endocrine
Clock system is responsible for the secretion of hormones that control our many func-
Theories tions, including reproductive, metabolic, and growth and repair processes. The
"endocrine system theory" of aging holds that these hormones dictate our aging
process, as well.

Immune System Theory. Another theory of aging focuses on the immune
system because as this system weakens, we become more susceptible to infectious diseases and also to cancer (see Chapter 15).

Cellular Clock Theory. *Replicative senescence* is the point at which, after a
finite number of cell divisions, a cell stops dividing. As a cell stops at this preprogrammed checkpoint, depending on the cell type, the organ, and the organism, the cell may remain functional but may not divide further. Eventually it
may undergo programmed cell death (*apoptosis*) after a variable amount of
time, sometimes many years. The organism may or may not begin to experience
age-related deficits. Scientists are actively investigating this process because it
may partly explain certain aspects of human aging.

The flip side of the replicative senescence process is uncontrolled cell proliferation, in which cells continue to divide indefinitely and in fact can cause
tumors to form and grow. Research is ongoing to better understand the relationships among genes that promote cell division, those that inhibit it, and those
that regulate cell death.

Damage **DNA Damage.** Deoxyribonucleic acid (DNA), a large molecule found in the
Theories nucleus of a cell, holds the codes for almost every protein of each cell. Damage
to the DNA occurs over time: Sections of the DNA may be destroyed, and its
genetic code may undergo mutations. Damaged DNA can result in abnormal
genes and proteins and other errors.

Our bodies usually can repair most of the damage done to the DNA throughout our lives, and our ability to sustain this complex repair process is central to
healthy aging. In contrast, an inability to sustain this DNA repair process may
be implicated in the development of a number of conditions or diseases associated with aging.

Antagonistic Genes. Genes are portions of DNA that contain the instructions
for how RNA (ribonucleic acid) and protein molecules should be made. Some
theorists have suggested that so-called "pleiotropic" genes that have an important and beneficial role in our younger years (such as those necessary for repro-
duction) may actually have harmful effects later in life. For example, such genes
may have a permissive effect in old age, such as allowing us to develop certain
diseases that bring about the symptoms associated with aging. We need to better understand how genes regulate the process of aging, and someday perhaps
we will identify those genes that may collectively promote longevity, as well as
those that promote age-related diseases.

Free-Radical Damage. A *free radical* is a chemically reactive molecule created in the process of normal cell metabolism. If left unchecked by the cell's defensive antioxidant enzymes, the free radicals can cause damage to cells. These molecules have been linked to the formation of cataracts, hardening of the arteries, arthritis, heart disease, neurologic disorders, and cancer. Just as with genes, scientists are trying to determine how free radicals are generated and utilized by the cell, and how they may lead to diseases associated with old age.

Research topics that hold substantial therapeutic potential include cardiovascular disease, cancer, neurodegeneration, metabolism, falls, osteoporosis, voiding disorders, gastrointestinal dysfunction, exercise physiology, nutrition, pharmacotherapy, joint and muscle disorders, strokes, dementia, delirium, and depression.

Promising Research Areas

One of the more promising future research areas is the genetics of aging. This area of research includes the study of the genetics of age-related diseases and the identification of gene variants associated with differences in susceptibility or resistance to disease. It also includes the study of longevity and the manipulation of longevity-assurance genes. Research on genetically engineered cells, intracellular signaling, host defense systems, DNA repair, stress response and cell maintenance, cell proliferation and senescence, as well as *pharmacogenomics* (the use of genetic engineering for making therapeutic compounds), are also of interest. These research efforts will probably lead to new fundamental information. They will also probably facilitate the development of improved prevention and healthy-aging treatment programs in the future.

Genetics and Gerontology

We need to understand the plasticity of living systems, the repair and regenerative processes of tissues, and the differences between reversible and irreversible changes in function. We need to discover new ways to help our tissues and cells repair themselves faster and more completely. We need to develop better assistive devices. We also need to understand the physiology of complex systems. In addition, we need to understand better how the brain works and how memory fails. For example, recent research suggests that cell transplantation or electrical stimulation could be effective for treating stroke, Parkinson's disease, depression, and epilepsy.

Researchers are making progress in isolating, mapping, and cloning genes that may increase one's risk for developing conditions or diseases of old age. With greater knowledge of how genes work, scientists may be able to assess how these genetic factors may be affected by environmental factors such as nutrition. An example of how basic science research has been applied to clinical efforts is the identification of genes that may be associated with age-related diseases. For example, apolipoprotein E, a gene that handles the movement of fats across membranes, is a "gene of permissiveness." That is, it may allow certain disorders to occur. Having certain subtypes or alleles of this gene (for example,

ApoE4 in some groups) may increase one's risk of developing late-onset Alzheimer's disease, as well as atherosclerosis. The subtype of this gene that is found in Alzheimer's disease appears to be found less often in some centenarians (those who live to the age of 100 years or more) than in younger individuals, while another subtype (ApoE2) appears to be more prevalent in those with extreme longevity. Another example is the finding in 1999 that a single nucleic acid difference in the clock gene in humans correlates with their preference for mornings or evenings as the optimal time of day. This partly explains how the circadian rhythm is governed by our genes in morning persons versus night owls.

Treatment of Cancers

Immunotherapy is currently being studied for the treatment of melanomas, kidney tumors, leukemias, lymphomas, breast cancer, prostate cancer, and colon cancer. Usually specific antibodies against a specific protein in tumor cells can be administered. Other methods may include use of lymphokine-activated cells (LAK) to kill tumors and the employment of fusion proteins that are toxic to tumor cells.

Recombinant vaccines use viruses designed against tumor cells expressing certain specific surface proteins (for example, carcinoembryonic antigen, or CEA). The vaccine then stimulates the body's T-cell antibody response to tumor cells that are positive for this protein and destroys the tumor cells. These vaccines may be effective for treating colon and lung cancers.

Gene Therapy

Genes can be used in different ways to help to treat diseases and potentially also retard aging. Currently efforts are under way to provide a composite picture of the groups of genes involved in the aging process. By enhancing the activity of genes in certain tissues that are reduced with age, for example, it may be possible to modulate the aging process. Conversely, a gene that has been mutated or is overexpressed with negative consequences during aging could be opposed by specific anti-sense or dominant negative gene therapy. For example, it may be possible to enhance memory function with increased expression of the NR2B gene. In the future, it also may be possible to treat anxiety disorders by modulating GABA-A receptor subunit gene expression.

Examples of genes that have been demonstrated to be potentially useful for treatment of age-related diseases include vascular endothelial growth factor (VEGF) for enhancing circulation and nerve growth factor (NGF) for regeneration of nerve and brain tissue in stroke and perhaps also other neurologic diseases. In addition, another gene, p53, is being used in studies of gene therapy for cancer (mesothelioma), where the tumor cells are made to express p53, thereby promoting apoptosis (cell death) of the tumor cells. Still other examples are the possible modulation of p16 expression for treating arthritis, and the possible treatment of Alzheimer's disease by preventing plaque formation through modulation of the beta amyloid protein gene. In the future, even hair regrowth may be potentially enhanced by modulating certain genes.

Alternative, or complementary, medicine is an area of growing interest for researchers and growing profit for entrepreneurs. Here, we give a few examples of the many preparations and therapies that are appearing in the news and in the supermarket each week.

Alternative or Complementary Approaches

Herbs

Ginkgo Biloba. The fruits, seeds, and extracts of the maidenhair tree, the oldest living tree species (200 million years), have long been used for many disorders. Recently ginkgo extracts were demonstrated to be beneficial in some people with cognitive impairment. More studies are needed to better understand the mechanisms of action of these compounds.

St. John's Wort. Currently, a rigorously designed study that is funded by the National Institutes of Health (NIH) is under way to test whether this compound may be beneficial for treating depression.

Antioxidants

Oxygen-free radicals, or simply free radicals, are potentially harmful reactive molecules that are produced when our cells produce energy (from food and oxygen) for the body's needs. These molecules are also produced by radiation, sunlight, certain chemicals, and smoking. As we mentioned earlier, one theory of aging is that an accumulation of free radicals in the body leads to cell, tissue, and organ damage. Free radicals may cause several diseases that are most prevalent in older people, such as atherosclerosis ("hardening of the arteries") and some forms of cancer, as well as certain immune deficiencies.

The good news is that our bodies create certain substances, such as the enzymes superoxide dismutase (SOD) and catalase, to inactivate free radicals. Foods such as carrots, oranges, and broccoli, which contain vitamins A, C, and E, can contain antioxidants, too. Blueberries, strawberries, tomatoes, peanuts, garlic, and soy products are good sources of antioxidants also. That's one reason why eating fresh fruits and vegetables is a healthful practice. However, as of this writing there is no definitive proof that taking very large amounts of antioxidants may reverse aging. In fact, ingesting excessive amounts of these or other substances may be harmful. As always, moderation is key, and you may wish to speak with your doctor if you have any questions about how much is right for you.

Caloric Restriction

Restriction of calories has been shown to be effective in maintaining function, reducing disease, and prolonging life in certain animals (fruit flies, mice, and rats). It is also being studied in monkeys, and preliminary results suggest that it may also have some beneficial effects.

Hormones

Human Growth Hormone (hGH). A hormone secreted by the anterior pituitary gland, hGH plays an important role in the metabolism of carbohydrates, proteins, and lipids (fats) in our bodies. Injected in the form of recombinant hGH, it may increase muscle size and reverse some signs of aging such as thickened skin and excess fat. The amount of hGH in our bodies declines as we grow older. Researchers currently are exploring whether supplements of hGH will help to make our bones and muscles stronger, and in doing so make us less frail. (Such supplements are already prescribed for children with a deficiency in this hormone.)

Just as with other hormones, there may be unpleasant or even dangerous side effects associated with taking too much hGH. These include the risk of developing diabetes, carpal tunnel syndrome, or high blood pressure. Therefore, it's a good idea to wait until we have more information about hGH before taking it.

Other substances that either increase production of growth hormone or enhance the effect of growth hormone are also being studied. Preliminary results suggest that these agents may have some beneficial effects for older women and men.

Estrogen and Testosterone. As we discussed in Chapter 5, levels of *estrogen,* the hormone that facilitates egg production in younger women, drop off dramatically after women go through menopause. Estrogen replacement therapy (ERT) can have protective effects against some of the downsides of estrogen loss in older women, such as osteoporosis and heart disease. This type of therapy may also improve our mood and brain function. ERT is not without its own risks, however (it may increase the likelihood for breast and uterine cancer), so talk with your doctor about whether ERT is the right choice for you. It may be that one of the selective estrogen receptor modulators (SERMs) may be used by some women, since they are associated with decreased risks for breast and uterine cancer.

Levels of testosterone, the male sex hormone, also tend to drop as people age, although this decline is not as dramatic as that of estrogen levels. Scientists are trying to determine whether replacement of this hormone can prevent weakness in frail older people by increasing bone and muscle mass.

DHEA (Dihydroepiandrosterone). This hormone, which is produced by the adrenal glands, is needed for the body to produce estrogen and testosterone. It has been found to boost the immune system and prevent some forms of cancer in animals. We don't quite know exactly how DHEA functions in the body, and it is unclear whether DHEA has beneficial effects on its own or mostly by means of the substances that it creates: estrogen and testosterone.

Because levels of DHEA in the body tend to fall gradually as we get older (especially after age 30), some people have proposed that increasing amounts of this hormone through hormone therapy may have a beneficial effect. Researchers are studying this option carefully. However, because liver damage and an increased risk of breast and prostate cancer may be linked to levels of DHEA that are too high, caution is recommended.

Since 1991, DHEA and the next hormone that we discuss—melatonin—have been available as over-the-counter nutritional supplements. However, because scientists are still investigating what DHEA does and how it works, we recommend that you speak with your physician before using such supplements.

Melatonin. Melatonin is a hormone produced by another gland—the pineal gland, located in the brain. Melatonin may help to induce sleep, and it may have some effect on our response to seasonal changes and to our biological clock (see Chapter 6). Research into the role and potential benefits of this hormone is ongoing.

"Antiaging" Cocktails

Currently, certain "antiaging" cocktails that contain minerals (magnesium, zinc, selenium, calcium, phosphorus, and chromium), enzymes (papain, bromelain, trysin, lipase, chymotrysin, rutin, pancreatin, and amylase), and vitamins and antioxidant nutrients (vitamins A, C, and E, glutathione, choline, pyroxidine, folic acid, cobalamin, and thiamine) are being tried with varying results.

Relaxation Response (Breathing Techniques)

This technique has been shown to be helpful for older as well as younger persons. It has been reported to enhance immune function, lower blood pressure in persons with hypertension, and promote a sense of well-being.

Tai Chi

This non-weight-bearing exercise program has been reported to improve balance and reduce falls. More research is under way to study its other effects.

> The Land of Faery,
> Where nobody gets old and godly and grave,
> Where nobody gets old and crafty and wise,
> Where nobody gets old and bitter of tongue.
>
> William Butler Yeats (1865–1939)

Other Areas of Future Research

Microtechnology

Scientists are trying to develop smaller and smaller microscopic and submicroscopic tools to manipulate cells and the proteins and other components such as DNA inside cells. This will allow doctors to treat disorders at the cellular and subcellular levels, thereby minimizing toxicity and enhancing specificity.

DNA Vaccines

DNA vaccines may one day become a standard form of immunization. Research in animals has demonstrated the ability of these vaccines to produce a good response. Other advantages of these vaccines include better stability and storage, as well as the flexibility to modify protein encoded by the DNA through genetic engineering. They may help to prevent Alzheimer's disease, rheumatoid arthritis, certain cancers, and heart disease. In the future, oral DNA gene therapy also may help to prevent allergic reactions.

Telomeres   *Telomeres* are the natural tail ends of the chromosomes of multicellular organisms. These tails usually get shorter each time a cell divides. Telomeres may have a more important role than simply marking a cell's duplication record, however. Indeed, they may serve as regulators of longevity, cell division, and cancer.

Further research will help us to better understand the processes of cell proliferation and aging. For now, be assured that in the majority of cases, there is more than enough reserve in our cells for them to keep dividing for 120 years or more—we don't have to become worried about our telomeres running out prematurely.

Tissue Engineering   Biologists, materials engineers, and clinicians are working together to develop new tissues to help the body better repair diseased or damaged tissues. For example, in cases of skin trauma, living skin equivalents that are produced by culturing together different types of skin cells within an artificial matrix have been used successfully for enhancing wound healing. Cultured cartilage cells within a matrix have now been successfully implanted in persons with joint cartilage damage, resulting in improved cartilage repair and healing. Tissue-engineered blood vessels and heart valves are also on the horizon. Studies of implantation of nerve cells into the brains of patients with stroke, Parkinson's disease, or epilepsy are currently under way; and early results appear to be favorable.

The 1999 reports of the finding of precursor cells, called "stem cells" in brain, liver, and bone-marrow tissues of adults, which can be stimulated to form organ tissue, have been greeted with excitement and intense interest. Research is ongoing to help to convert the stem cells into nerve cells and heart cells. Harvesting of tissues produced with these techniques has begun, and clinical applications may be possible in a few years. It is hoped that in the future, these and other advances, such as novel gene-delivery techniques, will enable our bodies to heal better and allow us to maintain our level of function and our independence longer.

Homes of the Future   Scientists, architects, and engineers are collaborating to design better homes and living environments that will allow each person to maximize and maintain the highest level of function. By using transgenerational, user-friendly design and state-of-the-art materials and technology, these advances will enable us to remain in our homes for as long as possible, so that we may age in place more easily in the twenty-first century. One major area to be developed would be improvements in the promotion of independence, through aids to assist with activities of daily living (such as help with toileting, dressing, feeding, and washing), and aids to assist with instrumental activities of daily living (for example, voice-activated, preprogrammed washing machines and computerized meal-preparation and house-cleaning options).

Another promising area would be technology development for the improved monitoring of early signs of weakness or illness, before a person gets ill or falls, for example, and suffers the consequences of a hip fracture or other similar events. This development would probably result in improved care and reduced health care costs.

Other potential areas of development could include use of photosensitive (light-activated) and thermosensitive (heat-activated) systems, as well as use of impact-safe materials to enhance safety and reduce injury in the home. Some of the other exciting research possibilities include reminders for taking medications and engaging in other activities; improvements in connectedness with family, friends, and loved ones; and means of addressing other social needs of the homebound.

> *If you are planning for a year, sow rice; if you are planning for a decade,*
> *plant trees; if you are planning for a lifetime, educate people.*
>
> Chinese proverb

Older people are living longer, with less disability, and many are more independent than ever before. Thus, an understanding of how we might achieve healthy aging is essential.

Although we don't yet fully understand exactly how or why we age, basic research has provided some insights into this area. In our efforts to study aging, we have grown to appreciate the need for separating disease from aging, where possible. Future research will improve our understanding of the molecular processes that underlie each and of their complex interactions.

In this book, we discussed the many steps that you can take to manage various conditions, prevent falls, and so on. We tried to stress the importance of key lifestyle factors: exercise, weight control, and diet. Research into the aging process is exciting, but don't wait for a miracle longevity drug to present itself. Even if a miracle drug were to be discovered, the best way to age well would still be to live well. To have lived well ultimately is to have appreciated and cared for the complex body mechanisms that make you one of the masterpieces of creation. Those of us who live well will not only attain personal fulfillment, but will undoubtedly also contribute towards the health and happiness of others.

APPENDIX A

State Agencies on Aging (includes commonwealths and territories)

Alabama
Region IV

Alabama Commission on Aging
RSA Plaza, Suite 470
770 Washington Avenue
Montgomery, AL 36130
334-242-5743, fax: 334-242-5594

Alaska
Region X

Alaska Commission on Aging
Division of Senior Services
Department of Administration
Juneau, AL 99811-0209
907-465-3250, fax: 907-465-4716

Arizona
Region IX

Aging and Adult Administration
Department of Economic Security
1789 West Jefferson Street, #950A
Phoenix, AZ 85007
602-542-4446, fax: 602-542-6575

Arkansas
Region VI

Division of Aging and Adult Services
Arkansas Department of Human Services
P.O. Box 1437, Slot 1412
7th and Main Streets
Little Rock, AR 72201
501-682-2441, fax: 501-682-8155

California
Region IX

California Department of Aging
1600 K Street
Sacramento, CA 95814
916-322-5290, fax: 916-324-1903

Colorado
Region VIII

Aging and Adult Services
Department of Social Services
110 16th Street, Suite 200
Denver, CO 80202-5202
303-620-4147, fax: 303-620-4189

Connecticut
Region I

Division of Elderly Services
25 Sigourney Street, 10th Floor
Hartford, CT 06106-5033
860-424-5277, fax: 860-424-4966

Delaware
Region III

Delaware Division of Services for Aging and
 Adults with Physical Disabilities
Department of Health and Social Services
1901 North DuPont Highway
New Castle, DE 19720
302-577-4791, fax: 302-577-4793

District of Columbia
Region III

District of Columbia Office on Aging
One Judiciary Square, 9th Floor
441 Fourth Street, N.W.
Washington, DC 20001
202-724-5622, fax: 202-724-4979

Florida
Region IV

Department of Elder Affairs
Building B, Suite 152
4040 Esplanade Way
Tallahassee, FL 32399-7000
904-414-2000, fax: 904-414-2002

Georgia
Region IV

Division of Aging Services
Department of Human Resources
2 Peachtree Street N.E., 18th Floor
Atlanta, GA 30303
404-657-5258, fax: 404-657-5285

Guam
Region IX

Division of Senior Citizens
Department of Public Health and Social
  Services
P.O. Box 2816
Agana, Guam 96932
011-671-475-0263, fax: 011-671-477-2930

Hawaii
Region IX

Hawaii Executive Office on Aging
250 South Hotel Street, Suite 107
Honolulu, HI 96813
808-586-0100, fax: 808-586-0185

Idaho
Region X

Idaho Commission on Aging
3380 Americana Terrace, Suite 120
Boise, ID 83706
208-334-3833, fax: 208-334-3033

Illinois
Region V

Illinois Department on Aging
421 East Capitol Avenue, Suite 100
Springfield, IL 62701-1789
217-785-2870, fax: 217-785-4477
Chicago Office: 312-814-2630

Indiana
Region V

Bureau of Aging and In-Home Services
Division of Disability, Aging and
  Rehabilitative Services
Family and Social Services Administration
402 W. Washington Street, #W454
P.O. Box 7083
Indianapolis, IN 46207-7083
317-232-7020, fax: 317-232-7867

Iowa
Region VII

Iowa Department of Elder Affairs
Clemens Building, 3rd Floor
200 Tenth Street
Des Moines, IA 50309-3609
515-281-5187, fax: 515-281-4036

Kansas
Region VII

Department on Aging
New England Building
503 S. Kansas Ave.
Topeka, KS 66603-3404
785-296-4986, fax: 785-296-0256

Kentucky
Region IV

Kentucky Division of Aging Services
Cabinet for Human Resources
275 East Main Street, 6 West
Frankfort, KY 40621
502-564-6930, fax: 502-564-4595

Louisiana
Region VI

Governor's Office of Elderly Affairs
P.O. Box 80374
412 N. 4th Street 3rd Floor
Baton Rouge, LA 70802
504-342-7100, fax: 504-342-7133

Maine
Region I

Bureau of Elder and Adult Services
Department of Human Services
35 Anthony Avenue
State House, Station #11
Augusta, ME 04333
207-624-5335, fax: 207-624-5361

Maryland
Region III

Maryland Office on Aging
State Office Building, Room 1007
301 West Preston Street
Baltimore, MD 21201-2374
410-767-1100, fax: 410-333-7943

Massachusetts
Region I

Massachusetts Executive Office of Elder
  Affairs
One Ashburton Place, 5th Floor
Boston, MA 02108
617-727-7750, fax: 617-727-9368

Michigan
Region V

Office of Services to the Aging
P.O. Box 30026
Lansing, MI 48909-8176
517-373-8230, fax: 517-373-4092

Minnesota
Region V

Minnesota Board on Aging
444 Lafayette Road
St. Paul, MN 55155-3843
612-296-2770, fax: 612-297-7855

Mississippi
Region IV

Division of Aging and Adult Services
750 State Street
Jackson, MS 39202
601-359-4925, fax: 601-359-4370

Missouri
Region VII

Division on Aging
Department of Social Services
P.O. Box 1337
615 Howerton Court
Jefferson City, MO 65102-1337
573-751-3082, fax: 573-751-8493

Montana
Region VIII

Senior and Long-term Care Division
Department of Public Health & Human
  Services
P.O. Box 4210
111 Sanders, Room 211
Helena, MT 59604
406-444-7788, fax: 406-444-7743

Nebraska
Region VII

Department of Health and Human Services
Division on Aging
P.O. Box 95044
301 Centennial Mall South
Lincoln, NE 68509-5044
402-471-2307, fax: 402-471-4619

Nevada
Region IX

Nevada Division for Aging Services
Department of Human Resources
State Mail Room Complex
340 North 11th Street, Suite 203
Las Vegas, NV 89101
702-486-3545, fax: 702-486-3572

New Hampshire
Region I

Division of Elderly and Adult Services
State Office Park South
115 Pleasant Street, Annex Bldg. # 1
Concord, NH 03301-3843
603-271-4680, fax: 603-271-4643

New Jersey
Region II

Department of Health and Senior Services
Division of Senior Affairs
P.O. Box 807
Trenton, New Jersey 08625-0807
1-800-792-8820, 609-588-3141;
fax: 609-588-3601

New Mexico
Region VI

State Agency on Aging
La Villa Rivera Building, 4th Floor
224 East Palace Avenue
Santa Fe, NM 87501
505-827-7640, fax: 505-827-7649

New York
Region II

New York State Office for the Aging
2 Empire State Plaza
Albany, NY 12223-1251
1-800-342-9871, 518-474-5731;
fax: 518-474-0608

North Carolina
Region IV

Division of Aging
693 Palmer Drive
Raleigh, NC 27626-0531
919-733-3983, fax: 919-733-0443

North Dakota
Region VIII

Department of Human Services
Aging Services Division
600 South 2nd Street, Suite 1C
Bismarck, ND 58504
701-328-8910, fax: 701-328-8989

North Mariana Islands
Region IX

CNMI Office on Aging
P.O. Box 2178
Commonwealth of the Northern Mariana
   Islands
Saipan, MP 96950
670-233-1320/1321,
fax: 670-233-1327/0369

Ohio
Region V

Ohio Department of Aging
50 West Broad Street, 9th Floor
Columbus, OH 43215-5928
614-466-5500, fax: 614-466-5741

Oklahoma
Region VI

Services for the Aging
Department of Human Services
P.O. Box 25352
312 N.E. 28th Street
Oklahoma City, OK 73125
405-521-2281 or 521-2327,
fax: 405-521-2086

Oregon
Region X

Senior and Disabled Services Division
500 Summer Street, N.E., 2nd Floor
Salem, OR 97310-1015
503-945-5811, fax: 503-373-7823

Pennsylvania
Region III

Pennsylvania Department of Aging
Commonwealth of Pennsylvania
555 Walnut Street, 5th Floor
Harrisburg, PA 17101-1919
717-783-1550, fax: 717-772-3382

Puerto Rico
Region II

Commonwealth of Puerto Rico
Governor's Office of Elderly Affairs
Call Box 50063
Old San Juan Station, PR 00902
787-721-5710, 721-4560, or 721-6121,
fax: 787-721-6510

Rhode Island
Region I

Department of Elderly Affairs
160 Pine Street
Providence, RI 02903-3708
401-277-2858, fax: 401-277-2130

American Samoa
Region IX

Territorial Administration on Aging
Government of American Samoa
Pago Pago, American Samoa 96799
011-684-633-2207,
fax: 011-684-633-2533

South Carolina
Region IV

Office on Aging
South Carolina Department of Health and
   Human Services
P.O. Box 8206
Columbia, SC 29201-8206
803-253-6177, fax: 803-253-4173

South Dakota
Region VIII

Office of Adult Services and Aging
Richard F. Kneip Building
700 Governors Drive
Pierre, SD 57501-2291
605-773-3656, fax: 605-773-6834

Tennessee
Region IV

Commission on Aging
Andrew Jackson Building, 9th Floor
500 Deaderick Street
Nashville, Tennessee 37243-0860
615-741-2056, fax: 615-741-3309

Texas
Region VI

Texas Department on Aging
4900 North Lamar, 4th Floor
Austin, TX 78751
512-424-6840, fax: 512-424-6890

Utah
Region VIII

Division of Aging
Adult Services
Box 45500
120 North 200 West
Salt Lake City, UT 84145-0500
801-538-3910, fax: 801-538-4395

Vermont
Region I

Vermont Department of Aging and
    Disabilities
Waterbury Complex
103 South Main Street
Waterbury, VT 05676
802-241-2400, fax: 802-241-2325

Virginia
Region III

Virginia Department for the Aging
1600 Forest Avenue, Suite 102
Richmond, VA 23219-2327
804-662-9333, fax: 804-662-9354

Virgin Islands of the United States
Region II

Senior Citizen Affairs
Virgin Islands Department of Human Services
Knud Hansen Complex, Building A
1303 Hospital Ground
Charlotte Amalie, VI 00802
809-774-0930, fax: 809-774-3466

Washington
Region X

Aging and Adult Services Administration
Department of Social & Health Services
P.O. Box 45050
Olympia, WA 98504-5050
360-586-8753, fax: 360-902-7848

West Virginia
Region III

West Virginia Bureau of Senior Services
Holly Grove, Building 10
1900 Kanawha Boulevard East
Charleston, WV 25305-0160
304-558-3317, fax: 304-558-0004

Wisconsin
Region V

Bureau of Aging and Long-term Care
    Resources
Department of Health and Family Services
P.O. Box 7851
Madison, WI 53707
608-266-2536, fax: 608-267-3203

Wyoming
Region VIII

Office on Aging
Department of Health
117 Hathaway Building, Room 139
Cheyenne, WY 82002-0480
307-777-7986, fax: 307-777-5340

State Long-term Care Ombudsman Programs

Ombudsman programs investigate and resolve complaints made by or on behalf of residents of nursing homes, board and care homes, and similar adult homes. The program also promotes policies and practices to improve the quality of life, health, safety, and rights of these residents. For information and/or issues and complaints regarding care of older persons in long-term care facilities, call the long-term care ombudsman program for your state listed below.

Alabama
State Long-term Care Ombudsman
Commission on Aging
RSA Plaza, Suite 470
770 Washington Avenue
Montgomery, AL 36130
334-242-5743, fax: 334-242-5594

Alaska
State Long-term Care Ombudsman
Older Alaskans Commission
3601 C Street, Suite 260
Anchorage, AK 99503-5209
907-563-6393, fax: 907-561-3862

Arizona
State Long-term Care Ombudsman
Aging and Adult Administration
Department of Economic Security
1789 West Jefferson, 950A
Phoenix, AZ 85007
602-542-6452, fax: 602-542-6575

Arkansas
State Long-term Care Ombudsman
Arkansas Division on Aging & Adult
  Services
1417 Donaghey Plaza South, Slot 1412
Little Rock, AR 72203-1437
501-682-2441, fax: 501-682-8155

California
State Long-term Care Ombudsman
Department of Aging
1600 K Street
Sacramento, CA 95814
916-322-5290, fax: 916-323-7299

Colorado
State Long-term Ombudsman
The Legal Center
455 Sherman Street, Suite 130
Denver, CO 80203
303-722-0300, fax: 303-722-0720

Connecticut
Acting State Long-term Care
  Ombudsman
Elderly Services Division
25 Sigourney Street, 10th Floor
Harford, CT 06106-5033
860-424-5200, fax: 860-424-4966

Delaware
State Long-term Care Ombudsman
Delaware Services for Aging-Disabled
Oxford Building, Suite 200
256 Chapman Road
Newark, DE 19702
302-453-3820 ext. 46,
fax: 302-453-3836

District of Columbia
State Long-term Care Ombudsman
AARP—Legal Counsel for the Elderly
601 E Street, N.W., 4th Floor, Bldg. A
Washington, DC 20049
202-434-2188, 202-434-2140,
fax: 202-434-6464

Florida
State Long-term Care Ombudsman
Florida State LTC Ombudsman Council
Holland Building, Room 270
600 South Calhoun Street
Tallahassee, FL 32301
850-488-6190, fax: 850-488-5657

Georgia
State Long-term Care Ombudsman
Division of Aging Services
2 Peachtree Street NW, 18th Floor, Suite
   18-129
Atlanta, GA 30303-3176
404-657-5319, fax: 404-657-5285

Hawaii
State Long-term Care Ombudsman
Executive Office on Aging
Office of the Governor
250 South Hotel Street, Suite 107
Honolulu, HI 96813-2831
808-586-0100, fax: 808-586-0185

Idaho
State Long-term Care Ombudsman
Office on Aging
P.O. Box 83720
700 West Jefferson, Room 108
Boise, ID 83720-0007
208-334-3833, fax: 208-334-3033

Illinois
State Long-term Care Ombudsman
Illinois Department on Aging
421 East Capitol Avenue
Springfield, IL 62701-1789
217-785-3143, fax: 217-524-9644

Indiana
State Long-term Care Ombudsman
Indiana Division of Aging & Rehabilitative
   Services
P.O. Box 7083-W454
402 W. Washington St., #W-454
Indianapolis, IN 46207-7083
317-232-7134, fax: 317-232-7867

Iowa
Interim State Long-term Care Ombudsman
Iowa Department of Elder Affairs
Clemens Building
200 10th Street, 3rd Floor
Des Moines, IA 50309-3609
515-281-4656, fax: 515-281-4036

Kansas
State Long-term Care Ombudsman
Office of the State Long-term Care
   Ombudsman
610 S.W. 10th Avenue, 2nd Floor
Topeka, KS 66612-1616
785-296-3017, fax: 795-296-3916

Kentucky
State Long-term Care Ombudsman
Division of Aging Services
State Long-term Care Ombudsman Office
275 E. Main Street, 5th Fl W.
Frankfort, KY 40621
502-564-6930, fax: 502-564-4595

Louisiana
State Long-term Care Ombudsman
Governor's Office of Elderly Affairs
State Long-term Care Ombudsman Office
412 N. 4th Street, 3rd Floor
Baton Rouge, LA 70802
504-342-7100, fax: 504-342-7133

Maine
State Long-term Care Ombudsman
21 Bangor Street
P.O. Box 126
Augusta, ME 04332
207-621-1079, fax: 207-621-0509

Maryland
State Long-term Care Ombudsman
Office on Aging
State Office Building, Room 1004
301 West Preston Street
Baltimore, MD 21201
410-767-1091, fax: 410-333-7943

Massachusetts
State Long-term Care Ombudsman
Executive Office of Elder Affairs
1 Ashburton Place, 5th Floor
Boston, MA 02108-1518
617-727-7750, fax: 617-727-9368

Michigan
State Long-term Care Ombudsman
Citizens for Better Care
416 North Homer Street, Station 101
Lansing, MI 48912-4700
517-886-6797, fax: 517-886-6349
In-state toll free: 1-800-292-7852

Minnesota
State Long-term Care Ombudsman
Office of Ombudsman for Older Minnesotans
444 Lafayette Road, 4th Floor
St. Paul, MN 55155-3843
612-296-0382, fax: 612-297-5654

Mississippi
State Long-term Care Ombudsman
Division of Aging & Adult Services
750 North State Street
Jackson, MS 39202
601-359-4929, fax: 601-359-4970

Missouri
State Long-term Care Ombudsman
Division on Aging
Department of Social Services
P.O. Box 1337
615 Howerton Court
Jefferson City, MO
800-309-3282 or 573-526-0727;
fax: 573-751-8687

Montana
State Long-term Care Ombudsman
Office on Aging
Department of Family Services
P.O. Box 8005
Helena, MT 59604-8005
406-444-4077, fax: 406-444-7743

Nebraska
State Long-term Care Ombudsman
Department on Aging
P.O. Box 95044
301 Centennial Mall-South
Lincoln, NE 68509-5044
402-471-2307, fax: 402-471-4619

Nevada
State Long-term Care Ombudsman
Division for Aging Services
Department of Human Resources
340 North 11th Street, Suite 203
Las Vegas, NV 89101
702-486-3545, fax: 702-486-3572

New Hampshire
State Long-term Care Ombudsman
Health and Human Services
Office of the Ombudsman
129 Pleasant Street
Concord, NH 03301-6505
603-271-4375, fax: 603-271-4771

New Jersey
State Long-term Care Ombudsman
101 South Broad Street, CN808, 6th Floor
Trenton, NJ 08625-0808
609-588-3614, fax: 609-588-3365

New Mexico
State Long-term Care Ombudsman
State Agency on Aging
228 East Palace Avenue, Suite A
Santa Fe, NM 87501
505-827-7640, fax: 505-827-7649

New York
State Long-term Care Ombudsman
Office for the Aging
2 Empire State Plaza
Agency Building #2
Albany, NY 12223-0001
518-474-0108, fax: 518-474-7761

North Carolina
State Long-term Care Ombudsman
Division of Aging, CB 29531
693 Palmer Drive
Raleigh, NC 27626-0531
919-733-3983, fax: 919-733-0443

North Dakota
State Long-term Care Ombudsman
Aging Services Division, DHS
600 South 2nd Street, Suite 1C
Bismarck, ND 58504-5729
701-328-8915, fax: 701-328-8989

Ohio
State Long-term Care Ombudsman
Department of Aging
50 West Broad Street, 9th Floor
Columbus, OH 43215-5928
614-644-7922, fax: 614-466-5741

Oklahoma
State Long-term Care Ombudsman
Aging Services Division, DHS
312 N.E. 28th Street, Suite 109
Oklahoma City, OK 73105
405-521-6734, fax: 405-521-2086

Oregon
State Long-term Care Ombudsman
Office of the Long-term Care Ombudsman
3855 Wolverine NE, Suite 6
Salem, OR 97310
503-378-6533, fax: 503-373-0852

Pennsylvania
State Long-term Care Ombudsman
Department of Aging
555 Walnut St., 5th Floor
Forum Place
Harrisburg, PA 17101-1919
717-783-7247, fax: 717-772-3382

Puerto Rico
State Long-term Care Ombudsman
Governor's Office for Elder Affairs
Call Box 50063, Old San Juan Station
San Juan, Puerto Rico 00902
787-725-1515, fax: 787-721-6510

Rhode Island
State Long-term Care Ombudsman
Department of Elderly Affairs
160 Pine Street
Providence, RI 02903-3708
401-222-2858, ext. 321, fax: 401-222-1420

South Carolina
State Long-term Care Ombudsman
Division on Aging
202 Arbor Lake Drive, Suite 301
Columbia, SC 29223-4535
803-253-6177, fax: 803-253-4173

South Dakota
State Long-term Care Ombudsman
Office of Adult Services & Aging
700 Governors Drive
Pierre, SD 57501-2291
605-773-3656, fax: 605-773-6834

Tennessee
State Long-term Care Ombudsman
Commission on Aging
Andrew Jackson Building, 9th Floor
500 Deaderick Street
Nashville, TN 37243-0860
615-741-2056, fax: 615-741-3309

Texas
State Long-term Care Ombudsman
Department on Aging
P.O. Box 12786 Capitol Station
Austin, TX 78711
512-424-6875, fax: 512-424-6890

Utah
State Long-term Care Ombudsman
Division of Aging & Adult Services
Department of Social Services
P.O. Box 1367
Salt Lake City, UT 84103
801-538-3910, fax: 801-538-4395

Vermont
State Long-term Care Ombudsman
Vermont Legal Aid, Inc.
264 North Winooski
P.O. Box 1367
Burlington, VT 05402
802-863-5620, fax: 802-863-7152

Virginia
State Long-term Care Ombudsman
Virginia Association of Area Agencies on
   Aging
530 East Main Street, Suite 428
Richmond, VA 23219
804-644-2923, fax: 804-644-5640

Washington
State Long-term Care Ombudsman
Washington State Ombudsman Program
1200 South 336th Street
Federal Way, WA 98003-7452
800-422-1384, 253-838-6810;
fax: 253-874-7831

West Virginia
State Long-term Care Ombudsman
Commission on Aging
1900 Kanawha Blvd. East
Charleston, WV 25305-0160
304-558-3317, fax: 304-558-0004

Wisconsin
State Long-term Care Ombudsman
Board on Aging and Long-term Care
214 North Hamilton Street
Madison, WI 53703-2118
608-266-8945, fax: 608-261-6570

Wyoming
State Long-term Care Ombudsman
Wyoming Senior Citizens, Inc.
953 Water Street,
P.O. Box 94
Wheatland, WY 82201
307-322-5553, fax: 307-322-3283

APPENDIX C

Resources

Administration on Aging
Department of Health and Human Services
200 Independence Ave., S.W.
Washington, DC 20201
202-619-0724, fax: 202-619-3759

Aging Network Services
Suite 907
4400 East-West Highway
Bethesda, MD 20814
301-657-4329

Alzheimer's Association
Suite 1000
919 North Michigan Ave.
Chicago, IL 60611
800-272-3900, 312-335-8700;
fax: 312-335-1110

**Alzheimer's Disease Education and
   Referral Center**
P.O. Box 8250
Silver Spring, MD 20907-8250
800-438-4380, 301-495-3311;
fax: 301-495-3334

American Association of Retired Persons
601 E Street, N.W.
Washington, DC 20049
800-424-3410, 202-434-2277

**American Bar Association
   Commission on the Legal
   Problems of the Elderly**
740 15th Street, N.W.
Washington, DC 20005-1022
202-662-8690, fax: 202-662-8698

Better Hearing Institute
5021-B Backlick Road
Annandale, VA 22003
800-327-9355, 703-642-0580

Better Vision Institute
1655 N. Fort Myer Drive, Suite 200
Arlington, VA 22209
703-243-1508, fax: 703-243-1537

Children of Aging Parents
Suite 302-A
1609 Woodbourne Rd.
Levittown, PA 19057
215-945-6900, fax: 215-945-8720

**Clearinghouse on Abuse and Neglect of
   the Elderly**
College of Human Resources
University of Delaware
Newark, DE 19716
302-831-3525

Consumer Information Center
Pueblo, CO 81009
719-948-3334

Elderhostel
75 Federal St.
Boston, MA 02110-1941
877-426-8056, 617-426-7788

Elder Craftsmen
610 Lexington Ave.
New York, NY 10022
212-319-8128, fax: 212-772-9717

Eldercare Locator
National Association of Area Agencies on
  Aging
927 15th St., N.W., 6th Floor
Washington, DC 20005
800-677-1116

Gray Panthers
733 15th St., N.W., Suite 437
Washington, DC 20005
800-280-5362, 202-737-6637;
fax: 202-737-1160

HIV/AIDS Treatment Information Service
P.O. Box 6303
Rockville, MD 20849-6303
800-448-0440, fax: 301-519-6616

Legal Counsel for the Elderly
601 E St., NW
Washington, DC 20049
202-434-2120, fax: 202-434-6464

Medic Alert Foundation
P.O. Box 819008
Turlock, CA 95381-1009
209-668-3333, fax: 209-669-2450

**Meeting the Special Concerns of Hispanic
  Older Women**
National Hispanic Council on Aging
2713 Ontario Road, N.W.
Washington, DC 20009
202-265-1288, fax: 202-745-2522

The National Aging Information Center
Administration on Aging
330 Independence Ave., W., Room 4656
Washington, DC 20201
202-619-7501, fax: 202-401-7620

National Association of Continence
P.O. Box 8310
Spartanburg, SC 29305-8310
800-252-3337, 864-579-7900;
fax: 864-579-7902

**The National Association of Professional
  Geriatric Care Managers**
1604 North Country Club Road
Tucson, AZ 85716
520-881-8008, fax: 520-325-7925

National Center for Vision and Aging
The Lighthouse, Inc.
111 East 59th Street
New York, NY 10022
800-829-0500, 212-821-9705;
fax: 212-821-9705

National Center on Elder Abuse
1225 I Street, N.W., Suite 725
Washington, DC 20005
202-682-2470, fax: 202-289-6555

National Center on Women and Aging
Heller Graduate School
Brandeis University
Mail Stop 035
Waltham, MA 02454-9110
800-929-1995, 781-736-3866;
fax: 781-736-3865

**National Committee to Preserve Social
  Security and Medicare**
10 G Street N.E., Suite 600
Washington, DC 20002-4215
800-998-0180, 202-216-0420;
fax: 202-216-0451

National Council of Senior Citizens
8403 Colesville Road, Suite 1200
Silver Spring, MD 20910
301-578-8800, fax: 301-578-8911

**National Council on Patient Information
  and Education**
Suite 810
666 11th Street, N.W.
Washington, DC 20001
202-347-6711, fax: 202-638-0773

National Hispanic Council on Aging
2713 Ontario Road, N.W.
Washington, DC 20009
202-265-1288, fax: 202-745-2522

National Hospice Organization
Suite 901
1901 North Moore Street
Arlington, VA 22209
800-658-8898, 703-243-5900

**National Interfaith Coalition on
  Aging**
National Council on the Aging
409 3rd Street, S.W., Suite 200
Washington, DC 20024
202-479-1200

**National Long-term Care Ombudsman
  Resource Center**
National Citizens' Coalition for Nursing
  Home Reform
1424 16th Street, N.W., Suite 202
Washington, DC 20036
202-332-2275, fax: 202-332-2949

**National Long-term Care Resource
  Center**
Institute for Health Services Research
University of Minnesota School of Public
  Health
420 Delaware St.
Box 197 Mayo
Minneapolis, MN 55455
612-624-5171, fax: 612-624-5434

**National Policy and Resource Center on
  Nutrition and Aging**
Department of Dietetics and Nutrition
Florida International University
University Park, OE200
Miami, FL 33199
305-348-1517, fax: 305-348-1518

**National Rehabilitation Information
  Center**
1010 Wayne Avenue, Suite 800
Silver Spring, MD 20910-3319
800-346-2742, 301-588-9284

**National Resource and Policy Center on
  Housing and Long-term Care**
Andrus Gerontology Center
University of Southern California
Los Angeles, CA 90089-0191
213-740-1364, fax: 213-740-8241

**National Resource and Policy Center on
  Rural Long-term Care**
Center on Aging
University of Kansas Medical Center
3901 Rainbow Boulevard
Kansas City, KS 66160-7117
913-588-1636, fax: 913-588-1464

**National Resource Center: Diversity
  and Long-term Care**
Heller School—Institute for Health Policy
Brandeis University
P.O. Box 9110
Waltham, MA 02254-9110
800-456-9966, 781-736-3930;
fax: 781-736-3965

**National Resource Center on Long-term
  Care**
National Association of State Units
  on Aging
1225 I Street, N.W., Suite 725
Washington, DC 20005
202-898-2578

**National Resource Center on Native
  American Aging**
P.O. Box 7090
Grand Forks, ND 58202-7090
800-896-7628, fax: 701-777-3292

National Rural Health Association
One West Armour Boulevard,
  Suite 203
Kansas City, MO 64111
816-756-3140, fax: 816-756-3144

National Self-Help Clearinghouse
25 West 43rd Street, Room 620
New York, NY 10036
212-642-2944

National Senior Citizens Law Center
1101 14th Street, N.W.
Suite 400
Washington, DC 20005
202-289-6976, fax: 202-289-7224

National Senior Sports Association
83 Princeton Ave.
Hopewell, NJ 08525
800-282-6772, 609-466-0022;
fax: 609-466-9366

National Women's Health Network
514 10th Street, N.W., Suite 400
Washington, DC 20004
202-347-1140, fax: 202-347-1168

Native Elder Health Care Resource Center
University of Colorado Health Sciences
  Center
4455 East 12th Avenue, Room 329
Denver, CO 80220
303-315-9228, fax: 303-315-9579

Older Women's League
666 11th Street, N.W., Suite 700
Washington, DC 20001
800-825-3695, 202-783-6686

SeniorNet
121 Second Street, 7th floor
San Francisco, CA 94105
800-747-6848, 415-495-4990

Volunteers of America
110 S. Union Street
Alexandria, VA 22314
800-899-0089, 703-548-2288

Wider Opportunities for Women
815 15th Street, N.W., Suite 916
Washington, DC 20005
202-638-3143, fax: 202-638-4885

SUGGESTED READINGS

Chapter 1: What Is Aging?

Harman D. Aging: Phenomena and theories, *Ann NY Acad Sci* (1998 Nov 20) 854:1–7.

Hayflick L. How and why we age, *Exp Gerontol* (1998 Nov–Dec) 33(7–8): 639–653.

Simon DK, Johns DR. Mitochondrial disorders: Clinical and genetic features, *Ann Rev Med* (1999) 50:111–127.

Vijg J, Wei JY. Understanding the biology of aging: The key to prevention and therapy, *Am Geriatr Soc* (1995) 43:426–434.

Westendorp RG, Kirkwood TB. Human longevity at the cost of reproductive success, *Nature* (1998 Dec 24–31), 396(6713):743–746.

Chapter 2: How to Age Successfully

Chee YK, Dash KR, Noguchi S, Levkoff S. Development and implementation of a train-the-trainer curriculum on successful and productive aging. *Educational Gerontology: An International Journal* (1998) 24:509–520.

Cohen GD. Creativity and aging: Ramifications for research, practice and policy, *Geriatrics* (1998 Sep) 53 (Suppl) 1:S4–8.

Edelberg HK, Wei JY. Primary-care guidelines for community-living older persons, *Clin Geriatrics* (1999) 7:42–55.

Goldberg TH, Chavin SI. Preventive medicine and screening in older adults. *J Am Geriatr Soc* (1997) 45:344–354.

Jaffe M. *Geriatric Nutrition and Diet Therapy,* 3rd ed. Englewood, CO: Skidmore-Roth Publishing, 1998.

Odenheimer G, et al. Comparison of neurologic changes in 'successfully aging' persons vs the total aging population, *Arch Neurol* (1994 Jun) 51(6):573–580.

Perls TT, Silver MH, Lauerman J. *Living to 100,* New York: Basic Books, 1999.

Rowe JW, Kahn RL. *Successful Aging.* New York: Pantheon Books, 1998.

Chapter 3: Making the Health System Work for You

Fried TR, Rosenberg RR, Lipsitz LA. Older community-dwelling adults' attitudes toward and practices of health promotion and advance planning activities, *J Am Geriatr Soc* (1995) 43(6):645–649.

Gillick MR. From confrontation to cooperation in the doctor-patient relationship, *J Gen Intern Med* (1992), 7:83–86.

Maxwell J, Levkoff S. Behavioral health care for the elderly: The promise and practice of managed care. *J Geriatr Psych* (in press).

Mechanic D. The changing elderly population and future health care needs, *J Urban Health* (1999 Mar) 76(1):24–38.

U.S. Department of Health and Human Services. *Clinician's Handbook of Preventive Services: Put Prevention into Practice.* Washington, DC: U.S. Government Printing Office, 1994.

Chapter 4: Your Heart

Cobbs EL, Ralapati AN. Health of older women. *Women's Health Issues,* Part I (1998) 82(1):133.

Oberman A, Wei JY. Older women and heart disease, *The Female Patient* (1998) 23:10–16.

Rich MW. Heart failure, *Cardiol Clin* (1999 Feb) 17(1):123–135.

Wei JY. Age and the cardiovascular system. *NEJM* (1992) 327:1735–1739.

Wei JY. Coronary heart disease, In Hazzard WR, ed., *Principles of Geriatric Medicine and Gerontology,* 4th ed. New York: McGraw Hill, 1999.

Wenger NK. *Cardiovascular Disease in the Octogenarian and Beyond,* London: Martin Dunitz, 1999.

Chapter 5: Your Reproductive System

Butler RN, Lewis MI. Sexuality in old age, In Tallis R, *Brocklehurst's Textbook of Geriatric Medicine and Gerontology,* 5th ed., New York: Churchill Livingstone, 1998.

Cobbs EL, Ralapati AN. Health of older women, *Med Clin North Am* (1998) 82(1): 127–144.

D'Amico AV, Desjardin A, Chen MH, Paik S, Schultz D, Renshaw AA, Loughlin KR, Richie JP. Analyzing outcome-based staging for clinically localized adenocarcinoma of the prostate. *Cancer* (1998, Nov 15) 83:2172–2180.

Emlet CA. HIV/AIDS in the elderly: A hidden population. *Home Care Provider* (1997) 2:69.

Janus SS, Janus CL. *Prevalence of Sexual Activity from Age 39 to 65 and Over: The Janus Report on Sexual Behavior.* New York: John Wiley & Sons, 1993.

Johnson SR. Menopause and hormone replacement therapy. *Med Clin North Am* (1998) 82(2):297–320.

Keller MJ, Hausdorff JM, Kyne L, Wei JY, et al. Is age a negative prognostic indicator in HIV infection or AIDS? *Aging Clin Exp Res* (1999) 11: 35–38.

Morgantaler A, et al. Occult prostate cancer in men with low serum testosterone levels. *JAMA* (1998, Dec. 18) 276: 1904–1906.

Chapter 6: Your Mind

American Psychiatric Association. *Diagnostic and Statistical Manual of Mental Disorders,* 4th rev. ed. Washington, DC: American Psychiatric Press, 1994.

Bachman DL, Wolf PA, Linn RT, et al. Incidence of dementia and probable Alzheimer's disease in a general population: The Framingham study. *Neurology* (1993) 43:515–519.

Chee YK, Levkoff SE. The invisible epidemic: Alcohol abuse and dependence in older adults, In Levkoff SE, Chee YK, Noguchi S, eds., *Successful and Productive Aging.* New York: Springer, in press.

Cummings JL, Benson DF. *Dementia: A Clinical Approach,* 2nd ed. Boston: Butterworth-Heinemann, 1992.

Duffy JF, Dijk DJ, Klerman EB, Czeisler CA. Later endogenous circadian temperature nadir relative to an earlier wake time in older people, *Am J Physiol* (1998 Nov) 275 (5 Pt 2):R1478–1487.

Edelberg HK, Wei JY. The biology of Alzheimer's disease, *Mechanisms of Aging and Development* (1996) 91:95–114.

Gillick MR. *Tangled Minds: Understanding Alzheimer's Disease and Other Dementias.* New York: Dutton, 1998.

Levkoff S, Marcantonio E. Delirium: A major diagnostic and therapeutic challenge for clinicians caring for the elderly. *Comprehensive Therapy* (1994) 20(10):550–557.

Neumann PJ, et al. Cost-effectiveness of donepezil in the treatment of mild or moderate Alzheimer's disease, *Neurology* (1999 Apr 12) 52(6):1138–1145.

Odenheimer GL. Cognitive decline in the elderly, In Wei JY, Sheehan MN, *Geriatric Medicine: A Case-Based Manual.* New York: Oxford University Press, 1997.

Ritchie K, Kildea D. Is senile dementia "age related" or "aging related"? Evidence from a meta-analysis of dementia prevalence in the oldest old. *Lancet* (1995) 346:931–934.

Chapter 7: Your Senses

Christen WG. Antioxidant vitamins and age-related eye disease, *Proc Assoc Am Physicians* (1999 Jan–Feb) 111(1):16–21.

Cohn ES. Hearing loss with aging: Presbycusis, *Clin Geriatr Med* (1999 Feb) 15(1):145–161, viii.

Richeimer SH, Bajwa ZH, Kahraman SS, Ransil BJ, Warfield CA. Utilization patterns of tricyclic antidepressants in a multidisciplinary pain clinic: A survey, *Clin J Pain* (1997 Dec) 13(4):324–329.

Schiffman SS. Taste and smell losses in normal aging and disease, *JAMA* (1997 Oct 22–29) 278(16):1357–1362.

Sommers MS. Speech perception in older adults: The importance of speech-specific cognitive abilities, *J Am Geriatr Soc* (1997 May) 45(5): 633–637.

Vernick DM. A comparison of the results of KTP and CO2 laser stapedotomy, *Am J Otol* (1996 Mar) 17(2):221–224.

Warfield CA, Kahn CH. Acute pain management: Programs in U.S. hospitals and experiences and attitudes among U.S. adults, *Anesthesiology* (1995 Nov) 83(5):1090–1094.

Chapter 8: Your Skin, Hair, and Nails

Edelstein C, et al. Oculoplastic experience with the cosmetic use of botulinum A exotoxin, *Dermatol Surg* (1998 Nov) 24(11):1208–1212.

Herd RM, Dover JS, Arndt KA. Basic laser principles, *Dermatol Clin* (1997 Jul) 15(3):355–372.

Khatri KA, Ross V, Grevelink JM, Magro CM, Anderson RR. Comparison of erbium: YAG and carbon dioxide lasers in resurfacing of facial rhytides, *Arch Dermatol* (1999 Apr) 135(4):391–397.

Stratigos AJ, Arndt KA, Dover JS. Advances in cutaneous aesthetic surgery, *JAMA* (1998 Oct 28) 280(16):1397–1398.

Sunderkotter C, Kalden H, Luger TA. Aging and the skin immune system, *Arch Dermatol* (1997 Oct) 133(10):1256–1262.

Chapter 9: Your Musculoskeletal System

Bludau J, Lipsitz L. Falls in the elderly, In Wei JY, Sheehan MN, *Geriatric Medicine: A Case-Based Manual.* New York: Oxford University Press, 1997: 67–79.

Fiatarone MA, et al. Exercise training and nutritional supplementation for physical frailty in very elderly people. *N Engl J Med* (1994) 330:1769–1775.

Greenspan SL, Myers ER, Kiel DP, Parker RA, Hayes WC, Resnick NM. Fall direction, bone mineral density, and function: Risk factors for hip fracture in frail nursing home elderly. *Am J Med* (1998) 104:539–545.

Hausdorff JM, Edelberg HK, Mitchell SL, Goldberger AL, Wei JY. Increased gait unsteadiness in community-dwelling elderly fallers, *Arch Phys Med Rehabil* (1997 Mar) 78(3):278–283.

Sewell KL. Arthritis in the elderly, In Wei JY, Sheehan MN, *Geriatric Medicine: A Case-Based Manual.* New York: Oxford University Press, 1997: 98–104.

Singh MA. Combined exercise and dietary intervention to optimize body composition in aging, *Ann NY Acad Sci* (1998 Nov 20) 854:378–393.

Chapter 10: Your Breasts

Balducci L, Phillips DM. Breast cancer in older women, *Am Fam Physician* (1998 Oct 1) 58(5):1163–1172.

Cummings SR, Eckert S, Krueger KA, Grady D, Powles TJ, Cauley JA, Norton L, Nickelsen T, Bjarnason NH, Morrow M, Lippman ME, Black D, Glusman JE, Costa A, Jordan VC. The effect of raloxifene on risk of breast cancer in postmenopausal women: Results from the MORE randomized trial, Multiple Outcomes of Raloxifene Evaluation, *JAMA* (1999 Jun 16) 281(23):2189–2197.

Dubey AK, Recht A, Come S, Shulman L, Harris J. Why and how to combine chemotherapy and radiation therapy in breast cancer patients, *Recent Results Cancer Res* (1998) 152:247–254.

Nixon AJ, Manola J, Gelman R, Bornstein B, Abner A, Hetelekidis S, Recht A, Harris JR. No long-term increase in cardiac-related mortality after breast-conserving surgery and radiation therapy using modern techniques, *J Clin Oncol* (1998 Apr) 16(4):1374–1379

Schapira L. Breast cancer and the older woman, In Wei JY, Sheehan MN, *Geriatric Medicine: A Case-Based Manual.* New York: Oxford University Press, 1997: 126–136.

Chapter 11: Your Urinary System

Avorn J, Monane M, Gurwitz JH, Glynn RJ, Choodnoviskiy, Lipsitz LA. Reduction of bacteriuria and pyuria after ingestion of cranberry juice, *JAMA* (1994) 271:751–754.

DuBeau CE, Levy B, Mangione CM, Resnick NM. The impact of urge urinary incontinence on quality of life: Importance of patients' perspective and explanatory style. *J Am Geriatr Soc* (1998) 46:683–692.

DuBeau CE, Yalla SV, Resnick NM. Identification and implications of the most bothersome symptom in prostatism, *J Am Geriatr Soc* (1995) 43:985–993.

Fonda D, Resnick NM, Kirschner-Hermanns R. Prevention of urinary incontinence in older people. *Br J Urol* (1998) 82(Suppl 1): 5–10.

Chapter 12: Your Respiratory System

Polakoff D. Pneumonia in the elderly, In Wei JY, Sheehan, MN, *Geriatric Medicine: A Case-Based Manual.* New York: Oxford University Press, 1997: 160–169.

Pope CA III, Dockery DW, Kanner RE, Villegas GM, Schwartz J. Oxygen saturation, pulse rate, and particulate air pollution: A daily time-series panel study, *Am J Respir Crit Care Med* (1999 Feb) 159(2):365-372.

Simon PM, Schwartzstein RM, Weiss JM, Fencl V, Teghtsoonian M, Weinberger SE. Distinguishable types of dyspnea in patients with shortness of breath, *Am Rev Respir Dis* (1990 Nov) 142(5):1009–1014.

Stang A, Glynn RJ, Gann PH, Taylor JO, Hennekens CH. Cancer occurrence in the elderly: Agreement between three major data sources, *Ann Epidemiol* (1999 Jan) 9(1):60–67.

Weiss JW, Remsburg S, Garpestad E, Ringler J, Sparrow D, Parker JA. Hemodynamic consequences of obstructive sleep apnea. *Sleep* (1996 Jun) 19(5):388–397.

Chapter 13: Your Gastrointestinal System

Barkin JS, Ross BS. Medical therapy for chronic gastrointestinal bleeding of obscure origin, *Am J Gastroenterol* (1998 Aug) 93(8):1250–1254.

Chen YY, Antonioli DA, Spechler SJ, Zeroogian JM, Goyal RK, Wang HH. Gastroesophageal reflux disease versus *Helicobacter pylori* infection as the cause of gastric carditis, *Mod Pathol* (1998 Oct) 11(10):950–956.

Harari D, Gurwitz JH, Minaker KL, Bohn R, Avorn J. How do older persons define constipation? Implications for therapeutic management. *J Ger Int Med* (1997) 12:63–66.

Kyne L, Merry C, O'Connell B, Keane C, O'Neill D. Community-acquired *Clostridium difficile* infection, *J Infect* (1998 May) 36(3):287–288.

Saltzman JR, Russell RM. The aging gut: Nutritional issues. *Gastroenterol Clin North Am* (1998 Jun) 27(2):309–324.

Chapter 14: Your Endocrine System

Gurwitz JH, Field TS, Glynn RJ, Manson JE, Avorn J, Taylor JO, Hennekens CH. Risk factors for non-insulin-dependent diabetes mellitus requiring treatment in the elderly. *J Am Geriatr Soc* (1994) 42(12):1235-1240.

Meneilly GS. Pathophysiology of type 2 diabetes in the elderly, *Clin Geriatr Med* (1999 May) 15(2):239–253.

Morrow LA, Minaker KL. Diabetes mellitus in the elderly, In Wei JY, Sheehan MN, *Geriatric Medicine: A Case-Based Manual.* New York: Oxford University Press, 1997, 87–97.

Rosen H. Thyroid disorders in the elderly, In Wei JY, Sheehan MN, *Geriatric Medicine: A Case-Based Manual.* New York: Oxford University Press, 1997: 67–79.

Seeman TE, Berkman LF, Gulanski BI, Robbins RJ, Greenspan SL, Charpentier PA, Rowe JW. Self-esteem and neuroendocrine response to challenge: MacArthur studies of successful aging. *J Psychosom Res* (1995) 39(1): 69–84.

Chapter 15: Your Immune System

John MD, Hibberd PL, Karchmer AW, Sleeper LA, Calderwood SB. *Staphylococcus aureus* prosthetic valve for endocarditis: Optimal management and risk factors for death, *Clin Infect Dis* (1998 Jun) 26(6):1302–1309.

Lesourd BM. Nutrition and immunity in the elderly: Modification of immune responses with nutritional treatments, *Am J Clin Nutr* (1997) 66:478S–484S.

Miller RA. The aging immune system: Primer and prospectus, *Science* (1996 Jul 5) 273:70–74.

Murasko DM, Gold MJ, Hessen MT, Kaye D. Immune reactivity, morbidity, and mortality of elderly humans, *Immunology and Infectious Disease* (1990) 2(3):171–179.

Yoshikawa TT. Perspective: Aging and infectious diseases, past, present and future, *J Infect Dis* (1997 Oct) 176(4):1053–1057.

Chapter 16: Your Mouth

Bivona PL. Xerostomia: A common problem among the elderly, *NY State Dent J* (1998 Jun–Jul) 64(6):46–52.

Jette AM, Feldman HA, Douglass C. Oral disease and physical disability in community-dwelling older persons. *J Am Geriatric Society* (1993 Oct) 41(10):1102–1108.

Joshi A, Douglass CW, Jette A, Feldman H. The distribution of root caries in community-dwelling elders in New England, *J Public Health Dent* (1994 Winter) 54(1):15–23.

Joshipura KJ, Douglass CW, Willett WC. Possible explanations for the tooth loss and cardiovascular disease relationship, *Ann Periodontol* (1998 Jul) 3(1):175–183.

Joshipura KJ, Rimm EB, Douglass CW, Trichopoulos D, Ascherio A, Willett WC. Poor oral health and coronary disease, *J Dent Res* (1996 Sep) 75(9):1631-1636.

Chapter 17: Retirement

Bosse R, Aldwin CM, Levenson MR, Workman-Daniels K. How stressful is retirement? Findings from the Normative Aging Study, *J Gerontol* (1991 Jan) 46(1):P9–14.

Bosse R, Spiro A, Kressin, R. The psychology of retirement, In RT Woods, ed., *Handbook of the Clinical Psychology of Aging,* John Wiley & Sons, 1996.

Caro FG, Morris R. Maximizing the contributions of older people as volunteers, In SE Levekoff, YK Chee, S Noguchi, eds., *Successful and Productive Aging.* New York: Springer, in press.

Ekerdt DJ, Bosse R, Levkoff SE. Adapting to retirement: Is there a honeymoon? *J Gerontology* (1984) 40:95–101.

Midanik LT, Soghikian K, Ransom LJ, Tekawa IS. The effect of retirement on mental health and health behaviors: The Kaiser Permanente Retirement Study, *J Gerontol B Psychol Sci Soc Sci* (1995 Jan) 50(1): S59–61.

Chapter 18: Your Home

Bassuk SS, Berkman LF, Wypij D. Depression symptomatology and incident cognitive decline in an elderly community sample, *Arch Gen Psychiatry* (1998 Dec) 55(12):1073–1081.

Bottum C, Balsam A. Community-based and educational services, In SE Levkoff, YK Chee, S Noguchi, eds., *Successful and Productive Aging.* New York: Springer, in press.

Hudson J, Dennis D, Nutter R, Galaway B, Richardson G. Foster family care for elders, *Adult Residential Care Journal* (1994 Fall) 8(2):65–75.

Mann WC, Ottenbacher KJ, Fraas L, Tomita M, Granger CV. Effectiveness of assistive technology and environmental interventions in maintaining independence and reducing home care costs for the frail elderly: A randomized controlled trial, *Arch Fam Med* (1999 May–Jun) 8(3):210–217.

Shannon K, Van Reenen C. PACE (Program of All-Inclusive Care for the Elderly): Innovative care for the frail elderly, comprehensive services enable most participants to remain at home, *Health Prog* (1998 Sep–Oct) 79(5):41–45.

Vailas LI, Nizke SA, Becker M, Gast J. Risk indicators for malnutrition are associated inversely with quality of life for participants in meal programs for older adults, *J Am Diet Assoc* (1998 May) 98(5):548–553.

Chapter 19: Risks and Rights

Bird PE, Harrington DT, Barillo DJ, McSweeney A, Shirani KZ, Goodwin CW. Elder abuse: A call to action, *J Burn Care Rehabil* (1998 Nov–Dec) 19(6):522–527.

Lachs MS, Williams CS, O'Brien S, Pillemer KA, Charlson ME. The mortality of elder mistreatment, *JAMA* (1998 Aug 5) 280(5): 428–432.

Weinberg AD, Wei JY (eds). *The Early Recognition of Elder Abuse: A Quick Reference Guide.* Bayside, NY: American Medical Publishing Co., 1995.

Wolf RS. Elder abuse. In SE Levkoff, YK Chee, S Noguchi, eds., *Successful and Productive Aging.* New York: Springer, in press.

Chapter 20: Making End-of-Life Decisions

Buckingham RW. *The Handbook of Hospice Care.* Prometheus Books, 1996.

Field MJ, Cassel CK. A*pproaching Death: Improving Care at the End of Life.* Washington, DC: National Academy Press, 1997.

Fried TR, Gillick MR. Medical decision-making in the last six months of life: Choices about limitation of care, *J Am Geriatr Soc* (1994) 307(2):451–459.

Fried, TR, Stein MD, O'Sullivan PS, Brock DW, Novack DH. Limits of patient autonomy: Physician attitudes and practices regarding life-sustaining treatments and euthanasia, *Arch Intern Med* (1993) 153:722–728.

Gillick MR. Ethical issues of the geriatric patient. In SE Levkoff, YK Chee, S Noguchi, eds. *Successful and Productive Aging.* New York: Springer, in press.

Mitchell SL, Kiely DK, Lipsitz LA. Does artificial enteral nutrition prolong the survival of institutionalized elders with chewing and swallowing problems? *J Gerontol A Biol Sci Med Sci* (1998) 53(3):M207–213.

Sheehan MN. Spirituality in later life. In SE Levkoff, YK Chee, S Noguchi, eds., *Successful and Productive Aging.* New York: Springer, in press.

Chapter 21: Loss and Bereavement

Carron AT, Lynn J, Keaney P. End-of-life care in medical textbooks, *Ann Intern Med* (1999 Jan 5) 130(1):82–86.

Gordon NP, Shade SB. Advance directives are more likely among seniors asked about end-of-life care preferences, *Arch Intern Med* (1999 Apr 12) 159(7):701–704.

Hanson LC, Earp JA, Garrett J, Menon M, Danis M. Community physicians who provide terminal care, *Arch Intern Med* (1999 May 24) 159(10): 1133–1138.

Irish DP, Lunquist KF, Nelsen VJ (eds.). *Ethnic Variations in Dying, Death, and Grief.* Bristol, PA: Taylor and Francis, 1993.

Schultz R, Heckhausen J. Aging, culture and control: Setting a new research agenda, *J Gerontol B Psychol Sci Soc Sci* (1999 May) 54(3):P139–145.

Silver MH. The significance of life review in old age. In SE Levkoff, YK Chee, S Noguchi, eds., *Successful and Productive Aging.* New York: Springer, in press.

Chapter 22: Helping Your Aging Parents

Camberg L, et al. Evaluation of simulated presence: A personalized approach to enhance well-being in persons with Alzheimer's disease, *J Am Geriatr Soc* (1999 Apr) 47(4):446–452.

Carter R. *Helping Yourself Help Others: A Book for Caregivers.* New York: Random House, 1994.

Given BA, Given CW. Health promotion for family caregivers of chronically ill elders, *Annu Rev Nurs Res* (1998) 16:197–217.

Gwyther LP. *You Are One of Us: Successful Clergy/Church Connections to Alzheimer's Families.* Durham, NC: Duke University Medical Center, 1995.

Haight BK, Michel Y, Hendrix S. Life review: Preventing despair in newly relocated nursing home residents—short- and long-term effects, *Int J Aging Hum Dev* (1998) 47(2):119–142.

Zang SM, Allender JA. *Home Care of the Elderly.* Philadelphia: Lippincott, 1999.

Chapter 23: "Healthy Aging" Research and Potential Therapies

Ames BN. Micronutrients prevent cancer and delay aging, *Toxicol Lett* (1998 Dec 28) 102–103:5–18.

Duffy JF, Dijk DJ, Hall EF, Czeisler CA. Relationship of endogenous circadian melatonin and temperature rhythms to self-reported preference for morning or evening activity in young and older people, *J Investig Med* (1999 Mar) 47(3):141–150.

Eisenberg, DM, Kessler RC, Foster C, Norlock FE, Calkins DR, Delbanco TL. Unconventional medicine in the United States: Prevalence, costs and patterns of use, *N Engl J Med* (1993 Jan 28) 328(4):246–252.

Isogai N, Landis W, Kim TH, Gerstenfeld LC, Upton J, Vacanti JP. Formation of phalanges and small joints by tissue-engineering. *J Bone Joint Surg Am* (1999 Mar) 81(3):306–316.

LeBars PL, Katz MM, Berman N, et al. A placebo-controlled, double-blind, randomized trial of an extract of ginkgo biloba for dementia, *JAMA* (1997) 278 (16):1327–1332.

Lee S, Wei JY. Molecular interactions of aging and cancer, *Clin Geriatr Med* (1997) 13(1):69–77.

Rudolph KL, Chang S, Lee HW, Blasco M, Gottlieb GJ, Greider C, DePinho RA. Longevity, stress response, and cancer in aging telomerase-deficient mice, *Cell* (1999 Mar 5) 96(5):701–712.

Trippel SB. Potential role of insulinlike growth factors in fracture healing, *Clin Orthop* (1998 Oct) (355 Suppl):S301–313.

Warner HR, Hodes RJ, Pocinki K. What does cell death have to do with aging? *J Am Geriatr Soc* (1997 Sep) 45(9):1140–1146.

Zund G, et al. The in vitro construction of a tissue-engineered bioprosthetic heart valve, *Eur J Cardiothorac Surg* (1997 Mar)11(3): 493–497.

INDEX